Socioling

Leabarl   prol íóč áča cliač

Theoretical Linguistics

General Editor
Pieter A. M. Seuren (University of Nijmegen)

Advisory Editors
Masaru Kajita (Tokyo University of Education)
Winfred P. Lehmann (University of Texas at Austin)
James D. McCawley (University of Chicago)
Anna Morpurgo Davies (University of Oxford)

Also published in this series:
Modern phonology
Alan H. Sommerstein

Sociolinguistics

A critical survey of theory and application

Norbert Dittmar
University of Konstanz

Translated from the German by
Peter Sand, Pieter A. M. Seuren and Kevin Whiteley

Edward Arnold

© Edward Arnold (Publishers) Ltd 1976

Authorized translation from the German
Soziolinguistik: Examplarische und kritische Darstellung ihrer
Theorie, Empirie und Anwendung
published by Athenäum Verlag GmbH, Frankfurt

This translated edition first published in 1976 by
Edward Arnold (Publishers) Ltd, 41 Bedford Square, London WC1B 3DQ
Reprinted 1981

ISBN: 0 7131 5837 9 (paper)

Printed in USA by
Whitehall Company,
Wheeling, Illinois

Preface to the English edition

This book was meant in the first place as a source of information for German readers concerning the state of research and theory in sociolinguistics. It seemed that, in a German context, where sociolinguistics was going through its first, tentative stages, the book could fulfil a useful function, the more so since early sociolinguistic work in Germany was heavily oriented towards Bernstein's theory. In this context, an attempt at a broader, perhaps even comprehensive, survey seemed appropriate. The immediate relevance of sociolinguistic work for important and pressing social problems connected with education and underprivileged groups was a further reason to produce the original book.

When the book was completed, however, it seemed that it might also be put to good use outside the Federal Republic of Germany, and in particular in the English-speaking world. The essential developments in sociolinguistics came, and still come, from there, witness the work of Uriel Weinreich, Charles Ferguson, Joshua Fishman, Basil Bernstein, Dell Hymes, John Gumperz, and, above all, William Labov. It is natural to assume that a survey of sociolinguistics should find a public in the Anglo-Saxon world.

This book has as its two principal focal points the work of Bernstein and that of Labov. My concern with Bernstein's theory and related investigations in the first three chapters is to be seen against the background of the Federal Republic of Germany, where this theory was dominant in the late 1960s and early 1970s. Apart from these local considerations, however, there seems to be ample justification for an extensive critique in English of this theory, which has had an immense influence, not only in sociolinguistics but also, and mainly, in education.

I would like to mention that the closing chapter of the book should be seen as a very succinct and incomplete account of questions which really need a much deeper and fuller treatment. Perhaps the chapter as it stands will provide material for thought and thus lead to further work in this area. Although I considered rewriting it completely for the English edition, I finally decided against doing so: a new book would have resulted. Some constructive contributions to the solution of the problems discussed in chapter 7 should be contained in the reports, to be made available shortly, on a project on Pidgin German of foreign workers in the Federal Republic of Germany, which is at present being carried out at Heidelberg.

That the present English edition is not only a correct but also an exemplary translation is due mainly to the very detailed care given to it by Pieter Seuren. By eliminating printing errors and stylistic ambiguities, and by giving his comments on various details, he has helped to bring about essential improvements over the German edition. I am, moreover, indebted to him for numerous suggestions concerning points of linguistic theory. The most manifest results of these suggestions are to be found in the sections on Fishman's use of the term 'diglossia' and on Labov's description of negation in Black English Vernacular. I have gratefully incorporated his suggestions into the text of this edition. Given the intensity with which Pieter Seuren has occupied himself with problems of sociolinguistics and linguistic variation, I would like to add a personal remark. There is nothing more satisfying for an author than to find that his work is read with care, and thoroughly discussed and evaluated on its merits and demerits. This satisfaction I had when Pieter Seuren visited me in Heidelberg for a whole week to discuss the book and its translation step by step. The final result is an English edition which has been revised and improved on numerous points.

Finally, I owe a word of appreciation to Peter Sand and Kevin Whiteley, without whose great personal dedication and very hard work the translation of the book in such a short time would have been unthinkable. If, by any chance, their study of Goethe and Schiller, so highly valued at Oxford, should have suffered because of this work, let them be forgiven: any such shortcoming would be testimony to their great engagement and to the importance and relevance of sociolinguistic problems.

Konstanz   Heidelberg
October 1974   ND

Contents

Introduction

'If linguistic research is to help as it could in transcending the many inequalities in language and competence in the world today, it must be able to analyse these inequalities. In particular, a practical linguistics so motivated would have to go beyond means of speech and types of speech community to a concern with persons, and social structure. . . .

Beyond the structure of ways of speaking, then, is the question of explanation, and beyond that, the question of liberation. . . .

The final goal of sociolinguistics . . . must be to preside over its own liquidation.'

Dell Hymes, *The scope of sociolinguistics*

'And this is where the sociolinguist faces his moral dilemma. He will perceive the ideal solution to a language problem, a solution which is certainly influenced by his liberal and moral values, and there will be very little possibility of such a solution ever being implemented by those directly faced with results—. . . the teachers, the parents and the children. What then should he do?'

Christina B. Paulston, *On the moral dilemma of the sociolinguist*

In the last decade sociolinguistics has become a powerful factor in promoting emancipation. Attempts have been and are being made to attenuate conflicts in schools and to remove the obvious inequality of opportunity of broad sections of the working classes and peripheral social groups by systematically exposing the connection between speech forms and class structure, and by application of the insights gained to specified social contexts. How this should come about, and whether it is at all possible, are the questions that have essentially motivated this work. We seek to convey the theoretical positions and empirical methods of sociolinguistics which, for reasons of educational policy, have arisen in Great Britain, in the USA and in the Federal Republic of Germany. It is our aim that these will thus be made available to a wide public for critical examination. For this reason unpublished material has been included as much as possible in this presentation.

We shall endeavour to demonstrate the extension of traditional methods of linguistic description by new sociolinguistic methods for the description of speech behaviour, variation and linguistic change. We shall, moreover, attempt to establish their correlation with the social system and with interests prevailing in it. From this we derive a twofold task: to achieve a comprehensive and accurate presentation of sociolinguistic theory, method and application; and to illustrate the discrepancies existing in the field as a whole, as well as the socially-conditioned contradictions inherent in certain approaches. As this study is primarily intended to supply basic information, only the barest outline of criticism can be provided: further critical consideration is called for. Essentially, therefore, the terminology of the works referred to has, in principle, been retained and has been criticized mainly in those sections where our critical opinion is given.

The book is divided into two main parts. The first part, chapters 1–3, deals with Basil Bernstein's Deficit Hypothesis. The second part, chapters 4–7, explains the theories of the Variability Concept which are based on linguistic notions and give the impression of being, sociologically speaking, value-free. These theories, which have arisen as a result of research into the speech behaviour of ethnic minorities in the USA, are as yet relatively unknown in the Federal Republic of Germany. In conclusion, a third part contains an annotated bibliography which is intended to provide a supplement to the book as well as easy access to information on specific questions and problems of sociolinguistics.

Chapter 1 is concerned solely with the presentation of the Deficit Theory formulated by Bernstein, which gave the first impetus to an investigation of speech barriers. In chapter 2, the Deficit Hypothesis is examined empirically, with detailed critical arguments, from the point of view of linguistics, psychology and sociology. In chapter 3 we pass from a rejection of the Deficit Hypothesis on internal grounds to an assessment of its sociopolitical significance, which is most clearly visible in its application to compensatory educational programmes. Chapter 4 sets out first to expound the differences between the Deficit Hypothesis and the Variability Concept, and then goes on to illustrate some basic concepts of the latter, putting them into the context of their linguistic and anthropological tradition. On the basis of this historical perspective, chapter 5 introduces the linguistic and sociological theories which describe and explain speech variation, linguistic change, bilingualism and multilingualism, touching on the socio-political reasons for their development. This section will concentrate on a résumé of linguistic methods. Chapter 6 demonstrates their application in the study of phonology, syntax and verbal interaction. The chief methods of empirical research in linguistic survey are discussed first, followed by an account of the results of correlative and functional studies of speakers' grammatical and communicative competence. In particular we shall consider the Urban Language Studies which were carried out by the Center for Applied Linguistics in Washington, whose most important exponent is William Labov. The discussion in chapter 7 centres upon recommendations for changing school systems that arise from these investigations. On the basis of an outline of the connection between social and educational policies in the USA, we formulate a criticism of the social categories assumed in the Variability Concept approach. We conclude that there is no essential difference between the programmes advocated by the proponents of the Deficit Hypothesis and those of the Variability Concept, given that both approaches fail in their avowed aim to eliminate social inequality. It is recognized, however, that the more cautious techniques of social adaptation of ethnic minorities to the American norm, developed in the context of the Variability Concept, represent a considerable improvement on the compensatory programmes of the Deficit Hypothesis.

Christina Paulston claims that the dilemma facing sociolinguistics is that, whilst it is able to supply idealistic solutions to sociolinguistic problems, the actual realization of its proposals still remains dependent on socioeconomic factors and on the power politics of a particular society. If one adopts her view one will agree that the central points of interest of the present work are:

1   to offer the basis for an answer to the question: What academically justifiable and socially necessary task can be assigned to sociolinguistics?
2   to convey an impression of the practical relevance of sociolinguistics, derivable from theoretical and empirical research.[1]

[1] For stimulation and criticism in compiling this book I am indebted to Peter Hartmann, Wolfgang Klein, Gudula List, Eberhard Pause, Rainer Schneewolf, Wolf-Dieter Stempel, Angelika Weyler and Dieter Wunderlich. Their comments, critical remarks and discussions have contributed to this book in many different ways. In particular I wish to thank Gisela Feurle for her comments and suggestions: she has followed the composition of the book from beginning to end. Her influence on the form of argument and presentation is unmistakable in various passages, and in particular in chapter 7.

Special thanks are due to Schwipsy, an unusual koala bear, who always looked at me with wise understanding and friendship whenever I found myself caught up in difficult formulations.

1 The Deficit Hypothesis: Bernstein's assumptions on the correlation between speech and socialization

1.1 Groundwork and orientation

This chapter deals with the theory of the British sociologist Basil Bernstein that the social success of members of a society, and their access to social privileges, is directly dependent on the degree of organization of their linguistic messages.

He starts from the principle that the speech habits of particular social groups in the low income bracket who have little social influence (in sociological terms the lower class) differ syntactically and semantically from those of other groups, who are assured powerful and influential positions because of their material and intellectual privileges (in sociological terms the middle class). Furthermore he assumes that the differences in expression of both classes are not neutral but are assessable in relation to the actual social position involved. In this sense the lower classes may be socially handicapped as a consequence of their inadequate command of language, which is limited in comparison with that of the middle and upper classes.

Successful organization of speech messages is thus defined by the social success of its users, i.e. of the middle class.

Instead of analysing the manifest differences between the two linguistic varieties according to their various functional capabilities, the linguistic characteristics which divide the speech behaviour of the lower class from that of the middle class are interpreted as a deficit phenomenon on the basis of an *a priori* normative scale of values. That is to say, they are interpreted as precisely those linguistic attributes which lower-class speakers lack, in order to achieve the same social success as the speakers of the middle class. This central assumption that the speech of the lower class is more limited in its competence than the speech of the middle class will be termed the *Deficit Hypothesis* throughout. Numerous sociologists and psychologists have, in the course of the last few years, attempted to verify this hypothesis empirically.

The theory of the restricted linguistic ability of particular social groups compared with that of others was first formulated by Schatzmann and Strauss (1955), who questioned members of the lower and middle classes about their impressions and experiences directly after the occurrence of a disaster. They established that members of the lower classes were taking it for granted in their verbal accounts that the interviewers had been present at the scene of the disaster which they themselves had just witnessed. This subconscious assumption was clearly demonstrated by the fact that they never gave any explicit indication of place, circumstances and people involved to the interviewers, who had not been present. On the contrary, they assumed these to be already known in that they used mainly nonspecific deictic particles in their referring expressions. Furthermore their verbal expressions were characterized by a display of emotion which gave rise to rapid speech and made their syntax elliptical and markedly paratactical. This gave the listener the impression that they were reliving the events of the disaster instead of giving the interviewers a comprehensive picture of what had happened.

The middle-class speakers, however, were able to do precisely this. They explained to the interviewers the events and circumstances of the disaster in a logical and chronological order, and gave detailed accounts of the people and place involved, taking into account the fact that the interviewers had not been present. The fluency of their apposite description reflected the emotional distance that they had maintained between themselves and the events observed.

Schatzmann and Strauss interpreted the difference between these two linguistic strategies in terms implying that the speakers from the lower class only conveyed their meaning implicitly, but those of the middle class did so explicitly.

This evidence together with additional observations led Bernstein in 1958 to distinguish between a 'public' language of the lower class and a 'formal' language of the middle class. In his later works (from 1962 onwards) he declared the public language to be the 'restricted' code and the formal language to be the 'elaborated' speech code. The 'restricted speech code' (approximately: limited range of linguistic expression), which is inferior to the 'elaborated speech code', capable of relatively complex and expressive linguistic organization, is considered by Bernstein to be a decisive cause of social inequality of opportunity. The theory behind Bernstein's distinction is that the different speech styles originate in the different psychological and social experiences of their speakers. He regards these experiences as being determined by membership of a particular social class.

The assertion of a dependency relation between ability of linguistic expression and sociopsychological experience is not a new one. As early as 1929 Sapir wrote that 'the "real world" is to a large extent unconsciously built up on the language habits of the group' (Sapir 1929, 209), and Whorf took this a step further when he stated that 'the background linguistic system (in other words, the grammar) of each language is not merely a reproducing instrument for voicing ideas but rather is itself the shaper of ideas, the program and guide for the individual's mental activity . . .' (Whorf 1956, 212). Whorf was of the opinion that different linguistic systems imply different social experiences. He also attempted to demonstrate this concept empirically by comparing Indian and European languages, thereby relying mainly on vocabulary and rules of grammar.

The colour adjectives are an extremely overworked example for demonstrating the dependency of thought on linguistic experiences. In different language communities the same colours are given varying verbal denotations. Thus English has only one adjective for the colour 'white', whereas the Eskimos differentiate linguistically between several shades of 'white'. The linguistic differentiation made by the Eskimos of the various shades of 'white' is clearly a result of their living conditions and their direct experiences, in particular of the daily necessity to distinguish between various types of snow.

The same correlation can be found in grammar, as in the example of the Hopi

Indians' concept of time. According to Whorf, the grammatical structure of the Hopi language does not exhibit any tenses in the way of our European languages (or any temporal adverbs or prepositions or indicators of time), which are based upon a physical concept of time. Whorf concludes from this absence of linguistic time indicators that in the life of the Hopis 'time' is not relevant to their experience.

Our examples are intended to illustrate in very simplified form the principle of Whorf's relativity theory, which, in his words, claims that 'users of markedly different grammars are pointed by their grammars toward different types of observations and different evaluations of externally similar acts of observation, and hence are not equivalent as observers but must arrive at somewhat different views of the world' (Whorf 1956, 221). In so far as linguistic structure, therefore, determines psychological social experience, and so creates diverging systems of social linguistic meaning in different language communities, Whorf's concept of language determinism is termed 'the linguistic relativity thesis'.

In many respects there are similarities between Whorf's and Bernstein's concepts of language. Both concepts are based on the theory that different linguistic forms produce different social experience. Whorf observed these differences chiefly in different language communities, but Bernstein transfers these observations to social barriers between classes within a society. Bernstein has added a decisive theoretical supplement to Whorf's relativity thesis with his assertion that it is primarily the social structure which determines linguistic behaviour and this in turn comes full circle to reproduce the former. The reproduction of the social structure by way of linguistic behaviour is a weaker formulation of Whorf's deterministic concept; it is in this weakened form, however, that it is integrated into Bernstein's wider conceptual scheme.

What the two concepts have in common is that they postulate a close relationship between language and the shaping of experience. According to Bernstein, however, this relationship is the reproductive part of a more vital relationship, which is the determination of linguistic behaviour through the social structure. Whereas Whorf's thesis is unilateral (grammar conditions experience), Bernstein's is circular: the social structure conditions linguistic behaviour, and this reproduces social structure. At this point, one should not overlook the fact that Whorf in no way denied the influence of society on language. Thus he writes: 'Which was first: the language patterns or the cultural norms? In main they have grown up together, constantly influencing each other' (Whorf 1956, 156). In the majority of his assertions, however, Whorf clearly opted for the causal primacy of language.

Bernstein has repeatedly stressed in his works the proximity of his concept to that of Whorf. He writes in his first essay: 'In this paper the valuable work of Whorf and Sapir has been used to explore the social implications of language' (quoted in Fishman 1968b, 226). The relative language-bound experience of speakers, and therefore the Sapir–Whorf hypothesis, remains present in the distinction between restricted and elaborated speech codes, which Bernstein upholds in all his works. Thus one reads in Bernstein (1971a):

'Whorf, particularly where he refers to the fashions of speaking, frames of consistency, alerted me to the selective effect of the culture upon the patterning of grammar together with the pattern's semantic and thus cognitive significance. Whorf opened up, at least for me, the question of the deep structure of linguistically regulated communication.'

Gumperz and Hymes also refer to the similarities between Bernstein and Whorf in their introduction to Bernstein (1972b):

'Bernstein places his work in relation to that of Whorf. Whorf, of course, did not consider the form of social relationships, or differences in function within a single language. He did, however, specify that it was not a language as such but rather a consistent active selection of its resources, a *fashion of speaking*, that was to be studied. Bernstein's delineation of communication codes can be seen as giving Whorf's insight new life and sociological substance.' (Gumperz and Hymes 1972, 471)

Since Bernstein's concept incorporates Whorf's relativist concept of language, we shall be concerned from now on solely with Bernstein's hypotheses. This can be justified on various grounds. From an empirical point of view, both theories deal with the demonstration of a dependency relationship between language and thought on the one hand, and language and social structure on the other. Up to this point what is valid for Bernstein in respect of this question is also valid for Whorf (with limitations). Historically, Whorf's work preceded that of Bernstein and was the subject of heated debate between 1950 and 1960. There is a vast range of critical literature on the subject of Whorf's relativity thesis; we shall not, therefore, resuscitate the issue.[1]

Considerations regarding the sociopolitical impact of scientific theories also necessitate a critical presentation of Bernstein's theories and their consequences.

In the wake of the general interest and application which Bernstein's theories have received, it is necessary to present a criticism of his ideas. It is, above all, the specific practical guidelines with respect to social application which motivate a critical examination of his theoretical position. In Bernstein's case it is not possible to separate theoretical conception from sociopolitical consequences, as will later become apparent. Finally, because Bernstein gave the crucial impetus to research into the problems of language behaviour specific to social classes, we must start our account of sociolinguistics with a discussion of his work.

First of all we shall explore the general theoretical concept of speech codes. We shall then examine their genesis during socialization. Finally, we shall deal with their sociological, psychological and linguistic correlates.

Between 1958 and 1972 Basil Bernstein published approximately 30 essays (cf. the bibliography) which reflects the basis of his theory with some considerable fluctuation in his attempts at definition and in the empirical material which he adduces.

He attempted to prove early formulations of his theory by means of empirical investigation (Bernstein 1962a, b). But while his work after 1962 is chiefly

[1] For a discussion of the Whorf hypothesis see Lenneberg and Roberts 1956 (empirical verification of the hypothesis); Hartig and Kurz 1971, 56–75 (survey of literature), Kutschera 1971, 280–340 (philosophically-oriented account) and Gipper 1972 (refutation).

directed at the demonstration of a generally valid theoretical framework, it was his followers (including Coulthard, Creed, Hawkins, Henderson, Lawton and Robinson) who concentrated on empirical attempts at validating his hypotheses.

The task of presenting Bernstein's theory is complicated considerably by the fact that, through his various publications, he often modifies, supplements or deletes terminologies, without providing any explicit indication as to the value of these alterations vis-à-vis earlier versions. It is thus impossible to obtain either explicit or coherent definitions from his work for the various speech forms he postulates. Because of the inconsistency and the contradictions in the formulations of his essays we shall not in what follows call their theoretical basis 'theory' but use instead the terms *hypothesis, theoretical approach* or *theoretical conception*, as appropriate.

Although his definitions of speech forms vary from one essay to another, Bernstein's hypotheses do contain an unchanging central idea which can be presented independently of the individual modifications. Thus the alteration of the terminology from 'formal language' and 'public language' to 'elaborated' and 'restricted speech codes' in the later works conceals the presence of one basic idea which we shall go on to develop. We shall thereby rely chiefly on Bernstein's least ambiguous accounts (in particular the essays of 1964; 1965; 1967; 1972b) and omit attempts at detailed interpretation.

1.2 Theoretical conception

1.2.1 Basic idea

Bernstein's idea of the significance of language for socialization[2] has a manifestly sociopolitical origin. His hypothesis of the existence of speech variation within a society is set on a definite line of thought. In the context of wealth as a variable privilege, which is greater for the upper but smaller for the lower classes, Bernstein regards access to privileges as a function of the use of different sets of communicative symbols determined in such a way that middle-class speakers (with a versatile verbal repertoire)[3] can attain considerably more privileges than speakers of the lower class (with a limited verbal repertoire). This means that speakers of underprivileged groups can only gain social success if they possess the particular linguistic ability which is considered as the norm and is controlled by the dominant class. In most societies the language controlled by the norms of the dominant class (through institutions, radio, television, newspapers, literature, etc.) is considered the standard language, and as such is taught in schools right from its basic phonological qualities to the rules of its significance in social contexts. The *Standard* is that speech variety of a language community which is legitimized as the obligatory norm for social intercourse on the strength of the interests of dominant forces in that society. The act of legitimizing a norm is

---

[2] By 'socialization' we mean the process of learning rules of social behaviour, which children have to undergo during their first years of life, and which is determined by persons of authority and by institutions.

[3] For the term 'repertoire', see the work of Gumperz.

effected by means of value judgements which have a sociopolitical motivation. In addition to the Standard, there exist in all societies speech varieties which can be termed *dialects* in the case of regional variation, or *sociolects* in the case of social variation (for a detailed discussion of these terms see 4.2). These regional and social variants frequently cause their speakers to be given a lower social valuation which is measured by the norms of the supraregional, and more highly valued Standard variety.

According to Bernstein, the requirements of linguistic performance, as demanded by the dominant middle class, can be taken to determine the Standard variety, which determines in turn the recognition and approval of speech behaviour, and thus decides the normative scale of valuation according to which other speech varieties, such as that of the lower class, can be described as deficient. Given that the linguistic literature on the functional description of dialects and sociolects shows that there are no linguistic criteria for making a classification of better and worse speech varieties, the originality of Bernstein's concept lies precisely in his assertion that the speech form of the middle class is superior to that of the lower class in explicitness, grammatical correctness and capacity for logical analysis, regardless of measured intelligence. For that reason he describes the speech of the middle class as 'elaborated' and that of the lower class as 'restricted'.

Restricted speakers lack that very range of expression which guarantees the success of elaborated speakers. The speech of the middle class (which in many respects should coincide with the Standard variety) thus represents a mechanism of selection which acts as a social filter in controlling social privileges through speech form.[4]

In principle, Bernstein equates social privileges and greater self-expression on the one hand, and social disadvantage and poorer speech on the other. The social barrier existing between the classes is ultimately due to the fact that some, apparently, cannot express themselves as well as others. This is the social and sociopolitical starting point of a *directed hypothesis* of speech behaviour specific to social classes and it will now be considered in detail. First of all we shall consider some of its basic theoretical ideas in isolation from the context of its substantiation and explanation.

1.2.2 Basic concepts

In his more recent essays (1965; 1967, 126), Bernstein distinguishes between language and speech.

Language, as a system of rules, is said to represent a *code*, but *speech* signifies an activity engaged in during actual speech encounters which serves to convey information by varying the application of the rules of the code. According to Bernstein, the code (the linguistic rule system) is capable of producing '*n* number of speech codes' which must satisfy its rules (Bernstein 1967, 126). These speech codes are realized through the system of social relationships, of which they are a function.

---

[4] Cf. Bourdieu and Passeron 1970, 133–66; especially the criticism of Bernstein, 146.

This can be represented as follows. Let C_1, C_2, ..., be *speech codes*, and $R_1, R_2,...,$ R_m *systems of social relations*. Then, according to Bernstein, a speech code C_i is a function of a system of social relations R_j, that is, $C_i = F(R_j)$, and a system of social relations R_j is a function of a speech code C_i: $R_j = G(C_i)$. It follows that $C_i = F(G(C_i))$,[5] which shows the unacceptable circularity of the definition of speech codes. The circularity of Bernstein's speech code definition has also been criticized by Kanngiesser (1972b, 89) as violating the following condition: 'No notion $B_i \in S_1$ $(i = 1, 2,..., n)$ may be defined by reference to a notion $b_j \in S2$ $(j = 1, 2,..., m)$, whose construction presupposes S_1 (*or* subsystems of S_1), and vice versa.' According to Kanngiesser this condition 'requires that S_1 and S_2 can be constructed independently of one another.'

Bernstein aims at making the term 'speech codes' (1967, 127) which he had first adopted more precise by terming these 'sociolinguistic codes' (1971a): 'The concept of sociolinguistic code points to the social structuring of meanings *and* to their diverse but *related* contextual linguistic realizations.'

Bernstein intends the sociolinguistic codes to be understood as linguistic planning strategies which, having been conveyed by the social structure on the level of actual speech, are realized systematically as speech form, i.e. relatively independent of the individual contexts. In certain respects they imply varying linguistic capabilities on the part of their speakers (systematic linguistic behaviour acquired by social rules); in other respects they express varying speech capabilities that depend on contextual constraints. Bernstein does not explain whether this is due to the varying underlying competence of the speakers, or rather to their varying fluency in performance. In 1972b (475) he writes: 'The codes refer to performance....', whereas in 1971a he identifies them with 'the deep structure of communication'. The speech/sociolinguistic codes are presumably to be thought of as existing on a level between competence and performance. Taking Houston's (1970) term, this level could be called *systematic performance*. It is essential for an adequate understanding to keep constantly in mind the frequently-repeated axiom: social structure intervenes between language and speech (Bernstein 1964 and 1967).

As the concepts 'code' and 'speech code' may well give rise to misunderstandings, we shall use the following terminology: *code* is the abstract linguistic rule system (we shall avoid using this term as much as possible); by *speech codes* we mean verbal strategies, which as a function of social relations have correlates on the linguistic and on the verbal planning level. The speech codes become manifest in 'elaborated' and 'restricted' speech forms.

The speech codes represent an abstraction from sociological, psychological and linguistic conditions and data. Their conceptual unity can be grasped by the term *range of alternatives* which is, on average, relatively large for the middle class and small for the lower class. In this sense, the middle class tends to realize more alternatives than the lower class (e.g. in elaborated speech).

---

[5] *F* and *G* are unspecified functions.

1.2.3 Three levels of analysis

The relationship between code and speech codes, as well as their correlates on the three planes, must be defined more precisely.

Theoretically speaking, the linguistic rule system can produce an infinite number of different speech forms. To the extent that social relations control communication, however, this conclusion would be wrong. To a large extent social relations depend upon economic conditions (and the imposition of authority connected with them). These are not distributed at random, but vary with the social class. According to Bernstein only two classes are relevant: the lower class and the middle class (he relates this extremely simplified division to England). Members of both classes diverge from one another in the use of communicative symbols of verbal and nonverbal nature. The differences are governed by social and psychological factors.

A speaker is employing an elaborated speech code when he can make extensive use of the structural possibilities of linguistic material, expressing himself in such a way that his verbal behaviour clearly identifies him as belonging to the middle class.

A speaker is employing a restricted speech code when he uses only part of the structural linguistic possibilities, and cannot correctly verbalize complex trains of thought or logical relationships. Frequently he has to resort to nonlinguistic signs in order to convey the message he has in mind. The resultant speech behaviour, which according to Bernstein can only bring about inadequate mental operations as a result of the insufficiency of the means, causes the speaker to be identified, from the middle-class viewpoint, as belonging to the lower class.

Depending on the class to which they belong, the speakers benefit from the same basic language in different ways. The elaborated variety enables its user to express complex relations in and with his environment, to solve conflicts and problems and to impart personal emotions and intentions. The speaker from the lower class, on the other hand, who has only a restricted command of language, does not use it to convey qualified information so much as to express common orientation and to maintain solidarity. From the angle of the middle-class speaker his speech behaviour seems characterized by numerous repetitions and diffused, incoherent argumentation. According to Bernstein, he thinks in a concrete rather than abstract manner.

Both speech codes can—in a vague borrowing of concepts from information theory—be distinguished according to the criterion of predictability. The restricted speech code should, in relation to lexical and syntactic options, be largely predictable, whereas the elaborated code should not.

Judging by the criteria of verbal planning, one is dealing with an 'elaborated' speech code, 'if it is difficult to predict the syntactic options or alternatives a speaker uses to organize his meanings over a representative range of speech' (Bernstein 1964, 57; cf. 1.4.1 below). Predictability relates therefore to the hearer's anticipation of the speaker's linguistic utterances.

The following diagram is intended to explain the correlation of linguistic rule system, social structure, verbal planning and speech forms in relation to the concept of speech codes:

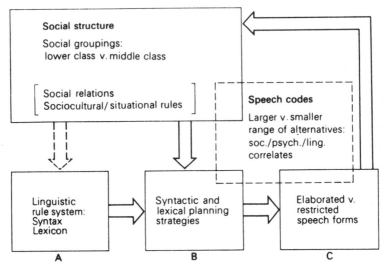

Fig. 1.1 Speech codes: diagram of the correlations between social structure, linguistic rule system, verbal planning and speech forms.

Figure 1.1 demonstrates that the linguistic rules in *A* are influenced by the social structure, and via the planning strategies in *B* are then realized in *C* as speech forms. A speaker from the middle or lower class (sociological correlates) selects via the specific planning strategies peculiar to him (high v. low level of verbal planning: psychological correlates) from syntax and lexicon in such a way that restricted or elaborated speech forms (linguistic correlates) become manifest. The feedback process lies in the fact that the social structure itself is again stabilized by the speech forms. It is in this process that the *circularity principle* of the speech codes is founded (cf. Oevermann 1970, 183–200).

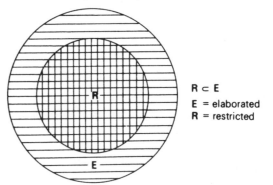

Fig. 1.2 The relation between 'restricted' and 'elaborated' forms of speech.

In order to specify the relationship of the two kinds of speech form with one another, we can imagine elaborated and restricted speech forms as two sets of communicative symbols, such that the elaborated incorporates the restricted as a subset. This means that everything which is expressed in the restricted form can also be realized in the elaborated form; the reverse, however, is not possible. In other words, elaborated speakers can also express themselves in the restricted form, though the restricted speakers cannot do so in the elaborated form. At the same time this inclusion relation makes it clear that restricted speech is limited compared with elaborated speech.

The concept illustrated in figure 1.1 differs from the generally-accepted notions in linguistics mainly in that the latter considers only a relation between A (the rule system of a grammar) and C (performance), which does not make it clear how aspects of performance can be systematically analysed. Linguistics, furthermore, considers the production of sentences in C by application of the rules from A to be unlimited in principle: C would allow for an infinite number of speech forms.

In Bernstein's conception, however, the essential idea is that a system of social rules intervenes between A and C via the planning strategies, which acts as a filter (as a type of secondary rule system) and divides the potentially infinite number of speech forms into two basic and systematically varying groups. Bernstein's argument as to how elaborated and restricted speech forms ultimately arise under the influence of the social structure, through the intervention of verbal planning, can be defined more precisely in the following way (Bernstein himself has never attempted to describe this correlation explicitly):

1   Let X and Y be speech forms such that $X = \{A_i/A_i$ has the features x_{l}, $x_{2},\ldots, x_{n}\}$, and $Y = \{A_j/A_j$ has the features $y_{l}, y_{2}, \ldots, y_{m}\}$, where A_i and A_j are sequences, and the x's and y's are their linguistic features.

2   Given in addition a social structure S consisting of the speakers $P = \{p_{l}, p_{2}, \ldots, p_{n}\}$, with classes L and M (where $L \neq M$), then the p_i of S have psychological planning strategies T for A's (depending in unspecified ways on L and M), so that $T(L)$ and $T(M)$ result. These then become manifest on the linguistic level (depending in unspecified ways on the T involved) as different speech forms $X_{T(L)}$ and $Y_{T(M)}$. Thus a social structure which is divided into two classes (sociological argument) produces two different verbal planning strategies (psychological argument) which in turn determine two different sets of speech forms (linguistic argument).

The above-mentioned formulations are restricted to the systematic correlation between social structure, planning strategies and speech forms.[6] To this extent they are independent of the illustration in figure 1.1, which takes into consideration the circularity of speech forms and social structure with the inclusion of time factors.

1.2.4 Bernstein's sources

Bernstein cites a series of authors in order to justify his distinction between restricted and elaborated speech codes, which are defined by sociological, psychological and linguistic criteria.

---

[6] No attention was paid in his account to the nonverbal aspects of behaviour. It should be pointed out, however, that Bernstein in no way distinguishes these from the verbal aspects. Since different forms of communication are at issue here, such a distinction ought to have been made.

He regards the division between mechanical and organic solidarity made by the sociologist Durkheim (cf. Bernstein 1965) as substantiating his theory that members of the lower class are status-oriented and dependent upon a maximum of reciprocal mechanical solidarity; linguistically, this is manifested in reassuring solidarity stereotypes and in a rapid but not very qualified speech form (cf. on this point Ehlich *et al.* 1971, as well as Negt 1971). Sapir and Whorf (cf. for example Bernstein 1965, 1971a and 1972b) strengthen Bernstein's initial view that 'language powerfully conditions all our thinking about social problems and processes . . .' (Sapir quoted in Bernstein 1965). Whorf's relativity thesis (cf. 1.1 above), which originated from ethnological studies, is transposed by Bernstein in a weakened analogy to the stratified English social structure. In so doing he is applying the relativity theory of exotic language communities to his own.

In his assessment of the psychological dimension relevant for acquiring language, Bernstein refers to Piaget, Luria and Wygotsky. According to the theory of the two latter authors, situations and events in the speakers' external environment are transformed by way of verbal planning strategies into manifest linguistic utterances:

> 'The speech system . . . , itself a function of the social structure, marks out selectively for the individual what is relevant in the environment. The experience of the individual is transferred by the learning which is generated by his own apparently voluntary acts of speech.' (Bernstein 1964, 56)

Bernstein's assertion that lower-class children use concrete meanings and middle-class children abstract meanings is based on Piaget, who has distinguished in the psychological development of the child between 'concrete' and 'formal' operations (Bernstein quoted in Hymes 1964a, 256). Piaget subdivides the development of the child into 'pre-operational', 'concrete-operational' and 'formal-operational' stages of thinking. These three phases of development in the child are described as cognitive universal features (cf. Ginsburg 1972, 127–9). Bernstein supports the theory, borrowed from Piaget, that lower-class children remain at the stage of concrete operations. This would mean that they are limited in their cognitive capabilities. Although Piaget did not exclude the possibility that children can remain restricted to concrete operations, he assumed at the same time a universal, cognitive development of the child that was independent of social class. Up to this time it had not been possible to give sufficient empirical proof of differences specific to social class in the cognitive development of children (cf. Ginsburg 1972, 95–239).

Bernstein takes his theory that speakers who are restricted to a small area of local conditions and social activities only have limited communicative possibilities at their command from Malinowski (1923), who in his opinion had shown what circumstances could give rise to a simplified syntax and a limited lexicon. We should like to point out here that Malinowski was concerned with so-called 'primitive languages', whose linguistic and social situation is not directly transferable to modern society. In his work of 1923 Malinowski places particular emphasis on the context (309–16) and pragmatic function (316–26) of speech. With these two differentiating factors in mind, he attempts to make conclusive statements on linguistic performance in 'primitive' languages. Bernstein appears to derive a supporting argument for the concrete speech of the lower class from the tendency of 'primitive' speakers to gear their language completely to concrete living conditions (on this difficulty cf. Cohen, Fraenkel and Brewer 1968).

In one of his last essays (1971a) Bernstein refers to Marx, in order to trace the reproduction of the class structure back to the influence of 'symbolic systems'. In his opinion 'access to, control over, orientation of and *change* in critical symbolic systems, according to the theory, is governed by power relationships as these are embodied in the class structure' (1971a). Here he must be postulating that 'manipulation and exploitation' occur not only 'in the strict economic sense' but also via the 'cultural capital', the language through which 'man can extend and change the boundaries of his experience' (*ibid.*: cf. the similar theory in Bourdieu and Passeron 1970). Bernstein bases his thesis 'on Durkheim and Marx at the macro level', without further dealing with the condition of economically-determined power relationships and their correlation with language (1971a).

The amalgamation of two authors, as is here evident, is typical of Bernstein's technique. He attempts to use extremely heterogeneous fragments, from works of various authors with very different scientific intentions, in order to support his own theory of the existence of two different speech codes and their social implications. Thus, without differentiation, Marx and Durkheim are fused for example with Mead, Piaget and Whorf.

Bernstein's argument, which disregards contradictions, has the advantage of making his conception difficult to criticize. If he is censured for his reference to Durkheim, he can always point to his interpretation of Marx, and vice versa. With regard to his sources, it seems that Bernstein does not want to commit himself to a particular standpoint; this is a basic characteristic which comes to light particularly when he refers to other works in his essays.

1.3   Origin of the speech codes and their social background

We have first developed the fundamental theoretical idea of Bernstein's conception so that on the basis of this further differentiations can be made. These concern the circumstances of socialization which are of central importance for the formation of different speech codes.

Bernstein supports his assumptions on socialization with the works of numerous authors who have considered this theory or have conducted experiments.

A comprehensive survey of literature on the correlation relevant to socialization between language, thought and social structure is to be found in Bernstein (1959a). Authors such as Weber, Mead, Sapir, Durkheim and Whorf, to whom Bernstein feels particularly indebted, are reviewed thoroughly in Bernstein 1965.

1.3.1   The process of socialization

'I shall take the term [socialization] to refer to the process whereby a child acquires a specific cultural identity, *and* to his responses to such an identity. Socialization refers to the process whereby the biological is transformed into a specific cultural being. It follows from this that the process of socialization is a complex process of control, whereby a particular moral, cognitive and affective awareness is evoked in the child and given a specific form and content.' (Bernstein 1971a)

The process of socialization takes place for the child under the control of the agencies of socialization: the family, the 'peer group' (the circle of friends and acquaintances), school and work, and these exert pressure on the child to adapt by means of the power of their authority (reward and punishment).

Socialization contains instructional phases in which individuals learn among other things their social identity, social interactions, role behaviour and, above all, speech and its rules. The child is oriented towards the use of the verbal or nonverbal channel when expressing its requirements by the manner in which the parents activate its cognitive, affective and intellectual behaviour, as well as by the habits which educational practice involves (e.g. explanation and justification of behaviour, metacommunicative remarks on the reasons for reward and punishment). When a middle-class child becomes acquainted early on with the verbal channel, it discovers the advantages of the 'elaborated' speech code: it learns to control a medium which can explain conflicts and problems as well as describe relations between objects and individuals. Bernstein adds that an early orientation towards 'elaborated' speech promotes logical thinking, whereby the relation between internal ideas and external objects can be recognized and processed by way of the complex organization of speech patterns. Thus strategies are formed by well-organized speech which favour the abstract comprehension of such relations. Furthermore, easy manipulation of linguistic structures seems to lead to greater motivation to learn.

These advantages are lacking in a process of socialization in which the predominant orientation of the child is towards the nonverbal channel as opposed to the verbal channel. According to Bernstein, socialization in the lower class takes place by way of few, short and rigid linguistic utterances; the authoritarian type of utterance, i.e. the command predominates, admitting of no explanatory motivation of action but only that which is founded on authority. Commands prevent all insight into causal relations, which in the educational practice of the middle class, however, is always provided explicitly. On the other hand, the intentional and emotional meanings in the lower class are transmitted to a large extent via the nonverbal channel. This means that they are conveyed by a less explicit inventory of signs. Accordingly, Bernstein also believes the scope of interpretation and therefore the possibility of misunderstanding to be greater. In contrast to the middle class, which is socialized by the abstract signs of language, the lower class concentrates rather on concrete, nonlinguistic signs, which have a certain unifying and emotional value. The nonlinguistic mode of expression, however, is an unreliable and inadequate means of communication for solving conflicts and expressing needs. For this reason Bernstein regards as advantageous the process of socialization by 'elaborated' speech.

A range of factors which govern the course of socialization is responsible for adjustment to verbal or nonverbal behaviour. Up till now Bernstein has only been able to describe them roughly. He distinguishes the most important of these as the social role, the family and the class (cf. Bernstein 1959a; 1961a; 1965; 1971a and b).

The family can be regarded as a community of interaction which leads to definite role constellations. According to the social roles which its members adopt (e.g. the father as breadwinner, the mother as housewife, the child as the person being socialized), their communicative forms are based on regular modes, which result from the internal family constellation, originate from psychological characteristics of their members, and are shaped by the general social enviroment and its values (past and present). These factors do not vary arbitrarily from one family to another. They display a series of common features which are decisively marked by the social structure. According to the social milieu the family structures can be systematically similar to or different from each other in distributing rights and duties, in assigning roles and in the type of interaction. Frequently these vary with the socioeconomic status and the level of education. In Bernstein's view, the different practices of socialization essentially covary with these two variables. 'Socioeconomic status' refers to the material position of the family in the social hierarchy; 'level of education' to the standard of command of intellectual strategies, upon which educational practice is based. Families are assigned to the lower or to the middle class depending on the criteria of socioeconomic status and level of education. Although Bernstein regards role as the social stage which brings about 'restricted' and 'elaborated' speech codes he concedes that class has a wider influence on speech. 'Without a shadow of doubt the most formative influence upon the procedures of socialization, from a sociological viewpoint, is social class' (Bernstein 1971a). Thus the significance of social class for the existence of 'restricted' or 'elaborated' speech forms lies in its 'prediction value' but it cannot be used to assign specific speech forms. The speech forms can be assigned to *types of transition families* ('transition family' describes a circular process: the exercise of educational practices by persons in authority— the assimilation of educational practices by children undergoing socialization as they grow up), which can be distinguished by the degree to which their role systems are status- or person-oriented. The *allocation of decision-making* is the characteristic which discriminates between these two role systems. If this is made in a hierarchical manner there is no possible communicative feedback between those in authority and the other members of the family; in the case of cooperative decision-making, on the other hand, maximum feedback is promoted by communicative interaction. This can be interpreted as follows: a status-oriented role system prevents the individual and communicative development (orientation towards the use of the restricted speech form); a person-oriented role system promotes behaviour determined by the individual, which gives rise to orientation towards the use of the elaborated speech form.

We shall come back to the sociological characteristics of the role systems that determine the speech codes; they lead to more precise distinctions between elaborated and restricted codes. Even in his most recent formulations, Bernstein (e.g. 1972b, 472–97) adheres to the view that status-oriented and person-oriented role systems (as extremes) should be related to the lower class and the middle class respectively.

For purposes of analysis Bernstein (1971a) distinguishes four contexts for the completion of the processes of socialization; they essentially determine which speech forms can be developed:

'1.   The *regulative context* (these are authority relationships where the child is made aware of the rules of the moral order and their various backings).

2.   The *instructional context* (where the child learns about the objective nature of objects and persons, and acquires skills of various kinds).

3.   The *imaginative* or *innovating contexts* (where the child is encouraged to experiment and recreate his world on his own terms, and in his own way).

4.   The *interpersonal context* where the child is made aware of affective states—his own, and others).'[7] (Italics mine.)

The consequences of these contexts are manifested in the linguistic characteristics of communication.

1.3.2 Language and social role

In Bernstein's later essays, social role assumes an increasingly important function. It is the smallest social unit by which the different speech codes are conveyed; at the same time it is the speech codes which generate the social roles:[8]

'As a person leans to subordinate his behavior to a linguistic code which is the expression of the role, different orders of relation are made available to him. The complex of meanings which a role-system transmits reverberates developmentally in an individual in order to inform his general conduct. On this argument it is the linguistic transformation of the role which is the major bearer of meanings; it is through specific linguistic codes that relevance is created, experience given a particular form, and social identity constrained.' (Bernstein 1967, 127)

The role is to be understood as 'a complex coding activity controlling both the creation and organization of specific meanings and the conditions for their transmission and reception' (Bernstein 1972b, 474). It can be empirically attached to manifest speech forms. By the process of social instruction, the role is acquired by communication symbols and conveyed by the lexical meanings relevant to a particular social structure and by its combinations in syntactic patterns.

Can meanings, which roles show to be relevant, be distinguished in any way? According to Bernstein (1971a) universalistic and particularistic meanings can be separated from one another by analogy to the distinction between the 'elaborated' and 'restricted' speech code. Universalistic meanings are formed by operations which, linguistically, are formulated explicitly and are not bound to concrete (extraverbal) contexts. Metalinguistic behaviour, for example, is borne by universalistic meaning. On the other hand particularistic meanings are context-tied to the extent that they are not intelligible on the basis of only the

---

[7] (1)–(4) have been adopted by Bernstein from Halliday 1969, with some modification.

[8] We shall give a critical account of the concept of roles and class later. Cf. the explanations of the concepts of role and class in Eichhorn *et al.* 1969, 388–94; cf. also Frigga Haug, 'Kritische Bemerkungen zu H.P. Dreitzels "Vorstudien zu einer Pathologie des Rollenverhaltens"', *Argument* **60** (1970), 217–22.

explicit linguistic structure but require also the support of the extraverbal context; in such a meaning system a certain local and sociostructural restrictedness of its speakers becomes linguistically evident.

It is clear from this that roles learnt by universalistic meanings promote non-context-bound speech behaviour whereas particularistic meanings generate context-bound roles. Bernstein takes the concepts 'universalistic' and 'particularistic' from an empirical examination by Hawkins (1969), who measured the use of pronouns in childrens' speech. An account of this is given in 2.3.5.

1.3.3 Language and school

The orientation towards an elaborated or restricted speech code gives rise to methods of selection at school, the secondary stage of socialization, which often have negative results for children of the lower class. According to the terminology used by Bernstein, lower-class children do have less verbal ability and less motivation to learn, and are inferior to middle-class children who use elaborated speech, in that the educational norms are tailored for the latter; and the teachers, who have been socialized by the norms of the same class, base their behaviour on its scale of values (cf. on this point Bourdieu and Passeron 1970; Bandelot and Establet 1971). The general behaviour of teachers seems to reward elaborated speakers and therefore middle-class children, and to penalize in an intuitive way restricted speakers (cf. Labov 1964b, 95f.; Seligman, Tucker and Lambert 1972). In a certain sense unequal opportunities of education result from this. Bernstein was the first to expose this situation and in so doing stimulated discussion on the analysis of the conditions which cause communicative behaviour to become a decisive factor in social injustice. This has led to suggestions which aim at changing the training of teachers and their methods as well as to progress towards linguistically based preschool programmes for lower-class children. Serious doubts have, however, also been expressed about the latter measures, in that, from the point of view of a comprehensive social analysis, the sense and the aims of such preschool programmes were questioned (cf. our arguments in 3.1; 3.2; 3.4.3 and 3.5).

1.4 Characteristics and predictability of the speech codes

Up till now we have discussed the theoretical factors and the conditions of socialization which determine the formation of restricted and elaborated speech. As a hypothesis Bernstein's theoretical conception can only have value if it indicates the characteristics which can classify the speech codes into two distinct types. As has been shown, one must be able to predict on the three levels (sociological, psychological and linguistic) which speaker is using elaborated or restricted speech and what the attributes are which determine this. Just as the three levels in the theoretical conception form a closed relation, so the characteristics analogous to these three levels are to be understood as a coherent mutually-conditioned complex of features. For reasons of analysis we shall consider the characteristics separately according to whether they belong to linguistic, psychological or sociological levels. Nevertheless we must bear in mind the fact that only when these are taken together do they predict the different speech codes.

1.4.1 Linguistic characteristics

An enumeration of the characteristics of speech forms is to be found only in Bernstein's earlier essays; in his more recent works there are only global characterizations which allow the reader much scope for interpretation.

We shall cite the characteristics of 'formal' and 'public' speech (later termed 'elaborated' and 'restricted' speech codes) not because we believe Bernstein's earlier arguments to be more precise but because there is a clear link between them; as a basis we have chosen the essay entitled 'Social structure, language and learning' (Bernstein 1961a). The characteristics that determine 'public speech' are as follows:

I

'1   Short, grammatically simple, often unfinished sentences with a poor syntactical form (stressing the active voice).
2   Simple and repetitive use of conjunctions (so, then, because).
3   Little use of subordinate clauses to break down the initial categories of the dominant subject.
4   Inability to hold a formal subject through a speech sequence; thus a dislocated informational content is facilitated.
5   Rigid and limited use of adjectives and adverbs.
6   Infrequent use of impersonal pronouns as subjects of conditional clauses.
7   Frequent use of statements where the reason and conclusion are confounded to produce a *categoric* statement.
8   A large number of statements/phrases which signal a requirement for the previous speech sequence to be reinforced: 'Wouldn't it? You see? You know?' etc. This process is termed *sympathetic circularity*.
9   Individual selection from a group of idiomatic phrases or sequence will frequently occur.
10   *The individual qualification is implicit in the sentence organization: it is a language of implicit meaning.'*

The characteristics of 'formal speech' are:

II

'1   Accurate grammatical order and syntax regulate what is said.
2   Logical modifications and stress are mediated through a grammatically complex sentence construction, especially through the use of a range of conjunctions and subordinate clauses.
3   Frequent use of prepositions which indicate logical relationships as well as prepositions which indicate temporal and spatial contiguity.
4   Frequent use of the personal pronoun 'I'.
5   A discriminative selection from a range of adjectives and adverbs.
6   Individual qualification is verbally mediated through the structure and relationships within and between sentences.

7   Expressive symbolism discriminates between meanings within speech sequences rather than reinforcing dominant words or phrases, or accompanying the sequence in a diffuse, generalized manner.

8   It is a language use which points to the possibilities inherent in a complex conceptual hierarchy for the organizing of experience.' (Bernstein 1961a, 169f.)

In the following critical discussion of these characteristics one should bear in mind that Bernstein could not refer back to any kind of preliminary linguistic study in his first attempts to differentiate between 'restricted' and 'elaborated' speech; it is therefore understandable that his criteria have a fairly arbitrary quality about them.

The characteristics of the two speech forms do not correspond either in their sequence or in their references to linguistic, psychological or other evidence. Statements such as I (9) and (10) or II (1), (7) and (8) are vague assertions, which do, however, have some suggestive value as global terms. Apart from the predominantly linguistic formulations, as in I (1), (2), (3), (5) and (6), there are also others which are both linguistic and psychological (e.g. I (4) and (7) or II (6) and (7)). In general, the value judgements associated with the use of particular linguistic expressions are based partly on logicogrammatical viewpoints (language must exhibit a definite minimal structure in order for it to be at all comprehensible); but they are also based on an *a priori* norm, which Bernstein considers to be the correct one. He believes that his concept of the norm is entailed by the results of objective sociological and psychological research which appear to enable him to distinguish between 'good' and 'bad'; yet he does not go into the question of the appropriateness of this application of the results. It is difficult to make out what, for example, I (5), 'limited use of adjectives and adverbs', is supposed to reveal about the linguistic capabilities of the speaker.

We can summarize our critique of Bernstein's characterization of the speech forms in the following way:

1   They only give us a very global idea of what kind of differences can exist between the two speech forms; the elasticity of these formulations makes it possible to verify them empirically by means of very different material.
2   The division between the linguistic level and other levels is not clarified.
3   The characterizations originate from normative concepts which are neither questioned from the social point of view nor justified by any explicit, empirically explanatory model.

By comparing the factors listed above, which are meant to define a 'public' and a 'formal' language, with Bernstein 1958, it can be seen that in the latter 'public' language has two criteria fewer and 'formal' language one criterion fewer. Furthermore, in Bernstein 1959 he differs from both these essays regarding points (3) and (9) on 'public' speech.

The later essays (e.g. Bernstein 1962a and b) makes these characteristics even more dubious, for they do not even attempt to give an accurate indication of the discriminating linguistic factors. On the contrary, there one sees an attempt, in vague association with information theory, to outline more precisely lexical and syntactic predictions for both speech forms by means of the notion 'speech code'. Thus Bernstein distinguishes (1965):

1   *'Restricted speech code (lexical prediction)'*
    'All the words, and hence the organizing structure irrespective of its degree of complexity, are wholly predictable for speakers and listeners'; it is a matter of 'ritualistic modes of communication', based on stereotypes; new information is conveyed by the extraverbal channel, which becomes the object of special perceptual activity.

2   *'Restricted speech code (syntactic prediction)'*
    Linguistic prediction is 'only possible at the syntactic level'; this type of speech consists to a large extent of solidarity utterances (commonly shared meanings and expectations); it is impersonal (in contrast to individual), conveys meanings only implicitly and is fast and fluent.

3   *'Elaborated speech code (low syntactic prediction)'*
    This speech code is the exact opposite of (1) and (2): verbally explicit, given to abstraction and individual qualification; its lexicon has a broad range and gives rise to many syntactic alternatives; it facilitates the verbal organization of experience and the transmission of affective and cognitive conditions.

It can be added here that the distinctions based on the criterion of prediction greatly exceed the bounds of any viable notion of linguistic prediction, It is, in any case, difficult to see how the evidence adduced can be predicted without reference to sociological or psychological dimensions. Consequently one can only speculate about the exact position and predictive value of these distinctions. In particular, there is no indication as to what grammatical theory should underlie the calculation of the degree of linguistic predictability, nor as to the exact nature of the quantifiable linguistic characteristics (syntactic as well as lexical) which lead to a discrimination between the two speech forms.

In an excursus we shall now consider linguistic predictability in more detail and show ways of specifying the notion 'speech code' more precisely.

Excursus: lexical and syntactic predictability of the speech codes[9]

The following exposé of the definition of the speech codes and their syntactic and lexical predictions can only reproduce to a very limited extent Bernstein's complex analysis. The sociological correlates are greatly oversimplified and the psychological correlates are reduced to plain 'probability'. Our formal representation can in no way grasp the connections that exist with respect to psychological and sociological factors, as we shall see in the following two sections. It is an abstraction of the 'elaborated' and 'restricted' speech forms dependent upon context and social structure. In this limited sense we can define a speech code more precisely as follows.

A linguistic system (e.g. English) can be represented by a number of lexical units $\{w_1, w_2, \ldots, w_n\}$ and by a set of syntactic rules $\{r_1, r_2, \ldots, r_m\}$.

[9] In the following section we shall draw on Norbert Dittmar and Wolfgang Klein, 'Die Codetheorie Basil Bernsteins', in Klein and Wunderlich 1972.

Speech acts, which can be produced with the help of such rules in particular situations, can now be characterized by means of two functions, which assign to each w and to each r a particular numerical value, reflecting a form of frequency. What value the functions assume for a particular lexical unit or syntactic rule depends to some extent on the *situational context t*, but essentially on the *social structure s*, to which the speaker belongs. Thus we obtain two functions:

$$f(w_i, s_k, t_l) = x_{i,k,l}$$
$$g(r_i, s_k, t_l) = y_{i,k,l}$$

$\qquad$ **1**

where f represents the *lexical* and g the *syntactic* function and x and y are values of certain frequency measures; they relate to the members of the functions (words or rules) and are not necessarily equally high. The functions formulated in (1) describe a speech code when the value of s is kept constant.

Of course, this definition disregards many details; it does not reflect the interdependence of s and t (particular contexts can be such that differences in social structure are removed) or the individual differences between speakers. On the other hand, it does take into account the fact that the realization of the speech code can vary according to the context. Thus Bernstein has repeatedly pointed out that elaborated speakers (e.g. at cocktail parties) can also use restricted speech. Nevertheless, context is a neglected factor in speech code determination, as will later become apparent in connection with our discussion of the empirical investigations.

On the basis of our definition in (1) we can distinguish the restricted from the elaborated speech code with the help of the predictability of lexical and syntactic selections. Speakers of the restricted speech code make a more restricted selection from a wide range of the entire repertoire of lexical units and syntactic rules; on the other hand, they make more frequent use of the units and rules they select.

If we write for the lexical units of English: $W = \{w_1, w_2, \ldots, w_n\}$ and for the syntactic rules: $R = \{r_1, r_2, \ldots, r_m\}$, then W can be divided into the disjunctive subsets W_m and W_l, whereby for each w_i from W_m

$$f_t(w_i, s_m) > f_t(w_i, s_l)$$

$\qquad$ **2**

and for each w_j from W_l

$$f_t(w_j, s_m) < f_t(w_j, s_l);$$

$\qquad$ **3**

by analogy, the same is true for R, divided into the disjunctive subsets R_m and R_l:

$$g_t(r_i, s_m) > g_t(r_i, s_l) \text{ for } r_i \in R_m$$

$\qquad$ **4**

and

$$g_t(r_j, s_m) < g_t(r_j, s_l) \text{ for } r_j \in R_l.$$

$\qquad$ **5**

B

The conditions (2) to (5) signify that in a constantly-maintained context t, w_i and r_i are used more frequently by middle-class speakers (denoted by m) than by lower-class speakers (denoted by l), whereas w_j and r_j are used by lower-class speakers more frequently than middle-class speakers.

A specific part of the characteristics of public speech (see I, p. 20 above) would therefore fall under W_l or R_l, whereas the characteristics of formal speech (II) should have been classed in part under W_m or R_m.

We have not, however, so far defined any form of 'greater linguistic predictability' with regard to the lower class. We should add to our statements in (2) to (5) the information that the lower class's high values are higher than the middle class's high values, and the lower class's low values are lower than the middle class's low values.

Accordingly, we say that:

$$f_t (w_j, s_l) > f_t (w_i, s_m) \qquad\qquad\qquad 6$$

$$f_t (w_i, s_l) < f_t (w_j, s_m), \qquad\qquad\qquad 7$$

whereby each w_j comes from W_l and each w_i from W_m, and

$$g_t (r_j, s_l) > g_t (r_i, s_m) \qquad\qquad\qquad 8$$

$$g_t (r_i, s_l) < g_t (r_j, s_m), \qquad\qquad\qquad 9$$

whereby each r_j comes from R_l and each r_i from R_m.

Using our expressions in (6) to (9) we can—with a little goodwill—interpret Bernstein's notion of 'greater predictability' as 'higher redundancy' in terms of information theory.

To put it simply, what the system illustrated above means statistically is that a speech code with n elements, of which some occur very frequently and others very rarely if at all, is more redundant than another speech code with the same elements, but which exhibit a more even distribution.

Up till now investigations have been able to demonstrate that conditions (2) to (5) are partly satisfied whereas conditions (6) to (9) could not be proved.

1.4.2 Psychological correlates of the speech codes

According to Bernstein (1965), the speech codes are 'established on a psychological level'. On this level they are generated 'by specific kinds of verbal planning'. The verbal planning takes place according to processes of

1   *orientation* (scanning by the hearer of the communicative utterances for a pattern of dominant signs);
2   *selection* (associations to the pattern of dominant signs which govern selections from a repertoire of verbal and extraverbal signs);
3   *organization* (the speaker's linguistic selections are adapted to a grammatical frame and integrated with extraverbal signs.

This planning is subject to two different governing activities which are themselves a function of the social structure and translate its meanings into speech forms. 'The [speech] codes, linguistic translations of the meanings of the social structure, are nothing more than verbal planning activities at the psychological level and *only at this level can they be said to exist*' (1965).

In spite of this description of the level of verbal planning Bernstein does not specify the characteristics which would enable the governing activities to be distinguished. In his empirical study of 1962 he attempts to ascertain the various levels of verbal planning by the number of speech pauses (per word and sentence).

As we shall show in 2.3.4, speech pauses are an inadequate scale for measuring processes of verbal planning.

1.4.3 Social correlates

The sociological conditions of speech codes have already been discussed in 1.3.1. A rough indicator, maintained in all Bernstein's works, is social class, which is ascertained by the criteria of socioeconomic status and level of education. Within the frame of social class the speech codes are generated in the family role system. Since the style of education in the family is dependent on the parents' verbal and nonverbal interaction with their children, Bernstein distinguishes (1972)[11] two types of families on the basis of the parents' sociological attributes: the *status-oriented* and the *person-oriented* family (cf. 1.3.1 above). The status-oriented type admits of few alternatives in communication; it is, therefore, described by Bernstein as a 'closed role system', which is characteristic for the genesis of the 'restricted' speech code:

'We could call a role system which reduced the range of alternatives for the realization of verbal meaning a closed type. It would follow that the greater the reduction in the range of the alternatives, the more communal or collective the verbal meanings and the lower the order and more rigid the syntactic and vocabulary selections—thus the more restricted the code.' (Bernstein 1972, 477)

On the other hand, in the person-oriented family there are many alternatives possible in communication; this type is therefore called and 'open role system', and produces the elaborated speech code:

'However, we could call a role which permitted a range of alternatives for the realization of verbal meanings an open type. It would follow that the greater the range of alternatives permitted by the role system, the more individualized the verbal meanings, the higher the order, and the more flexible the syntactic and vocabulary selection and so the more elaborated the code.' (Bernstein 1972, 477f.)

---

[11] We must here point out a difficulty which is to be found in most of Bernstein's essays: there are various versions of one and the same essay. The essay 'A sociolinguistic approach to socialization, with some reference to educability' appears in different versions in Williams 1970a, and in Gumperz and Hymes 1972. Until one version is endorsed by Bernstein we can only roughly reproduce the distinctions he makes.

The concept of the family as a role system is fundamental for different varieties of elaborated and restricted speech. Whether the role system is open or closed depends on the way linguistic meanings are related to persons or objects; equally the degree of elaboration or restriction is affected by particular speech acts (appeals, commands), by which social control is exerted within the family.

The sociological characterizations given by Bernstein can be understood as explanatory attempts to narrow down the social conditions of different speech codes. This can be inferred both from their breadth of variation and from a certain globality in the argumentation which from the outset seeks to avoid the necessity of further specification.

In our attempt to enlarge upon Bernstein's linguistic, psychological and social correlates for the restricted and elaborated speech codes we encountered the difficulty of not being able to find any uniform characteristics; it is true that these correlates are all bound to the restricted-elaborated dichotomy, yet the numerous different subclassifications in various essays do not provide a clear picture of exactly which is correct. We shall now catalogue the numerous distinctions, and at the same time pursue the development of Bernstein's conception as reflected in his successive essays.

1.5 Catalogue of speech-code determinants

Bernstein's early distinction between a formal and a public language (1958) is altered to a distinction between an elaborated and a restricted speech code from 1962 onwards. The adoption of these terms represents a tendency to specify two conditions:

1   The speech codes have systematic attributes, i.e. particular forms of social relations determine different verbal planning strategies, which are manifested in constant speech forms.
2   It should become clear in the terminology that restricted speech codes are limited in relation to elaborated codes.

In his further differentiations Bernstein continues to dichotomize. One of the first subdivisions is to be found in Bernstein 1964 (65): 'It is possible to distinguish two modes of an elaborated code. One facilitates relations between *persons* and the second facilitates relations between *objects*.'

The distinction made for the elaborated speech code is later also applied to the restricted code. Bernstein (1972b) surveys the most recent state of the distinctions relevant to the speech codes. The term 'range of alternatives' can be regarded as a central concept or link between role systems, types of social control, planning strategies and speech forms. At the same time this concept is the criterion which differentiates the analytical units.

Role systems are open or closed according to the range of linguistic meanings which inhere in them. Families are person- or status-oriented, depending on the type of decision-making, i.e. according to whether decisions can be made on the basis of individually varying opinions or whether they are decreed by hierarchically determined status persons. Communication systems are *open* or *closed* according to the types of social control (appeals, commands). The linguistic meanings governed by the verbal planning can be *object-* or *person-bound*; they can, moreover, still be differentiated according to whether they are used as *means* or for particular *aims*.

Eight speech codes can be distinguished, finally, on the basis of these differentiations: four person-oriented and four object-oriented codes, which can again be divided according to whether they are elaborated or restricted and whether they are aims or means. These speech codes depend on the forms of social relations in the families, that is to say, on whether families promote person orientation or object orientation; it also depends on whether their role systems are open or closed. The diagram below, which we have modified from the one in Gumperz and Hymes (1972, 470), reproduces the possible combinations; on the basis of this the specific speech code of a group, a family or an individual can be determined.

| | | | | (Family with) *Object orientation* | | | |
| | | | | Elaborated | | Restricted | |
				Aims	Means	Aims	Means
(Family with) *Person orientation*	Elaborated	Aims	{	El (P, A) El (O, A)	El (P, A) El (O, M)	El (P, A) R (O, A)	El (P, A) R (O, M)
		Means	{	El (P, M) El (O, A)	El (P, M) El (O, M)	El (P, M) R (O, A)	El (P, M) R (O, M)
	Restricted	Aims	{	R (P, A) El (O, A)	R (P, A) El (O, M)	R (P, A) R (O, A)	R (P, A) R (O, M)
		Means	{	R (P, M) El (O, A)	R (P, M) El (O, M)	R (P, M) R (O, A)	R (P, M) R (O, M)

P = person-oriented; O = object-oriented; El = elaborated; R = restricted; A = aims; M = means.

Fig. 1.3 Possible combinations of the eight speech codes.

Figure 1.3 shows Bernstein's most recent position on the speech-code determinants. The question remains as to what linguistic criteria should correspond to these speech codes. For a critical discussion on the state of these differentiations, see 3.4.1 below.

1.6 Summary

In conclusion, we shall summarize some aspects which to us appear to be characteristic of Bernstein's ideas of the different speech codes.

1   *Basic idea*
    Communication, acting through the social structure, can contribute decisively to the methods of selection which govern the distribution of privileges in a society. The 'elaborated' speech code provides access to social privileges, whereas the 'restricted' speech code prevents this; the difference

between the 'elaborated' and 'restricted' codes is precisely the deficit which prevents the social success of 'restricted' speakers.

2   *Theoretical aspects*

   i   The social structure intervenes between language as a rule system and speech as performance, and determines specific speech codes by way of specific planning strategies. The 'elaborated' speech code is to be found in the middle class, the 'restricted' code in the lower class.

   ii   The speech codes have social, psychological and linguistic correlates. They are defined by their lexical and syntactic predictions.

   iii   By speech code is meant the constant speech strategies of speakers. They refer to capabilities of speakers, which are determined not genetically but socially.

   iv   The speech codes develop during the phase of socialization. While they are generated by social roles they themselves also mould the social roles. This is what constitutes the circularity principle of the speech codes.

3   *Implications of the theoretical concept*

   i   A close correlation exists between speech and thinking. A linguistic deficit implies at the same time a cognitive deficit.

   ii   Differences in the communicative behaviour of speakers are not established from speech acts but from the predictability of linguistic sequences.

   iii   It is primarily linguistic (and not, for example, socioeconomic) differences that are blamed for social inequality.

   iv   Social inequality (of opportunity) can be compensated by raising the standards of speech.

4   *Theoretical method*

   i   In most cases the definitions are imprecise and metaphorical. The terminology is altered from one essay to another.

   ii   Bernstein's conception should be regarded as a hypothesis. As such, however, it has never been explicitly formulated. This causes considerable problems for its verification.

   iii   The concept of theory formation is normative rather than descriptive. Above all, it is oriented towards values of bourgeois sociology. (This is evident from the positive evaluation attached to notions such as 'individual', 'family', 'educated speech'.)

The discussion of Bernstein's works has yet to arrive at conclusive results or unequivocal empirical judgements, as is shown by the numerous publications on the hypothesis of speech codes specific to social class. We are still waiting for the results of current empirical investigations. At present there is a marked tendency to regard Berstein's work as a contribution to research into the communicative competence of speakers (cf. Hymes and Cazden in Cazden, John and Hymes 1972).

2 Empirical verification of the Deficit Hypothesis: normative investigations into the correlation between speech and socialization

Bernstein's hypotheses on speech behaviour specific to social class have stimulated numerous inquiries in Europe as well as in the USA aimed at testing their accuracy empirically. In addition to the purely academic interest, there is another deeper-lying factor which must be regarded as giving impetus to these investigations: the increasingly urgent necessity in Western society to mobilize educational reserves in order to maintain the prevailing levels of production. Empirical investigation was considered the right way to gain the knowledge of lower-class speech behaviour which is necessary for restructuring the education system and for maximizing the yield of the educational potential in schools (cf. 3.5).

An example of this correlation is provided by the development of inquiries into class-specific speech behaviour in the USA. The results are arrived at on the basis of arbitrarily-fixed norms and value scales; they serve, however, the requirements of prevailing forces in society in that they aim at showing ways of developing unused educational reserves. Similar tendencies are to be seen in the UK; we shall come back to this point.

The fact that the empirical verification of Bernstein's hypotheses leaves appreciable room for normative and ideological padding is a result of its inexplicit formulation (there is great scope for variety in the form of the investigation), although it should not be forgotten that *each* empirical inquiry can be manipulated in a number of possible ways (cf. Garfinkel 1967; Slama-Cazacu 1971). Because Bernstein's thesis is so unsystematic, it allows a considerable degree of arbitrariness in the determination of the measurable characteristics that are to verify the differences postulated in speech behaviour on the sociological, psychological and linguistic level of analysis. As we shall see for each of these three levels of analysis, the direct (and not surprising) consequence of these inexplicit formulations is that the results of experiments and quantifications conducted in completely different ways can nevertheless be interpreted as corroborating the hypotheses. We shall also be concerned with the problem of how and with what instruments empirical research is conducted: that is, with what intentions, in what situations and with what methods empirical investigations are carried out. The following are perhaps questions which will enable us to acquaint ourselves with some aspects of the issues at hand, as well as with the value and significance of the empirical results.

1   What is the value of the tests for the assessment of linguistic and intellectual capabilities of lower-class children? What do the tests measure: superficial or basic capabilities?

2   What are the norms underlying the quantifications and the interpretation
       of their results? In this connection we must also question the selection of the
       situation in which the test is performed.
3   How is different speech behaviour explained? What is the correlation
       between speech and thinking? What assumptions are made in respect of the
       socialization of the child?

Of course we cannot possibly deal with these questions exhaustively. We shall
discuss some more precise theories in the next chapter.

With the help of specific empirical investigations, we must first of all develop
clearer notions of the problems at hand. The empirical analyses of class-specific
speech behaviour with which we shall be concerned represent English, American
and German forms of research; sociopolitically speaking, they are motivated by
inequality of opportunity, a key-word which has, however, not been further
specified; their empirical aim is the verification of Bernstein's hypotheses.

As examples, we shall select a few typical investigations; first we shall deal with
the correlation between intelligence and social class; then the results of
investigations into the intellectual and linguistic capabilities of lower-class
children will be described and related to their class-specific socialization.

A considerable part of the literature relevant to these questions will not be
mentioned, since we prefer to give more detailed accounts of individual case-
studies. Elsewhere, of course, the available literature has been discussed from
various points of view (see Bernstein 1959b; Cazden 1966 and 1968; Lawton 1968;
Oevermann 1969a).

2.1   Correlation between social class, intelligence and speech behaviour

One of Bernstein's fundamental assumptions is that speech differences specific to
social class are *independent of nonverbal intelligence test scores*. Linguistic
differences exist therefore not because of different genetic aptitude, but because of
the social structure.

In order to prove this, Bernstein (1960) predicts that the results of a language
test for the working class would be severely depressed in relation to those of a
nonverbal test.

In testing this prediction two groups were selected from different social
backgrounds:

1   *Working-class group:* 61 boys between the ages of fifteen and eighteen, who
       were comparable in their level of education, social background, occupation
       (they were messenger boys), and domicile.
2   *Middle-class or 'public school' group:* 45 schoolboys who were comparable
       with the boys in (1) in age; they went to one of the six major 'public schools'
       in London.

The two groups were given the Raven's Progressive Matrices Test (a nonverbal
intelligence test) and the Mill Hill Test (test of the range of vocabulary).

For both tests the differences between the groups are clear in a regression analysis:[1]

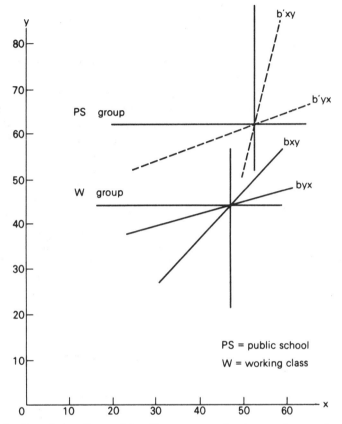

Fig. 2.1 Regression lines of intelligence tests for lower-class and middle-class groups. This figure 'indicates the position of the regression lines of the tests for both groups. For both the public-school and the working-class group the slope of the regression lines *byx, b'yx* (the regression of the vocabulary upon the Matrices score) is similar. This is not the case for *bxy, b'xy*, which indicates the regression of the Matrices upon the language score for the two groups. The difference in the slopes of *bxy* and *b'xy* indicates differences in the distribution of the language scores in the two groups. The distribution of the working-class language scores in relation to those of the public school is depressed at the higher ranges of the Matrices score'. (Source: Bernstein 1960)

The following differences in marks can be seen between the two groups: if one assumes an average age of 16 years for the groups, in the nonverbal Matrices Test the difference is roughly 8–10 marks, whereas in the vocabulary test it is 23–4 marks.

According to Bernstein, this clearly demonstrates a difference in verbal

---

[1] The statistical terms used are those of McCollough and Atta, *Statistik programmiert* (Weinheim, Berlin, Basel 1970); cf. also the glossary in the appendix to the present book.

performance which is related to class; in answering the questions of the nonverbal test, both the working and the middle classes displayed equal ability, whereas the decline of the *W* group in the verbal tests makes it plain that they were not capable of an adequate command in verbal exercises. 'There can be no doubt that a different relationship exists between the nonverbal and verbal group measures of intelligence for the two social groups.'

How does Bernstein interpret these results?

First of all he goes into the different evidence yielded by the tests. He interprets the fact that members of the *W* group were unable to reach the upper ranges of the verbal test as proof of their inferior command of concepts and linguistic rules vis-à-vis the members of the *PS* group. The higher assessment of linguistic performance is clearly visible in the higher value given to the verbal test:

'... a score on the Matrices may not indicate anything except the score; but a score on a reliable verbal test often serves as a guide to educational and occupational performance.'

Here the interpretation of a test is made on the basis of a preconceived norm of social performance: verbal intelligence is more important for the 'occupation' than non-verbal intelligence.

In his explanation of the fact that the *W* group was inferior to the *PS* group in verbal performance, Bernstein considers two alternatives:

1   the inferior verbal ability of the working class is a function of their deficient education (that is to say, of their worse instructional environment);
2   the inferior performance can be traced back to a genetic deficiency in linguistic ability.

Bernstein interprets the results in the light of (1). With this, his investigation has brought a new element to the discussion of the existence of two different speech codes: they are independent of measured nonverbal intelligence and are therefore a function of socialization processes. This means they are a result of different instructional environments. This is in fact the first inkling of the call for compensatory programmes which was to be made later: if different verbal behaviour can be attributed to different socialization processes, then it must be possible to correct and compensate these whenever they do *not* conform to the prevailing social norms.

It is of course nothing new in sociopsychological research that differences exist between social classes in measured intelligence. As early as 1942 McNemar was able to demonstrate a correlation between the type of occupation of the parents and the intelligence of their children. Two- to five-year-old middle-class children scored on average 20 IQ marks more than working-class children of the same age (this was based on the Stanford Binet Intelligence Test). An equally large discrepancy between the classes was found in the 15–18 age bracket.

Eels *et al.* (1951) and Ravenette (1963) arrived at similar results. Furthermore these two investigations clearly demonstrate that the verbal tests have a greater correlation with social class than the nonverbal test. (In connection with this Eels *et al.* establish, moreover, that the verbal intelligence test handicaps the lower classes.) Bernstein's work reinforces the view that class differences exist above all in the sphere of speech. According to Bernstein (1960), it is an undisputed postulate in sociopsychologically-oriented, class-specific linguistic research that speech differences determined by the social structure can only be regarded as valid if the nonverbal IQ level between the classes is a constant. Robinson (1965), Lawton (1968), Brandis and Henderson (1970) and also (to a certain extent) Oevermann (1970), amongst others, proceed along these lines.

We shall now make a few brief comments on Bernstein's study and its implications; they will be discussed in more detail in 3.3. It should be clear from the insufficient attention paid to the available material and from our primarily linguistic orientation that we do not intend to do more than merely touch on problems raised by the intelligence test. The following remarks are also relevant to the majority of intelligence tests in the frame of class-specific linguistic investigations according to Bernstein (1960).

First, it is apparent that Bernstein gives no indication of the way in which the subjects were tested. Were the tests conducted at school? Were the questions set to each subject individually or as a group? In connection with this we must know what motivated the boys to take the test. The bare results have very limited value if we are not told more about the relation between the results and the motivation with regard to the problem-solving required.

Secondly, the value attached to the tests is based on the assumption that the verbal part has more significance than the nonverbal part. If this is valid as a general assumption for the intelligence test, then we must, together with Eels *et al.* (1951), object that this very premise inflicts an unfair handicap on lower-class children. Even if we ignore the question of general intelligence the following problem remains: what bearing do the tests have on the everyday life of the boys? From research into socialization and the lower class, it follows that tests as a social situation are comparable with the problem-solving behaviour of middle-class children in the early stages of socialization (cf. for example Palmer 1970, 9).

This leads us to a third problem: what do the IQ scores reveal about the capabilities of lower-class children if there is reason to assume that the test situations made them feel insecure and that the required norms had no bearing on their social reality? Does the discrepancy of about 20 marks between the two groups in the verbal test imply a difference in the *factors connected with the problem-solving set-up* or in *linguistic competence*? Although Bernstein points out that the differences stem from different instructional environments, he still does not answer the question as to whether they should be regarded as differences in the linguistic ability of the speakers.

Fourthly, the test results reveal group features without giving any information about the construction of the group values from the individuals' aptitudes. A poor, below-average performance which stands out from the group average can, for example, considerably distort the score of the group as a whole.

Even if we do not fully go into the general value of intelligence tests, it is already clear that what measurement of verbal and nonverbal intelligence reveals about the capabilities of lower-class children is more than obscure (3.3 deals with this in greater depth). In order to avoid over-hasty conclusions on tests of this type, which nevertheless are the cornerstone of Bernstein's evidence, we shall turn to investigations which deal in more detail with the intellectual capabilities of lower-class children and support the Deficit Hypothesis on the psychological level.

2.2 Investigations into the intellectual capabilities of lower-class children

2.2.1 The work of Gray and Klaus

The work of Gray and Klaus (1968) serves as a starting point for our assessment of the intellectual capabilities of lower-class children. It is characteristic of a series of similar investigations in two respects:

1   Their investigation starts from the assumption that lower-class children are multidimensionally deficient.
2   The preconceived aim of their investigation is compensatory education.

Gray and Klaus conducted their survey in Tennessee, where there are many towns with slum areas, widespread poverty and a critical lack of education. Their subjects were exclusively children in Black families who lived in neglected, dilapidated houses; their parents were unskilled or semiskilled workers with a very low income and little education. The authors describe the deficit of the children in perception and concept formation in the following way:

> 'The children, when they came to us [at the age of four] were noticeably deficient in all three areas [perception, concept formation and speech]. This is easily understandable when one remembers that across all modalities, the sensory stimulation provided in the deprived home is basically unstructured and unordered. . . . In the spatially and temporally disorganized homes, full of noise in all modalities, from which our children came, the only coping mechanism readily available to them was "tuning out". . . . Exploration of the qualities of objects and events is difficult for the child in the deprived home. Not only does the disorganization lead to this, but so also do the reinforcement patterns in the home—withdrawing and passive behavior are much more apt to be reinforced positively than is active exploratory behavior . . . . Such exploration is essential for the development of adequate perception.' (Gray and Klaus 1968. 15–6)

The children exhibit little perception activity and are incapable of the simplest discriminations: thus they cannot tell the difference between various primary colours or geometric figures. Their concrete thinking is reflected in their type of concept formation: their answers are emotional and bear no trace of abstractions. Gray and Klaus regard the incapacity for differentiated perception of the environment as well as for abstract thinking as the reason for underprivileged children's failure at school. From this they derive the need for compensation. These formulations may well suffice to bring us back to the classic version of the Deficit Hypothesis: little perception activity, concrete thinking and emotional speech belong to the topical observations in sociolinguistic research since the time of Schatzmann and Strauss and Bernstein.

Without going into the conclusions which are drawn, from this assessment of the intellectual capabilities of lower-class children, as to the type and nature of compensatory programmes (see 3.1), we shall turn to investigations which substantiate this classic interpretation with empirical material. First of all we refer to a survey which considers *cognitive* deficit to be directly linked to *linguistic* deficit. The work of Robinson and Creed (1968) is particularly important in this respect because it contains empirical support for the theory of the correlation between language and perception ('this is the first demonstration that general differences in language samples . . . are associated with perceptual and verbal discriminations', Robinson and Creed 1968, 193), and at the same time asserts the success of compensatory speech education. The claims of this analysis are supported in an investigation made by the psychologist Martin Deutsch, who identified correlations between social class and intellectual capabilities in a series of tests with a total of more than 100 variables. Deutsch's results have been obtained from an unusually broad random sample and have been evaluated with great statistical accuracy. The significance of these results will be considered in detail.

2.2.2 The investigations of Robinson and Creed

Robinson and Creed (1968) set out to verify Bernstein's theory that restricted speakers can observe and perceive their environment with less discrimination than elaborated speakers as a result of their limited linguistic possibilities. Contrary to earlier attempts at verification, the authors are concerned with examining the correlation between perception activity and expressive ability by means of specifically-designed tests set in a well-controlled situation.

For this analysis they chose 24 predominantly working-class girls and tested them on their verbal and nonverbal capabilities before they entered primary school. During their first year at school, half the girls were given a speech training programme lasting 20 minutes per day (these girls were classed as a group of elaborated speakers), whereas the other girls in the sample test did not take part in such training (they formed the control group of restricted speakers). The investigation took place about 18 months after they had entered the school, and its object was to show differences in the correlation of perception and speech between trained elaborated speakers and untrained restricted speakers.

The survey was designed to give information on (1) the children's curiosity and attentiveness, as well as on their (2) perceptual and (3) verbal capacity for discrimination.

It was predicted that the elaborated speakers would gain higher scores for the following three variables than the restricted speakers:

'1   his greater facility for cognitive experience will lead him to spend more time studying and analysing a new situation,

2   as a further consequence he will see more relationships between objects in a new situation; he will notice more attributes, and similarly,

3   these discriminations are more likely to have effective verbal correlates which can be used to communicate the discriminations to a second person.' (Robinson and Creed 1968, 183)

How were these predictions put into practice by the problems set in the tests? First of all we must accept the fact that what the predictions called a 'new situation' was simulated in the tests by showing the children pictures. The 'objects', the relationships between them which the child should have noticed, and the 'attributes' referred to things shown in the picture; the communication by which the child conveyed her impressions after looking at the picture was directed at the examiner—a person unknown to the child who demanded an answer from her.

The examiner set the child the following problems in order to obtain the scores which were to verify the predictions: she was told to look at the picture for as long as she wanted and then to recount what she had seen. After this she was shown a second, almost identical picture which was slightly different from the first. The child was supposed to point out these differences and later she had to name them.

Quantitative scores were applied to the qualitative solution of these problems, which were set in order to verify the predictions in the three areas specified earlier. The degree of attentiveness and curiosity of a child was established by

1   measuring the time in seconds that the child took to look at the first picture;
2   noting the length of time that the child looked away from the picture;
3   counting the number of times the child took her eyes off the picture and looked elsewhere (Robinson and Creed 1968, 188).

The perceptual capacity for discrimination was made to follow simply from the number of differences which a child pointed out in comparing the pictures. To evaluate the verbal capacity for discrimination a scale of marks was introduced (0–3), which graded the statements made into four categories:

'i   simple statement of difference;
ii   recognition of relevant variable (shape, colour etc.);
iii   recognition of variable plus a statement of the value of the variable in one picture ("It's round there");
iv   recognition of both values of variable ("That is red and that is green").'(188)

The quantitative scores for the variables were checked for their significance and submitted to various analyses of variance and covariance. As this investigation is concerned not so much with details of the quantitative scores as with the presuppositions underlying the way they were obtained, we shall only add that the quantifications were carried out with accuracy. Generally, the predictions were confirmed by the results. None of the differences ran counter to the predicted trend.

How do Robinson and Creed interpret these results? In a narrow sense they conclude that 'elaborated' speakers perceive and communicate more precisely and efficiently (this was concluded from an additional error analysis). Their better performance can be accounted for by their superior command of speech. They must be classed as more curious and more attentive than 'restricted' speakers, although this is not absolutely clear from the test scores. In a broader sense, Robinson and Creed ascribe theoretical and practical significance to their investigation: first they claim to have proved that a change in speech implies a change in perception, and secondly, they claim success for a speech training programme.

What relevance does this study have for our inquiry into the intellectual capabilities of lower-class children? We shall consider only three aspects of this question.

First, in the same way as we objected to Bernstein's investigation (1960), we must object to the way in which pictures are substituted for real-life situations and used as the basis for evidence about curiosity, attentiveness, and perceptual and verbal performance: what was the relation of the test situation to the children's social reality? What stimulated the children's curiosity and attentiveness? (It must surely be indisputable that motivation is an essential factor in both these aspects of behaviour.) It is a matter of arbitrary decision that a relation is posited between the child's looking away from the picture and her attentiveness, or between her naming differences in the two pictures and her perceptual capacity. But apart from this, the results can tell us nothing new about 'restricted' speakers while we know as little about the children's basic motivation to solve the problems—and this stems from their needs—as we do about the relation of these problems to such needs.

Secondly, Robinson and Creed evidently believe that the correlation between speech and perception is reflected in the child's ability verbally to name differences between two pictures, or merely to point them out. It should be added that the perceptual capacity can remain passive and does not necessarily have to be verbalized. Moreover, the degree to which the perceptual capacity can be intensified depends on the motivation to verbalize.

Our third point is concerned with the role played by the speech-training programme in the test results. It is not at all surprising that the trained children were significantly superior to the untrained children in the test. They were trained for a whole year to solve problems that were based on the same standards as were those set in the tests: to recognize the object world with as great a distinction as possible (normally this requires more time) and to name the distinction that they recognize. Thus the test results show that, after appropriate training, lower-class children can perform without difficulty according to certain norms (that is, the test conditions and the acclimatization to differentiated verbalization etc.). This proves on the one hand that a good performance in the test presupposes a certain familiarity with the test norm and values, and on the other that lower-class children have the necessary ability to acquire it. Although this confirms Bernstein's thesis that restricted speech is a function of social class, it does not support the implicit judgement that at the same time it contains fewer resources, either in a verbal or a cognitive sense. The following seem to us to be the essential aspects of the investigation carried out by Robinson and Creed:

1   The problem-setting and solving in the tests are of no real significance for the assessment of lower-class children's capabilities, nor do they say anything about the relation between speech and perception.
2   The children trained along the lines of the test norms performed significantly better than the untrained children.
3   The conclusion to be drawn from (2) is that it is *not* the capability but the

tests and their *norms*, with which the lower-class children are not acquainted, that make them appear more limited.

As Robinson and Creed do not give any convincing proof of a relation between perception and speech, or of the inferior ability of lower-class children, we shall now turn to the extensive investigation carried out by Deutsch and his assistants.

2.2.3   Deutsch's investigation

Deutsch (1967)[2] is concerned chiefly with the correlation between social class and intellectual ability. Together with his assistants he examined a total of 292 Black and White children in their first and fifth years at school (the children were aged between 6 and 11) and, by means of approximately 100 variables, correlated their intelligence and their ability in speech, thinking and reading with their race and social class. The children came from schools in various cities of the USA. The results obtained from the investigation were to serve as a guide for constructing compensatory programmes. We shall select and elucidate the following from among the numerous tests conducted with the schoolchildren:[3]

1   the *Verbal Identification Test*
2   the *Concept Sorting Test*.

The problem-setting of the two tests is listed in figure 2.2, as well as some variables according to which they are subdivided, so as to facilitate judgement of their content (the numbers in the left-hand column denote the original numbering of the variables).

The problems set and the variables for the other tests are similar to those given above. The Verbal Identification Test requires the child to identify correctly objects in the pictures, and then to name what he sees with a single-word concept which should be as apposite as possible. The same thing is required in the Peabody Picture Vocabulary Test. The Concept Sorting Test makes two different demands on the child: first, he must be able to handle concepts—that is, he must be capable of establishing certain similarities in different objects (thus, for example, that pears, plums and bananas are fruits); secondly, he must be able to give the correct terms for the concepts.

The first two arguments in 2.2.2—in which we objected to Robinson and Creed's investigation—apply basically to both tests described here. With specific regard to these tests, we can add that a verbal measurement of concept formation seems inappropriate for two reasons. First, concepts can also exist on the nonverbal level, which means that a child does not necessarily lack concepts when he verbalizes them only sparingly. Secondly, there are investigations which show that a child has a command of concepts before he is able to express them verbally (cf. Piaget 1946; Ricciuti 1965; Lenneberg 1967).

[2] This section is based on a summary of the important results of these investigations in Deutsch 1965 and Ginsburg 1972, 112–16.
[3] The most important of these are the PPVT IQ Test, Verbal Identification Test, Concept Sorting Test, Concept Formation Test, Verbal Fluency Test, Orientation Scale Test, Word Association Test and the Cloze Test (cf. Deutsch 1965, 81–3).

Variables	Identification

Verbal Identification Test

The child is shown 20 simple drawings one at a time and is asked to enumerate the objects in each of the pictures. The child is then shown the 20 pictures a second time and asked to give the one word that best describes each picture.

9   Noun enumeration score:
The number of items identified correctly on those stimulus cards best described by a noun, e.g. *kitchen*.

10   Action enumeration score:
The number of items identified correctly on those stimulus cards best described by a verb, e.g. *saluting*.

11   Combined enumeration score: 9 + 10.
All the items identified correctly on the stimulus cards of the Verbal Identification Test.

12   Noun gestalt score:
The measure of the child's ability to describe a scene with a single word when the scene is best described by a noun.

13   Action gestalt score:
The measure of the child's ability to describe a scene with a single word when the scene is best described by a verb.

14   Combined gestalt score: 12 + 13.
The measure of the child's ability to describe the scenes of the Verbal Identification Test with a single word.

15   Peabody Picture Vocabulary Test (PPVT), raw score:
The number of words tried minus the number incorrect.

16   PPVT IQ score:
Obtained from the appropriate tables in the PPVT manual.

Concept Sorting Test

The child is presented 16 cards in random order (four sets of four, each representing modes of transport, housing, occupations or animals) and asked to sort the cards into piles. He is also asked to explain this grouping.

17   Number of Piles score:
The exact number of piles sorted. Four would be best. Usually anything above four indicates inadequacy at the task. The number has been primarily intended as a denominator for the other scores.

18   Sort score:
This score reflects the implicit quality of the child's sorting; e.g. sorting by class generalization receives more credit than functional pairings. Generally, the higher the score the better the quality.

19   Verbalization score:
For this score the child is asked to explain the basis of his sorting procedure. The basis of his sorting is evaluated and scored. Higher forms of classification, such as generalization v. functional pairing, get higher scores.

20   Verbal score ratio:
Verbalization score over Number of piles score (19/17).

21   Sort score ratio:
Sort score over Number of piles score (18/17).

Fig. 2.2 Deutsch's Verbal Identification and Concept Sorting Tests. (Source: Deutsch 1965, 82)

Variables	Correlations with SES[1]	
	Grade 1 (N=127)	Grade 5 (N=165)
1 = Age in months		−0·21
2 = L-T IQ Score	0·42	0·38
3 = L-T Subtest 1	0·35	0·25
4 = L-T Subtest 2	0·26	0·32
5 = L-T Subtest 3	0·26	0·38
6 = L-T raw score	0·34	0·37
7 = WISC Vocab. score	0·22	0·49
8 = Gates score	(test not given)	0·44
9 = Verbal Ident., noun enumer. score		
10 = Verbal Ident., action enumer. score		
11 = Verbal Ident., combined enumer. score		
12 = Verbal Ident., noun gestalt score	0·33	0·24
13 = Verbal Ident., action gestalt score	0·24	
14 = Verbal Ident., combined gestalt score	0·32	0·27
15 = PPVT raw score	0·32	(test not given)
16 = PPVT IQ	0·33	(test not given)
17 = Concept Sort., # piles score		
18 = Concept Sort., verbal score	0·23	
19 = Concept Sort., verbal score # piles ratio		0·23
20 = Concept Form., percept. similarities scores		0·22
21 = Concept Form., verbaliz. score, class specificity	0·26	0·20
22 = Concept Form., verbaliz. score, class generalization		0·21
23 = Concept Form., total verbaliz. score		0·21
24 = Word Knowledge score (Verbal Fluency)		
25 = Verbal Fluency, all rhymes score	0·24	0·28
26 = Verbal Fluency, meaningful rhymes	0·28	0·33
27 = Verbal Fluency, sentence fluency	0·25	
28 = Orientation Scale	0·36	0·51
29 = Wepman test of auditory discrimination[2]	−0·24	
30 = Word Assoc., form class score		0·27
31 = Word Assoc., latency score		
32 = Cloze test, grammatical score	0·26	0·33
33 = Cloze test, correct score	0·25	0·33
34 = Cloze test, popular score	0·30	0·37

[1] Higher index denotes higher SES. [2] Error score.

Fig. 2.3 Test results for 34 variables of Deutsch's Verbal Survey (1965): comparison of the sample groups from the first and fifth grades—significant correlations with socioeconomic status (SES). (Only correlations significant at $p < 0.01$ are shown.)

Thus Deutsch's tests are in essence only superficial measurements, which attach too much importance to verbalization.

Figure 2.3 gives the complete test results of his study of the correlation between social class and intellectual capability. We have not included the correlations with race (although Deutsch listed them simultaneously), since they are not essentially relevant to the question at hand.

Deutsch bases his assertion (similar to that of Bernstein) that lower-class children have a *cumulative deficiency* on the significant results of this table. This concept implies that already in the early stages of socialization the child is handicapped almost beyond hope by the extent of his intellectual deficiencies, and that this early disadvantage is further increased, i.e. accumulated, by the secondary agents of socialization such as kindergarten and school. With the help of the data in figure 2.2, we shall take a closer look at Deutsch's assertion that lower-class children are intellectually deficient.

In order to understand the results correctly, it is important to realize that correlations are possible between -1.0 and $+1.0$. The closer the correlation approaches 0, the less significant the relation between the variables in question. If, on the other hand, the correlation is at $+1.0$ or -1.0, a *strict* relation must be implied between two variables. Statistically, all the results obtained by Deutsch are significant at the level 0.01.

The first 8 variables relate to intelligence tests. The correlations with social class are between 0.2 and 0.4. These correlations could easily have been predicted from a knowledge of the norms that are measured by the Lorge-Thorndike intelligence test: the higher the social class, the greater the IQ score.

The variables 9–14 represent the results of the Verbal Identification Test. Less than half the variables yield significant correlations with social class. The higher the social class, the easier it is for the child to find the suitable word to describe a detail or an event on the picture shown to him during the test (variables 12–14). The significant scores lie between 0.2 and 0.3: they do not therefore really enable us to make an accurate prediction of the child's intellectual capacity from a knowledge of his social class. The variables 15 and 16, which refer to the Peabody Picture Vocabulary Test, apply only to the first grade and show that lower-class children perform significantly worse than middle-class children. No test was given to the fifth grade. There is also nothing surprising about what the variables 17–23 of the Concept Sorting Test reveal: approximately half the variables point to significant differences that are related to class. Variable 22 of the class generalization score, for example, does not show any differences in the first grade in identifying 'abstract similarities'. In the fifth grade, on the other hand, middle-class children perform better.

We could continue to examine the remaining statistical scores in this way, but we would not learn anything new. Correlations between social class and intellectual ability exist for about half of all the variables, although the scores themselves are relatively low (generally between 0.2 and 0.3). It is highly questionable that these scores could tell us anything about the intellectual capabilities of lower-class children. We shall now summarize some essential aspects of Deutsch's investigation.

First, only half the variables produced significant differences, and these are so small that we can hardly speak of different capabilities.

Secondly, the test norms are oriented to verbalization. The child must be able to understand the examiner's language and to manipulate his own speech according to the norms set by the tests.

Thirdly, the test problems assign too much value to speech. A bad performance in the test shows that the child has a small vocabulary rather than that he is unable to conceive or form the appropriate concepts. It is clear, moreover, that in this respect the tests measure superficial and not basic capabilities.

The investigations of Gray and Klaus, Robinson and Creed and Deutsch profess to corroborate empirically Bernstein's theory that restricted speech behaviour greatly impairs the intellectual capabilities of lower-class children. We saw that this is partly true for formal test conditions and particular test problems. Precisely because of this we must conclude, however, that the tests do not measure *normal* but only *artificial* behaviour, and that they reflect capabilities tested in unfamiliar conditions. Furthermore, they confuse 'thinking' with 'differentiated vocabulary'—in short, they measure value standards but not basic intellectual capabilities.

The investigations show a marked tendency to evaluate cognitive achievement on the basis of verbal performance. Verbal expressive ability is repeatedly taken to be the crucial point for various aspects of behaviour relevant to the Deficit Hypothesis. We shall turn now to the central part of this hypothesis: empirical investigations into speech behaviour as dependent on social class.

2.3 Analyses of class-specific speech behaviour

2.3.1 Lower-class speech as discussed by Schatzmann and Strauss

Schatzmann and Strauss (1955) describe the speech behaviour of lower-class speakers whom they had questioned after a disaster caused by a tornado (cf. 1.1 above). Their formulations suggest a mode of assessment of such speakers' verbal ability which is still widely practised today:

> 'Often terms like "we" and "they" are used without clear referents. The speaker seldom anticipates responses to his communication and seems to feel little need to explain particular features of his account. He seldom qualifies an utterance, presumably because he takes for granted that his perceptions represent reality and are shared by all who were present. Since he is apt to take so much for granted, his narrative lacks depth and richness and contains almost no qualifications and few genuine illustrations.' (331f.)
> 'At worst he cannot talk about categories of people or acts because, apparently, he does not think readily in terms of classes. . . . The organizing of [his] description is very poor. . . . Speakers think mainly in particularistic or concrete terms. . . . In communicating to the interviewer, class terms are rudimentary or absent and class relations implicit: relationships are not spelled out or are left vague. Genuine illustrations are almost totally lacking. . . .' (333)

'The respondents did not give long, well-organized, or tightly knit pictures of what happened to them during and after the tornado. . . . Stylistic devices further this kind of organization [linguistic organization of the narrative]: for instance, crude connectives like "then", "and" and "so". . . .' (334)
'Among the devices readily observable are the use of crude chronological notations (e.g. "then . . . and then"), the juxtaposing or direct contrasting of classes (e.g. "rich" v. "poor"), and the serial locating of events. But the elaborate devices that characterize middle-class interviews are strikingly absent. . . .' (335)

From this characterization of lower-class speech we can extract the most important hypotheses which appear in the investigations: they relate without exception to the verbal inadequacy of members of the lower class.

We have already dealt in detail with Bernstein's linguistic characterization of lower and middle-class speech in 1.4.1. It was also made clear there that the explicit, abstract, well-organized and qualified speech of the middle class is judged as a guideline for good speech. Such a judgement should be regarded as dangerous in that it is based, without any further explanation, on the argument of greater communicative efficiency. Insofar as communication is measured according to the bourgeois values of middle-class speech, our concern will be with *normative* speech studies; that is, where the definition of what a communication should or should not achieve is already provided by a preconceived normative understanding. We shall examine the results of further empirical studies of speech behaviour from this point of view as well as from that of the linguistic ability of lower-class speakers.

2.3.2 Templin's investigation[4]

Templin's investigation (1957) is one of the first extensive, carefully-planned analyses of class-specific speech behaviour. She took a sample of 480 White, monolingual children aged between three and eight, half of them male, half of them female. 70 per cent were members of the lower class (their parents were semiskilled or unskilled workers) and 30 per cent were members of the middle class. The social classification of the sample was based on the Minnesota Occupational Scale, which takes the father's occupation as the essential criterion. The sample was divided into 8 age groups of 60 children each, with average age of 3, 3·5, 4, 4·5, 5, 6, 7, respectively.

The five- to eight-year-old children were subjected to the Stanford–Binet intelligence test. As Templin says explicitly (1957, 7f.), the IQ values of the children were unusually high: for seven-year-old middle-class children the average IQ was 117·1; for lower-class children of the same age it was 102·6.

The following two main aims underlie Templin's investigation:

1   the description of the development of linguistic skills in three- to eight-year-old children in relation to the areas of (i) sound articulation, (ii) sound discrimination, (iii) sentence structure, and (iv) vocabulary.

2   determination of the relation between age-specific speech norms and class-specific speech differences in these areas.

---

[4] The critical account in 2.3.2 and 2.3.3 is based on Ginsburg 1972, 64–73.

Templin stresses that she is concerned with normative aspects of linguistic development, leaving out of account functional aspects or any consideration of human needs to be satisfied by linguistic means (4f.).

Given the extraordinary mass of data resulting from this investigation, we shall limit ourselves to part iii of the analysis, which deals with sentence structure. This part is relevant to our problem area insofar as an attempt is made at measuring class-specific complexity of sentence constructions.

How does Templin obtain her data? In principle, she adopts the method given in McCarthy (*The language development of the preschool child*, Minneapolis 1930), according to which the interviewer first establishes a natural rapport with the child (with the help of books and toys), and then tries to elicit utterances, which are recorded. From the moment that a relatively good relationship with the child could be said to exist, the first 50 successive utterances of each child were counted and taken as material for the analysis. Unfortunately, no further indications are given by Templin as to how the data were elicited,[5] and what the interaction and role relations were between child and interviewer.

For the measurement of sentence complexity, analytic categories developed by McCarthy and Davis were used (Templin 1957, 81ff.). The utterances were divided into complete and incomplete ones; for the latter the type of incompleteness was defined; for the former the sentence type was determined, as well as any type of subordination that occurred. The typology was as follows:

1   *Functionally complete but structurally incomplete sentences*
     This covers utterances which give a meaningful, or at least appropriate answer to a preceding question. (Example: when a child, in answer to the question: 'Is the car going *this way* or *that way*?', replies, 'That way'; however, grammatically incorrect utterances such as 'Saw a train yesterday', instead of 'I saw a train yesterday', were also counted as incomplete (83).

2   *Simple sentence without phrase*
     Sentences such as 'He goes.'

3   *Simple sentence with phrase*
     Sentences such as 'He runs *with great speed.*'

4   *Complex sentence*
     A sentence is complex when it contains a main and a subordinate clause.

5   *Compound sentence*
     By this is meant a type of sentence in which two main clauses are joined by a conjunction to form a *single* sentence, e.g. 'He runs to school *and* she leaves the room.'

6   *Elaborated sentence*
     Sentences with more than one stratum, such as 'He ate the cat *who bit the dog who lived in Jack's house.*'

7   *Incomplete sentence*
     Sentences in which syntactic and semantic information essential for understanding is omitted (e.g. pronouns, verbs, prepositions).

[5] 'Elicit' is the current sociological term for the way in which an interviewer can induce the subject to behave naturally.

For the quantitative data analysis the following values were assigned to these construction types: *0* for all incomplete utterances (types 1 and 7), *1* for simple sentences (type 2), *2* for simple sentences with complements (type 3), *3* for complex and compound sentences (types 4 and 5), and *4* for all complex and compound elaborated sentences (type 6).

Figure 2.4 displays the results of the analysis of sentence types.

| Type of sentence | Age | | | | | | | |
	3	3·5	4	4·5	5	6	7	8
Middle class								
1 Functionally complete, but structurally incomplete	26·0	20·2	18·4	11·6	16·2	12·0	9·1	7·0
2 Simple sentence without phrase	36·4	39·2	38·6	40·2	32·2	36·0	29·5	—
3 Simple sentence with phrase	15·3	21·5	19·3	18·3	17·6	17·4	22·2	18·0
4 + 5 Complex and compound sentence	4·2	5·3	6·0	8·0	8·8	10·4	12·7	19·0
6 Elaborated sentence	4·7	4·9	6·0	9·0	8·4	13·1	14·0	16·0
7 Incomplete sentence	13·3	8·6	11·4	12·0	15·8	9·9	12·3	8·8
Lower class								
1 Functionally complete, but structurally incomplete	27·7	24·1	20·9	21·8	16·5	8·5	8·6	10·0
2 Simple sentence without phrase	33·2	37·7	35·9	34·7	52·1	37·4	34·4	30·6
3 Simple sentence with phrase	12·5	13·5	17·3	15·1	15·7	21·9	23·2	22·8
4 + 5 Complex and compound sentence	2·2	2·9	6·7	5·3	8·6	9·9	9·9	12·6
6 Elaborated sentence	2·3	2·1	6·8	6·6	7·6	10·9	12·5	11·2
7 Incomplete sentence	17·1	15·1	10·6	12·0	10·6	7·6	7·7	9·8

Fig. 2.4. Mean score of speakers for types of sentence used in relation to age and social class. (Source: Templin 1957, 88f.)

The scores differ only slightly between the social classes. The results for the five-year-olds, for example, show a small difference between the two classes for the variable 7 and only for the variable 2 a relatively large difference. The other sentence types do not reveal any significant differences.

When the other columns are compared for class differences, it becomes clear that they are just as small as in the case of the five-year-olds. In short, it appears that lower-class children tend to use simpler sentences than middle-class children.

Templin (1957, 92f.) adds the subordinate clause as a further important variable in the class-specific distinction between the children's speech forms. She classifies subordinates into three types:

1 *nominal clauses* ('*What is needed* is rigour')
2 *relative clauses* ('We all live in a submarine *which is yellow*')
3 *adverbial clauses* ('I sink *when I float*')

The results can be seen in figure 2.5.

	Middle class %	Lower class %
Nominal subordinate clauses	2·7	2·0
Relative clauses	0·9	0·8
Adverbial clauses	4·1	2·7

Fig. 2.5 The use of subordinate clauses in the two classes (irrespective of age). (Source: Templin 1957, 94)

The class differences are small; moreover, none of the results is statistically significant. All in all, Templin's data hardly show any real differences between the classes in their use of various sentence types. Where they do exist, it is to the advantage of the middle class.

What relevance do the data have for the assessment of the linguistic ability of lower-class children?

In any case they do not support the Deficit Hypothesis. Bernstein predicted that lower-class children were scarcely capable of forming subordinate clauses. Templin's results show that this assertion is not true for three types of subordinate clause.

Furthermore, Templin's evidence was obtained in an unreliable way. The sentence types are inadequately defined and do not relate to any explicit linguistic model. Neither do we know exactly how the data were elicited.

2.3.3 Loban's long-term survey

In contrast to Templin, Loban (1963) carried out a long-term investigation into the speech behaviour of children, which one would expect to provide revealing information.

Once a year a total of 338 Black and White children from California were individually given certain standard tests and interviews from the time they were at kindergarten until they completed their sixth year at school. The investigation was centred on speech behaviour.

In order to establish a rapport with the child and to get him to speak, the interviewer began by asking him questions about his friends, favourite games, television, illnesses and particular wishes. Then, during the remainder of the interview, the child was shown six pictures which he should describe as best he could (Loban 1963, 3–4). The analysis of this linguistic material was mainly limited to aspects of the lexicon and the sentence construction. In the following we shall take into account only data of oral speech behaviour.

In this connection it should be observed that (as in Templin's case) no further information is given as to exactly how the data were elicited and the reliability of their evaluation.

The results of the data analysis should mainly serve the purpose of comparing two groups selected from the total sample of 338 children according to a vocabulary test and the subjective evaluation of teachers: (1) a group of 30 children with above average linguistic capabilities and (2) a group of 24 children with particularly deficient linguistic achievements. Roughly the same weight was given to the two criteria used for the selection of the children.

Since Loban had established the socioeconomic status of all test subjects according to paternal occupation (Minnesota Scale for Paternal Occupations), he could observe that the children of the high achievement group (1) came mostly from the middle class and those from the group with poor results (2) mainly from the lower class. These groups were not selected on the basis of strictly social criteria; we do not know, however, what the proportions were of middle- and lower-class children in the two groups. Thus Loban commits an error when he equates membership of these groups with class membership and compares the two groups for class-specific differences. The comparisons are liable to produce distorted results, since middle-class children could just as easily belong to the less gifted group as lower-class children could belong to the particularly competent group. We must not forget this when we come to analyse the results themselves.

The analysis of sentence constructions forms the central part of the investigation. For the quantitative evaluation of the data 'communication units' were distinguished, which were defined as groups of words that cannot be further divided without essential semantic loss (6f.), and were opposed to 'mazes' which are defined as 'unattached fragments or a series of unattached fragments which do not constitute a communication unit and are not necessary to the communication unit' (8).

Loban differentiates between the following sentence types (10ff.):

1   *Simple sentence*, e.g. 'Mary eats.'
2   *Simple sentence with direct object*, e.g. 'Mary eats strawberries.'
3   *Sentence with subject, copula and phrase*, e.g. 'Blue strawberries without stems are unusual.'
4   *Sentence with subject, verb, dative and accusative object*, e.g. 'Mary threw the dog some biscuits.'
5   *Sentence with 'here is' or 'there are' plus phrase*, e.g. 'There are four horses in the street.'
6   *Incomplete sentence*

The quantitative results of the analysis of these structural sentence types ('first level of analysis') are summarized by Loban on pp. 44 and 45 of his report.[6] Crucial class differences existed only for variable 5, incomplete sentences: during the first years at school children in the less competent group formed more incomplete sentences than those in the other group. There was a detectable but insignificant difference between the two groups for sentence type 3. Taken together, these differences have no significance.

On the second level of analysis, Loban (1963, 15, 59ff.) investigates whether the two groups differ in the use of subordinate clauses. Three types of clause, noun-complement clauses, relative (adjective) clauses and adverb clauses, were counted for frequency of occurrence. The results of this analysis are given in figure 2.6; they show clearly that the superior group produced more subordinate clauses (for each of the three types) than the inferior group.

---

[6] Loban's analysis of speech acts (questions, commands, invitations) (15) is not included here.

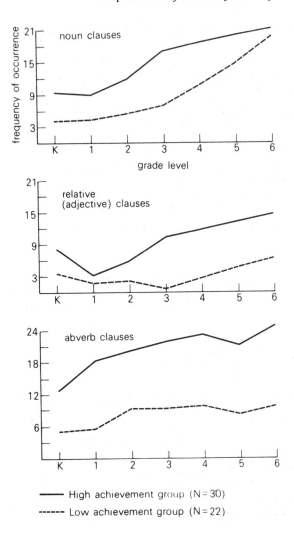

Fig. 2.6 Frequency of three types of subordinate clause according to group membership and school grade. (Source: Loban 1963, 60)

These results are supported by Loban's further analysis of subordinate clauses in terms of a 'weighted index of subordination' (61f.). Quite clearly, Loban's results contradict those of Templin which did not show differences for this construction.

We shall only comment on three aspects of Loban's investigation. The first is concerned with the reliability of the data. The remarks made about Templin's analysis also apply here: the sentence types are constructed according to ad hoc criteria; there is no information as to how the data were classified.

The second relates to the tenability of the class comparisons. The results are distorted because the utterances of all the middle-class children were not compared with the utterances of all the lower-class children. From this point of view the differences in the number of subordinate clauses used do not have any serious significance.

The third aspect refers to the significance of the results for the assessment of the children's linguistic competence. What does Loban mean by his observation that the children in the less competent group only formed a smaller number of subordinate clauses? Perhaps that they were not capable of forming subordinate clauses? This conclusion would be wrong since they did produce *some* subordinate clauses, and this proves that they had that ability.

But even if they had not produced any subordinate clauses, this would not necessarily mean that they were incapable of forming them. It could be that they readily understood sentences of this type, yet lacked a disposition towards producing them. In other words, Loban's speech data give an impression of how children usually use language under test conditions or at school; however, they do not reflect the range of the children's linguistic ability either in competence or in performance.

The investigations of Templin and Loban were carried out in the USA. We shall now see to what extent the results of European inquiries are similar to or different from them. We shall consider investigations which Bernstein, Hawkins, Oevermann and Robinson conducted in order to verify the code conception.

2.3.4 Bernstein's investigation

Bernstein's investigation of 1962 is divided into two parts: the first deals with aspects of verbal planning (1962b), and the second is devoted to grammatical aspects of speech use (1962a). The speakers selected for the analysis are the same as the subjects Bernstein used for his analysis in 1960 of the correlation between social class, IQ and speech behaviour (see 2.1 above). The data of this intelligence survey form the basis of the analysis made in 1962.

From the total sample of 61 lower-class and 45 middle-class speakers, five groups were selected (five speakers per group) of which groups 1 and 2 were composed of middle-class speakers and groups 3, 4 and 5 of lower-class speakers. The two major class-correlated groups made up of the five subgroups permitted Bernstein (1962b) to make the following comparisons:

'1   General interclass comparison.
2   Class comparisons with nonverbal intelligence held constant.
3   Class comparisons with verbal and nonverbal intelligence held constant.
4   Comparisons between different IQ profiles holding class constant.'

A discussion was held with the groups on the topic of 'the abolition of capital punishment'. Unfortunately we are not told where and in what atmosphere the discussion took place. However, Bernstein assures us that the discussion was 'relatively undirected' and that the research worker only intervened, 'when a boy was monopolizing the discussion or when voluntary contributions came to an end. The number of such interventions,' Bernstein continues, 'was considerably greater for the working-class groups for the last-mentioned reason' (1962b).

The data used in the analysis consisted of approximately 1800 words, which followed the first five minutes of discussion in each of the five groups. For reasons of analysis the utterances were divided into long and short: sequences containing 40 or more syllables were considered long, and sequences containing between 10 and 40 syllables were considered short. Only long utterances were taken into account for analysing the speakers' level of verbal planning (the reason for this was that the distribution of so-called 'hesitation phenomena' associated with short utterances seemed to be unstable).

We should bear in mind another important point with regard to the organization of the experiment and the evaluation of the results: the composition of the groups. The fact that a member of group 4 was absent on the day of the discussion and that a member of both groups 4 and 5 had to be excluded from the analysis because they did not produce any long utterances is not so vital as the exchange of individual boys between the groups. *After* the discussion was over, that is after 1800 words had been recorded for each group, 'one subject each from group 1 and group 2 were exchanged, two subjects were shifted from group 4 to group 3 and one from group 3 was placed in group 4' (1962b). This subsequent manipulation of the original groupings is one reason to doubt the validity of the results.

Before going into the results in more detail, we shall comment briefly on the way in which the experiment was conducted (as a necessary condition for an adequate evaluation of the individual analyses).

First, the exchange of group members after the discussion must cast doubt on the validity of the speech data which had initially been systematically obtained. This is not the only point, however, which makes us question the reliability of the investigation.

In the second place, it is not really possible to assess the actual linguistic performances of the lower-class* boys, as Bernstein conducted two practice discussions with them before the test discussion. It is difficult to judge the extent to which the practice discussions influenced the performances in the test.

Thirdly, Bernstein emphasizes that during the discussions the research worker had to intervene far more frequently for the working-class groups than for the middle-class groups. This can be interpreted in two ways. Either it is possible that the boys did not have enough motivation to speak on the set topic, or the reason for their lack of motivation could have been that they had already had two practice discussions. At any rate, we cannot exclude the possibility that in these circumstances the boys had no inducement to display their actual linguistic capabilities in the discussion.

Fourthly, the declared aim of the investigation was to show certain grammatical characteristics and qualities of verbal planning to be *common*, mutually corresponding characteristics of either speech form. One of the prerequisities of this aim is that the sets of utterances on which the two analyses are based should have the same range. This, however, is not the case since short utterances (less than 40 syllables), which were excluded from the evaluation of the data to judge verbal planning, were accepted for the grammatical analysis (1962a) of the working-class groups.

Thus in two of the four respects mentioned here there is the possibility of the results being considerably distorted.

Let us first consider the results of the analysis of verbal planning.

By quantifying certain hesitation phenomena (pauses) during speech, Bernstein intends to draw conclusions about the verbal planning activity of speakers. He bases this on the work of the phonetician Goldmann-Eisler, who showed that there was a certain relationship between sentence-planning activity and hesitation behaviour in speakers. Bernstein interprets the work of Goldmann-Eisler as meaning that, in relation to the number of subsequent words, the length of speech pauses represents a certain index of the structural organization of a sentence and of its degree of abstraction. We shall come back to the problems raised by this interpretation. The utterances which were recorded on tape were analysed according to the following six variables:

'i   the number of words
ii   the number of syllables
iii   the articulation rate: this time is based on the rate of vocal speech
        utterance exclusive of pauses
iv   the mean number of words per pause (W/P). . . . , a measure of the
        phrase length or frequency of pauses
v   the mean pause duration per word utterance (P/W)
vi   the mean word length in number of syllables.' (1962b)

Bernstein makes four predictions for the outcome of the experiment:

'1   Holding verbal and nonverbal IQ constant, working-class groups
        would pause less frequently and spend less time pausing than middle-
        class groups.
2   Holding nonverbal IQ constant, working-class groups would pause
        less frequently and spend less time pausing than middle-class groups.
3   Irrespective of nonverbal IQ the hesitation phenomena of working-
        class subjects would be similar.
4   A general relationship would be found between the two IQ tests for
        the working-class group: the verbal scores would be severely
        depressed in relation to the scores at the higher ranges of the
        nonverbal test. It was expected that this general relationship would
        not hold for the middle-class group.' (1962b)

The results of the evaluation of the data (we shall not reproduce a numerical list; cf. 1962b) can be summarized as follows: there are no significant differences for the *articulation rate* (variable iii); these do exist, however, for the two major groups $(1 + 2$ v. $3 + 4 + 5)$ in respect of *phrase length* (variable iv: $p > 0.005$), *pause duration per word* (variable v: $p > 0.005$) and *word length* (variable vi: $p > 0.025$). Individual comparisons between the groups, disregarding the two major groupings, produced hardly any significant differences, if any.

In one particular respect it is not possible to check the data, as individual scores for groups are not listed.

The three main results of the investigation appear to confirm the most important predictions:

'1   Overall social class differences were found. The working-class subjects

> used a longer mean phrase length, spent less time pausing and used a shorter word length.
>
> 2   Holding nonverbal intelligence constant, social class differences were found in the same direction.
>
> 3   Holding verbal and nonverbal intelligence constant, social class differences were again found in the same direction, but not for word length.' (1962b)

What do the results reveal about the verbal planning activity of lower-class speakers? First of all it is not clear in what sense one can deduce a high or low planning level from pause frequency and duration. According to Bernstein, a high structural organization corresponds to a high planning level. The planning activity which leads to the latter can therefore be demonstrated by pause variables. Let us consider variable v, 'mean pause duration per word'. Bernstein uses this scale to predict the structural organization of the utterances. Goldmann-Eisler, however, considers the 'duration of hesitation pauses to be a function of the predictability of the words which follow them' (Coulthard 1969, 42). Consequently Bernstein's scale is only suitable 'for measuring the quantity of *lexical* information in a sentence' (*ibid.*).

The second objection concerns the results being treated as collective data specific to groups. Bernstein presupposes that the speech speed of the individual group members is the same and that it only varies according to the content. Goldmann-Eisler points out that the speech speeds can vary from one speaker to another (cf. Coulthard 1969, 42). Bernstein is therefore wrong to hold the speech speed constant.

Generally, 'pause frequency' and 'pause duration' can only be superficial measurements of verbal planning. We can reduce Bernstein's assertion to this: as the pauses become progressively shorter and more infrequent, so too does the speech become more disorganized and incomprehensible. It depends, of course, to a great extent on the situation whether speakers talk rapidly or in a calm and collected manner. Bernstein's standards tell us little about the ability to communicate satisfactorily.

We shall now consider the grammatical aspects of his analysis. Bernstein obtained scores for the following variables:

1   *Subordination*   A sequence containing a finite verb whether or not the subject was explicit or implicit was counted as a proposition; if a subject was associated with two finite verbs this would be counted as two propositions. The mean proposition length was obtained by dividing the finite verbs by the total number of words.

2   *Complexity of the verbal stem*   The count was based on the number of units in the verbal stem; adverbial negations were excluded from the count; verbal stems containing more than three units were counted for each subject and expressed as a proportion of the total number of verbs uttered; a verb plus an infinitive was counted as a complex verbal stem.

3   *Passive voice*   The proportion of passive verbs to the total number of finite verbs.

4 *Uncommon adverbs* Counted according to arbitrary classification; excluded from the analysis were 'just', 'not', 'yes', 'no', 'then', 'how', 'really', 'when', 'where' and 'why'; the remainder was expressed as a proportion of the total number of analysed words used by each subject.

5 *Total adjectives* Their proportion to the total number of words.

6 *Uncommon adjectives* Arbitrary classification: all adjectives (excluded from the analysis were numerical and demonstrative adjectives, and 'other', 'another' and repetitions) in proportion to the total number of analysed words used by each subject.

7 *Prepositions* Total number of prepositions in proportion to the total number of analysed words; the relative use of 'of' in relation to 'in' and 'into' was assessed by the proportion to the total number of 'of', 'in', and 'into'.

8 *Uncommon conjunctions* Arbitrary classification: all conjunctions other than 'and', 'so', 'or', 'because', 'also', 'then', and 'like' in proportion to the total number of conjunctions.

9 *All personal pronouns* 'I' in proportion to the total number of personal pronouns; 'you' and 'they' in proportion to the total number of personal pronouns.

10 *Selected personal pronouns* The pronouns, minus the pronouns in 'I think', in 'sociocentric sequences' and in direct speech sequences in (9).

(From Bernstein 1962a, 225–31.)

We cannot check the validity of the data in detail, since Bernstein does not give the group scores for the individual variables in their raw state but in most cases only mentions whether the results are significant or not. We shall therefore summarize the results as a whole.

The middle class (groups 1 and 2) used variables, 1, 2, 3, 4, 5, 6 and 8 with greater frequency; they used more 'egocentric sequences'(i.e. they used 'I' more often in proportion to all personal pronouns, in proportion to the total number of words and in proportion to all selected pronouns) and more prepositions 'of' (variable 7). The working-class groups (3, 4 and 5) employed variables 9 (total number of personal pronouns) and 10 (predominantly the pronouns 'you' and 'they') with greater frequency; wider use of 'sociocentric sequences' was linked with more frequent employment of personal pronouns ('you' and 'they'). The results were only significant for the differences between the two major groups. The significance level varied between $p > 0.001$ (e.g. subordination) and $p > 0.05$ (e.g. for the pronoun 'I').

Bernstein regards his predictions in relation to the general characteristics of the restricted and elaborated speech codes as being confirmed. The results of the grammatical analysis, however, do not corroborate his hypothesis any more than the works that have been considered so far. As was mentioned earlier the data look less reliable as a result of subjects changing from one group to another. The majority of the variables correspond to normative value judgements that have no bearing on communicative efficiency. More frequent use of 'I' or of 'unusual adjectives' is supposed to have a greater value, on the assumption that frequent mentioning of 'I' implies 'being able to make an individual judgement', and frequent use of 'unusual adjectives' implies 'being able to express oneself in different ways'.

We must bear in mind that to make such a valuation is to condemn the speech of members of the lower class without any consideration of their communicative requirements. Equally, only superficial attributes are measured: this is evident in the variable 'passive voice'. It was selected because in Bernstein's view passive forms reflected a 'more elaborated' form of speech than active forms. This disregards the linguistic point of view, which is that both forms are superficially different but identical in their basic meaning.

Bernstein claims to have proved that certain elements of verbal planning and certain aspects of sentence planning are *common* characteristics of the limited expressive ability of lower-class speakers. This interpretation is in various respects untenable: the random tests were distorted by uncontrollable factors, the variables were chosen *ad hoc* and obtained on the strength of ideological norms. In short, only external appearances were measured and not capabilities.

The linguistic part of Bernstein's investigation (1962a) was repeated by Lawton (1968, part 6) under similar conditions and with only a few alterations (Lawton's subjects, for example, were 12 years old, and Bernstein's were 15). As Lawton uses basically the same variables (only the subordination index is improved according to Loban's model), he arrives at results similar to those of Bernstein. We can make the same criticism of Lawton's investigation as we did of Bernstein's.

2.3.5 Hawkins's pronoun analysis

In a broader investigation into the complex of socialization and language, Hawkins selected 124 children from a middle-class and 139 from a lower-class background, according to strict criteria of social classification and intelligence quotient. The average age of the children was five years (in contrast to earlier investigations, they were meant to come from the primary phase of socialization which is decisive for speech development); they were tested approximately three weeks after they had started school.

The children were set two verbal tasks: to tell a story from a series of four picture cards; and to describe three postcard-size reproductions of the work of a Belgian painter. Hawkins was concerned solely with the analysis of the use of pronouns. In contrast to the speech analyses described up till now, he indicates the grammatical model which defines the position of pronouns and which is taken as the basis for deciding on the variables: this is Halliday's grammatical categorization.

Excursus: The nominal group in Halliday

According to Halliday (1961), the position of pronouns is defined in the frame of the nominal group. Its central category is what Halliday calls the proposition, which consists of a noun or pronoun. When the proposition is a noun, modifiers can stand *before* it, and these can be subdivided into deictic expressions (e.g. 'the, a, some'), ordinatives ('two, three, first, next'), epithets ('little, red, naughty') and nominals (e.g. 'stone' in 'a stone wall'); qualifiers can occur *after* the subject and can again be subclassified into one-word qualifiers ('all, else, both'), group-qualifiers (e.g. 'the dog in the window') and clause-qualifiers (e.g. 'the man who owned the house'). The proposition is obligatory, the modifiers and the qualifiers are optional. A modifier can be strenghtened by an intensifier, as for example in 'very long'.

A phrase such as 'these two very long railway trains' can be analysed according to Halliday's categories in the following way:

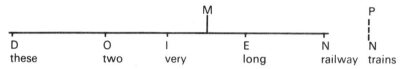

M					P
D	O	I	E	N	N
these	two	very	long	railway	trains

Fig. 2.7 Halliday's structure of the nominal group. (Source: Hawkins 1969, 129)

In the diagram M stands for modifier, D for deictic expression, O for ordinative, I for intensifier, E for epithet, N for nominal expression and P for proposition. The example illustrates that only modifiers can stand before the proposition, and only where the latter is a noun. Pronouns cannot be modified but only qualified and this to a limited extent.[7]

Hawkins concludes from the structure of the nominal group that in the case of a full noun in the position of head more meaningful alternatives are possible than in the case of a pronoun in that position. In the latter case, the possibilities of phrase expansion are greatly reduced. Referential relations to external context can be ambiguous; modifications are not at all possible and qualifications only to a limited extent.

Hawkins's hypothesis is that middle-class children use nouns, but working-class children use pronouns, with greater frequency.

For the purpose of quantification Hawkins distinguishes the following types of pronoun (the distinction is presented as relevant from the points of view of reference to extraverbal context and the structural linking of phrases in narrative texts):

1   *anaphoric pronouns* (these refer backwards: 'the boy kicked the *ball* and *it* broke the window');
2   *cataphoric pronouns* (these refer forwards: '*it* was the *ball* that broke the window');
3   *exophoric pronouns:* relation of the pronouns to the external context (i.e. they relate to concrete external objects or persons).

The children's narrations and descriptions were analysed according to the frequency of nouns on the one hand, and of anaphoric, cataphoric or exophoric pronouns on the other. Items were also included in the quantification which permitted a choice between anaphoric and exophoric reference:

1   'this', 'that' as head of the nominal group (anaphoric: 'go away, that's what she said'; exophoric: 'that's a little boy');

---

[7] For a critical discussion of Halliday see Paul Postal, *Constituent structure: a study of contemporary models of syntactic description* (Bloomington, Indiana 1964), 97–114.

2   'this', 'that' as modifier (anaphoric: 'the boy broke the window . . . so the
     lady told that boy off'; exophoric: 'these boys were playing football');
3   'here', 'there' as head of the group after a preposition. This referent is always
     exophoric, e.g. 'on here', 'up there', 'along there'.

The frequency of anaphoric pronouns hardly varied between the classes, both in
the narration and in the descriptions. There were considerable differences,
however, in the use of exophoric pronouns. The middle class used on average
2·84, and the working class 4·12 (Hawkins 1969, 132). But the difference was not
significant, since most children of both classes used at least *one* exophoric
pronoun. All the remaining categories of exophoric pronouns, listed in (1) to (3),
did reach the significance level (0·05 was taken as statistically significant and 0·01
as highly significant); this applies to 'this' and 'that' as modifiers and to 'here' and
'there' at the beginning of a sentence after a preposition.

Moreover, it was established that middle-class children used more nouns and
in various respects elaborated the nominal group better. In particular, they made
heavier use of the following categories:

1   Epithets as qualifiers of the proposition ($p < 0.001$), e.g. 'the boy was
     hungry'.
2   Epithets as modifiers, other than 'little' and 'big' ($p < 0.001$), e.g. 'the
     naughty cat'.
3   Two or more ordinatives ($p < 0.01$).
4   Intensifiers before epithets ($p < 0.001$); words such as 'so', 'very', 'too'.
5   Rankshifted clauses as in 'she saw *them running away*' or 'he thought *it was a
     fish*' ($p < 0.02$).

We can summarize Hawkins's interpretation and the conclusion he draws from
these results in the following way.

Middle-class children not only use more nouns but also display more varied
elaboration of the nominal group. Lower-class children, on the other hand, are
seriously limited in their possibilities of modification and qualification, as they
use pronouns instead of nouns far more frequently than middle-class children.
This wide use of pronouns requires the hearer to have a good knowledge of the
situation (that is to say he must know to what persons or objects the speaker's
pronouns refer).

We quote Hawkins's general interpretation of the results:

'With this evidence we have shown very considerable differences between the
type of speech produced by middle class children and that of working class
children, which may well have important cognitive consequences. . . . These
findings substantiate the predictions derived from Bernstein's theory of
restricted and elaborated codes. . . .' (Hawkins 1969, 135)

The significance of Hawkins's investigation is that it reveals certain characteristics
of lower-class children's pronominal usage—characteristics which might lead to
communicative misunderstandings.

There are three points to which we should draw attention. First, Hawkins does
not list all the data which would allow us to have a general view of the scores for

the individual variables. We are only told the significance level of certain differences. We cannot check the way in which the data have been manipulated. Thus, for example, the mean duration of the utterances of middle-class and working-class children is not known. This could be relevant, since the greater frequency of pronouns in the texts of the working-class children could be a function of the longer mean duration of their utterances.

Secondly, the frequency of pronouns is not related to the mean number of nominal groups, nor is there any indication of the number of nominal groups which allow for pronominal substitution. It should have been made clear in what cases nominal groups could be replaced by either anaphoric or exophoric pronouns. This information would have been interesting in that only exophoric pronouns revealed class differences (cf. also Coulthard 1969, 46f.).

Thirdly, we do not know whether Hawkins's test situation was such that an unspecified use of exophoric pronouns can justifiably be interpreted as poor communicative behaviour. The children were shown picture cards and asked to say what they had seen. Since we can assume that the child and the interviewer had the same opportunity to look at the picture, there is no reason why the child could not have described details in the cards which the interviewer was not able to recognize and identify.

Finally the differences that were established do not tell us much about the children's ability to express referential relations. There was not one child who used *only* exophoric pronouns.

The analytical accuracy of Hawkins's 1969 investigation has been surpassed by Ulrich Oevermann's comprehensive speech analysis (1970), which was carried out in secondary schools in Frankfurt. Oevermann's analysis is the first major survey of class-specific speech behaviour undertaken in the Federal Republic of Germany. It was preceded only by Regine Reichwein's (1967) study of 'public' and 'formal' speech which is based on Bernstein's work. It combines a linguistic analysis of 132 essays written by Berlin schoolchildren in the seventh, eighth and ninth grades with recommendations for linguistic education. (Reichwein recommends compensation by means of instruction in set theory.) Reichwein's work professes to be a 'preliminary investigation into the problem of the correlation between social background, linguistic structure and mental ability.' Technically, it is not so advanced as the works that have been discussed. Within the framework that has been defined here, the work cannot be regarded as anything more than an attempt to verify Bernstein's theory, since the author's use of the terms 'public' and 'formal' speech is not part of an explicit hypothesis, nor are significance tests carried out for the value scales.

Oevermann's investigation, on the other hand, is theoretically and empirically one of the most serious works in the context of the Deficit Hypothesis. This is true above all for the technical accuracy with which it was conducted. Oevermann describes his investigation as a 'study with an explorative function' (Oevermann 1970, 49), since he was the first to carry out a major analysis of speech behaviour specific to social class in the German-speaking countries. He could not therefore refer to previous linguistic or other works in this field which could have corroborated his findings. In contrast to the practice of works already discussed, he refuses 'to provide an explanation in the strictest sense for descriptively

obtained results [the results of the quantification of linguistic variables]'
(Oevermann 1970, 183). Even if he does not give a strictly sociological
explanation, he still intends to validate Bernstein's hypotheses.

2.3.6 Oevermann's investigation

Influenced by Bernstein's works, Oevermann pursues two basic aims: to make a
contribution to a general 'theory of socialization' and of 'processes of social
classification'; and to devise 'a programme for rationally planned, permanent
educational reform with regard to creating equality of opportunity' (Oevermann
1970, 10).
For his analysis Oevermann selected four Frankfurt secondary school classes
in the sixth grade. The total of 124 children was divided into lower class, lower
middle class, middle class and upper middle class according to Scheuch's[8]
classification model. The division into the social strata was effected by so-called
filters: the first and most important filter was the father's education; the second
filter, the mother's education, could only *improve* the child's classification. The
overall classification of the children on the socioeconomic scale showed that the
social distance between the families of the lower class and those of the middle class
was unexpectedly small. Only for one of the four school classes, class A, did the
division of the children correspond with any reasonable accuracy to the four
strata. Oevermann therefore only lists the results of this one class. The four social
strata originally selected were reduced for the purpose of linguistic analysis to the
poles middle class—lower class to reach more conclusive results.

The empirical analysis was based on two hypotheses:

1   'There are differences in speech behaviour between middle- and lower-class
children which correspond to the theoretical interpretation of the
distinction "restricted"–"elaborated".'
2   'These differences between the middle and lower classes are independent of
the level of measured intelligence.' (Oevermann 1970, 51)

Bernstein's theory that 'characteristics of social structures ... are manifested in
the structure of speech forms' forms the theoretical basis of the general hypothesis.
Oevermann conducted the following tests with the children in order to verify
this general hypothesis:

1   They were given a group intelligence test and vocabulary test (100 minutes).
2   They had to write two essays, each in 45 minutes, on the subjects of:
     i   'It is not always easy to get on with grown-ups.'
     ii   'How I imagine my life in ten years' time.'

The analysis of written linguistic material is one of the fundamental points on
which Oevermann's investigation differs from that of Bernstein (1962).
Oevermann selects *essays* as a basis for his linguistic analysis in order to make
controlled measurements of the performance of each individual (this condition

---

[8] Erwin K. Scheuch, 'Sozialprestige und soziale Schichtung', in D. V. Glass and R. König (eds.),
Soziale Schichtung und soziale Mobilität (Cologne and Opladen 1961), 65–103.

was not fulfilled in the group discussions conducted by Bernstein; cf. 2.3.4 above).
He takes up arguments of Lawton and Robinson and justifies his decision in the
following way: class differences can be expected to stand out even more sharply
because of the necessarily greater discipline demanded by written formulations;
'written linguistic material' should not 'cause the lower-class children to be
artificially handicapped in respect of the hypotheses' (52ff.). We shall come back
to the problems raised by the choice of written material. First of all we shall take a
closer look at the principles of the linguistic analysis and its results.

In accordance with the task he sets himself, Oevermann primarily intends 'to
establish differences in the rules of linguistic construction, that is, the selection
patterns of the possibilities afforded by the rule system of a written language.'
Consequently, the author asserts, his method of linguistic analysis cannot be one
of 'analytical deduction' as demanded by Chomsky's grammatical theory, but,
from 'the point of view of linguistic theory', must result from 'empirical induction'
(95). Oevermann has 'therefore had to give up the attempt to formulate the
linguistic variables strictly in terms of one of the existing linguistic models' (96).
What he does do is to derive the 'linguistic variables from theoretical
determinants developed by Bernstein' (95f.).

The requirements formulated by Oevermann for a linguistic analysis have two
prominent characteristics:

1   The linguistic material in question should be analysed for its formal means
     of construction and not for its expression content (96).
2   The method of linguistic analysis 'is based on the conception that sentences
     are to be considered as sequences of linguistic elements, which can again be
     regarded as indicators of intrapsychological verbal planning acts. These
     sequences are divided into various levels of structural elements with vertical
     and horizontal logicolinguistic dependency relations. Each structural
     element and each planning position in the sequence is a potential conveyer
     of new structural elements' (96).

In (1) we can detect the influence of modern linguistic work, which is mainly
concerned with the formal qualities of language. (2) is an attempt to reconcile the
formal linguistic concept with Bernstein's theory, which is essentially that speech
is a product of verbal planning strategies. From this point of view, certain
elements in the linear succession of the sentence sequence become 'potential
conveyers of new structural elements', in that 'vertical and horizontal
logicolinguistic dependency relationships' can be derived from them.

It is important to regard this theoretical approach in the light of a conception
of language known as 'Information Theory': 'Each structural element . . . as a
potential conveyer of new structural elements' guarantees the possibility of
applying linguistic probability measures (this corresponds roughly to Bernstein's
definition of the speech forms which relies mainly on Information Theory).

Even if it is not explicitly stated that the 'horizontal and vertical' grammatical
dependency relationships are to be thought of 'as indicators of intrapsychological
verbal planning acts', the psychological correlates of the manifest speech forms
(i.e., the verbal planning strategies) can be reduced to a scale of grammatical
complexity. This leads Oevermann to the statement that 'the variables of speech

behaviour ... are constructed in such a way that they allow plausible conclusions to be drawn with regard to their significance for cognitive behaviour' (51). Bernstein and Oevermann both agree that the complexity of the cognitive dimension can be inferred from the complexity of the linguistic dimension.

The linguistic variables used to analyse the essays should be so designed as to 'be plausible operational elements following from the theoretical definitions of the "elaborated" and "restricted" codes' (97). For this Oevermann chooses five 'defining factors' which he has taken from Bernstein:

'1 Complexity of the syntactic and grammatical construction, divided into (a) complexity of the relations between sentences and (b) complexity within the sentence structure. This point of view is related expressly to the greater predictability of the constructional elements in the "restricted" code. However, this factor is also closely connected with the following.
2 Differentiated comprehension of structural correlations in the object world vis-à-vis isolated over-concrete relations and juxtaposition of facts.
3 Individualized speech by explicit semantic specifications in descriptive elements and interpretation of psychological states.
4 Individualized speech by signalling subjective intentions.
5 Level of abstraction.' (Oevermann 1970, 101)

These principles for the selection and construction of the variables clearly reflect Bernstein's normative linguistic concept; it is thus not surprising that the 89 variables, which Oevermann takes from Hinze's *Deutsche Schulgrammatik* (1966), are essentially similar in character to Bernstein's variables, although they are far more numerous and varied. A few examples should illustrate this.

Thus some of the variables for the fourth 'defining factor' of the speech forms, 'individualized speech by signalling subjective intentions', are quantified as follows (Oevermann 1970, 139–44):

Variable 66: verbs of emotion and verbs of intention in proportion to the total number of verbs

Variable 61: number of auxiliary verbs acting as main verbs in proportion to the total number of verbs

Variable 62: number of model auxiliary verbs (except for 'may') in proportion to the total number of verbs

Variable 68: total number of personal pronouns inclusive of the impersonal pronouns 'it' and 'one' in proportion to the total number of words

Variable 69: personal pronouns in the first person singular in proportion to the total number of personal pronouns

Variable 70: personal pronouns in the first person plural in proportion to the total number of personal pronouns

Variable 71: personal pronouns in the third person plural in proportion to the total number of personal pronouns

Variable 71a: number of personal pronouns in the first and third person plural together in proportion to the total number of personal pronouns.

These and other variables are founded on the same normative concept as we have already seen in Bernstein (1962). In Oevermann's work, too, subordinations (first defining factor), use of adjectives and adverbs (third defining factor) and level of abstraction (fifth defining factor) play a central part. There is therefore no need to reproduce a detailed list of the variables.

Oevermann's general hypothesis is divided into as many individual hypotheses as there are linguistic variables. The hypothesis for a variable was considered proved when the variable showed a significant discrimination between the two social classes.

We shall now summarize the essential results of Oevermann's linguistic analysis and relate them to the five defining factors for which the linguistic variables were brought into play; by analogy we shall also obtain results for five subsections:

1 A 'greater syntactic complexity in middle-class children has been statistically attested.' This is based 'almost exclusively on the construction of subordinate clauses, i.e. on subordination' (Oevermann 1970, 114).

2 The analysis revealed no consistent class-specific differences. Although middle-class children use syntactically more complex sentences, they do not differ from lower-class children in the use of 'qualitatively different subordinate clauses' (124). 'They do not use, contrary to expectation, more causal or final constructions . . .' (124). Despite this finding, Oevermann considers his hypothesis to be indirectly confirmed in that the middle-class children's use of 'causal, final and concessive conjunctions' was 'very significantly' greater than that of the lower-class children. This difference seems to be closely connected with the tendency of middle-class children 'to use the more analytical, causal, final, instrumental, concessive and consecutive phrases more frequently when planning adverbial determinants' (124). These results, however, were *not* significant.

3 'In this section a test was made to see whether there were differences between the classes in the degree of individualization of speech by means of specification of meaning and interpretation of inner mental conditions, as well as differences resulting from the rigidity and type of word selection' (138). The variables measured here concerned semantic aspects of verbal planning. The evaluation of some of the variables was based on an 'interpretation of meaning and context' (138).

'Differences in the relative use of all factors counted as specifying meaning were not found to conform to the prediction.' In his commentary, however, Oevermann remarks that there was an indication 'that the middle-class children used more evaluative adjectives or adjectives describing mental states to convey social, moral, emotional and aesthetic meanings.' (Of course these differences could not be statistically attested.)

4 'The relative use of verbs of intention and verbs of emotion as well as the relative frequency of personal pronouns in the first person plural' (145) were adopted as criteria for the analysis in this section.

Here Oevermann saw an 'impressive confirmation' of the hypothesis: 'In proportion to the total number of verbs used, middle-class children used verbs of intention with significantly greater frequency than lower-class children' (145). The personal pronouns only revealed class differences to the extent that the middle-class children used more personal pronouns in the first person singular; 'the lower-class schoolchildren, on the other hand, used more pronouns in the first and third person plural' (145). (These results were interpreted completely along the lines of Bernstein.)

5   The level of abstraction was to be measured in this section. It was not possible to develop any suitable operational methods for the variables relevant to this. The quantifications that were carried out, however, run counter to the expectations of the hypothesis.

Thus only in sections 1 and 4 were there significant differences. The variables in (4) consider the psychological characteristics of members of the lower class: insufficient awareness of purposeful action and too little emphasis on the self; these attributes are derived particularly from the infrequent use of 'verbs of intention', of 'modal auxiliary verbs' and 'pronouns in the first person singular'. Once more, it is inviting disaster to maintain a normative point of view together with a simple analogy between speech and thought: a person who uses many verbs of intention appears to be motivated and dynamic in his action; if, in addition, he employs many 'I' forms then his action must be regarded as self-assured and individualized. The valuations implied in the selection of the variables and the conclusions naively drawn from the analogies make it clear that in *this* perspective the suggested role of speech in social behaviour is greatly overestimated; on the other hand, Oevermann does not pay enough attention to the general correlations between speech and behaviour.

The range of variables in (1) concerns subordination. In most of the works referred to up till now it was the most reliable indicator of class differences. We have already seen in connection with Loban's investigation, however, that infrequent use of subordinate clauses reveals little about the linguistic capabilities of members of the lower class. After all, in Oevermann's investigation, as in the others, all the schoolchildren produced *some* subordinate clause constructions. This is adequate proof that they were capable of using them (for a discussion on 'syntactical complexity', see Schulz 1971).

Less than half the approximately 90 variables yielded statistically significant differences. These results do not justify Oevermann's conclusion that Bernstein's 'characterizations of the two types of speech forms have been proved suitable for describing speech forms specific to social class' (158). But also in other respects the validity and significance of his investigation must be questioned.

Of all the analyses of class-specific speech behaviour that we have so far mentioned or discussed, Oevermann's is the first to analyse written linguistic data. It is, however, a mistake on his part to equate written linguistic material with spoken utterances, since the conditions of oral and written communication differ considerably. Unless the inherent differences between oral and written linguistic behaviour are adequately described it is inadmissible to draw conclusions about oral behaviour from written material (cf. Wunderlich 1970).

Oevermann's investigation, like most of the others, was carried out at school. This must be regarded as essentially restricting the children's spontaneity of expression, in addition to the fact that they were compelled to express themselves in writing.

Basically Oevermann has two aims: (1) to make a contribution to a 'theory of socialization and processes of social classification' which are to specify the 'different conditions of general psychological and cognitive development in socialization processes with reference to social class'; (2) this theory should devise 'a programme for rationally-planned, permanent educational reform with regard to creating equality of opportunity' (Oevermann 1970, 10).

What does his investigation achieve in the perspective of these aims? It does not reveal much about the nature of socialization processes specific to social class because the subjects were secondary schoolchildren. In the first place they had already successfully passed through the basic social selection filters; secondly, they were in the *secondary* socialization stage, which is profoundly affected by an orientation towards established institutions, and not in the primary phase which is crucial for the formation of class-specific socialization processes—and therefore of speech behaviour (cf. also Wunderlich 1970). An additional factor is that in Oevermann's sample test the lower class was not adequately represented.

These arguments are one reason why the investigation cannot provide any meaningful contribution to a programme for 'rationally-planned educational reform'. We can see in the normative valuations of the analysis a second reason, which calls into question the very basis of such an educational reform. Oevermann has in some way ascertained the existence of socially different speech strategies. But he has done so on the basis of a bourgeois assessment of communicative behaviour, which implies that the differences in speech behaviour should be levelled out according to the prevailing speech norms, i.e. that speakers who deviate from these norms should be adjusted to them. In basic terms this means that lower-class speakers should learn to produce more subordinate clauses, verbs of intention, passives and 'I' forms.

The fact that these and other values apparent from the choice of variables are pseudo-objectively neutralized and clouded by the term 'rational' shows how ideological such a concept of rationality is. In principle, it appears merely to justify the maintenance of class interests and therefore opposes the promotion of emancipation as a task of academic work. Furthermore, equal opportunity of education is identified with a command of 'similar speech strategies'. Here the overestimation of speech serves as an alibi for a radical change in the field of education, which should not be seen in isolation from the changes necessary in other social spheres.

Oevermann's investigation is not the only one to analyse written linguistic patterns of behaviour. Robinson (1965) had already done this, and had accounted for his preference of written rather than oral material with a critique of Bernstein's and Lawton's works. Robinson's critique, which was adopted in part by Oevermann was concerned chiefly with two aspects: the first objection to Bernstein's investigation of 1962 was that in the group discussion the structure of the situation was not formal enough to require the speakers to use markedly 'elaborated' speech; the second objection was that restricted and elaborated speakers always talked amongst themselves; such an arrangement must have encouraged restricted speech amongst the lower-class speakers.

These objections led Robinson to carry out his own investigation, and his starting point is that the written form of expression is a better medium for

c*

distinguishing between the two speech forms. Robinson's analysis is the last investigation of class-specific speech behaviour that we shall consider. Its importance lies in the fact that it intends to examine empirically the extent to which changes in the situation help to provoke the use of one speech form or another. In the works studied up till now, situation has always been neglected as a factor determining different speech behaviour.

2.3.7 Robinson's investigation

For the investigation 15 pairs of boys and 16 pairs of girls were selected from a random sample of 120 12- to 13-year-olds; they all belonged to either the lower or middle class and were comparable in their verbal and nonverbal IQ scores. The subjects had to write a formal and an informal letter at school. In the first case the children were to imagine that the school had enough money to enable some of them to go on a journey. As numbers had to be limited, the letters were to serve as the basis for selection. The children were asked to explain as well as possible the reasons why they in particular wanted to undertake the journey.

In the case of the informal letter the children were asked to tell a good friend their personal news and the latest events. One of the things they were told in connection with this letter was:

> 'All that is important is that you write *naturally* to him in the way you would if this were a real letter. This is not an English exercise of any sort, so just be yourself. If you'd normally write differently from how you write in English lessons, carry on and do so.' (Robinson 1965, 245)

In this way Robinson wanted to create an informal situation which allowed restricted expression and a formal situation which demanded elaborated formulations.

The letters were analysed according to numerous variables, most of which were the same as those used by Bernstein and Lawton. Unfortunately only a few results are given, so that we have to rely on Robinson's general comments and are unable to assess the empirical significance of the investigation. Contrary to expectation, the analysis of the formal letters revealed no significant differences: Robinson writes: 'The formal letter imposed constraints on the subjects. . . . Under these conditions virtually no social class differences appeared' (Robinson 1965, 250). The informal letters, on the other hand, showed differences of the nature predicted by Bernstein. It must however be borne in mind that there were significant differences only in relation to the diversity of the lexical units used (the number of various adjectives, nouns etc.).

From his analysis Robinson concludes that the choice of speech code is to a large extent a *function of the object of communication and of the situation*. Working-class children also had access to 'elaborated' speech when there was sufficient motivation.

Apart from the weaknesses of this investigation, which as in the other works discussed reside in the choice of the linguistic variables, the test situation and the unreliable analogy between written material and oral behaviour, it does nevertheless contain an important indication which enables us to relativize the value of all other speech-behaviour analyses. This will concern us again below: Robinson's work draws attention to the influence of motivation, topic and situation on speech behaviour.

We have now discussed enough data on different forms of speech behaviour to enable us, in conclusion, to summarize their implications for the assessment of the verbal capabilities of lower-class speakers. The hypothesis of deficient linguistic ability among the lower class has not been conclusively proved in any empirical investigation.

First, none of the six investigations was conducted accurately enough to provide supporting evidence for the existence of different speech codes. The investigations of Loban, Bernstein and Oevermann were distorted by the samples they selected. Templin's investigation shows only small class differences, whereas Hawkins's data were in various respects too dubious for us to be able to derive from them differences in verbal capabilities. Four investigations dealt with oral linguistic behaviour and two with written behaviour. As written and spoken language require different expression strategies (specific to media), the written tests cannot be compared with the oral tests. Moreover, in the analyses of oral linguistic behaviour we have no knowledge of the way in which the data were elicited.

Secondly, speech motivation and context are not adequately reflected in any of the studies. Thus it is unclear to what extent the subjects' natural behaviour was impaired by the conditions of the test. In any case, the test situations seem to correspond far more to the expectations of the middle class than to those of the lower class.

This leads us to the third point, which concerns the value judgements implied in the analyses. What we said about the tests of intellectual capabilities also applies to the linguistic tests: speech behaviour is measured by middle-class-oriented norms which are employed, without further justification as a criterion of communicative efficiency and aptness. Thus a speech form is considered superior if it exhibits a high frequency of subordination, or of linguistic expressions which show the speaker to possess subjective judgement capable of qualification.

The most uniform differences revealed by the investigations are those in the use of subordination. This cannot imply differences in verbal capabilities, however, as there was still no lower-class speaker who did not produce at least one subordinate clause. Furthermore, no attention was paid to the fact that hypotaxis can often be replaced by parataxis without impairing the function of communication (cf. Schulz 1971 and 1972).

The normative evaluation of 'individualized' and 'well-qualified' speech prompts a fourth objection, which arises from the latent implications of this value judgement for the correlation between speech and cognition. It can in no way be proved that children who use a smaller range of qualifying adjectives can perceive with less differentiation. Authors such as Furth (1966) and Lenneberg (1967) have produced empirical material which opposes such an oversimplified conclusion.

Fifthly, it should be emphasized that the investigations suppress an important factor which is connected with the competence of speakers in constantly interpreting utterances and producing new utterances on the basis of these interpretations. Until account is taken of this dynamic aspect of all types of communication, i.e. dialectic interaction and argument, in assessing the speaker's ability, only superficial judgements can be made.

Our general conclusion about the above arguments is that the hypothesis of the linguistic deficit of lower-class speakers lacks substantial evidence. Admittedly, there is proof that under certain test conditions class-specific differences exist between speakers in some normatively-defined aspects of speech; yet these differences relate without exception to phenomena of superficial linguistic organization and tell us little about the basic 'communicative competence' of speakers.[9]

The fact that no linguistic deficit of speakers has been proved makes it unnecessary for us to discuss further the *reasons* that are given for the origin of any such deficit. Since there are, however, works which claim to support Bernstein's hypotheses with empirical material on class-specific socialization processes, we shall consider two studies which attempt to demonstrate how parents' speech behaviour is transmitted to their children during the process of socialization.

2.4 Empirical material on class-specific socialization

Bernstein (1970a, 117–33; 1972b) blames the family role system for the inferior verbal and intellectual performance of lower-class children in comparison with middle-class children. We have already given an account of his distinctions in role behaviour in 1.3 and 1.4.3. In accordance with the central concept of a range of alternatives, we emphasized that closed-role systems (status-oriented families) admit of fewer alternatives in communication than do open-role systems (person-oriented families).

The studies on linguistic socialization are centred on the mother-child hypothesis which is based on Bernstein's theses and has been expounded in recent years by a series of sociopsychologists (cf. Hess and Shipman 1965 and 1967; Bernstein and Henderson 1969; Henderson 1970; Olim 1970). The reasoning of these authors is summarized by Olim in the following way:

'The behavior which leads to social, educational, and economic poverty is learned; it is socialized in early childhood. This socialization takes place in large measure by way of language. Since the mother is the primary socializing agent in most instances, the learning takes place in the context of the mother-child communication system. The deprivation that leads to poverty is a lack of cognitive meaning and cognitive and linguistic elaboration in this communication system. The family control system of the socially deprived is one in which appeals to status and role predominate and this type of system, by offering the child predetermined solutions and a narrow range of alternatives of action and thought, limits the child's cognitive development.' (Olim 1970, 212)

Lower-class mothers therefore elaborate their speech less than middle-class

---

[9] For the term 'communicative competence', see Hymes 1968a.

mothers; they determine their child's behaviour to a great extent by appeals to status and give the child little stimulation for a rational and cognitive development of thought.

2.4.1 The analysis of Bernstein and Henderson

The investigation of Bernstein and Henderson (1969) represents an attempt to verify the mother-child hypothesis. Its aim is to examine what relevance lower- and middle-class mothers each attach to speech in different hypothetical cases.

50 lower-class and 50 middle-class mothers were given a list of 11 statements on various aspects of socialization, and an interviewer asked them the following question: 'If parents could not speak, how much *more* difficult do you think it would be for them to do the following things with young children who had not yet started school?' (2f.) Then, from the point of view of 'mute parents', the mothers had to indicate for each statement the degree of difficulty (the scale was divided into six ratings: 'very much more difficult','much more difficult', 'more difficult', 'not too difficult', 'fairly easy', 'easy') involved in coping with each of the situations named without resorting to speech. We shall list the most important of the eleven statements together with the corresponding psychological field into which, according to Bernstein and Henderson (1969, 2), they fall:

1	teaching them everyday tasks like dressing and using a knife and fork	(motor skill)
2	helping them to make things	(constructional skill)
3	drawing their attention to different shapes	(perceptual skill)
5	showing them what is right and wrong	(moral principles)
7	showing them how things work	(cognitive)
9	disciplining them	(control)
11	dealing with them when they are unhappy	(child-oriented affective)

Four of the statements were concerned with the transmission of skills (skill-related statements), five dealt with aspects of social control (person-related statements). The following three hypotheses, derived from Bernstein (1972), were to be tested:

1   Both middle class and working class would place greater emphasis upon the use of language in inter-personal aspects of socialization than the emphasis placed upon language in the socialization into basic skills.
2   The shift in emphasis in the use of language from the skill to the person area would be much greater for the middle-class group.
3   Within the skill area the middle-class group would place a greater emphasis upon language in the transmission of principles.

These three hypotheses were fully confirmed in the analysis of statement-grading by the mothers according to the theory of Bernstein and Henderson (1969, 17f.). The results can be summarized in three points:

1   *All* mothers, independent of class membership, thought it was more difficult to cope with person-related interaction situations without speech than with those in which instruction in skills was relevant.

2   Within the person-related sphere, middle-class mothers placed more emphasis than did lower-class mothers on language.

3   Within the skill-related sphere, lower-class mothers considered language to be more relevant than did middle-class mothers.

The results referred to in (1) to (3) are significant at the level 0·001.

The explanation of the results corresponds exactly to Bernstein's premises: social control is exercised in lower-class families by restricted speech; the children learn correspondingly few role alternatives, and their role autonomy and role distance is correspondingly small.

Is this explanation adequate in relation to the way in which the investigation was designed and carried out? We shall only make two observations. The first concerns the frivolity with which the authors drew conclusions about the mothers' actual socialization behaviour from their behaviour in the test. The mothers had to imagine a situation which had nothing to do with everyday reality, namely having to socialize their children without language. Seen in this light it was an unusual task to have to answer the 11 statements: it was difficult for them to assess situations of which they themselves had no experience. Thus their reactions to the statements are likely to reflect anything (e.g. their wishful thinking) *but* their natural behaviour in everyday situations of socialization. Secondly, it is inadmissible to draw conclusions from the mothers' reactions in the test about the verbal and intellectual stimulation which their children experience during socialization. Since the behaviour of the children was not observed in direct correlation with that of the mothers, nothing at all can be inferred about the cognitive development of the child from this investigation.

The results of this study were included in a more comprehensive investigation into mother-child relations, carried out by Henderson (1970); however, there is just as little explanation here of the correlation between the mother's behaviour and the cognitive development of the child as there was in the work of 1969. Moreover, the data for the mother-child interaction were obtained by questionnaires. But as Garfinkel (1967 and 1972) amply demonstrates, questionnaires are an inadequate means of obtaining information on natural behaviour.

2.4.2 The empirical data of Hess and Shipman

Hess and Shipman (1965 and 1967) place more emphasis on particular speech acts of the mother in interaction with her child in their investigation, which is highly regarded in the field of the mother-child hypothesis.[10] These studies were based on Bernstein's early works, and were intended to validate his hypotheses.

163 non-employed Black mothers with their 4-year-old children were selected for the investigation. The sample was divided into four groups: group A comprised 40 mother-child pairs from prominent professional positions (academics, civil servants, high employees); group B (42 pairs) came from the milieu of skilled workers with more than elementary education; group C consisted of mothers with elementary school education, whose husbands were

---

[10] For the following arguments cf. Ginsberg 1972, 140–54.

mainly unskilled workers; group D (41 pairs) had the same status as group C, with the difference that the husbands did not live at home; these families received unemployment benefit.

The investigation was conducted in three phases:

In the first phase, the mothers were given two interviews (the first of one hour, the second of half an hour) at home on questions of socialization which concerned the intellectual stimulation of their children and their attitudes to school. In the second phase, mothers and children were given various tests at the University of Chicago (intelligence tests, concept-formation and curiosity tests, etc.). In the third phase, mother-child interactions were observed in a special room by means of a two-way mirror. The mothers were encouraged to teach the children certain tasks.

Hess and Shipman analysed their sets of data according to a series of different viewpoints. We shall only be concerned here with those aspects of the investigation which deal with the education strategies of the mothers and their influence on the cognitive development of the child. The main question thereby is what the relation is between the observed behaviour of the mother and the intellectual capabilities of the child.

In their investigation of 1965 Hess and Shipman distinguish three types of speech acts used by mothers to get their children to behave in certain ways, and therefore to exert social control over them (cf. Bernstein's distinction of 'status-oriented' and 'person-oriented' in 1.3.1, 1:3.2 and 1.4.3 above):

1   *Appeals to authority (commands)*
    The mother imposes her will on the child on the strength of her authority, e.g. 'You must do this because I say so.' These imperative utterances appeal to status norms; they cannot be called into question and prevent the child from reflecting on his actions and their moral foundation.

2   *Subjective-personal appeals (invitations, encouragements, advice)*
    In situations of conflict between the child and the family, the subjective emotional dispositions of the child are taken into account. The control through speech acts is directed at specific individuals and appeals to cooperation, in contrast to (1), so that the child learns to imagine the role of another person and to see his own behaviour in a different perspective. Take the case of a child who has been lazy and risks being late at school. A mother who prefers commands might say 'Hurry up! You mustn't be late at school!'; but a mother who is in the habit of taking the child's emotional reactions into account would rather say something like 'You're late. What do you think you'll feel like when you arrive in the class-room and all the others are already there?'

3   *Cognitive-rational appeals (justifications, motivations)*
    Forms of behaviour are justified and alternative sources of action are rejected on rational grounds. Presuppositions and consequences of actions are made conscious or explicit. This is given greater value than the subjective emotional dispositions of the child. Appeals to reason are founded rather on some pragmatically-oriented logic. In a case such as given in (2), a mother might say, 'If you're late you'll miss part of the

teaching and you won't be so well prepared for a written test.' This type of control enables the child to develop strategies for sensible argument and to evaluate better the pros and cons of actions. According to Bernstein, appeals to reason are typical middle-class socialization practice.

In their interview, Hess and Shipman (1965) designed various questions to measure these different types of social control. One of them asked the mother what she would say to her child before the first day at school. Another concerned the child's potential misbehaviour at school. The mothers' answers were recorded on tape and coded according to various categories. The appeals 1 to 3 were mainly taken into account. As for the significance of the data, the following should be observed: the mothers gave a verbal account of how they *would* behave in hypothetical situations; yet their *idea* of such behaviour may differ considerably from what they *actually* do (cf. Labov 1966a, 405–80). The following diagram shows some of the results for frequency of use of the three types of speech act in reaction to the two specific questions mentioned above.

Type of control	A Upper middle class	B Upper lower class	C Lower lower class	D Families on unemployment benefit
1 Question on misconduct at school				
Imperatives	27·9	37·4	42·6	52·2
Subjective- personal	37·5	31·5	25·9	21·7
2 Question on behaviour before first day at school				
Imperatives	14·9	48·2	44·5	46·9
Cognitive- rational	8·6	4·6	1·6	3·1

Fig. 2.8 Class differences in appeals of social control. (Source: Hess and Shipman 1967, 65f.)

Part 1 in figure 2.8 shows that in the case of the hypothetical question on their child's misbehaviour at school, middle-class mothers would use fewer imperative and more personal appeals than any other group. No data were given for appeals to reason as these did not occur frequently enough. Part 2 reveals similar results in the mothers' advice for the first day at school. Middle-class mothers used fewer imperative appeals and more appeals to reason than any other group. However, for *all* mothers imperative or personal appeals prevailed over appeals to reason. These results appear to support Bernstein's hypotheses if it is assumed that personal appeals are rational teaching techniques on the part of the mothers with respect to their children.

Next we must examine the effect that the mothers' control had on the children's behaviour. According to the results given in figure 2.8, we must expect that children of mothers who exert their control through imperative appeals achieve less well than children whose mothers exert control through subjective-personal or cognitive-rational appeals. Figure 2.9 shows the correlations in certain tests between various aspects of the mothers' linguistic control and the children's performance. The correlations reflect the connection between the scores for the solution of the test problems and those for the answers to the two interview questions (see figure 2.8).

Intellectual performance	Control techniques		
	Imperatives	Subjective-personal	Cognitive-rational
Verbalization score for the sorting of 8 blocks	-0.32^2	0.18^1	0.30^2
Physical sorting of the 8 building blocks	-0.26^2	0.12	0.25^2
Binet IQ	-0.32^2	0.22^1	0.18^1
Sigel's nonverbal test	0.36^2	-0.17^1	-0.09

[1] Significant at $p < 0.05$
[2] Significant at $p < 0.01$

Fig. 2.9 Correlations between the mothers' control techniques and the children's intellectual performance. (Source: Hess and Shipman 1967, 66)

The verbalization score measures the child's ability to verbalize the principles for his way of sorting blocks. The score for physical sorting of the 8 building blocks reflects the child's skill in correctly sorting the blocks withou. recourse to speech. The Binet IQ score measures certain specified intellectual capabilities, whilst the Sigel test establishes to what extent the child is *unable* to explain verbally the principles for block sorting.

The test results show that the children attain relatively good intellectual performances when the mother appeals to reason or employs personal appeals; on the other hand, the performances are weak when the appeals are imperative. From this, Hess and Shipman conclude that the data confirm Bernstein's hypotheses: lower-class mothers use more imperative appeals and thereby curb rather than stimulate the intellectual development of their children.

We shall comment briefly on this part of the investigation. Hess and Shipman base their results on data from interviews. Interviews cannot in any way replace observations of actual natural behaviour. Often they are imprecise, and moreover they raise the well-known question of bias. Crandall and Preston (1955) compared psychologists' assessments of mothers' behaviour with the mothers' self-assessment. They discovered that there was little correlation between the two judgements. Similar results were obtained by Zunich (1962). This means that we should judge interview data on mother-child relations with a certain degree of scepticism.

The correlations between the control techniques of the mothers and the intellectual performance of the children are relatively small. They exceed the score 0·3 only for imperatives. Whereas some variables have a significant correlation, others show little or no connection between the mother's behaviour and that of the child. Moreover, it must be emphasized that statistical significance cannot simply be equated with psychological significance. In the work of Hess and Shipman a number of factors other than the mothers' control techniques could have been responsible for the different intellectual performances of the children.

In the third phase of their investigation, Hess and Shipman (1967, 67ff.) observed the interactions between mother and child directly. In a special room the mothers were asked to teach their children three simple tasks, which the interviewer had explained beforehand. The first consisted in the sorting of a number of toys (spoons, cars, chairs) that were coloured red, yellow or green, in three groups according to function and colour, and moreover in explaining the grounds for the sortings ('all these are spoons', 'these have the same colour', etc.).

The second task (the block-sorting task) was a little more difficult than the first. The child had to be taught to apply two criteria at once in the sorting of blocks. It should group the blocks in such a way that they had the same height (high or low) and had the same mark on them (x or 0). As in the case of the first task, the mother should explain the principles according to which the groupings should be made.

The third task, finally, was to be solved by mother and child in collaboration. They were asked to copy five geometric drawings.

The point of the test was that the mother should show the child what had to be done and explain her demonstration as clearly as possible with corresponding verbalization. The precise way of teaching the tasks was left entirely to the mothers themselves. They were also given as much time as they needed.

When the mother had finished her explanation, the child was tested by the test leader on his skill in carrying out the various operations without help: in this case the mother was not allowed to help the child. This was designed to establish the effect of the mothers' teaching on the intellectual behaviour of the children.

Hess and Shipman (1967, 69ff.) analysed large sets of data. We shall, however, deal mainly with the block-sorting task, whose results are characteristic for the other tasks as well. The mother's teaching style in the sorting task was measured according to the following categories (which correspond in principle to certain specific types of speech act):

1   *Informing*
     Certain utterances concerning the blocks, such as 'these blocks are the same height', or 'this block belongs here'.
2   *Motivating*
     Utterances which seek to arouse the child's interest and cooperation in problem solving by promises, rewards, or by emphasising the particular value of the task. E.g. 'we're going to play a game' or 'now listen carefully and learn this so we can tell Daddy how smart you were'.
3   *Orienting*
     Utterances which prepare the child to solve the problem, such as 'I'm going to show you how to put these blocks in the right place', 'let's try it once more'.
4   *Seeking physical feedback*
     The mother tries to induce the child to physical action: 'where does this block go?', 'put this with the other blocks that are tall and have an x on them'.

5 *Seeking verbal feedback*
   Utterances which urge the child to explain his actions, such as 'is this tall or short?', 'why did you put that block there?'
6 *Positive reinforcement*
   Speech acts of confirmation, such as 'that's right', 'yes, that's an *x*'.
7 *Negative reinforcement*
   Negative utterances which accompany the actions of the child, such as 'that's not right', 'no, this is a tall block'.
8 *Specific language when requiring discriminations*
   Speech acts which invite the child to discriminate certain aspects of external shape, colour, etc., e.g. 'find a tall block with an *x* on it', 'find the block that goes here'.

Hess and Shipman set out with the assumption that middle-class mothers would give more precise instructions than lower-class mothers and would thus motivate the child to a more intellectual analysis of the tasks. Figure 2.10 summarizes the class differences in the mothers' teaching style.

Types of speech act	*Groups*			
	A Middle class	*B* Upper lower class	*C* Lower lower class	*D* Lower class (father absent)
1 Informing	23·46	22·87	20·82	22·26
2 Motivating	5·3	3·46	2·73	3·08
3 Orienting	8·12	6·45	5·78	5·44
4 Seeking physical feedback	8·17	13·91	13·16	14·06
5 Seeking verbal feedback	21·05	20·45	20·89	19·65
6 Positive reinforcement	53·1	35·37	40·75	46·27
7 Negative reinforcement	44·73	44·8	53·82	58·24
8 Specific language when requiring discriminations	48·2	42·56	44·72	39·17

Fig. 2.10 Mean class differences in maternal teaching behaviours. (Source: Hess and Shipman 1967, 72; cf. Ginsburg 1972, 146)

Except for variables 1 and 5, figure 2.10 shows significant differences between the middle-class group and the other groups. We shall examine the significant results in greater detail. For variables 2 and 3 the differences are still fairly small. Middle-class mothers used an average of eight speech acts of orienting; mothers from class D about five. Variable 8 shows a moderate differentiation: there is a difference of nine score points between group A and group D. Therefore, there are *substantial* differences only for variables 4, 6 and 7.

In general we can establish that middle-class mothers requested their children less frequently to sort the blocks and encouraged them more often in their actions but admonished them less. For four of the eight types of behaviour the differences are small, and there are not insignificant differences for variables 4, 6, 7 and 8.

In order to examine the importance of these differences, we should compare the scores for the maternal teaching behaviour in the block-sorting task with the children's individual performance in this test. Figure 2.11 shows correlations between the mothers' behaviour and that of the children irrespective of the social class. Thus the data only reflect the impression made by the mothers' behaviour on the intellectual behaviour of the children.

Speech-act types	Placement score	Verbal score
2 Motivating	0·06	0·07
3 Orienting	0·2[2]	0·16[2]
4 Seeking physical feedback	−0·39[1]	−0·3[1]
5 Seeking verbal feedback	0·18[2]	0·24[1]
6 Positive reinforcement	0·12	0·01
7 Negative reinforcement	−0·09	−0·03
8 Specific language when requiring discriminations	0·16[2]	0·3[1]

[1]$p < 0.05$ [2]$p < 0.01$

Fig. 2.11 Relation of maternal teaching variables in the block-sorting task to children's learning scores. (Source: Hess and Shipman 1967, 74)

The data show little correlation between the mothers' behaviour and that of the children. We shall deal mainly with variables 4, 6, 7 and 8 in which, according to figure 2.10, the middle and lower classes differ from one another. There is no correlation for variables 6 and 7, and the class differences for these variables are therefore unimportant as they have no influence on the child's behaviour. On the other hand, there was a consistent correlation for variable 4 between mother and child behaviour, which means that the child's sorting was poor when his mother pushed him too much. However, this result can hardly be regarded as confirming Bernstein's hypotheses. What we should conclude is that children react negatively to pressure (cf. Ginsburg 1972, 147).

Only variable 8 correlated positively with the performances in the sorting test. It supports Bernstein's hypotheses. But as the remaining correlations are small, we must conclude that the class differences in the use of speech-act types revealed in figure 2.10 are of hardly any consequence, if at all.

The results of the investigation conducted by Hess and Shipman can be summarized as follows. In some aspects of maternal behaviour the social classes do differ (e.g. negative behaviour reinforcement), but not in others (e.g. prompting the child to verbalize). The differences that do exist sometimes have no effect on the child's intellectual behaviour (in the case of positive and negative reinforcement) and sometimes only a small effect (in the case of prompting discrimination).

Overall, Bernstein's hypotheses find little confirmation.

We shall now make a general assessment of the significance of the empirical material on the mother-child hypothesis.

First, we established that there are some differences in maternal behaviour. However they are frequently insignificant, sometimes small, or even trivial.

Secondly, the methods of the investigations often have considerable weaknesses. We must be sceptical about the data of the assessment test of Bernstein and Henderson (1969). They can only tell us little about the actual interactions between mothers and their children.

Our third point concerns the investigation conducted by Hess and Shipman (1967) into interaction behaviour. It reveals more about the relation between the mother's instructional style and the child's behaviour than do the other investigations. Nevertheless it has the disadvantage that the observations were made in the laboratory. We need more evidence on the ways in which mothers stimulate their children to learn in natural situations.

There is a further disadvantage in this investigation, which leads us to the fourth point. Hess and Shipman do not attach enough value to the *process* of interaction. It is not enough merely to count the actual utterances of the mothers; what we really need is more information about the reciprocal communicative reactions of mother and child. On the one hand, it should be appreciated that the theory of speech acts is used for the analysis of behaviour (cf. Austin 1962; Searle 1969). On the other, however, it should be recognized that the theory of speech acts is still in such a primitive and unempirical state that it would be grossly premature to attempt to quantify over types of speech act (cf. Labov 1970a and 1972a).

Finally, none of the investigations are able to explain *what influence maternal behaviour has on the cognitive development of the child*. It is not even clear whether there is a strong influence at all. It is remarkable that there should be absolutely no proof of these correlations when one considers that all these studies presuppose a close relation between mother and child behaviour and even intend to make it the basis of compensatory programmes.

What is certain is that up till now no convincing proof of the mother-child hypothesis has been forthcoming.

2.5 Further development of Bernstein's theoretical conception

Some of the weaknesses of Bernstein's hypotheses have already become apparent through the empirical investigations aimed at their verification. These created an awareness of the problems which arise for such hypotheses in concrete surveys and analyses of linguistic material. These works either supplemented or corrected Bernstein's theories.

We shall now deal with certain considerations which have brought about a modification of Bernstein's assumptions. Robinson (1965) and Lawton (1968, 103–43) pointed out that the conditions in which sociolinguistic investigations are carried out should not be neglected. Whereas Robinson doubts that the concept of codes has any validity at all beyond the immediate situation (248), Lawton (138f.) argues that the results of sociolinguistic investigations are only relevant with respect to the particular test from which they were obtained.

Cazden (1968, 603) writes on the problems concerned with the test situation:

'Whenever differences in code use are found, it can be claimed that they would not have appeared in some other experimental situation. Since the number of experimental situations is infinite, this is a difficult claim to dispute.'

Cazden (1970) concentrates on the role played by situation in investigations into speech behaviour. He proves that the Deficit Hypothesis is inadequate on this point.

Williams and Naremore (1969a and b), who base their work on linguistic material from the social dialects project in Detroit (cf. the comments on Williams and Naremore 1969a in the Bibliography), emphasize that account must be taken not only of the speech situation but of the communicative function of utterances in general. Consequently Williams and Naremore are no longer concerned with classifying speakers into categories of restricted or elaborated speech but with a general analysis of different forms of communication. They believe, however, that these are easier to grasp not by categories but by assuming a *communicative continuum* which reflects the different effects of function and form in communicative behaviour (Williams and Naremore 1969b, 97).

Williams and Naremore see the necessity for investigations into the communicative development of children which should record primarily their ability to use linguistic utterances in the functionally appropriate context (100). This leads them to the following view of lower-class speech:

'More realistic is the view that children's linguistic development differs mostly in the demands for communication that are placed upon them. Thus it could be argued that the distinctive language behaviors of the lower class child are more a function of the communicative experiences in general, and by his early family life in particular, than they are of linguistic exposure. His language behavior will most directly reflect what he has learned of language in a functional sense, and that will typically be what his environment has required of him in the role of an active speaker-listener.' (100f.)

Oevermann (1970) adds general theoretical considerations on class-specific speech behaviour to his critical comments on Bernstein's hypotheses. Before we turn to his theoretical discussion, we shall look briefly at Oevermann's critique which can be divided into four points (cf. Oevermann 1970, 197–216):

1   Bernstein has not paid sufficient attention to the *non-verbal factor of behaviour*. If empirical analyses are to have any meaning, however, a distinction must be made between verbal and nonverbal use of symbols.

2   The definition of the 'linguistic codes' is *circular*. The first aspect of the circularity is that 'an adequate description of the interaction situation . . . always presupposes the theory of the linguistic codes; but, on the other hand, the situation is always needed to verify the theory.' Oevermann describes this state of affairs as a general methodological dilemma of sociological measurements. The second problematic aspect of this circularity concerns the unspecified definition of the 'linguistic codes' on the sociological, psychological and linguistic levels (cf. 3.4.1 below). 'Bernstein . . . does not make it clear whether the various linguistic codes should be

defined by sociological concepts, by psychological concepts involved in analysing cognitive processes or by concepts of linguistic analysis.'

3   The correlative connection between speech forms and roles on the one hand and speech forms and verbal planning strategies on the other should be separated. This gives rise to the urgent sociolinguistic task 'of discovering the system of rules by which the role relations determined by the social structure coincide with concrete linguistic patterns.' If it were possible to determine the covariation of nonlinguistic with linguistic characteristics in role behaviour, 'the next step would be to establish the psychological consequences of these forms of symbol use.'

4   There is a difference between 'linguistic code' and 'dialect'. Apart from the 'codes' which are primarily relevant to class differences, dialects can act solely as a *secondary* filter of intellectual capabilities.

From his critique of Bernstein, Oevermann derives the theoretical question of how 'the concept of the linguistic codes . . . can be systematically linked to basic assumptions on role theory.' He sees two possibilities for such a link, both of which one should be able to integrate into a wider concept of 'sociological pragmatism'. Oevermann suggests a 'simplified and a complex version of the linguistic code theory'. The simplified version 'leaves out of account all determining factors that do not fall directly under its scope' and predicts 'identical speech for all members of a social system in identical social situations' (190). Oevermann assigns the 'simplified version' to an 'objective, quantitative sociology', which attempts to embrace 'objectively' the phenomena of reality by describing these according to an externally-imposed pattern of categories. This version, however, ignores the fact that a given situation is affected by an individual's historically-conditioned experiences and subjective patterns of interpretation. The complex version takes account of precisely this factor (191). Only this version can 'incorporate the conception of verbal strategies as these are determined by factors beyond the immediate situation, characterizing the social biography of an individual in a general sense' (191).

Both versions reflect the methodological problems of the social sciences and they have been fully discussed by Habermas (1967). Oevermann considers that both theories are justified and that they should complement one another: micro-analyses that have been carried out by systematic variation of individual variables must be extended in accordance with the complex version by including the relevant historical dimensions of role behaviour. Furthermore, it seems to Oevermann that there is at least a possible tendency for the two versions to coincide when the linguistic codes are analysed from the point of view of 'intra-family socialization processes specific to social class'.

Oevermann reckons Bernstein's works as well as his own to belong to the complex version.

2.6. Summary

We have discussed in this chapter a series of empirical investigations which attempt to verify the Deficit Hypothesis, which led to a critical examination of their validity and significance. We shall give a short résumé of some of the results of our dicussion, which will be dealt with in greater detail in the next chapter.

First, no investigation was able to prove conclusively that lower-class children have an intellectual or linguistic defiicit. Such a conclusion is dubious not only because of the type of tests and the way they were carried out but also because the methods used to analyse linguistic and cognitive differences were shown to be largely inadequate.

Secondly, the hypothesis concerning the origin of class-specific behaviour (mother-child hypothesis) is also inadequate. It cannot explain how the mother's behaviour is transmitted to the child, and it also overlooks the fact that children are to a certain extent self-taught (cf. Piaget 1946 and Ginsburg 1972, 154–66, 173–89). Precisely this point reveals that children seek stimuli in their environment themselves and do not rely solely on stimuli provided by the mother.

Thirdly, it has been demonstrated that the majority of investigations on the Deficit Hypotheses are founded on normative methodological principles determined by middle-class values. The middle-class bias shows that differences are not analysed in a functional sense but according to preconceived valuations. Such a procedure must support our supposition that research into class differences, as it is promoted by society, is intended not so much to emancipate the lower class as to integrate it into the existing hierarchical structure of society (cf. 3.1, 3.2 and 3.5).

Fourthly, the implicit basic assumptions of the Deficit Hypothesis have still not been proved. The mother-child hypothesis as well as the insistence on a linguistic and cognitive deficit are based on the assumption of a close relation between speech and thinking. At the present stage of research, however, this relation has not yet become clear.

Fifthly, the central issue of social behaviour is excluded from all the investigations. It is only in the frame of a social pragmatics which is both structurally and historically oriented that we can meaningfully interpret the linguistic and cognitive aspects of behaviour.

③ Social consequences of the Deficit Hypothesis: function and evaluation

We have two aims in this chapter: on the one hand, to summarize the criticisms that have been formulated from various angles with regard to the Deficit Hypothesis; on the other, to go into the sociopolitical reasons which have caused it to have such wide repercussions, particularly in the USA. We shall begin with a concrete example—the linguistic programme proposed by Bereiter and Engelmann—to show how the results of Deficit research are crystallized in compensatory programmes. This brings us to a discussion of the connection between theory and application, both of which have sociopolitical implications. With this in view we shall reduce the Deficit Hypothesis to the myth of verbal deprivation and finally show its social function, which has been exposed mainly in Marxist works.

3.1 An example of compensatory education: the speech programme of Bereiter and Engelmann

We have already established that in essence the Deficit Hypothesis blames harmful influences in the social environment for the limited functionality of lower-class verbal and intellectual performance in the context of middle-class values. The term 'environmentally harmful' covers all those social values of the lower class which bring the child into conflict and confrontation with the prevailing social norms (a typical example of this is *school*). Where 'environmental harm' causes a certain deficiency in ability and, in the words of Bernstein, a 'cultural deprivation' (Bernstein in Gahagan and Gahagan 1970), the concept of 'compensation' is put forward. Many supporters of compensatory programmes assume that lower-class children simply do not acquire in their families the capabilities essential for success at school (cf. Blank 1970, 63f.). They seek to explain the child's insufficient stimulation and retardation by the mother-child hypothesis (cf. 2.4). It is the family in general and the mother in particular who are held responsible for the fact that the child is subjected to certain restrictions. Thus the *aim* of compensatory programmes is to 'promote a planned development which will balance out the deficiencies in stimulation and experience that are caused by the environment' (Deutsch 1970, 20). It is both remarkable and significant that although Deutsch sees the 'social environment' as being the cause of the 'deficiency in experience', his conclusion is not that the environment itself should be changed, but that the people who live in it should be constantly compensated for the harmful effect it has on them. This strange logic is only comprehensible when we look more closely at the social system which Deutsch represents when he comes to this conclusion. An analysis of the social framework, from which the necessity for compensatory education is derived, will be given in the next section in connection with the evaluation of the Deficit Hypothesis. Here we need only say that the basic idea of compensatory education is not to blame the miseries of the lower class on the social system with its norms and principles of unequal distribution of poverty and wealth, but rather to make the lower class itself the scapegoat of its own condition. It is thus a prerequisite of compensatory work that the poor performance and inability of the lower class should be proved. Once this has been achieved (the representatives of the Deficit Hypothesis are trying to do just this), the State can intervene (with compensatory programmes) to try and adapt the lower class to the norms of the middle class. Although these programmes are claimed to be charitable measures designed to create equality of opportunity, they provide in fact the foundation for mobilizing the workforces which have become necessary to maintain the processes of production.

First of all we shall deal with the prerequisite of compensatory work by giving an account of the functional correlation between formulations of the Deficit Hypothesis and their immediate practical consequences. There are many examples which demonstrate this correlation. We shall choose the speech compensation programme of Bereiter and Engelmann (1966), which is a typical example and one of the most well-known and popular compensatory programmes in the USA.

Bereiter and Engelmann take as their basis Bernstein's theory that only elaborated speech enables lower-class children to climb the social ladder. It is an implicit presupposition of their programme that more complex speech automatically facilitates a more differentiated comprehension of the social environment.

According to Bereiter and Engelmann, the poor intellectual ability of Black lower-class children is reflected in their inadequate speech; among the fundamental characteristics of their speech behaviour are the following:

1   The children answered questions either with an incomplete sentence or merely with a simple 'yes' or 'no'. In the authors' view, this shows first that they were unable to form complete sentences, and secondly that they had probably not understood the questions correctly.

2   The children's utterances frequently lacked prepositions, conjunctions and above all the copula 'be'. According to Bereiter and Engelmann, these are essential linguistic means for establishing logical relations; if children are limited to the use of only few prepositions/conjunctions, this is reflected in an insufficient capacity for logical analysis.

   The absence of the copula 'be' seems to have an even more serious effect. In the authors' view, the copula is necessary to establish the relation of the sentence to reality (126).

On the basis of these observations Bereiter and Engelmann paint a grim picture of the verbal capabilities of the lower-class children:

   they are indifferent to the content of verbal utterances;
   in their social environment (family) they have not experienced the linguistic

stimuli necessary to be able to use language with any degree of meaning-fulness;

they lack the ability to grasp and reproduce with linguistic adequacy correlations, processes etc.;

their retarded development is accounted for by a 'dissociation' of speech and behaviour similar to that which is assumed for mentally-retarded or psychologically-disturbed children. (Bereiter and Engelmann 1966, 37ff.)

It is no wonder that such observations bring Bereiter and Engelmann (1966, 39) to the general conclusion that lower-class children show 'a total lack of ability to use language as a device for acquiring and processing information. Language for them is unwieldy and not very useful.'

Bereiter and Engelmann believe that nothing can increase the self-assurance of the underprivileged child so much as the correct reproduction of the middle-class linguistic norms. Their conclusion is that this should be attained by purely behaviouristic speech drills.

The authors formulated 15 minimal goals which are required for a speech compensation programme; of these we shall list points 1 to 9, 12 and 14, which indicate the linguistic learning aims for the children:

'1   Ability to use both *affirmative* and *not* statements in reply to the question "What is this?"—"This is a ball. This is not a book."

2   Ability to use both *affirmative* and *not* statements in response to the command "Tell me about this——(ball, pencil, etc.)"—"This pencil is red. This pencil is not blue."

3   Ability to handle polar opposites ("If it is not ——, it must be ——") for at least four concept pairs, e.g. "big-little", "up-down", "long-short", "fat-skinny".

4   Ability to use the following prepositions correctly in statements describing arrangements of objects: "on", "in", "under", "over", "between". "Where is the pencil?—The pencil is under the book."

5   Ability to name positive and negative instances for at least four classes, such as tools, weapons, pieces of furniture, wild animals, farm animals and vehicles. "Tell me something that is not a weapon"—"A cow is not a weapon." The child should also be able to apply these class concepts correctly to nouns with which he is familiar, e.g. "Is a crayon a piece of furniture?"—"No, a crayon is not a piece of furniture. A crayon is something to write with."

6   Ability to perform simple *if—then* deductions. The child is presented a diagram containing big squares and little squares. All the big squares are red, but the little squares are of various other colors. "If the square is big, what do you know about it?"—"It's red."

7   Ability to use 'not' in deductions. "If the square is little, what else do you know about it?"—"It is not red."

8   Ability to use 'or' in simple deductions. "If the square is little, then it is not red. What else do you know about it?"—"It's blue or yellow."

9   Ability to name the basic colors, plus white, black, and brown.

12   Ability to recognize and name the vowels and at least 15 consonants.

14   Ability to rhyme in some fashion to produce a word that rhymes with
            a given word, to tell whether two words do or do not rhyme, or to
            complete unfamiliar rhyming jingles like "I had a dog, and his name
            was Abel; I found him hiding under the ———.'"

The main points of these minimal goals are correct replies to the set questions
using complete sentences, correct formation of the negative in Standard English,
correct use of certain prepositions, practice in the application of *if—then*
sequences, knowledge of vowels and consonants in Standard English and ability
to make simple rhymes. Speech training, on which the compensatory
programmes are based, is carried out according to the principle of dialogue by
means of question-and-answer games. Only questions that are answered with
complete sentences are accepted. Within the dialogue, importance is attached to
repetitions, minimal linguistic contrasts ('Is this a book?'—'No this is *not a* book')
and contrasting qualifications ('This pencil is *red*'—'This pencil is not *blue*').

The grammatical drill is supposed to lead to a logical precision in the way the
child expresses himself, whereas the practice in linguistic modification and
qualification is expected to produce changes in cognition.

Our discussion of other empirical investigations into the speech behaviour of
lower-class children will have already caused the reader to view the minimal goals
proposed by Bereiter and Engelmann with a certain scepticism. As a prelude to a
more fundamental criticism of compensatory programmes of this and similar
types, we will begin by looking at the ideological foundation on which a
programme such as this is based.

The comprehensive analysis made by Labov *et al.* (1968) on Non-Standard
English has shown to what extent Bereiter and Engelmann have misrepresented
and misunderstood the verbal capabilities of lower-class children.[1] Labov
demonstrates that lower-class children speak a *different kind* of English which, in
many respects, deviates systematically and regularly from the middle-class
Standard. From his speech data on Non-Standard English he arrives at the exact
opposite conclusion from Bereiter and Engelmann: lower-class children live in a
verbally rich subculture, where the child is 'bathed in verbal stimulation and
verbal contests from morning to night' (Labov *et al.* 1968, II, 343; also Labov
1970b, 11); they speak and hear well-formed sentences; there is no linguistic
ground which prevents the children's logical capability for analysis being
developed. Labov (1970b, 2) reveals the 'myth of verbal deprivation' as pure
middle-class ideology by examining the assertions made by Bereiter and
Engelmann on the speech behaviour of Black children from two points of view:
the *eliciting* of the linguistic utterances and their *grammaticality*.

According to Labov, linguistic utterances must be observed in the speakers'
social surroundings and in natural situations; they must be functionally
connected with their communicative needs and their social actions. Contrary to
these principles, Bereiter and Engelmann tested the ghetto children in a situation
that was totally unfamiliar to them and in which they would not have had the

---

[1] The methodological consequences of this investigation are set out in the essay 'The logic of
Nonstandard English' by William Labov (1970b). I base some of the following arguments on his
comments in the German translation in Klein and Wunderlich 1971, 80–83.

slightest motivation to speak naturally. The interviewer was a White adult and consequently the children must have felt themselves to be in a totally asymmetrical situation. When the interviewer put questions to them, they replied with the self-consciousness of an inferior who realizes that anything he says can literally be held against him. In the test situation the children only answered with a 'yes' or 'no' and their behaviour revealed, moreover, what Bereiter and Engelmann describe as a 'total lack of ability to use language' (39). The defensive, monosyllabic behaviour of the child is a direct reaction of the child to the test situation: 'If one creates an alien and threatening situation, children will react appropriately' (Labov *et al.* 1968, II, 342). The observations made by Bereiter and Engelmann are simply unusable because they are related to unnatural test situations and can therefore tell us nothing about the verbal capacity of the child. In order to obtain information about the linguistic capability of a child, 'it is necessary to discriminate between the child's underlying ability or competence and the amount of attention or effort he puts into a test situation' (Labov *et al.* 1968, II, 341).

Consequently, Labov conducted his investigation into the speech behaviour of ghetto children in natural speech situations. What Bereiter and Engelmann had considered defective speech proved in reality to be a consistent and systematic type of speech which follows the grammatical rules of Non-Standard English (cf. our more detailed account (methods of analysis, results) of the investigation conducted by Labov *et al.* (1968) in 6.2.6, 6.3.3 and 6.3.4). We shall take four examples which demonstrate that Bereiter and Engelmann have no grammatical knowledge of Non-Standard Negro English (NNE), or rather, as it is preferably called today, Black English Vernacular (BEV).

Our first example concerns the use of *negation*. Contrary to the simple negation in Standard English (SE), BEV uses double negation ('nobody knows nothing') and Bereiter and Engelmann consider this to be a severe violation of the grammar and logic of English. However, it is easy to show that sentences with double negation are based on the same deep structure as sentences with simple negation (cf. 6.2.6, 'Negation in BEV'). The negation drill in the programme put forward by Bereiter and Engelmann must therefore lead the Negro children into verbal conflict with their mother tongue. Double negation is penalized, although it is functional and valid in BEV.

Another difference between SE and BEV is manifested in the use of the copula 'be'. Bereiter and Engelmann assess sentences such as 'they mine', in which the cupola, mandatory in SE, is missing, as proof of the verbal deficit of ghetto children. However, it is a systematic characteristic of most BEV utterances to leave out the cupola. The omission of the copula 'be' in BEV is a consequence of its contraction in SE. The contracted SE form 'they're mine', derived from the uncontracted SE form 'they are mine', becomes 'they mine' in BEV. Whenever the copula can be contracted in SE it can be removed in BEV (cf. 6.2.6). Although linguists have not as yet agreed upon a description of the copula, it is plausible, as Labov *et al.* argue, that the copula is present in the deep structure of BEV. In any case, Bereiter and Engelmann are wrong when they maintain that the omission of the copula implies a disturbed relationship of the child to reality.

An example of the use of the interrogative conjunction *if* also demonstrates that BEV systematically deviates from SE. The repetition tests of SE sentences carried out by Labov with BEV speakers show that BEV speakers automatically replaced *if*-clauses by a construction with *do*. Thus the sentence 'I asked Alvin *if* he knows how to play basketball' would be altered by BEV speakers and repeated as 'I ax Alvin *do* he know how to play basketball' (cf. Labov *et al.* 1968, 3.9). It is clear from this as well as from the earlier examples that BEV uses different syntactic possibilities for the same semantic material. We must question the function of a programme that is designed to teach the children to produce *if*-clauses when these children are already capable of expressing the notions corresponding to these *if*-clauses.

Our last example concerns the use of pronouns in BEV. Bereiter and Engelmann found that BEV speakers left out relative pronouns ('This here is one family eat nothing') but that they did use pronouns pleonastically ('My sister *she* play piano'). It is a part of their compensatory programme to adapt BEV children to the norms of pronoun use in SE. As Smith (1969) has already shown, however, such a measure would bring the child into verbal conflict. The reason for this is that there is a close correlation between the omission of the relative pronoun in BEV and the pleonastic use of the subject pronoun. In such sentences where the relative pronoun is omitted, the pleonastic pronoun is applied to remove any ambiguities. If, therefore, the programme of Bereiter and Engelmann is supposed to teach the children to omit the pleonastic pronoun, this will cause communicative interference within BEV usage.

These examples amply demonstrate that BEV does not have fewer or worse possibilities of expression, but that it uses other, equivalent linguistic forms. We must stress here that BEV speakers use the Non-Standard language rather than the 'correct' one for various linguistic games which require a great deal of verbal dexterity on the part of the speaker. An example of this can be taken from the verbal duels or 'ritual insults' which are customary between members of the peer group; these contain a rich variety of taboo words and often rhyme (cf. Labov *et al.* 1968, 4.2.3 and Labov 1972a; this is discussed in 6.3.3 below). We can clearly establish from this that any desire to 'compensate' children for the capabilities which they possess in their natural speech behaviour (e.g. the ability to rhyme) already reveals a naive and careless assessment of their capacity. The political background of speech compensation programmes becomes apparent in the unthinking, blind eagerness to adapt lower-class children to the middle-class standards as efficiently as possible. In the end, it is not so much a question of helping the child to get out of his social situation as of preparing his efficient adaptation to the dominant norms of society. In order to achieve this, the lower class must be made to feel so insecure that they will approach a pathological state (cf. Bereiter and Engelmann 1966, 38: 'The culturally deprived child then shows much the same *dissociation between language and action* that has been observed in mentally retarded children' (italics mine)). We must now take a closer look at the underlying reasons for these attitudes and value judgements in correlation with the social function of the Deficit Hypothesis.

3.2 Reasons for the controversy about the Deficit Hypothesis

Why did Bernstein's works have such a widespread effect? Some of the reasons can be seen if we take the USA as an example, where it must be realized that we are only able to give a rough outline of the entire social fabric underlying the problems at hand. From this angle, the controversy about the Deficit Hypothesis will become more comprehensible, including its academic and sociopolitical dimensions.

Bernstein's work has awakened hopes, first in the USA and then increasingly in Europe, of being able to solve the socioeconomically-conditioned class conflicts by large-scale State intervention in the family socialization processes of the lower class. There are two main reasons why it became necessary in the USA as early as 1960 to remove children from the 'harmful' environment of the lower class and to adapt them to the values of the middle class. In the first place industrial production required more technically-trained workers if it was to guarantee the competitiveness of American industry; secondly, a potential conflict developed in the slums and ghettos between lower-class Whites and Blacks, and the dominant class did not want to lose control of the situation. The American government's answer to the 'chronic poverty' of 77 million Americans (two-fifths of the entire American population) was a 'war against poverty' (du Bois-Reymond 1971, 25) that was initiated by President Kennedy at the beginning of the 1960s and intensified by President Johnson. The social sciences (particularly sociology, psychology and linguistics) were given the task of conducting numerous investigations into the behaviour of the lower class. Projects were undertaken, at great financial cost, on the socialization practices of the lower class (e.g. Hess and Shipman 1965 and 1967) as well as on their intellectual and linguistic behaviour (Deutsch *et al.* 1967; Labov *et al.* 1968; Williams and Naremore 1969a and b). Similar attention was paid to the peripheral ethnic groups that were neither economically nor culturally integrated into society (cf. Fishman 1966; Fishman *et al.* 1968). At the end of the 1960s, the market was flooded with volumes containing comprehensive analyses on the question of the 'disadvantaged child' (among the standard works are: Bloom, Allison and Hess 1965; Coleman *et al.* 1966; Keach, Fulton and Gardener 1967; Miller 1967; Passow, Goldberg and Tannenbaum 1967; Williams 1970a). The spectrum of abstract labels given to the socially disadvantaged increased in proportion to the number of investigations into the behaviour of the lower class: 'culturally deprived', 'socially disadvantaged', 'educationally deficient', 'undereducated', 'underachiever' etc. (cf. Iben 1971, 11). It is remarkable that not one of these labels mentions the actual socioeconomic position of those concerned.

The reasons for the rapid success of Bernstein's socialization theory are self-evident: it names factors preventing full utilization of cultural reserves and proposes a way of rectifying this without calling into question the structure of authority and production in a capitalist society. What can still be seen as a charitable and humanitarian concern in Bernstein's works becomes, in the formulations of other research workers, more clearly a concern with the *economic* situation of a society. We quote from Olim (1970, 213f.) who is representative of this point of view:

'The economy is expanding most rapidly in those service industries that demand high educational attainment and highly developed skill in the use of symbol systems. At the same time, as a result of increased productivity, there has been only moderate expansion in manufacturing employment in the United States in the past twenty years. Unskilled jobs are rapidly disappearing as more and more physical work is assigned to machines. The economy is being converted from one in which workers produce physical products to one in which they produce services. Many of the new services deal with the management of information. *Society, therefore, is accelerating its need and demand for persons who have developed highly skilled elaborate methods of processing information* and who are able to manipulate the environment, not directly as in factory work, but representationally, by *symbolic means*—the means essential for coping with the conditions of an advanced technological civilization.' (Italics mine.)

From this description it is clear that the basic motive for teaching the lower class to use complex and flexible communication symbols is *to equip them better to meet the present demands of production.* Thus the function of elaborated speech is evident: 'elaborated codes maximize the range of alternatives of thought and action, and the possibility of this maximization should be open to all. . . .' (Ohm 1970, 224).

Although Bernstein in one essay (Rubinstein and Stoneman 1970, 114) emphatically rejects the idea of compensatory education—'I suggest that we should stop thinking in terms of "compensatory education"'—his introduction to Gahagan's (1970) compensatory programme expresses quite the opposite view. Although he has 'severe doubts' about compensatory programmes, he nevertheless has the 'feeling that the attempt to run a language programme could hardly fail to be informative. Since little was known about the problems involved in setting up and implementing such programmes, useful practical knowledge was certain to be gained. This was also the feeling of the then Ministry of Education, who were extremely anxious to see a trial language programme implemented.'

Taken together, these quotations suggest the conclusion that the social production situation and the Deficit Hypothesis on the one hand, and the Deficit Hypothesis (as a theoretical concept) and compensatory education (as its practical consequence) on the other, belong functionally together. This doublesided relationship explains the correlation between the dominant social production situation and the necessary measures in the training sector which help to maintain the former. A certain connection between the Deficit Theory and the idea of compensation arises from this situation: the latter, as the application of the theory, must be successful so that production can be increased and the production factors stabilized according to economic development. Seen from this point of view, when social attentiveness is awakened, unsuccessful programmes can become the cause of critical discussions about the concept of compensation itself. In fact, one observes that controversy about the Deficit Hypothesis is provoked when the failure of compensatory programmes places the theoretical premises in a sociopolitical and politicoeconomical light. In the USA, where the first compensatory programmes were carried out, the expected results were hardly achieved in spite of the considerable financial cost involved (one example of this is the largest interregional programme that was carried out, Operation Headstart; cf. Labov 1970b, 28 and du Bois-Reymond 1971, 93f.). If we intend to pursue the causes of the criticisms of the Deficit Hypothesis, we must do so on the basis of the fact that it was primarily the fruitlessness of compensatory efforts (practice) that showed the defects of the hypotheses (theory) on which they were based, and this made the hypotheses the subject of sociopolitical and politicoeconomical controversy. In Bernstein's essay 'A critique of the concept of "compensatory education"' (1970), we can detect a certain degree of politics coming into the discussion. It was written with a knowledge of the fact that the American compensatory programmes had little success and that the basic conception of these programmes was based on his own theories. Bernstein deals with the political side in order to disassociate himself from the failures of American educational psychologists. He claims that it is the misuse of his works that has resulted in what seems to him to be bad programmes. He chooses new terms in order to distance himself from the earlier ones but nevertheless retains the old concept from both the theoretical and the practical points of view. The positions adopted by Baratz (1969), Baratz and Baratz (1970), Coulthard (1969), Labov (1970b) and Bernstein (1970a) clearly show that the controversy about the Deficit Hypothesis has moved from a phase of general acceptance to one of political discussion.

The *failure* of programmes would falsify the hopes of State and industrial interests in relation to compensatory programmes. As we shall shortly see, this not only leads to the necessity of refuting the basic theoretical conception (the problem must be solved in another way); the failure of compensatory measures also uncovers the immanent contradictions of a society which mobilizes the cultural reserves of the production force but which must, at the same time, prevent the realization of true equality of opportunity. In any case, the controversy about the Deficit Hypothesis that arose in 1969–70 can be regarded, in certain respects, as the catalyst for the defects of this theory in the academic and social sphere. Bernstein's problem (1961c, 309) of the practical consequences of his hypotheses comes into the discussion rather belatedly: restricted speakers from the lower classes can be helped (1) by modification of the social structure, and (2) by school training.

Bernstein recognizes only the school as the agent of change, which implies that room for change is necessarily restricted to speech therapy. Such a therapy can only be meaningful 'under suitable conditions or methods', which in turn imply a suitable methodological theory (1961c, 309).

Our following criticism is concerned either implicitly or explicitly with points 1 and 2. It is evident that those who see the necessity for 'changing the social structure' do so on the basis of a broad social analysis, whereas those who merely want to expose the logical defects of the Deficit Hypothesis at least are not opposed to a 'change effected through the school' in terms of existing theory (for it is only when the theory is proved wrong that one can talk in terms of developing new strategies, and the schools can then be given new lines to follow). We shall first deal with criticism relating to the Deficit Hypothesis from the point of view of

D

individual disciplines, and then we shall discuss works that analyse Bernstein's conception from the point of view of society in general.

3.3 Criticism of the measurements of intellectual ability

3.3.1 Four myths concerning the intelligence test

The newest and the best-founded discussion of the psychological dimensions of the Deficit Hypothesis is that of Ginsburg (1972). Ginsburg gives a critical survey of the theoretical and empirical studies on the intelligence test, on speech behaviour relative to social class and on the development of the intellectual abilities of lower-class children. We shall single out some of the points from his work that concern the validity of measuring intelligence.

The function and achievement of intelligence tests were subjected by Ginsburg (1972, 18–57) to a detailed analysis on the basis of extensive data. This led him to formulate four myths concerning the intelligence test (Ginsburg 1972, 26–7) which we shall list, taking into consideration additional arguments according to the pattern of 'thesis foundation'.

'The first myth is that the IQ test measures an intelligence which is a unitary mental ability'. It is still widely believed that there is a fundamental ability called 'intelligence' which dominates the entire intellectual activity. The amount of 'intelligence' varies from individual to individual, and this is confirmed by the difference in the IQ scores.

This standpoint overlooks the fact that the intelligence test measures various mental operations but not a closed-unit 'intelligence'. This can be demonstrated by a simple example, such as when the interviewer requests the subject to solve an identification problem by saying: 'Pick out this or that object'. The subject must first of all be able to understand the individual words and then the whole sentence; he must perceive the form and colour of the object and be able to link it with the corresponding word category. Even for simple tasks, complex mental operations are frequently necessary: perception, comprehension and memory.

Once this has been realized, it follows that a particular IQ score is difficult to interpret. According to the number of necessary mental operations, it may have been arrived at by totally different ways. In any case, it is not clear exactly what intellectual ability it reflects.

'The second myth is that differences in IQ scores reflect fundamental differences in intellect.' It is usually assumed that differences in IQ reflect abilities that are of prime importance for intellectual capacity. Again this is an erroneous proposition.

First, in no way does the IQ test measure *creativity*, Getzel and Jackson (1962) found that at most there was only an extremely small correlation between IQ scores and tests of creativity.

Secondly, the emphasis of the tests was on verbalization. For the most part, however, only passive linguistic knowledge is required in verbalization problems; absolutely no attention was paid to linguistic creativity.

Thirdly, IQ differences show that middle-class and lower-class children differ from one another in many respects. However, this assessment does not account for the fact that although there are some differences between them, they are in fact *similar* in most of their fundamental abilities. There are cognitive universals which are at the disposal of all children, irrespective of their class.

It follows from these three points that the IQ differences of 10 to 20 points, which have been considered relevant up till now, are of little significance. They do, at any rate, not reveal any serious differences in the command of important intellectual operations.

'The third myth is that the IQ test measures intellectual competence.' Since performance in the IQ test depends essentially upon the motivation to solve the problems and since this differs according to class membership, it follows that the IQ test does not measure competence under the same conditions. Lower-class children are always at a disadvantage in formal tests, as the problems in the IQ test are constructed according to middle-class values which play only a small role in the socialization of the lower class; lower-class children are correspondingly less motivated to deal with problems which they experience as alien to their style of life.

Eels (1953) discusses the middle-class bias of the intelligence test in great detail. He names three criteria which must be fulfilled if the intelligence test is to be freed from the middle-class bias:

> '(a) the test must be composed of items which deal with materials common to the various sub-cultures in which it is to be used, (b) the test must be expressed in language and other symbols which are equally familiar to the children growing up in different sub-cultures, and (c) the test must be so organized and administered as to stimulate equal degrees of interest and motivation for the children of different sub-cultures.' (292f.)

Eels concludes: 'To the extent that an intelligence test does not meet these three qualifications, it cannot be said to be a culturally "fair" test.' On the basis of empirical investigations, Ginsburg (1972, 38–44) demonstrates that the intelligence test does not measure the competence of lower-class children.

'The fourth myth is that the IQ test measures an innate ability which is relatively unaffected by experience.' It is a traditional view that the intelligence of a child is innate and that later environmental influences have little effect on IQ. Except in rare cases, intelligence cannot be raised or lowered. This view is incorrect. The level of intelligence is not predetermined at birth. All children, irrespective of the influences of environment or social class, share in their development certain cognitive universals (Piaget 1946). Beyond the frame of these universals, there are some differences that are conditioned by environmental experiences. At the present time, all we can say about the problem of innate and environmentally-influenced abilities is that heredity and environment are in constant interaction with one another (cf. Ginsburg 1972, 44–52).

An example of the still widespread belief in the heredity of intelligence is Arthur Jensen. On the basis of numerous intelligence measurements, he undertakes to prove (Jensen 1969) that the Blacks in the USA are genetically inferior. The discussion of his ideas in academic journals and in the press shows the seriousness with which his results were received. Respect for the intelligence test still seems to lie so deep that it is almost universally accepted as a valid measuring instrument.

The IQ test holds a key position in the class-specific investigations of the Deficit Hypothesis (cf. its significance in the most important investigations: Bernstein 1962b; Deutsch 1965 and 1967; Hawkins 1969; Oevermann 1970). For instance, in investigations into speech behaviour, groups are selected according to criteria of class and given verbal as well as nonverbal IQ tests. As a rule the nonverbal IQ profile between the classes is kept constant, whereas the verbal IQ discriminates between them. The intelligence test is the foundation of linguistic research into class differences; it turns out that it creates false preconditions for differentiating speech forms and, at the same time, the results of this research are doubtful. Our distrust of this method of research becomes more acute if we compare the contents of the verbal intelligence tests used in class identification with the verbalization test-problems occurring in the more representative studies of class-specific speech behaviour. There is frequently not much difference between the two. It seems strange that groups which are differentiated by verbal IQ should once more be differentiated with similar verbal tests.

The four myths show that the intelligence test is not capable of measuring the intellectual capacity of lower-class children; all it can do is point out that these children have less ability in operating with certain middle-class attributes that are favoured at school.

3.3.2 Self-teaching activity of the child and cognitive universals

We have already mentioned in 2.4.2, in connection with the mother-child hypothesis, that it is relatively unknown what influence the mother's behaviour has upon the cognitive development of the child. It is not clear how strong the verbal effect is compared with the nonverbal one. We are also not quite sure what role is played by the peer group in the child's learning. The main objection to the mother-child hypothesis is that the child himself takes an active part in his cognitive development. It is chiefly the studies of Piaget (1946) and Lenneberg (1967) that deal with this. This view was corroborated by the work of Ginsburg, Wheeler and Tulis (1971). In a so-called 'open classroom' (anti-authoritarian style of education), the authors taught five- and six-year-old lower- and middle-class children to read and write in a totally unconventional way. The children were only guided in their initiative to acquire skills in reading and writing. For more than a year they were split up into small groups and left for the most part to their own devices. Their self-teaching process and their individual creative activity were unbelievable. The results obtained show that the children did not exhibit any class-specific differences in the acquisition of reading and writing skills. This state of affairs can be traced back on the one hand to their motivation to learn, and on the other to their individual creative initiative.

These results are further supported by a series of cross-cultural studies, with which we cannot concern ourselves more deeply (cf. Ginsburg 1972, 122–39; Slobin 1967). They were carried out according to Piaget's methods, and they demonstrate that abilities, in the sense of basic intellectual capacities, are not seriously impaired by the factor of social class. There are a multitude of cognitive universals (Vernon 1965; Greenfield 1966; Lenneberg 1967), which are not influenced by social class and ethnic membership. The fact that there still are some differences occurring consistently in superficial measurements can be interpreted in a way which has already been mentioned several times: it is not the *common abilities* but the *norms* for those abilities that are different. (On the tests/intellectual abilities/middle-class norms complex, see the contribution of the group 'Psychologie' in Sprachbarrieren 1970, 75–110).

3.4 Linguistic critique

3.4.1 Code definition

The subject of the code concept has already been raised in 1.2.3 and 1.4.1. We shall supplement the discussion with arguments that have been formulated by Coulthard (1969) and Labov (1971a).

According to Coulthard, Bernstein divides language, with his dichotomous code concept, 'apparently into two levels, three times, using his sociological, linguistic and psychological definitions, and then gives each of the pairs the same names.' Bernstein thus 'neatly sidesteps the problem of proving that a code originating in a certain social environment will have a certain grammatical structure and a cognitive effect—it has these three features by definition.' Apart from the contradictorily-formulated definition of the code concept, it is still unclear to Coulthard by what linguistic characteristics the further subdivisions of the codes (object v. person division, means v. aims, etc., cf. figure 1.3) can be diagnosed. In the face of this new (undefined) subdivision of the code concept, Coulthard becomes thoroughly perplexed and resigns himself to this conclusion:

> 'The theory now has three binary divisions, producing eight codes, but there is no reason why it should stop here. The reader should soon be struggling to separate an Elaborated code object (means) non-striving managerial, from a Restricted code person (ends) upward-striving clerical.' (Coulthard 1969, 48)

Labov (1971a, 201f.) deals with the implications of the code concept for grammatical theory. In his view, the idea of a limited vocabulary in Bernstein's restricted code implies a limited output of utilized grammar, which would raise the degree of predictability for the occurrence of vocabulary items. The question of greater predictability in the case of the restricted code can only arise when the speakers have a command of a grammar capable of generating only a *finite* number of sentences.[2] However, as all speakers of English can produce sentences from an *infinite* set of different sentences, Bernstein cannot possibly infer a restricted code from the quantification of lexical units such as rare adjectives, pronouns etc. (it should be borne in mind that with a basic vocabulary of 850

[2] Labov's actual words are: 'this increase in predictability would be realized only if we had a finite state grammar which produced a finite number of different sentences.' Here Labov is in error: a 'finite state' grammar can generate an infinite number of different sentences (cf. Chomsky 1957, 18–25); from Labov's argument it is apparent that he means a grammar which can only generate a finite number of sentences.

words, the speaker of English can already produce an unlimited number of sentences).

Further critical remarks on the code concept, which do not however add anything new to the arguments we have put forward, can be found in Wunderlich 1970, Oevermann 1970, Niepold 1970, Ehlich *et al.* 1971 and Bühler 1972.

3.4.2 Linguistic parameters

Wunderlich (1970) assumes that a speech form can be regarded as restricted 'when certain linguistic parameters have a low or a high value' (cf. 1.4.1 and Dittmar and Klein 1972). From the point of view of this definition, the empirical work that has been done can be criticized in that the 'linguistic parameters . . . were obtained from a very naïve standpoint' (Dittmar and Klein 1972, 37). Not only do the measurements emanate from normative evaluations, they also use linguistic criteria which are in no way independently defined. It is characteristic that 'reference was only made to aspects of linguistic surface structure', whereas those of the deep structure were ignored. If indeed linguistic complexity is measured according to surface criteria, the fact is overlooked that 'there are several alternative constructions which would at least lead to other values of complexity (e.g. coordination/subordination, adverb/subordinate clause, particle/conjunction, adjectival attribute/relative clause . . . are such alternatives which are expressed in the surface structure but not in the basic functional organization of a sentence)' (*ibid.* 37).

Wunderlich formulates two objections against the 'use of complexity as a linguistic indicator of class-specific differences'. Complexity can only be used meaningfully as a gauge 'when it is measured against the basic deep structures of sentences and when all nonverbal possibilities of expression are radically separated'; at the same time it cannot be an independent gauge but must be seen in correlation with 'the processes of linguistic production and perception', of which it is actually a function. (For three different possibilities of defining the notion 'linguistic complexity', see Bartsch 1973.)

In a verification of the criterion 'syntactic complexity' used by Oevermann to describe the 'restricted' code, Schulz (1971 and 1972) comes to the conclusion, following the texts of the *Bottroper Protokolle* (1968), that lower-class speakers possess, not fewer, but equivalent possibilities of complex linguistic organization. Schulz shows this in an example of conjunctions and coordination in lower-class speech, where they have other functions than in middle-class speech, but nevertheless correspond to equivalent deep structure notions. Thus expletives (e.g. 'doch', 'surely') in a causally coordinating function occur as proper conjunctions and must be treated as the normal conjunctions 'und' and 'denn' in standard speech. Expletives are, therefore, not redundant but functionally necessary in lower-class speech. Schulz draws the conclusion from her description of lower-class speech that it is not defective but merely different.

Labov comes to the same conclusion on the basis of his comprehensive study on Non-Standard English in New York City (Labov *et al.* 1968); we have already singled out some of the points of this work in the previous section. Drawing on examples from this work, he considers the view that lower-class speech is less logical and less complex to be a myth. He demonstrates (1970b) the ability of lower-class speakers to argue objectively and logically by taking the example of a Black boy from a New York ghetto area. In contrast to this, he conducted speech tests on a middle-class speaker who is consistently verbose. Labov concludes:

> 'Whatever problems working-class children may have in handling logical operations, they are not to be blamed on the structure of their language. There is nothing in the vernacular which will interfere with the development of logical thought, for the logic of standard English cannot be distinguished from the logic of any other dialect of English by any test that we can find.' (Labov 1970b, 25f.)

It should, furthermore, be emphasized that BEV speakers possess a highly-developed verbal culture. An analysis of lower-class stories (answers to the question 'Were you ever in serious danger of being killed?') revealed that lower-class speakers produced complex linguistic structures in order to produce certain desired effects upon the hearer (Labov *et al.* 1968, 4.8; Labov and Waletzky 1967; and Labov 1972c, 354–96; cf. also 6.3.4 below). Finally, Labov recapitulates his arguments in order to show the myth of verbal deprivation in relation to its social consequences.

3.4.3   Theoretical bias and effects of the Deficit Hypothesis

The observations made by Labov to refute the theory of verbal deprivation and thus also speech compensatory efforts, can be summarized in six steps; these clearly demonstrate the transition from the academic to the sociopolitical sphere:

'1   The lower-class child's verbal response to a formal and threatening situation is used to demonstrate his lack of verbal capacity, or verbal deficit.

2   This verbal deficit is declared to be a major cause of the lower-class child's poor performance in school.

3   Since middle-class children do better in school, middle-class speech habits are seen to be necessary for learning.

4   Class and ethnic differences in grammatical form are equated with differences in the capacity for logical analysis.

5   Teaching the child to mimic certain formal speech patterns used by middle-class teachers is seen as teaching him to think logically.

6   Children who learn these formal speech patterns are then said to be thinking logically and it is predicted that they will do much better in reading and arithmetic in the years to follow.' (Labov 1970b, 26)

Paradoxically, the theoretical conception whose object it was to ensure equality of opportunity for deprived children achieves in practice exactly the opposite, owing to ignorance of linguistic factors. One of the reasons for this is the theoretical bias, and the other is the consequences which result from the failure of compensatory efforts.

Theoretical bias

The assumptions of the Deficit Hypothesis have enormous implications for educational methods in schools. By implying that the children have no language at all (an implication based on the results from inappropriate test situations) and, in connection with this, by demanding speech drills in the standard language as compensation, they have labelled the first acquired language of the child dysfunctional and bad. The teachers are given 'a readymade theoretical basis' (Labov 1970b, 27) for their prejudice, which they already have in any case vis-à-vis lower-class children. As a result, all BEV forms are penalized. Thus the child is discriminated against, not only in society but also at school, because of his speech: as soon as he opens his mouth, the teacher hears and identifies 'the primitive mentality of the savage mind' (*ibid.*).

This leads directly to the role allotment which Rosenthal and Jacobson (1968) have described in their essay on 'self-fulfilling prophecies in the classroom'. When children are referred to as intellectual bunglers and their 'everyday language ... is stigmatized as "not a language at all" and "not possessing the means for logical thought", the effect of such a labelling is repeated many times during each day of the school year' (26f.).

The theoretical bias of the Deficit Hypothesis is also shown by its judgement of the role of the peer group in the child's failure at school. It is suggested that the child turns to the peer group as compensation for poor performance and lack of support at school, a view that shows an extraordinary ignorance of the subculture. Against this, it must be stated that the domestic environment and the school represent for the child totally different social spheres with specific rules of reward and punishment, which imply different value systems (Rosenthal and Jacobson 1968, 28f.). For this the following evidence is given: 'Children who are rejected by the peer group are quite likely to succeed in school'; whereas it is precisely those children who are healthy, vigorous, intelligent and integrated into the peer group who fail 'all along the line'. Labov considers that from a linguistic viewpoint the peer group has a greater influence on the behaviour of the child than the family. This also casts doubt on Bernstein's thesis that the speech behaviour of the child is primarily determined by the family (cf. also Ginsburg 1972, 140–89). The fallacy of the proponents of the Deficit Theory lies in their tracing the failure of the child at school to his personal deficiencies, to the 'harmful' environment of the peer group:

'It is traditional to explain a child's failure in school by his inadequacy; but when failure reaches such massive proportions, it seems to us necessary to look at the social and cultural obstacles to learning, and the inability of the school to adjust to the social situation. Operation Headstart [a large-scale pre-school programme] is designed to repair the child, rather than the school; to the extent that it is based upon this inverted logic, it is bound to fail.' (Labov 1970b, 28)

According to Labov, there is nothing to repair or to compensate for in lower-class children; what should be done is to change the school so that it offers equal opportunities of learning to lower-class children.

Social consequences of the Deficit Hypothesis

Labov points out the consequences that arise from the failure of compensatory programmes: the same academics who advanced the notion of compensatory programmes also judge their results; they do not look for mistakes in the theory or in the data, but lay the responsibility for their failure on the children's inability. Up till now, then, three causes have been named for the failure of compensation programmes:

1   The good performances that were obtained in the first instance were lost again due to 'bad' school teaching that followed.
2   The environment has already had such a harmful effect on the children that operation Headstart could not help.
3   As a result of heredity, the children could not profit from the programmes.

(3) is the genetic interpretation of Jensen (1969) which attempts to prove the racial inferiority of Blacks by means of the intelligence test. This last hypothesis shows very distinctly what has been the result of the Deficit Hypothesis: instead of removing social discrimination against the children, it has in fact created the conditions, thanks to a bad theory, for increasing discrimination even further. The connection mentioned in 3.2 between pure theory and its sociopolitical consequences is evident here. Insufficient knowledge of linguistics has led to a false and negligent theory which inevitably broke down when put into practice (cf. Labov 1970b, 31–4). Instead of the failure of the theory being openly admitted, it is attributed not to the theory itself but to the children. In the end, the unavoidable conclusion is that these children cannot be helped at all since they are 'genetically inferior'.

This is where the academic and social task of the linguist comes into play. Linguistics refutes the theoretical presuppositions of the Deficit Hypothesis and its methods. Its starting point is that Standard and Non-Standard are two different systems which have their own equivalent possibilities of expression and correspond to an equivalent logic. A linguistic analysis will give a *functional* description of different forms of speech behaviour through interviews and participant observation of speakers in their domestic and social environment, taking into account social pressures and situations. Then it will give an adequate portrayal of the social values correlating with linguistic utterances. Only such a functional description can be the basis for changes in the school. The teachers must be given an insight into the systematic functioning of BEV so that they can adjust their behaviour to the communicative habits of the children (cf. Labov 1970b, 31–4). To tie this up with our argument in 3.2, we can say that the Deficit Hypothesis is inadequate not only on account of its false presuppositions and its methodological deficiencies, but also, and evidently so, because it is not at all able to realize the necessary integration of lower-class children.

Labov, however, does not deal with the problem that is still with us of deciding to what purpose and on the basis of what social conception lower-class children ought to be integrated. The answer is obviously that account should be taken in the school of the values that they have acquired during socialization. What cannot be answered is whether the school as an institution in a capitalist society such as the USA can ever bring about real emancipation. Exactly this problem is raised in the Marxist critique of the Deficit Hypothesis.

D*

3.5 Marxist critique

Marxist critique in sociolinguistics is directed against the analysis of speech barriers as sketched by Bernstein and taken further by Oevermann, in so far as such analyses form part of a bourgeois sociology.

Negt (1971, 59–82) undertakes to rework the code theory by evaluating the 'sociocentric sequences' or 'social topoi' (62) of the lower class in a Marxist sense as a positive beginning to a collective consciousness and thus as a basis for creating class consciousness. Negt sees 'contradictions in existing class society' (78) in the speech barriers between the working and middle classes and demands an 'education for the workers that will transform attitudes and consciousness alike'; in this education the 'teaching material will be organized in an exemplary manner', and will be determined by a 'dialectic reconciliation between "formal" and "public" language' (82).

Whereas Negt still tries to assign to the results of speech barrier research a positive evaluation in the light of workers' education, Ehlich *et al.* (1971a and b) submit all Bernstein-oriented work to a radical methodological and sociopolitical critique, which we shall summarize, in connection with other arguments, from three points of view:

1   sociolinguistics as bourgeois elitist knowledge;
2   social stratification model and role theory;
3   function of compensatory education.

3.5.1 Sociolinguistics as bourgeois elitist knowledge

Sociolinguistics as a line of research must be seen in correlation with the entire social conditions in society. We shall here concentrate in particular on the Federal Republic of Germany.

On account of the new generation's rising requirements in production, the educational reserves must be mobilized and the educational system must be made more efficient. This trend, which can be shown to exist by a number of quotations, may be illustrated by a passage from Iben *et al.* (1971, 9):

> 'In the mid-1960s, preschool education, which had been a long-neglected sector of the educational system, was rediscovered. . . . This rediscovery was a delayed effect of the unrest resulting from the educational disaster, and was, on the other hand, stimulated by the results of American research. . . . It was not until knowledge about the correlations between class membership, speech behaviour and success at school, which was propagated by the works of B. Bernstein, P. M. Roeder, R. Dahrendorf and U. Oevermann, had significantly increased, that a discussion came about on the possibilities . . . of compensatory education. With the search for talent reserves, the question about the possibilities of their utilization also became relevant.'

What Iben refers to as a 'rediscovery' of preschool education is not, however, a chance 'effect' that was to solve the contradictions in the social development of the Federal Republic of Germany, but proves to be in fact the third phase of a consistent rationalization policy in the Federal Republic in the sphere of research and education (see Hirsch and Leibfried 1971, 17–94). The first phase of the Federal Republic's cultural policy after 1945 was designed to bring about an increased overall efficiency of instructional organization. This was extended in the second phase to some kind of 'alliance system' (e.g. by establishing a complex network of intimate connections between the German Research Society, the Max-Planck Institute and the Ministry for Science). In the third stage of this development, State planning activities have become necessary, and their task is to solve, 'by means of "compensatory planning" in its broadest sense', (e.g. planning for the training and supply of specialists in communication and of social workers) the various contradictions of capitalist societies that have arisen due to economic development' (Hirsch and Leibfried 1971, 9).

According to Ehlich *et al.* (1971a), the works of Bernstein and Oevermann serve the dominant production forces because they reveal barriers to the mobilization of the educational reserves among workers. As these reserves are meant to be activated by preschool programmes in response to sociolinguistic research, a preparation is made for the subtle integration of workers into the production process: with differentiated (middle-class-oriented 'elaborated') speech it ought to be possible to achieve differentiated thinking and thus also the flexible handling of roles and the individual adaptation to social relationships.

'In essence, Oevermann and Bernstein propagate the connection of linguistic and intellectual performance with ability in role behaviour, which lies at the base of petty bourgeois and bourgeois social relations. In this view, they are in agreement with an educational policy that is designed to combine a greater utilization of the cultural reserves of the workers with the propagation and implementation of bourgeois aims and norms of behaviour.' (Ehlich *et al.* 1971a, 38)

3.5.2 The social stratification model and role theory

The Marxist critique of the works of Bernstein and Oevermann concentrates on the social stratificational model and on the role theory of 'bourgeois sociology'. Both are considered inadequate as correlates of the linguistic codes in so far as they regard a series of empirical quantities (in the case of 'class') and individual characteristics (in the case of 'role theory') as intrinsic features of different forms of speech behaviour. However, neither the class nor the role concepts reflect the 'true differentations and dynamic laws' of 'bourgeois-capitalist society' (Ehlich *et al.* 1971a, 42). Thus, the concept of 'lower class' covers both the proletariat and the lumpenproletariat, whereas the petty bourgeoisie and the bourgeoisie are combined under the term 'middle class'. The allotment of members of a society to a particular class according to such criteria as 'profession, career, prestige, income, education' is, in this view, unsuitable and misleading in that it is not guided by an 'analysis of the classes that are present in a capitalist society'. One way of ascertaining the membership of individuals to a particular class is to look at their 'position in the production process' (*ibid.*, 42f; see also Hahn 1968). To the extent that the class concept only measures superficial social appearances, it is incapable of explaining their basic laws. An adequate explanation[3] of socially-determined forms of speech behaviour can, in this view, only be given in the frame of a Marxist analysis which relates the 'concrete class analysis to certain speech forms'. On the basis of this, it would be possible to understand 'the distortions which are to be expected in an analysis carried out in terms of the stratification model' (Ehlich *et al.* 1971a, 43). It should be added that an adequate class analysis will also always proceed historically; yet most investigations of social classification leave out this aspect (cf. the entry 'Schicht' (class) in the *Wörterbuch der marxistisch-leninistischen Soziologie* (Berlin 1969, 393f.).

Next to class, social roles are regarded as elementary correlates of speech forms in bourgeois research into speech barriers (above all Oevermann 1970; cf. 1.3.2 and 1.4.3).

As Hahn (1968) and Haug (1972), amongst others, have shown, the role theory is based on normative concepts such as role ambivalence, role distance, identity of the self etc. which result from middle-class ideas and which cannot claim adequacy either in a functional or in a descriptive sense. These concepts are supposed to outline the sphere of interaction of allegedly 'freely moving' individuals who are able to shape their roles in an 'ambivalent' or 'distant' manner, whenever 'ambivalence' or 'distance' are required.

As Hahn (1968) shows, *roles* are understood in bourgeois sociology as the effects of the norms and rules of social institutions. Social development is explained as the spontaneous deviation of actual behaviour from the institutionally-determined norms and rules; it is accounted for in the dimension of the individuals who are thus variables, whilst society is considered a constant. Such a conception, which is also applied in research on socialization, is static; it ignores dynamic social development, which, in Marxist sociology, is included in the dialectic contradiction that exists between the social determination of the individual and his active participation in the formation of social relationships. Roles are not primarily moulded by the institutions, but much more by the type and manner of material production which is the individual's existential expression and his form of self-activation. The question about the 'product' of the process of social determination can only be deemed answered when the reasons why the product of this determination was different at various times and under various historical conditions have been brought to light. A meaningful discussion of roles is only possible in terms of an analysis which gives a total picture of the position of the individual in the production process and his dialectic relationship with the group and with society.

The determination of individuals by material and social conditions is considered the result of the overall system of value scales of the *superstructure*. The norms existing in the superstructure are derived from the material forms of existence of a society and are thus secondary. A materialist role theory would have to analyse the interaction between the individual, the group and society (Hahn 1968, 105–53). In bourgeois sociology, however, the comprehensive social and material basis of individual roles is not reflected. There, certain contradictions of capitalist society are not located in its overall system of social relations and its production conditions, but are accounted for by means of

[3] On the concept of explanation, cf. *Erklärung in der Soziologie,* in Hahn 1968, 219–57.

concepts developed in role theory. Role theory 'attempts to come to terms conceptually with the contradictions of capitalist society, provided they are interpreted as problems of the individual, which it is up to him to solve. The preservation of the system becomes the point of reference for the functionality or dysfunctionality of role handling' (Ehlich *et al.* 1971b, 101). Thus role theory 'in effect places the onus on the individual to neutralize within himself the contradictions of his, or more precisely of capitalist, society' (*ibid.*, 45). The high assessment of the elaborated code is to be seen in close correlation with the positive values in role theory (cf. especially Oevermann 1970). We have already pointed this out elsewhere.

3.5.3 The function of compensatory education

We have already listed a series of critical attitudes towards compensatory programmes in 3.1 and 3.2. We shall now supplement the arguments that were developed in those sections.

Compensatory education is the method proposed for the emancipation of the lower class, whilst in effect it is meant to adapt the lower class to the capitalist conditions of production. It is part of the shortsighted logic of this view that no attempt is made to promote emancipation of the lower class by consistently changing their economic and social situation. Instead, they are to be given compensatory help which is based on the assumption that communication in lower-class families is defective. It is not the conditions of social production and the institutions deriving from them that are made responsible for the situation of the lower class; on the contrary, the lower class is blamed for its own failure. Compensatory education is intended to resolve the conflict between wealth and poverty by giving a hope for equality of opportunity to those 'who, because of their socioeconomic position, have no opportunities' (du Bois-Reymond 1971, 21).

A further contradiction of compensatory education lies in the fact that the education of the masses must be increased and improved in the interest of production, whereas it must be suppressed 'in the interest of a bourgeois-dominated class system' (Ehlich *et al.* 1971a, 53). As Labov has already concluded, compensatory education draws attention away 'from the failure of the existing school system that threatens to become dysfunctional' and looks instead for 'misery within the family system of roles and interaction' (*ibid.*). 'In this respect, the bourgeois methodological approach proves to be narrow-minded, and intent on stabilizing the system in that it does not try to eliminate the fundamental causes of role systems, but seeks to alleviate the symptoms by compensation in terms of the existing system' (*ibid.*, 54).

In his vehement rejection of compensatory education, Bernstein (1970a) advocates nothing more than to transfer the task of compensatory education to education itself: 'The introduction of the child to the universalistic meanings of public forms of thought is not compensatory education—*it is education.*' It is up to the school to provide 'education' in its broadest sense: 'The school attempts to transmit knowledge' which is 'socially acceptable knowledge'. This 'socially acceptable knowledge' transmitted via the school is called by Bernstein 'universal'. Emancipation should ensue within the framework of the existing institutions, that is to say that everyone has a right to be taught that which is 'socially acceptable'.

Bernstein's hopes for the emancipation of the working class within the framework of the existing institutional value systems are an illusion.

'What reformers deplore as a failure due to the school's neglect of progressive programmes is mainly the expression of capitalist contradictions. The funds are insufficient, since short-term structural measures do not bring in any profit. And even if more money was made available, the class school will always be a class school.' (Ehlich *et al.* 1971b, 106)

On the whole, our argument at the beginning of the section has been confirmed: an ill-founded and socially naïve Deficit Hypothesis cannot succeed in integrating the working class into the dominant social production conditions. This is why, in general, the discussion has been shifted to the schools. With their help, it is hoped that a 'potential for change' will be produced.

Our discussions have made it clear that children with fully-developed abilities need no compensation. Our efforts should be redirected, therefore, at making them aware of these abilities.

The class-determined value systems (working class v. bourgeois class) clash when the children come to school and it becomes evident that they are meant to adapt to the norms of the school, which are in fact fixed by the balance of power in society.

There is a dilemma, namely that if a child adapts to the norms of the school because of middle-class-oriented instruction, it may happen that he will become involved in conflicts of value and identity with his parental milieu, and this in turn could lead to psychological difficulties. On the other hand, if the child retains the values of his parental milieu, he will predictably fail at school and in later life. The dilemma is inescapable: the child founders on *value conflicts* and these reflect *class conflicts*. He founders on the contradiction that although he has a recognized right to the full development of his abilities, he may nevertheless in practice develop these abilities only in so far as the reproduction of social inequality is not jeopardized.

It is not a question, therefore, of 'maximizing the range of alternatives of thought and action' (Olim 1970, 224) by means of the 'elaborated' code (what arrogance lies in the idea that one is able to substitute social experiences by increasing someone's ability to form subordinate clauses!) but of making the lower class aware of the potential of their abilities so that they can determine and decide their own interests. This defines a programme which should start with the concrete living conditions of the lower class and their historically-transmitted values.

3.6 Summary

In this chapter we have discussed critiques of the Deficit Hypothesis, its reflection in compensatory programmes and its social function. Our comments on Bernstein's theoretical assumptions, their validation and their practical consequences have now come to a conclusion. We shall briefly summarize some of the main points.

First, it became clear how academic work is tied to sociopolitical developments. The relatively fruitless application of the Deficit Hypothesis leads to critical reflection, which not only discloses its methodological deficiencies, but also unmasks the contradictions of capitalist society, whose motto is: compensation rather than emancipation.

Secondly, our critical account of empirical work in chapter 2 could be supplemented by supporting arguments:

The validity of the intelligence test proves to be a myth. It measures certain normative skills in formal test situations, but not ability. By implicit value judgements, it handicaps the lower class.

The factor of social class plays a secondary role in the cognitive development of the child. Children display a self-instructional activity which is relatively free of environmental influences and is connected with certain motivations to learn.

The myth of verbal deprivation can be traced back to normative measurements of speech behaviour. Lower-class children reveal linguistic creativity in their home environment: this has been sufficiently proved by Labov (1970b) and Labov *et al.* (1968)—cf. in 6.2.6 and 6.3.3 below; this creativity can only be observed in natural situations and results from their functional communication needs.

Thirdly, it became clear in the compensation programme developed by Bereiter and Engelmann how false theoretical assumptions and deficient eliciting of speech material lead to bad practical applications. The defensive behaviour of children in what they feel to be a threatening test situation is put down to their deficient competence which requires compensation. Thus they are expected to learn Standard patterns for things which they are already able to express equivalently in Non-Standard. They are forced to adopt a type of speech that brings them into conflict with their first language and which must, moreover, alienate them from the people with whom they have primary contact. This kind of compensation programme promotes alienation rather than emancipation.

Fourthly, the example of the social stratification model and of role theory showed that bourgeois sociology cannot have an adequate grasp of the dynamic laws of capitalist society. Both of these are based on static and not on dynamic notions; to a large extent they exclude the historical dimension. In the case of the stratification model, people are assessed according to their external attributes, not according to their function in the production process. Finally, in role theory the contradictions of capitalist society are interpreted as contradictions of the individual.

Fifthly, the true function of compensatory programmes has become clear. Instead of real emancipation aimed at improving the living conditions of the lower class, they contribute to the integration of the lower class in such a way as to stabilize the system. 'Emancipation' thus becomes nothing more than a farce: it is the misleading expression of a basic equation: Emancipation = (verbal) Elaboration = (system-stabilizing) Integration.

4 The Variability Concept: basic ideas and tradition

In this chapter we shall deal with the fundamental concepts and the presuppositions of the alternative to the Deficit Hypothesis, namely the Variability Concept. First of all we shall expound some of the main points which differentiate the Variability Concept from the brand of sociolinguistics that has been discussed in the first three chapters; then we shall introduce some of its basic ideas and give an account of its actual linguistic and anthropological tradition. Finally we shall distinguish in the complex of traditional linguistic and anthropological interests four areas of research which play an important role in the legitimization of sociolinguistic research as it is now carried out.

4.1 Deficit Hypothesis v. Variability Concept

The fundamental differences between the Deficit Hypothesis and the Variability Concept are not only sociopolitical, which was the aspect we emphasized in the last chapter; they are also methodological.

In the first place, the claims of the Variability Concept are formulated in a much more modest and circumspect manner. It is in full agreement with the insights of grammatical theory as far as the structural description of speech variations is concerned, and it hardly exceeds the proven results (phonology, syntax). It is characteristic of this level of description and its solid results that the psychological dimension is essentially excluded from the analysis.

On the general level of interaction of language varieties over and beyond the behaviour of individuals and small groups (i.e., national languages, standard languages, regional and social dialects, linguistic minorities) in situations of conflict or coexistence, it is assumed, unless proved to the contrary, that from a linguistic point of view they are functionally equivalent in their expressive possibilities and their capacity for logical analysis. This view can be traced back to numerous structural linguistic descriptions and comparisons as well as to the well-established linguistic and anthropological interest to discover and define the different social norms which underlie different speech behaviour.

Speech variation is analysed impartially (neutrally, in the descriptive sense) rather than on the basis of normative value scales (or directed hypotheses).

Since the study of the covariance of linguistic characteristics with social and other parameters is still in its first stages, and only a modest number of methodologically valid results have been submitted (e.g. Labov 1966a; Ma and Herasimchuk 1968; Wolfram 1969; Lindenfeld 1969; Cedergren 1973b; G. Sankoff 1973), a large part of the discussion about description and explanation of speech variation is heuristic. It is partly crystallized in the development of practical methods of conducting functional and context-specific research into natural speech behaviour (unconstrained speech in unconstrained situations). It is only the knowledge of natural speech which permits an adequate explanation of the processes of speech acquisition, linguistic identification and linguistic change. From this point of view, it is clear that the Variability Concept will, if possible, consider the results of formal tests on speech behaviour as secondary data.

The following are the characteristic differences that can be established between the Variability Concept and the Deficit Hypothesis:[1]

Variability Concept	Deficit Hypothesis
Descriptive procedure. The discovery of socially-determined speech norms.	Normative procedure. Starting point is the speech norms.
Investigation of speech variation on the micro level (description of the features of verbal interaction between individuals in small groups), and the macro level (distribution and function of language varieties in a society).	One-sided concentration on the analysis of class-specific speech behaviour (lower class v. middle class).
In relation to the possibilities of expression and the logical capacity for analysis, language varieties are functionally equivalent.	Middle-class speech accomplishes more than lower-class speech from a rhetorical as well as a logical point of view.
Relative neglect of the cognitive aspects of speech behaviour.	Crucial inclusion of the cognitive aspects. Heavy dependence on Whorf's concept of linguistic relativity.
Investigation of the formal/informal continuum of natural speech behaviour in different social situations.	Description of speech behaviour in one-sided formal test situations (mostly in the context of schools).
Primary data are mainly those which are obtained through participant observations.	The data of the formal tests serve as primary data for judging linguistic ability.
The aim is theory construction, and explanation of all linguistic differentiations caused by the intervention of social parameters, and of their correlations with the social structure. Undirected hypotheses.	Theory and explanation of the role of speech in the social success potential of the speakers at school and in other institutions. Consideration of a limited number of social parameters. Directed hypotheses.

[1] These two concepts differ also in their implications, and in particular in their scope of application. The Deficit Hypothesis has a wider range of explanation due to its fundamental inclusion of the psychological dimension, even though this dimension is, in fact, not exploited since no adequate descriptive methods are made available for it. In the Variability Concept, on the other hand, the psychological component is left out of account in order to maximize comparability of the different linguistic varieties. Although its explanatory scope is thus more restricted, its theoretical position is more highly developed to the extent that various factors determining speech behaviour are taken into

Some of the points that have been summarized in this comparison have already been discussed in chapter 3. At this stage it must be emphasized that the Variability Concept can primarily be traced back to linguistic research and interpretation. Empirical evidence for an old linguistic postulate, namely that it is impossible to distinguish between 'good' and 'bad' speech (Bloomfield 1927), has led from about 1965 onwards (cf. the provisional results of Labov *et al.*) to an elaboration of the Variability Concept (Bailey 1965; Dillard 1968; Labov *et al.* 1968; Baratz 1969 and 1970a; Cazden 1970). One result of this has been a polemical campaign against proponents of the Deficit Hypothesis (Baratz and Baratz 1970; Labov 1970b; cf. also the discussion of 'social Darwinism' in Stewart 1970b, 216ff.). The proponents of the Variability Concept emphasize three main points over and over again:

1　　Any meaning which is relevant to the understanding between people can be expressed in any language.
2　　In accordance with (1), socially-determined speech differences are of a non-cognitive type unless there is empirical proof to the contrary. The non-cognitive analysis of speech differences is based on the idea that for each linguistic utterance in *A* there is a corresponding utterance in *B* (*A* and *B* can represent styles, Standards, dialects or functional varieties), which conveys the same semantic information (synonymy). Differences beween *A* and *B* in respect of certain linguistic features are only understandable on the basis of a comprehensive contrastive analysis of *A* and *B* on all levels of grammar.
3　　In the sense of (2), the description of speech variation is concerned with the type and degree of structural and functional interference, as well as the social relation and interaction between two given linguistic systems.

In the framework of the linguistic orientation of the Variability Concept, descriptions of speech variation aim to explain how and in what function language systems are divided (regional, social, functional language varieties), how speech realizations are evaluated (privileged v. stigmatized status of speech forms) and how they change on the basis of such evaluations (revaluation v. devaluation of Standards, dialects, speech behaviour of minority groups). The descriptions also have to explain to what extent language systems interfere with one another on the phonological, syntactic and semantic levels, how they are acquired, conserved and modified on these levels and, finally, on the basis of what relationships they coexist or come into social conflict. The aim of research into speech variation is thus to describe and explain the entire social network of speech

---

account more comprehensively so that a better basis is created for a general theory of linguistic variation and linguistic change. Recently, the Deficit Hypothesis and the Variability Concept have usually been represented as mutually exclusive theories (cf. Ammon 1974), which has led to little more beneficial for sociolinguistic theory than a flurry of polemics. One should rather seek to integrate both concepts into a comprehensive sociolinguistic theory. The Deficit Hypothesis would then be a part of such a theory; it would have to be given a descriptive foundation of verifiable data and would have to be validated in the light of the influence of class-specific differences on linguistic behaviour. The theoretical foundations of the Variability Concept would have to be supplemented with a sociopsychological component relating to the social aspects of language acquisition.

practice and the complex competence that speakers have at their disposal for communication, in correlation with the social norms and parameters. This should be done in such a way that a basis is formed for a comprehensive linguistic theory which is able to explain linguistic developments and changes and can help to avoid the conflicts that may arise from them.

However illuminating these aims may be, they are still far from being realized, as appears not only from the still vague theoretical concepts (chapter 5) and the modest empirical results (chapter 6), but also from the largely imprecise definitions of the notions involved in describing speech variation. We shall now list some of these.

4.2 Some basic concepts

Structural descriptions of speech variation, which are linked only very marginally to social parameters, on the whole follow concepts and descriptive methods as they have been worked out in theoretical linguistics over the last ten years in the fields of phonology, syntax and semantics. This is not the place to introduce them; instead, we shall refer the reader to introductions to the terminology and descriptive methods of linguistics which give an account of the present position: Langacker 1968; Fowler 1971. Whilst the concepts of theoretical linguistics and its descriptive methods are constructs for which exact procedures can usually be indicated, in the case of the wider terms concerned with linguistic variation tied to social parameters, it is a question of expressions which do not as yet admit of any unequivocal definition. In other words, they are heuristic concepts whose validity has not yet been fully discussed. Although it is possible to classify speech varieties according to their distinctive linguistic characteristics (phonology, grammar, lexicon), such a procedure, which excludes other than purely linguistic elements, is unable to explain either the causes or the functions of speech variation (cf. Weinreich 1953 and Weinreich, Labov and Herzog 1968).

Neglecting, on the whole, problems raised by the interaction of language and social structure, we shall content ourselves here with saying that language varieties differ from one another in respect of certain linguistic characteristics which have resulted from the historical process of the mutual influence of language and social structure. In order, however, to be able to associate speech variants with speakers, it is necessary to have more comprehensive terms also covering social and other elements. There is a series of research reports and general articles in which a certain unity is achieved in the terminology for the description of linguistic variation (Weinreich, Labov and Herzog 1968; Gumperz 1968; Ervintripp 1969; Fishman 1971a and b; Grimshaw 1971a; Labov 1970a, 1971a and b). In the following, we shall make a first approach at explaining some of the concepts that appear in this literature, such as speech community, language variety, Standard, and verbal repertoire.

Language systems are founded on, and vary with, social structures represented by social groups, institutions, interaction communities with specific needs, nations etc. In so far as linguistic events are to be analysed 'within a socially-defined universe', they must be studied with regard to the extent in which they reflect the general norms of behaviour (cf. Gumperz, in Giglioli 1972, 219). The term 'speech community' has gained rights in traditional linguistics as a comprehensive label for such a 'social universe' and the collection of social norms linked with it. According to Gumperz (*ibid.*), it refers to 'any human aggregate characterized by regular and frequent interaction by means of a shared body of verbal signs and set off from similar aggregates by significant differences in language usage.' Under this definition, speech communities can be classified according to their linguistic similarities and differences. Social groups which show constant communicative interaction, such as a gang whose members are linked in 'face-to-face' communication, or groups that belong together through work that they have carried out in common over a long period of time, can be designated as speech communities just as well as nations that are split up into various regions. The only precondition for their classification as speech communities is that they must show certain linguistic features in which they are similar to, and different from, one another. The idea that underlies the definition of a speech community given here is that social communication creates a regular relationship between language usage and social structure. Before we can judge the social information carried by an utterance, and the intention of the speaker, we need to know something about the social norms which define the appropriateness of linguistic variants for individual types of speakers. These norms vary with the economic and ideological power relations between groups and the social environment. When it is possible to give an explicit account of the connection between the choice of variants and the rules of social appropriateness, it is also possible to classify styles, dialects, technical languages, etc., according to their distinctive linguistic features (cf. Gumperz, in Giglioli 1972).

We can differentiate between homogeneous speech communities, where the verbal indicators of social differences are essentially limited to phonological, syntactic or lexical peripheral phenomena, and other speech communities, where various literary standards and grammatically different local dialects are to be found. Speech communities can either correspond to the national unity of a people, or they can represent certain communicative networks of interaction in which one or several languages are employed as coexisting means of communication. Again, this is something which is determined by regional factors or by supranational or sociopolitical interests.

Whatever differences may exist between speech communities, varieties *within* a speech community form a system that is made up of a number of shared social norms. One example will serve to show the difficulty of defining the notion of a 'speech community' (in the end, of course, definitions always depend on the interest of particular case studies). Switzerland can be considered a speech community in the full sense of the word, in that it has integrated three languages into the force field of national interests, and the barriers that do exist are overcome by supra-regional communicative networks (radio, television) and by bilingual or trilingual education. However, all speakers of Italian can also be classed as a speech community, for although they are not of the same nationality, they all belong to one linguistically continuous geographical area.

Speech communities are, however, rarely homogeneous. In most cases, they are composed of varieties which are connected with the speech community as a whole by a number of shared social norms; at the same time, they reflect historically-based discrepancies determined by differences of interest and region. The term 'variety', in accordance with the descriptive view of linguistics, is a neutral concept.

We shall distinguish four forms of linguistic variety, which can be further differentiated as the need arises:

1   Standard variety
2   regional variety
3   social variety
4   functional variety.

1   Standard variety

The Standard variety is that variety of a speech community that is legitimized and institutionalized as a supraregional method of communication as a result of various sociopolitical and power-political circumstances in the historical process. Frequently, as for example in the case of the European languages, it has a long historical tradition. The Standard variety is to some extent codified by means of a series of norms which lay down the correct written and oral usage. It serves as an intersubjective conveyor of information and is most frequently used in the context of official and social institutions, as well as in all formal contexts where sanctions can be expected if it is not used correctly. The Standard is taught in schools, and its use normally secures prestige and favours the acquisition of social privileges. Other language varieties may be subordinated to the Standard variety. However, this depends essentially on its social rating.

Garvin proposes three types of criteria to indicate the degree of standardization of a Standard variety: '(i) intrinsic properties of a Standard language, (ii) the functions of a Standard language within the culture of a speech community and (iii) the attitudes of the speech community towards the Standard language' (Garvin 1964, 522). The most important features of the Standard are its 'flexible stability' and the degree of its 'intellectualization'. With reference to (ii), it can be judged according to four functions: (a) its *unifying* function (domination or control of various dialect areas); (b) its *separating* function (demarcation vis-à-vis other languages); (c) its *prestige* functions and (d) its function as a normative *'frame-of-reference'* to guide its speakers (norms of correctness). The attitudes of speakers to the Standard (iii), which can be assessed by considering their language loyalty, their language pride and their awareness of the norm, are related to these four functions: language loyalty to the unifying and separating function (and thus also to the degree of national consciousness), language pride to the prestige function, and awareness of the norm to its function as a guiding normative frame-of-reference (Garvin 1964).

Taking German as an example, Deutrich and Schank (1972, 15f.) have attempted an operational definition of the Standard for a particular area, a particular time and particular speakers. See Table on page 108.

As can easily be seen, this proposed definition can only be approximate. For example, it fails to take into account the characteristic distribution of the Standard over particular social domains ('public communication' and 'roles' are insufficient as criteria for the use of the Standard: its specific *functions* in administrative, political, economic, sociocultural and subcultural domains will

Characteristics	Suggested method of operation
1 Areas with German as the primary language	Nationality; persons with German as their primary language.
2 Time	The spoken German after 1945 of speakers who came under (1).
3 Passive command	Evidence of an educational background with 'German' as the primary language.
4 Relation to standardization: language in strict dependence on codified normalizations (with partly accepted gross regional variations).	High German phonetic norms; 'officially' codified language normalization, e.g. Duden grammar, school grammars.
5 Active application (i): limited to particular speakers under the conditions of (7) and (8) (special restrictions for the German part of Switzerland).	Speakers with positions and roles, e.g. text writers, teachers, authors of radio lectures, politicians, journalists, trades-union functionaries, managers, clergymen, judges, doctors.
6 Active application (ii): guidelines for active application amongst the remaining speakers under the conditions of (7) and (9) in communication with the speakers mentioned under (5) (special restrictions for Switzerland)	All those positions and roles not included under (5), in particular speakers with few supraregional and/or intergroup speech contacts, e.g. peasant or small-scale industrial population.
7 Supraregionality	Application in mass media.
8 Application in public acts of communication.	Public acts of communication: e.g. lectures, public discussions, parliamentary debates.
9 Applied, or aspired to, in public acts of communication between various social speakers, predominantly in upward direction.	Cf. examples in (6).

also have to be specified). Neither does it take account of the social communication networks, which ensure its legitimacy through certain interest groups, and thus stabilize its elitist function. More precise knowledge of the functions of the Standard will have to be gained through detailed empirical investigations of particular social domains.

2　Regional variety

Regional varieties are classed as *dialects* when they are developed in particular areas of settlement and are historically conveyed. Their major role is in oral communication, i.e., in contrast to the Standard variety, they are not rigidly codified (in the normative sense). Sometimes dialects are raised to the level of Standard and sometimes they disappear under the influence of the mass media or as a result of economic conditions necessitating the migration of the population into other linguistic areas. Dialects can be further differentiated according to their geographical diffusion into regional and local dialects. A diagram, which we have taken from Labov (1971a, 191), will clarify the relation of dialects to the Standard language:

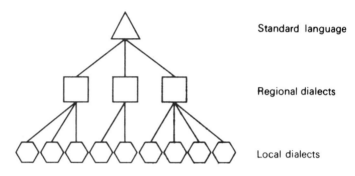

Fig. 4.1 The relation of regional and local dialects to the Standard.

Regional varieties can also become social varieties. When immigrants of a geographical area *A* represent the lowest socioeconomic class in area *B*, and are therefore generally handicapped, then their dialect can be considered the symbolic expression of their low social status (cf. Fishman 1971a, 22).

3 Social variety

Social varieties or *sociolects* are those speech conventions of groups that are frequently subjected to a large-scale prestige evaluation by other social groupings (e.g. socioeconomically or ideologically repressed classes) and can become the subject for conflict between them (Occitan v. Parisian French; Catalonian v. Castilian; Serbian v. Croatian, etc.). This is how language minorities (e.g. French Canadians), social classes (the Non-Standard dialects of Whites and Blacks in the USA) or groups bound by a rigid ideology can be affected. Social varieties or sociolects often stand in a relation of sociopolitically-motivated asymmetry to other language varieties. This asymmetry is expressed in the negative social evaluation of certain linguistic expressions, as appears, for example from efforts to keep these expressions out of public institutions and to refuse to accept their written codification in public life. Even the Standard variety can be a sociolect in certain speech communities. This partly applies, for example, to young African states which, although they have designated a certain variety to be the Standard, do not use it publicly because of its lack of prestige, since the old colonial languages still carry greater prestige (cf. Samarin, in Bright 1966a; Hymes 1971; Whiteley 1971).

4   Functional variety

Functional varieties differ from the other varieties that have been mentioned in that their usage runs straight across the dimensions set by the Standard variety, the sociolect or the dialect. They can be connected with specific interactions, with institutions or with conditions of the place of work, with formal or informal situations, with the speaker's idiosyncracies, etc. Speakers use the varieties that they have command of in a functional manner: they will use variety *A* in one context and variety *B* in another. Thus German students who have been brought up on dialect generally use High German at university, whilst they continue to talk dialect with their family. Functional varieties are frequently technical languages, special languages, slang or commercial languages. Amongst the latter, English and French 'Pidgin' have become well-known; they are still spoken in ex-colonies (cf. for example Decamp 1971b).

As a result of the increased occurrence of Pidgin languages in Europe, caused by the vast movements of immigrant labourers in countries such as Germany, France and Switzerland, this problem is being studied more and more in linguistics. The description of these linguistic varieties leads, at the same time, to a better insight into the processes of second-language learning.

Functional varieties are the smallest variety unit. There is no other than a practical limit to the number of functional varieties that can exist in a speech community.

Our definitions, which are to be seen in a sociological perspective, were directed, in the cases of (1) to (3), towards supraregional, regional and social regularities in speech behaviour, whilst in (4) a form of speech was considered that can vary with a large number of heterogeneous parameters. The acquisition and usage of these latter varieties is bound up with verbal interaction in correlation with social activity. We can term the uses of speech that vary with roles and situations the *verbal repertoire* of speakers (Gumperz, in Giglioli 1972, 230f.; Fishman 1971b, 235f.). In the tradition of Firth, English linguistics calls the different styles of the speakers *registers* (cf. Halliday, in Fishman 1968b, 149–56; Davies 1969).

A detailed account is given in 5.3 of the components of speech and speech situations, as well as an analysis of those factors in speaker-hearer situations that are fundamental for the genesis of the verbal repertoire. We shall content ourselves here with stating that the total verbal repertoire or register of a speech community normally reflects its role repertoire. This applies not only to its range but also to accessibility and the extent of command achieved. It determines the actual communicative appropriateness that varies with social roles and situations, and with the forms of behaviour and attitudes of speakers (cf. Gumperz 1968). Verbal repertoire and language varieties can be investigated on a micro level in so far as they originate in the dynamic process of speakers' social communication, and they can also be analysed on a macro level in so far as they stand as different social symbolic systems in specific contact or conflict.

Sociolinguistic investigations carried out on the micro level can be understood as those which attempt to describe the regular speech conventions that are manifested in speech acts occurring in verbal interaction between speakers. The task of linguistics is to carry out analyses on the micro level: ideally, certain systematically-recurring traits in the utterances of speakers (sociolects) should be correlated with their social attributes (e.g. age, position in the production process etc.). This can also be done in a dynamic time-specific perspective when groups of speakers are investigated for their linguistic changes over relatively long periods of time by participant observation (linguistic change due to the effect of constant social factors, e.g. the development of children's language). The next chapter will discuss the theoretical and empirical requirements underlying the rules which will fulfil these descriptive aims.

Depending on the state of knowledge of theoretical linguistics, the intention on the micro level is to give an explicit description of regular speech occurrences. However, on the macro level it is less a question of the contrastive description of different speech forms on the various levels of grammar than of a sociologically-oriented analysis of the social and sociopolitical function of varieties in speech communities, leaving individual linguistic facts out of account. This field of research has been called the 'sociology of language' (Fishman 1968b, introduction), whilst linguistic (micro) analyses have been described by Labov (1970a) as 'the study of language in its social context'.

Connected with the problems of the description of speech variation is the question of the *social norms* which determine the homogeneity or heterogeneity of speech behaviour. The question of the linguistic norm originates in the socioeconomic and ideological dominance relations in a society, and the social values of groups, which produce distinct varieties in correlation with various parameters. It is an essential problem of sociolinguistics to discover what this norm is. The problem of the norm has become a constant matter for discussion in German linguistics in the last few years—although the sociopolitical dimension has been largely ignored (cf. Polenz 1972 for a summary). All we shall say at this point is that grammatical structures are of such a nature that they allow for a virtually unlimited range of realizations of speech acts. Social norms of the widely different types determine, however, through a system of social controls and sanctions, what can be realized from the potential possibilities of a linguistic system and what is to be treated as deviant (cf. Coseriu 1967).

So far we have compared the linguistically-motivated Variability Concept to the Deficit Hypothesis as an empirical position which is descriptive rather than normative in its orientation. We shall gain a better understanding of the foundation and methods of the Variability Concept and its historical legitimacy by taking a brief look at its linguistic and anthropological tradition.

4.3 The linguistic tradition

More recent concepts relating to the study of language in its social context[2] have their methodological and historical roots in structuralism, in the tradition of dialectology, and in the study of languages in contact.

---

[2] Except for some classics, and also for the development of Soviet sociolinguistics (see Girke and Jachnow 1974 and Dittmar 1975), sociological interest in language has only existed for about a decade. Cf. Fishman 1971b and Grimshaw 1971a.

4.3.1 Structuralism

Structuralism developed from the systematic division by Saussure of language into *langue* (system) and *parole* (language-use, speech), and of linguistic studies into synchronic and diachronic analysis. The *langue* is 'un produit social de la faculté du langage' (Saussure 1949, 25), which is developed in speech communities into a rule system of linguistic conventions. The *langue* postulated by Saussure was treated by his successors less as the result of different types of social processes than as an abstract system of rules whose *ideal* homogeneity was presupposed.

This tendency towards 'idealization' in linguistic theory can be traced back to Saussure's text: 'Tandis que le langage [a concept that is placed above *langue* and *parole* and embraces them both] est hétérogène, la langue ainsi délimitée est de nature homogène' (1949, 32). Although Saussure himself emphasized that the '*langue* exists perfectly only in the whole community' (*ibid.*, 30), most linguists have understood him to mean that it should be investigated independently of actual speech behaviour. The contradiction which has arisen as a result of Saussure's specific words, and which consists in the fact that 'the social aspect of language is studied by observing any one individual, but the individual aspect only by observing language in its social context' (Labov 1970a, 32), has remained unsolved in the context of structuralism.

Saussure's definition of *langue* as a system of rules stimulated the development of structuralism, which sought to discover the immanent laws of linguistic structures, neglecting their variation. The following are some of the essential features of structuralism which characterize its different schools, independent of individual divergences (cf. Helbig 1971, 46–118 and in particular 94–9):

1   The description of linguistic structures must take place according to empirical principles, i.e. it must be descriptive (as opposed to normative). For reasons of analysis, the descriptive levels of phonology, syntax and semantics are kept strictly separate.
2   Descriptions must be related to a well-defined corpus of linguistic utterances that have been obtained from an *informant*, the 'native speaker'. The informant is to give information about normative aspects of speech usage (for example pronunciation) and to judge whether two utterances to be compared are the same or different. Although many of the claims of the structuralists about individual speech behaviour are empirically based, it has become an established custom amongst linguists to act as their own informants. It should be remembered that structuralism attempted to make empirical discoveries about speech behaviour through the questioning of informants. This has led, moreover, to considerable progress in field work.
3   The central method of structuralism is the *distributional analysis*, according to which a linguistic element is analysed in relation to the entire set of linguistic environments—on some level of description—in which it (or rather its members) can occur.[3] This formal procedure excluded to a large extent an analysis of meaning, or reduced it to the more or less trivial statement that linguistic elements can have different meanings in different

[3] Cf. Harris 1951.

positions. Phonology was the main area of application of distributional analysis. Here, three types of distribution were distinguished:

i *Contrastive distribution* of different elements at the same level (bat—bit): the informant responds to this minimal opposition of the two phonemes in the same environment.

ii *Complementary distribution* of members of a single higher-level element: a member of a linguistic element appears in one context where another member cannot appear (e.g., *le* and *la* in French as members of the higher-level element Definite Article Singular). Complementary units are called allophones or allomorphs of the higher-level element.

iii *Free variation* of members of a single higher-level element: various members can appear in the same linguistic (phonetic or phonological) environment without any particular response from the informant (e.g. different variants or /r/ in English and in German).

This structural procedure, which has only briefly been touched upon here, has had a decisive influence on the more recent development of the study of language in its social context; at the same time, it has been further developed and supplemented by new techniques.

The analytical aims (descriptive, empirical, form-oriented (in contrast to meaning-oriented), behaviouristic) introduced into linguistics by Bloomfield (1933) are the same in many respects for proponents of the Variability Concept, such as Labov, Decamp and Wolfram. The Variability Concept (different languages possess equivalent possibilities of expression), with its postulate of the descriptive analysis of language, is in agreement with the views that have generally been adopted in linguistics. In his now famous article of 1927 on literate and illiterate speech, Bloomfield shows that in public opinion, 'literate' and 'illiterate' English are classed as 'good' and 'bad' respectively, whilst empirical analysis shows that neither of the two varieties is disadvantaged with respect to the other:

'. . . what we find is not well-informed and regulated activity opposed to ignorant and careless, but rather a conflict of definite, fixed locutions, one of which, for some reason, is "good", while the others are "bad". . . . The scientific view . . . will bring us farther. It has the advantage of being based on a more extensive survey of various languages and of their history than any one person could make; also it has the advantage of methodical approach. This last means that we shall not operate with the terms "good" and "bad" language, or their equivalents, since it is precisely these which we are trying to define. . . . In this way, wherever there are lines across which communication is hampered— water, mountains, deserts, political boundaries, and the like—we find *differences* of speech.' (Bloomfield 1927, 433–4—italics mine)

Long before the whole discussion about speech barriers, Bloomfield suggested that the notion 'good' and 'bad' speech was a question of social evaluation: 'the nearest approach to an explanation of "good" and "bad" language seems to be this, then, that, by a cumulation of obvious superiorities, both of character and standing, as well as of language, some persons are felt to be better models of conduct and speech than others' (439) and not one of systematic, linguistically-determined inferiority. (This traditional view is referred to in Labov *et al.* 1968).

Bloomfield's behaviouristic approach has been adopted in the sociolinguistic works published during the last few years by the Center for Applied Linguistics (Washington, D.C.). Here, as in most structural linguistic work, the view prevails that the correlation between linguistic forms and their cognitive meanings should be left out of account (cf. Labov 1966a; Wolfram 1969; Labov 1971a, where this is frequently emphasized). With their new technique of correlating linguistic and social parameters, these works have, on the other hand, been able to achieve a much greater precision of the insufficiently-defined structuralist notion, 'free variation'.

There is a further parallel between the form-oriented procedure, introduced by Bloomfield, and the newer works of descriptive sociolinguistics, in that the latter have essentially been limited to analyses of phonological and syntactic aspects. It is only recently that speech acts were included in the semantic explanation of communication processes.

Although the structuralists have frequently worked with individual native speakers, they have hardly developed adequate techniques for research into the speech behaviour of speaker *groups*. One of the main reasons for this is that they were only oriented towards *one* of the poles of the Saussurean paradox, namely' that the social aspect of a language (taken as a homogeneous system) is observable in each individual. That the isolated description of an individual's speech in this sense should be the object of linguistics has been proposed by one of the most important American structuralists, Bernard Bloch, in his article, 'Set of postulates for phonemic analysis' (1948), where for the first time he introduces into linguistics the concept of an idiolect, defining it in the following way:

> 'The totality of the possible utterances of one speaker at one time in using a language to interact with one other speaker is an *idiolect*. . . . The phrase "with one other speaker" is intended to exclude the possibility that an idiolect might embrace more than one style of speaking: it is at least unlikely that a given speaker will use two or more styles in addressing a single person. . . . Phonological analysis of a given idiolect does not reveal the phonological system of any idiolect belonging to a different dialect.' (Bloch 1948, 7–9)

Descriptive sociolinguistics has criticized this side of structuralism which denies or overlooks the stylistic variation of speakers in verbal interactions. The reduction undertaken by Bloch was supposed to exclude all types of variation. However, he overlooked the fact that language varies regularly with social parameters.

There are two further structuralist schools that must be mentioned, apart from American structuralism, as they have influenced modern sociolinguistic work: British contextualism (Helbig 1971, 109–12) and Prague functionalism.

Under the influence of their most important analyst J. R. Firth (1958; 1964), the British school of structuralism related linguistic utterances to their occurence in social contexts. Sentences were not simply classified grammatically but according to their function in situational contexts. Firth stresses his chief concepts: the *function* and the *meaning* of linguistic utterances. He constantly repeated that his concept of function should be understood as dynamic (Firth, 20ff., 26f., 32f.). His work has, above all, influenced the anthropological linguistics of the group around Hymes and Gumperz.

Firth's ideas were adopted more recently by Halliday, and taken a great deal further (cf. Halliday 1964; 1969). During the last few years, Halliday and his followers (for example Hawkins) have worked out linguistic procedures of analysis for the description of class-specific speech differences (cf. 2.3.5); they were put into practice in the language surveys conducted by the sociological research unit headed by Bernstein. More recent works in the tradition of contextualism are concerned with features of verbal interaction (Sternberg 1970) and with the stylistic register of speakers (Davies 1969).

In addition to British contextualism, Prague structuralism placed emphasis on the investigation of language as a social method of communication. Although during its heyday (1929–39), this school largely limited the object of its investigation to phonology, it later developed serious concepts for syntactic analysis (Sgall, Hajičová and Benešová 1973). Mathesius investigated utterances in the functional perspective of their information content, and exposed their universally valid Theme-Rheme organization (cf. Beneš and Vachek, in Kochan 1971, xivf.). The Prague structuralists also showed great interest in sociological questions of language. Contrastive analysis of written and oral language has lately been given new impetus by Havránek (cf. Kochan 1971). He makes a firm distinction between the language *norm* (the convention developed in the speech community) and the *codification* of the norm (the more or less arbitrary sociopolitical determination of the norm). The contrastive description of written and spoken language—a factor, for example, that was totally neglected in the work on speech barriers initiated by Bernstein—also led to more intensive research into style (Hausenblas, Jelínek, in Kochan 1971). Despite these sometimes penetrating analyses (see Vachek 1964), Prague structuralism has not succeeded in backing up its analytical concepts with empirical evidence. Nevertheless, it must be stated that one of the first empirical investigations into language norms (Reichstein 1960) was greatly influenced by the Prague school. A comprehensive account and appraisal of the achievements of the Prague school can be found in Vachek 1966.

4.3.2 Dialectology

One of the oldest linguistic disciplines concerned with the analysis of speech variation is *dialectology*. Its methods were on the whole statistical, aimed at explaining early language states, but the end of the nineteenth century saw the preparation of the first systematic dialect atlases. Dialect research attempted to pin languages and their varieties down to geographical areas; by questioning speakers (fieldwork), it was possible to identify regional areas in which certain grammatical rules applied or certain speech variants were used. The dialect atlases marked mostly sound shifts, but they also sometimes included grammatical changes. Lines indicating such shifts were called *isoglosses*. Dialectologists have produced fundamental works on linguistic variation which teach us that speech communities are essentially heterogeneous. The necessity to select representative samples of speakers and linguistic utterances according to standardized principles ensured that dialectology became the branch of linguistics which least excluded the application of the empirical methods of the social sciences.

The selection of speakers was mainly representative of age groups; they helped to demonstrate the change in grammar and pronunciation that resulted from the speakers' identification with linguistic prestige patterns. The speaker selection, however, was rarely effected according to strict sociological criteria.

Linguistic material was obtained by questionnaires and interviews, which concentrated on lexical usage and grammatical selection habits. Interviews frequently helped to record pronunciation habits, which were either transcribed phonetically by a competent interviewer, or which, in more modern times, were recorded on tape. In trying to record pronunciation, dialectologists came up against the main problems of field research: what was to be taken as the normal pronunciation of speakers? How could it be established whether this was used in a given interview? Dialectologists reached the conclusion that the pronunciation of speakers in the situation of an interview represented—in most cases—the *formal* style of their verbal repertoire. This problem of style selection in an interview situation has remained unsolved till the present day. One is agreed, however, that a speaker varies his style depending on whether the context is formal or informal, and that what matters is precisely to have speech samples of both extremes of the style continuum (cf. the discussion of this problem in Labov 1966a, 90–131 and Wolfram 1969, 8–9). In any case, dialectologists have traditionally been alert to the question of the influence which the interview situation exerts on the quality of speech data.

Descriptive sociolinguistics has borrowed some of the methods of dialectology; the type of speaker and corpus selection, the procedure of questionnaires and interviews are but a few of the most important (cf. on this Shuy, Wolfram and Riley 1968). Dialect research, which has been conducted in recent years in conjunction with work on socially-determined speech behaviour, has become known in the USA under the name 'social dialectology' (Shuy 1964).

Although dialectologists have collected a vast amount of valuable speech material, there are weaknesses in this approach which reduce its general linguistic interest:

1   It was limited to phonology and grammar (cf. Fishman 1971b, 378f.).
2   Linguistic variation was related only to geographical conditions, although innovations, divergences etc. *can*, but not necessarily *must*, coincide with geographical boundaries; finally, even dialectologists became increasingly aware that speech variation is a result of the processes of interaction of a series of factors (social, economic etc.) other than geography (cf. Weinreich, Labov and Herzog 1968, 151–9).
3   Dialectology was unable to develop a comprehensive theory capable of explaining speech variation.

More attention has been paid by dialect research in recent times to theoretical viewpoints (Weinreich 1954; McDavid 1970). However, it ought to be included in a more comprehensive sociolinguistic perspective now that more is known about the subject. This is one of the conclusions that have emerged from the analysis of languages or dialects in contact.

4.3.3 Languages in contact

Sociolinguistic reseach in the last decade has been strongly influenced by the theoretical works of Weinrich (1953 and 1954) and Ferguson (1959). Some of their basic ideas should, therefore, be mentioned.

Weinreich (1953) devotes himself to the entire problem range of 'languages in contact' (e.g. the coexistence of German, French and Italian in Switzerland). The mutual interference of two languages in contact is determined (1) by structural linguistic factors and (2) by nonlinguistic factors.

Structural linguistic factors
The potential structural linguistic factors of interference are predictable from a comparison (differences and/or similarities) of the phonological, grammatical and lexical systems of both languages. Certain possibilities for linguistic interference will become apparent if it is accepted that speakers can take over and integrate grammatical elements of a secondary language (phonemes, morphemes, lexemes) into the system of their primary language.

Among the types of *phonological interference* there are (Weinreich 1953, 18f.):

1   the *underdifferentiation* of phonemes (2 sounds, which are not different in the primary system (*PS*), are confused in the secondary system (*SS*));
2   the *overdifferentiation* of phonemes (when 2 sounds, which are not distinct in the *SS*, are differentiated in the *PS*);
3   *reinterpretation of distinctions* (phonemes in the *SS* are differentiated by features which are redundant in this system, but are relevant in the *PS*);
4   *phone substitution* (phonemes that are identically defined in both languages but whose pronunciation differs).

Whether processes 1 to 4 actually take place depends on factors that either favour or prevent the adoption and propagation of interference phenomena.

Statements about *grammatical interference* presuppose that both language systems have been described separately. They can then be differentiated according to whether they have more or fewer grammatical categories, and whether the morphemes in them have a stronger or weaker syntagmatic link. Contrastive linguistic analyses are prerequisites for such an undertaking.

Some types of grammatical interference are (Weinreich 1953, 30f.):

1   the use of morphemes of a language *A* in a language *B*;
2   the use of grammatical relations in *A* for morphemes in *B*, or the neglect of *B* relations;
3   the identification of a *B* morpheme with an *A* morpheme (transformation of the *B* morpheme according to the pattern of *A*).

The probability of *transfer* is to be noted: the more a morpheme is integrated into one system, the less the probability of its transfer. 'Integrated' also implies 'syntactically linked': Weinreich sees morpheme classes as a continuously-ordered series, which begins with the syntagmatically most strongly linked inflection endings, and leads, via prepositions, articles etc., to complete words (nouns, verbs, adjectives) and non-integrated interjections (Weinreich 1953, 29f.).

The result of the principle that the facility of transfer depends on the degree of grammatical linkage is that isolated words represent the greatest fluctuation potential in interference processes.

Mechanisms of *lexical interference* are manifested in that:

1   morphemes are transferred from *A* to *B*;
2   *B* morphemes are employed in a new or extended function according to the model of *A* morphemes and are identified with the latter's content;
3   when lexical elements are combined into a new unit, processes 1 and 2 can occur together.

Thus loan-words are mainly integrated into the system of a language at the point where the structure of the vocabulary is at its weakest.

Weinreich claims that quantification is a necessary component of work on interference. The various types of interference should be sorted according to their frequency of occurrence, and tests of language competence carried out on bilingual (multilingual) speakers.

Tests of language competence (mostly word-naming and word-association tests) are today commonly used in measuring the degree of bilingualism (cf. Fishman *et al.* 1968). Further knowledge about the development and situation of Creole and Pidgin languages can also be gained from interference studies of languages in contact (see Hymes 1971).

Nonlinguistic factors
Typical forms of interference can only, however, be predicted from *sociolinguistic* descriptions which relate structural linguistic features to extralinguistic factors. The most important factors determining the kind and degree of bilinguality are:

1   *The role of sociocultural setting*   This covers the factors that make one language the *dominant* one for the bilingual person (usefulness of the language, role for social mobility, literary and cultural values etc.); the environment (social, economic, cultural) determines the predominance of the one or the other language in particular speech situations (Weinreich 1953, 83; cf. the importance of this point in Fishman *et al.* 1968).

2   *Language functions in bilingual groups*   These can be classified according to the *conservatory* effect they have on speech behaviour. Which language is favoured in the educational system is crucial in 'conservation' (see also 5.4.3).

The conservatory effect determines the degree of uniformity and, at the same time, the emergence of functional varieties; a measurement of its strength would open the way for a classification of the importance of the various functions in which the one or the other language dominates (Weinreich 1953, 87f.).

3   *Congruence of linguistic and sociocultural divisions*   In each concrete contact situation, the separation of mother-language groups coincides (or is congruent) with one or several divisions of an extralinguistic nature. *Types of congruence* are: (a) geographical separation; (b) indigenous v. immigrant language; (c) cultural and ethnic groups; (d) religion; (e) race; (f) sex; (g) age; (h) social status ('language shift' is often stimulated by socially-differentiated

groups, especially in socially-differentiated towns); (i) occupation; (j) rural v. urban population (Weinreich 1953, 89–97).

These categories have guided a series of sociolinguistic surveys. Investigations on (h), social status, have brought forth particularly rich empirical material (cf. amongst others Labov 1966a; Labov *et al.* 1968; Wolfram 1969; Trudgill 1974).

4   *Standardized language as a symbol of language loyalty*   The standardized and regulated—and thus also nationalized—language is given a high sociopolitical and national political value in order to protect it and set it apart from other languages. Language loyalty prevents 'language shift' and interference; in contact situations it is the symbol of group integrity (Weinreich 1953, 99).

5   *Duration of contact between languages*   The rapidity of linguistic change often depends crucially upon the duration of contact. The time factor responsible for the process of linguistic interference can be analysed in two ways: by *relative* association of the interferences with different age-groups living at the same time, and by measuring the *absolute* time of the occurrence of individual interference phenomena (Weinreich 1953, 103).

6   *Crystallization of new languages*   Specific factors in the contact situation can contribute to the emergence of new languages:

i   the degree of difference between two languages (a third one can spring up between the other two);

ii   the degree of stability: the emergence of patterns of interference is beyond strictly linguistic causation: a language may not possess sufficient linguistic prestige or may not exert strong enough social pressure;

iii   the function range: it is only when the crucial function of language is its use in the family that it can develop as another language;

iv   the speakers' own rating of their language; this depends upon sociocultural and political factors (Weinreich 1953, 104–6).

7   *Language shift*   Language' shift is entirely extrastructural since the linguistic structure of two languages in contact does not determine which language yields its function to the other. Language shift depends upon the social value and the prestige of the languages involved (Weinreich 1953, 106–8; cf. Fishman 1966).

Weinreich's reflections on the analysis of languages in contact have created the preconditions for the formation of three main fields of research:

1   studies on the structural comparison of languages: contrastive analyses and the analysis of coexisting language systems;

2   sociolinguistic investigations in a narrower sense: the correlation of linguistic characteristics with extralinguistic factors;

3   sociological investigations into language loyalty, language shift, bilingualism, language minorities etc.; these investigations deal with the social and political functions of language varieties and not with concrete material from a single language.

Weinreich's work has combined in an ideal fashion the structuralist and dialectological approaches with others from the neighbouring behaviourist sciences. From the theoretical and empirical point of view, he is the Nestor of sociolinguistics.

One of the problem areas pointed out by Weinreich is the subject of work by Ferguson (1959), who discusses the situation of two functionally different language varieties in a speech community under the title of *diglossia*. This is the term given to a relatively stable language situation with primary regional dialects, the *L* (low) variety, and a superimposed variant, the *H* (high) variety. The *H* variety is used for writing and, in general, in formal speech situations; it is usually learnt in educational institutions and has a high prestige value. Grammatically, it is markedly different from the *L* variety, which is intended for oral communication and conversation. *L* is acquired as the mother language and is not subjected to any normative control.

H and *L* are strictly divided according to their functions. Thus *H* is employed, for example, in radio news broadcasts, public institutions, literature, political speeches, church etc.; *L* serves as a means of understanding in all informal and unstructured situations, e.g. for conversing with friends and colleagues, at home, or as a language for giving instructions to employees and workers. *H* and *L* produce a comical effect when they are not used in the right function and in the right context. *H* is considered to be the prestige language and consequently superior to *L*.

The differences between *H* and *L* are manifested in (1) *grammar*, (2) *lexicon* and (3) *phonology*:

1   *L* has fewer grammatical (morphological) categories and a reduced system of inflection; *H* has a greater grammatical (morphological) complexity.

2   *H* and *L* have, in the main, a complementary lexicon. It is a particular characteristic of the diglossia situation that lexical pairs are used situation-specifically with the same meaning in the *H* variety or the *L* variety.

3   *H* and *L* share one single phonological system, in which the *L* phonology represents the basic system, and the deviant characteristics of the *H* phonology form a subsystem or parasystem.

The diglossia situation differs in two basic aspects from the relationship between Standard and regional dialects: in the diglossia situation, nobody uses *H* in normal conversation; in the Standard dialect situation, the Standard is often identical with the variety of a regional or social group.

Ferguson and others found diglossia situations in overseas speech communities which used to be European colonies (e.g. in Haiti). Conversational and higher strata speech variants coexist in the speech community in such a way that the use of the one or the other variant is subjected to strict situation-specific rules. Thus Pidgin counts as a commercial language with a limited and often ill-defined syntax and vocabulary, and is used for communication in economically-defined situations; Creole is the *L* variety and the mother language that has resulted from interference of the colonialists' European languages and Pidgin (different hypotheses have been put forward to explain the origin and development of Pidgin and Creole; cf. Decamp 1971b). In most cases, the colonial languages (French, English, Dutch, Spanish, Portuguese) are still considered the *H* variety in Creole speech communities. The sociolinguistic situation of Creole languages can (but does not necessarily) correspond to the diglossia situation described by Ferguson. Frequently, the *H* variety is the language of social mobility, required for climbing the social ladder, whereas 'Creole is inseparably associated with poverty, ignorance and lack of moral character. . . . A Pidgin or Creole almost invariably has low social status' (Decamp 1971b, 26). Creole is thus immediately dependent on norms of social prestige in its formation and development. On account of their low social status, Creole languages can disappear; or else they can be raised to the status of national Standard (as happened recently in Australian New Guinea). How long they will exist in a long-term, stable diglossia situation depends on sociopolitical factors. In modern linguistic research, the prevailing view is that Pidgin, Creole and Standard varieties represent a developmental continuum which cannot be divided up into rigid linguistic fields (cf. Decamp 1971b, 18–25 and Decamp 1971c).

Weinreich (1954) devotes himself to the question of how linguistics can give a structural description of the relationships between linguistic varieties. Structural linguistics, which had so far only dealt with one single homogeneous variety, would have to combine its principles with those of dialectology, which had up till now only considered heterogeneous speech phenomena from a regional, temporal and social point of view. Weinreich considers it possible to include both these fields in a *structural dialectology* by the construction of a system on a higher level, made up of discrete homogeneous systems. Such a system, which would reveal partial intrinsic differences (phonology, syntax, semantics) of the varieties in the framework of partial similarities, is termed by Weinreich a *diasystem*. This describes the competence of speakers of languages in contact (Weinreich 1954, quoted in Fishman 1968b, 307). Weinreich considers that the difficulties of a structural dialectology lie mainly in the fact that it must find criteria for the division of continuum into discrete varieties. This brings him to the conclusion that structural linguistic descriptions should include extralinguistic factors: diasystems, as an empirical reality, should give an integrated description of linguistic facts, beyond pure constructs, taking account of extralinguistic criteria (*ibid.*, 317).

Weinreich's suggestions have been further developed, and, in more recent times, some solutions have been proposed (cf. Weinreich, Labov and Herzog 1968).

4.4 The anthropological tradition

Just as recent sociolinguistic research in the USA was given a decisive impetus by the racial conflicts between Whites and Blacks, the development of anthropological linguistics is connected with the interest in American Indian languages: 'We can trace an involvement of linguistics in anthropological study to the early interest in American Indian languages as indicative of the origins and character of the natives of the New World' (Hymes 1964a, 6).

The main interest of linguistically-oriented anthropologists remains the investigation of exotic languages in connection with the social behaviour of their speakers: 'Anthropological linguists are personally excited about the intellectual systems of primitive and peasant peoples—particularly . . . their languages' (Friedrich 1971, 167).

The extraordinarily broad perspective observed in anthropological linguistic studies, which means that social, geographical and psychological factors are taken into account, has inevitably made it an eclectic science. The old anthropological notion, that languages and cultures are *relatively* different, on account of their different social value systems, seems to be upheld also in its theoretical relativism (cf. Friedrich 1971, 168). Anthropologists adopted from structuralism its taxonomic descriptive methods and its widely-practised ahistorical procedure.[4]

It was in field research that techniques and methods of participant observation were developed ('ethnomethodology'), which are of prime importance today and are used with increasing frequency (cf. Garfinkel 1967 and 1972). From the psychological perspective, the main problem was how far the grammatical categories of a language determine the cognitive strategies of speakers. Whorf's relativity theory, which deals with this question, provoked a heated discussion among linguists during the 1950s. Today, Whorf's thesis is considered to be unproved (cf. Lenneberg and Roberts 1956). Nevertheless, it is still of interest to anthropologists to find out what influence different grammatical systems and lexica have on the cognition of speakers (Gumperz and Hernandez 1971).

The main areas of anthropological linguistics are:

1   The systematic description of forms of address and their social significance (e.g. Brown and Ford 1961).
2   The semantic analysis of lexical systems. There is a vast amount of literature on the description of kinship terminology and colour adjectives. In the framework of the analysis of kinship terms, the so-called 'componential analysis' was developed.
3   The functional linguistic description of exotic or so-called 'primitive' languages. Following the old tradition, sociocultural and cognitive factors are frequently included in these descriptions.

The material found in the linguistic studies of linguistically-oriented anthropologists supports the view that language must be considered empirically and theoretically from the aspect of heterogeneity. Linguistic diversity implies that it is part of the competence of the speaker to be able to change regularly from one style or speech form to another.

The development of anthropological linguistics is connected with such names as Boas, Sapir, Kroeber, Malinowski and Whorf, whose works are continually mentioned by Hymes (cf. Hymes 1964a, 3–14), who is the discipline's most important representative at the moment. They all demand an analysis of language which is embedded in the social context. Apart from numerous programmatic pronouncements, which were never followed up by actual empirical work, some anthropological axioms have once more become fully significant. Malinowski's insistence that language be investigated as a component of social action, and that

4 Cf. for example the polemic of Lévi-Strauss against Sartre in *La pensée sauvage* (Paris 1962).

an analysis be given of its role as a means of social control (1923), has never ceased to be relevant. It was also he who insisted on what is now a theory accepted by most linguists and anthropologists and can be considered part of their programme. The task of that theory is to explain

> 'what is essential in language and what therefore must remain the same through the whole range of linguistic varieties: how linguistic forms are influenced by psychological, mental, social, and other cultural elements; what is the real nature of meaning and form, and how they correspond; a theory which, in fine, would give us a set of well-founded plastic definitions of grammatical concepts.' (Malinowski, quoted in Hymes 1964a, 4)

4.5 Four areas of research relevant to sociolinguistics

Our presentation of the linguistic and anthropological tradition of the Variability Concept shows up four areas of research which are of prime importance for the constitution of sociolinguistics. They are justified by the necessity of having a universal linguistic theory, which has, as an important part of its overall mandate, the task of providing the general terms for the description and explanation of the processes of appropriation, development, diffusion, conservation and change of linguistic forms in speech communities. The explanatory function of such a linguistic theory would include the processes of (1) speech variation, (2) linguistic change, (3) language acquisition, and (4) social communication.

Work on these areas could be limited to the investigation of internal linguistic processes; this would give us at best, however, an explanation of the phenomena in limited, purely linguistic terms, not in the wider context of social dynamism. This is clear when one considers the relationship of linguistic to extralinguistic factors that is inherent in the processes listed above. In many cases, linguistic elements are affected by speech variation and linguistic change in proportion to the degree to which they are *not* embedded in the framework of a stable grammatical structure: most resistant to change are those elements which are integrated into a hard and fast system of syntactic rules. On the other hand, the syntactically less bound elements (such as the lexicon) show a greater inclination towards change. Thus the internal linguistic situation plays a part in the process of linguistic change. At the same time, there is sufficient evidence to show that extralinguistic factors also have a decisive effect. The effects of both mechanisms (linguistic and extralinguistic) must be specified and kept separate from one another. It must be emphasized, however, that only an analysis of the mutual relationship between linguistic and extralinguistic factors will give an adequate explanation of 1 to 4 above (cf. Weinreich, Labov and Herzog 1968, 188). Possible explanations depend on a series of social parameters: the sociopolitical and power-political situation; the agents of socialization such as the family, the circle of friends, the school; the nature of the regional and social communication networks; the flexible as opposed to rigid observance of the norms, etc. From this angle, we shall discuss the question of what aims the areas of investigation 1 to 4 could serve in the context of sociolinguistic analysis.

4.5.1 Speech variation

A number of very different languages, which are in direct contact with one another, may show sharp grammatical contrasts; but they can still form closely-connected functional communication networks. The question is, what are the social and political processes that are responsible, in a speech community, for homogeneity or heterogeneity; does structural heterogeneity make communication more difficult or, on the contrary, does its absence render communication *dysfunctional*? (Cf. Weinreich, Labov and Herzog 1968, 101.) Analyses of linguistic variation must tell us in what way languages and dialects coexist; they must tell us what the need to control and distinguish varieties means for the linguistic competence of the speaker, and what the social, sociopolitical and power-political mechanisms are by which language varieties are formed or disappear.

Thus, from the point of view of linguistic variation in a social context, neutral (non-discriminating) varieties must be differentiated from those varieties which put a social stigma on a speaker and prevent his emancipation. In this context, the problem of how far language varieties imply cognitive differences remains unsolved.

4.5.2 Linguistic change

Origin, diffusion, disappearance of linguistic varieties—these processes have a strong influence on linguistic change. It should be the aim of an empirically-based theory of linguistic change to establish to what extent it is possible to predict linguistic usage and its development for particular social groups for a given time and a given place (cf. Weinreich, Labov and Herzog 1968, 98–105). Although it may appear difficult, even unrealistic at the present time, to satisfy this empirical requirement of the theory, academic norms and standards make this a necessity. An adequate insight into the mechanisms of linguistic change will, moreover, be of invaluable help in formulating practical policies regarding rational linguistic planning in the area of standardization and normalization of existing varieties. Such knowledge could also contribute to a politically sensible policy of enforcement of linguistic norms, in particular in the case of coexisting language systems.

The task of empirical analyses is to show the various stages of linguistic developments and to specify the social and sociolinguistic pressure situations that caused them (essentially the 'actuation problem' of linguistic change; see on this point Weinreich, Labov and Herzog 1968, 186f.). The 'actuation problem'—at what point in time, in what environment and under what conditions does a linguistic system change?—is one of the main problems of linguistic change. Its solution depends on the answer to four further questions:

1   the problem of the pressure situation (social or political pressure on linguistic structures to change);
2   the transition problem (the transition from one linguistic stage to another);
3   the problem of how linguistic changes are embedded in the matrix of

linguistic and extralinguistic accompanying factors (cf. Weinreich, Labov and Herzog 1968, 101);

4   the problem of assessment (the assessment of linguistic variants which, in their social usage, can become either prestige forms or stigmatized expressions).

4.5.3 Language acquisition

The processes of language acquisition play an important role in the explanation of linguistic change and variation. Questions of language acquisition relevant to sociolinguistics are (1) to what extent and in what intensity is children's language learnt in the family and in the group of friends, and (2) what influence do institutions such as kindergarten, school, etc., have on the child's linguistic competence? The question of language acquisition raises the whole problem of linguistic socialization. In this respect, it must be clear what verbal stimuli the children receive, to what extent and in what functions their communicative competence is developed (cf. L. Bloom 1970), what sociolinguistic values allow prestige forms to be produced amongst young people, etc. The analysis of language acquisition, seen from the sociolinguistic point of view, is concerned with the learning of linguistic rules specific to class and to groups, and not with the purely psychological learning processes. It must specify the stages and ages of language acquisition in correlation with the learning conditions created by the social structure, and indicate whether, and at what point in time, rules are acquired in a variable and/or categorical manner.

4.5.4 Social communication

Sociolinguistic work can help to reveal strategies of social communication in correlation with social action. In this field, sociolinguistics has the task of exposing the norms of social communication and of comparing these with the norms of the social system. It must draw attention to the extent to which divergences are caused by the social system or by the typical speech behaviour of individuals.

The illuminating sociolinguistic work on the speech behaviour of Black and lower-class speakers (cf. Labov *et al.* 1968, I and II) has shown how extraordinarily important it is to have an adequate understanding of this task: psychologists called it 'pathological' speech behaviour which needed to be subjected to the control and therapy of the 'speech clinician' (cf. Raph 1967). Here, linguists could demonstrate that the communication forms of lower-class children were only termed pathological on the basis of bourgeois norms.

4.6 Summary

In this chapter, we contrasted the Deficit Hypothesis with the more serious and more solidly grounded Variability Concept. Then we pursued the latter's linguistic and anthropological tradition and named four fields for which sociolinguistic research is of primary importance: speech variation, linguistic change, language acquisition and social communication. The following are the most important points of our exposé.

1   In contrast to the normative Deficit Hypothesis, which is restricted to class-specific speech behaviour, the Variability Concept offers certain clear advantages: its procedure is descriptive, it assumes the functional equivalence of different languages and uses neutral concepts in its description; it separates cognitive aspects from the analysis of linguistic variation; and it investigates speech behaviour in specific contexts in correlation with a large number of social and regional parameters in specific situations.

2   From the point of view of the concept of the speech community, four different types of language variety can be distinguished:

i   the *Standard* variety as a supraregional means of communication which is legitimized and given prestige as a result of the distribution of power;
ii   the *regional* variety as a dialect;
iii   the *social* variety as a sociolect subjected to authority or to sanctions;
iv   the *functional* variety as a part of the verbal repertoire specific to context and situation.

These varieties make up together what we regard as linguistic variation and contribute to its transmission.

3   The aims and methods of present sociolinguistic research are to be understood in the perspective of its linguistic and anthropological tradition.

The empirically-based, non-cognitive form of linguistic analysis, which excluded the semantic aspect and was limited to individual informants, can be traced back to the general structuralist paradigm. Although it did bring technical progress for the study of language in social context, it had its disadvantages in so far as it was restricted to the description of idiolects. The experiences of dialectologists in field work (selection of informants, the collecting of well-defined corpora of utterances) were utilized for the direct observation of linguistic behaviour. Finally, the anthropological tradition awakened interest in a broader spectrum of sociolinguistic questions, in particular, questions about the speech situation, the social background and the psychological regulation of communication, about the social significance of forms of address and kinship terms and, above all, about the pragmatic functions of language. In this respect, anthropological research has led to differentiated techniques of participant observation.

4   Particular emphasis must be placed on the influence that the work of Weinreich (1953), on languages in contact, has had on attitudes to sociolinguistic problems, on the methodology of investigation and on theory. In this work, the problem is raised of the relationship of internal linguistic factors to extralinguistic factors, and material is produced to demonstrate that linguistic interference, change and variation cannot be explained without taking into account sociocultural situations and the interaction of various social groups. Weinreich's work provided the stimulus for an amount of important research on the coexistence of language systems (mostly linguistically-oriented) and on the social and political functions of languages in contact (mostly sociologically-oriented).

5 Theoretical concepts of speech variation in the framework of the Variability Concept

The last chapter dealt with the foundations and traditions of the Variability Concept; we shall now devote our attention to theoretical questions of sociolinguistics.

In accordance with linguistic and sociolinguistic interests, we shall discuss the literature from essentially two points of view: first, the extent to which sociolinguistic data can be linked to a linguistic theory, and the changes which thereby become necessary in this theory; and secondly, the theoretical approaches to a sociology of language. Theoretical aspects of bilingualism and multilingualism will be considered in a separate section emphasizing the necessarily interdisciplinary character of sociolinguistic research, not because the problems they raise are fundamentally different, but because they require special treatment.

Before we give some reasons for the recent interest in theoretical concepts of sociolinguistics, however, we should make a brief comment on the relation between theory and empirical investigation. In so far as sociolinguistics can be considered part of the social sciences, there is a strong interaction between theoretical and empirical inquiry. Most of the theoretical concepts we shall deal with have been preceded by empirical investigations, and it might therefore have been desirable to describe the latter first. We prefer the opposite way, however, as for a systematic account this has the advantage that when the theory has been explained in advance empirical results can be more easily described and understood.

5.1 Sociolinguistics—the genesis of a new branch of science

Even though the need for analysis of language in its social context was felt by many authors, mainly linguists but also sociologists and psychologists, as early as the first half of this century (for more detailed information cf. Hymes 1964a, 3–14 and Weinreich, Labov and Herzog 1968 for the USA; Lencek 1971 for the USSR) the name 'sociolinguistics' does not appear until 1952 in a work by Haver C. Currie, whose intention was to encourage investigation into the relation between speech behaviour and social status:

> 'The present purpose is to suggest ... that social functions and significations of speech factors offer a prolific field for research. ... This field is here designated *sociolinguistics*.' (Currie 1952, quoted in Williamson and Burke 1971, 40)

At first, Currie's formulations projecting an interdisciplinary field of research

r*

remained merely a programme. Ten years later the terms *sociolingvistika* and *social'naja lingvistika* came into use in the USSR (Lencek 1971), and in 1964 sociolinguistic research also gained broader interest in the USA, even though at first this was in many respects of a programmatic nature.[1] Hymes, who at first describes the analysis of language in its social context as the 'ethnography of speech' Gumperz and Hymes 1964), declares in his reader, *Language in Culture and Society*, which was published in the same year, that sociolinguistics is a main area of interest for anthropologists: 'Indeed, the main foci of interest . . . would seem to be semantic description or sociolinguistics or both' (Hymes 1964a, 11).

Hymes's large volume contains the first studies on the social significance of language to have been made since the 1920s: Firth's programmatic essay of 1937 on sociological linguistics (also in Firth 1958), Bloomfield's comparison of literate and illiterate speech (1927), McDavid's observations of 1948 on the social significance of post-vocalic -*r* in South Carolina (also in Bright 1966a), Fischer's analysis of inflections as social markers (1958), the investigation of social dialects (Bright 1966b and Gumperz 1964) and Garvin's attempt of 1959 to classify factors of linguistic standardization. Similarly, the advance of dialectology into the social dimensions of dialectal colouring can be seen in the volume on social dialects edited by Shuy (1964), where Labov's essay (1964b) provides new insight into the acquisition of language specific to social groups.

Finally, it should be noted that the first conference actually on sociolinguistics under that name took place at the University of California in Los Angeles in 1964. In the conference publication that appeared two years later, Bright formulated seven dimensions of research for sociolinguistics: (1) the social identity of the speaker and (2) that of the hearer involved in the process of communication; (3) the social environment in which speech events take place; (4) the synchronic and diachronic analysis of social dialects; (5) the different social assessments by speakers of speech behaviour forms; (6) the degree of linguistic variation; and (7) the practical applications of sociolinguistic research (Bright 1966a, 12–14). However, 1964 marks not only the programmatic propagation of a new discipline but also the turning-point in empirical research. Labov's dissertation on the social stratification of English in New York City (1964, published 1966) proves for the first time a regular variation of linguistic variables with social parameters.

Thus, although its realization was characterized by varying academic interests and by a certain vagueness, it was in 1964 that a place was carved out for a new discipline which in subsequent years caused a boom in what became known as 'sociolinguistics' and 'sociology of language'. Before inquiring as to the reasons behind this boom, we shall briefly outline its further development.

In the last eight years the number of empirical, theoretical and practically-oriented works has grown to immense proportions. Grimshaw (1966), Hymes (1967a and b) and Fishman (1968a and b) are concerned with a programmatic discussion of, amongst other things, linguistic, anthropological and sociological contributions to sociolinguistics. Hymes makes a plea for an integrated field of research that goes beyond the discipline itself, whilst Fishman (1968b,

---

[1] We shall be dealing solely with the genesis of sociolinguistics in the USA, which is symptomatic in that similar tendencies may be expected in Europe.

introduction; 1971b) and Labov (1970a) aim to extend their traditional disciplines, the former through his interest in the sociology of language, the latter by linking linguistic analysis to social context. An insight is given into the factors stimulating the production of publications by mentions of 'personal communications' in Grimshaw (1971a), which identify the initiators of inquiries along these lines (admittedly brought about also by the research needs of American society); the 'personal communications' of Gumperz, Hymes, Labov and Lieberson which he quotes date from 1967 and 1968, i.e. the time when discussion was centred on the question of the discipline and its subject.

Of course, the programmatic phase came to an end as empirical investigations gradually made it possible to demarcate sociolinguistic research with more precision.

The inquiries into speech behaviour made by Deutsch, Hess and Shipman among others (cf. 2.2.3 and 2.4.2) were partially refuted by linguistic investigations conducted by the Center for Applied Linguistics (cf. Shuy, Wolfram and Riley 1967; Labov *et al.* 1968; Wolfram 1969). They had been sparked off by Bernstein's early work, which had been disseminated by the essays in Gumperz and Hymes 1964, another fact which shows that 1964 marks the beginning of sociolinguistics in the USA. These investigations have led to technologically-oriented recommendations for a continuous and systematic method of adapting speakers of linguistic minorities to the American standard (Baratz and Shuy 1969; Fasold and Shuy 1970a; cf. chapter 7 below). Similar analyses were carried out for bilingual speech minorities which made possible the development of integrated sociolinguistic techniques of description (cf. MacNamara 1967a and b; Lambert 1967; Fishman *et al.* 1968). These case studies provided, amongst other things, the basis for recommendations for bilingual education. They were preceded by a comprehensive sociological examination of the position of language minorities in the USA since the second world war, which resulted in a more precise assessment of their present size and their relation to the American standard (Fishman 1966). In recent years the amount of empirical work has greatly increased in several fields. Thus there are investigations into reading and speech (Levin and Williams 1970), analyses of the correlation between language and poverty (Williams 1970a), studies on the strategy of social communication (Gumperz and Hymes 1972) and inquiries into the Pidgin and Creole languages (Hymes 1971).

Every single sociolinguistic inquiry in the USA after 1964 has been financed by the Ministry for Health, Education and Welfare (Deutsch 1967; Shuy, Wolfram and Riley 1967; Labov *et al.* 1968; Fishman *et al.* 1968). The intention has been throughout that sociolinguistic research should enable the schools to integrate, by careful planning, the linguistic minorities into a monolingual American society (see amongst others Cazden, John and Hymes 1972), their Non-Standard language being a symbol both of their solidarity and of their disintegration. It has been official American policy to neutralize the system-resistant and potentially explosive character of these linguistic minorities by educational means directed at their deviant speech forms. For this purpose, empirical results and solid theories are necessary. We should bear in mind that the development of sociolinguistic theory in the USA has been motivated by concrete sociopolitical reasons. Although it is not until chapter 7 that we give a coherent account of the cycle from sociopolitical needs to sociolinguistic research and the development and application of theoretical concepts, we can say here that an account of these theories should anyhow be based on the premise that their development serves specific interests of the prevailing forces in a society. In the case of the USA these interests are concentrated in an attempt to avoid conflicts by apparent *conciliation* but not *elimination* of class contrasts.

In order to avoid any misinterpretation of what follows, however, it should be made clear that the demonstrable correlation between sociopolitical interests and the evolution of theoretical concepts should not be interpreted as implying that these concepts are *per se* unsuitable or unusable. We do not object here to theoretical or formal procedures which can find practical application in promoting emancipation, but only to their ideological premises (chiefly those of bourgeois sociology) and their abuse. We object to the fact that sociopolitical interests behind their evolution are obscured or kept out of the discussion, and are thus not subject to rational social control.

Bearing this correlation in mind we shall select two trends from the wealth of analyses, both of which are characteristic of the theoretical discussions in sociolinguistics in recent years:

1   regarding sociolinguistics as an interdisciplinary branch of research;
2   conceiving sociolinguistics as an extension of the traditional disciplines of sociology or linguistics.

The interdisciplinary conception stresses that a simple amalgamation of two disciplines (linguistics and sociology) cannot provide the explanations which an integrated treatment is capable of supplying. Hymes, who has repeatedly subscribed to an integrated theory of sociolinguistic description, formulates this as follows:

> 'It should be clear that a mechanical amalgamation of standard linguistics and standard sociology is not likely to suffice. . . . Adding a speechless sociology to a sociology-free linguistics can yield little better than post-hoc attempts at correlation between accounts from which the heart of the relevant data will be missing.' (Hymes 1967b, 640f.)

This can perhaps be interpreted, in agreement with Kanngiesser (1972b, 88f.), as meaning that an integrated theory should provide not only an explanation of correlated data, which would be biased to the linguistic or sociological side, but should also be able to treat *fresh* data resulting from the correlation.

> 'The only theoretical system that can be justifiably regarded as a component of a sociolinguistic theory (i.e. an explanatory system) is that which goes beyond the bounds of both sociology and linguistics, and which therefore is also able to provide an explanation for "fresh kinds of data" (Hymes) (those sets of data which are not dealt with in either of the disciplines concerned).' (Kanngiesser 1972b, 88f.)

The interdisciplinary concept contrasts with a more recent development, which distinguishes between a strict and a more general sociolinguistic interest.

Fishman describes the sociology of language as a comprehensive field of research which should integrate the most varied methods and most widely differing ways of investigating the social significance of language: linguistic studies, the 'ethnography of speaking' (Hymes 1962), correlative and functional linguistic investigations, analyses of bilingual and multilingual speech communities, questions of language planning, etc. In contrast with this, the tendency to evolve sociolinguistics as a counterpart to traditional linguistics is regarded by Fishman as a 'self-liquidating prophecy' (Fishman 1971b, 9): 'Sociolinguistics has been viewed . . . as a means of widening the contextual horizons of linguistics, beyond the phrase, beyond the sentence, beyond the utterance, to the speech act, the speech event and the speech occasion' (*ibid.*, 8). Once it has been accepted that speech descriptions should take account of the social context—a demand constantly made by sociolinguists—this extended notion of speech analysis will be termed 'real linguistics'. This 'real linguistics' will not have to be identified with a 'sociology of language' which can, if it wishes, dissociate itself from purely linguistic analysis and description. The 'self-liquidating prophecy' is that initially programmatic *socio*linguistics will increasingly give rise to a contextually and functionally oriented linguistics.

There are many authors who appear to confirm Fishman's assessment. Thus Labov writes (1970a):

'In what way, then, can "sociolinguistics" be considered as something apart from "linguistics"?

'One area of research which has been included in sociolinguistics is perhaps more accurately labelled "the sociology of language". It deals with large-scale social factors and their mutual interaction with languages and dialects. There are many open questions and many practical problems associated with the decay and assimilation of minority languages, the development of stable bilingualism, the standardization of languages and the planning of language development in newly-emerging nations. The linguistic input for such studies is primarily that a given person or group uses language *X* in a social context or domain *Y*. . . .

'There is another area of study sometimes included in "sociolinguistics" which is more concerned with the details of language in actual use—the field which Hymes has named "the ethnography of speaking" (1962). There is a great deal to be done in describing and analysing the patterns of use of languages and dialects within a specific culture: the forms of speech events, the rules for appropriate selection of speakers; the interrelations of speaker, addressee, audience, topic, channel and setting; and the ways in which the speakers draw upon the resources of their language to perform certain functions. This functional study is conceived as complementary to the study of linguistic structure. . . .

'If there were no need to contrast this work [sociolinguistic treatment of questions concerning phonology, morphology, syntax and semantics] with the study of language out of its social context, I would prefer to say that this was simply *linguistics*. It is therefore relevant to ask why there should be any need for a new approach to linguistics with a broader social base. It seems natural

that the basic data for any form of general linguistics would be
e as it is used by native speakers communicating with each other in
╰╴╴╴ ay life.'

'Self-liquidating prophecies' are also to be found in other authors. Whereas Kanngiesser, for example, still seeks initially to define the bounds of an interdisciplinary sociolinguistic theory (cf. above), he concludes:

> 'Linguistics . . . is . . . *ipso facto* also "sociolinguistics"; for, like all behaviour, linguistic behaviour takes place in a social context. . . . Accordingly, linguistics cannot have any special subdiscipline called "sociolinguistics", as the nature of linguistics is already sufficiently restricted by the term "communicative practice".' (Kanngiesser 1972c, 13)

The different conceptions of the scope of sociolinguistics clarify the procedure we shall follow: it will be assumed that there are *strict* and *more general* sociolinguistic problems and interests. As 'strict' we count those that aim to extend linguistics on the lines of a 'study of language in its social context' (Labov 1970a); the 'more general' questions are concerned with all conceivable investigations on the subject of 'Who is speaking to whom, in what speech variant, where, when, on what topics and with what intentions and social consequences?' (Fishman quoted in Kjolseth 1971, 18). It is evident that investigations in this 'more general' sense need an 'integrated, interdisciplinary approach on additional levels and involving a plurality of methods' (Kjolseth 1971, 21), of which (*socio-*)linguistic research can only form a part. It should be equally clear that every analysis of language in its social context, if it is to be related to the social sciences must in a certain sense go beyond the bounds of the discipline itself. The extent to which it does this will depend on the individual case (scope, aim of the investigation etc.).

In accordance with the distinction made here between the 'strict' and the 'more general' perspectives (which corresponds roughly to our distinction between micro- and macro-levels in 4.2), we shall discuss first of all the way in which sociolinguistic data can be associated with a linguistic theory.

5.2 Sociolinguistic data within a theory of grammar

Up till now, possibilities of sociolinguistic theory have been discussed only in linguistics, which is the most theory-conscious discipline of the social sciences. This has inevitably led to a certain restriction in its range of interest, which is concentrated on the problem of representing in *grammars* speakers' different speech behaviour. The problem of describing socially-conditioned speech variation has led to the two following questions in linguistics:

1   What linguistic data should be correlated with what extralinguistic data?
2   What theory, with what modifications, can provide an adequate description of speech variations and afford meaningful explanations?

Most answers to the above questions agree on one point: the transformational grammar model, first proposed by Chomsky (1957; 1965) and later extended, must be the starting point of all theoretical discussion. But this only establishes a certain platform with regard to fundamental conventions of description. The root of the problem is deeper, and concerns the presuppositions and assumptions which decide the answers to possible ways of linking sociolinguistic data to the transformational theory, and which also determine the degree to which these descriptive conventions must be modified. Such further problems can only be solved in cooperation with the social sciences; they can be formulated as follows:

3 What correlation is there between speech structure and social structure? Should one start from categories of social structure and relate speech data to this structure, or should speech variants that are classified according to internal linguistic criteria not be correlated with social parameters until after their linguistic classification?

4 To what extent do the speech behaviour data observed in normal speech reflect the verbal capabilities of speakers? Does a symmetrical relationship exist between speech and hearing—that is, do speech and hearing imply one and the same level of competence in speakers—or an asymmetrical one?

5 Is speech variation governed more or less by chance external incidents, or does it occur systematically? Do speakers have the competence to shift between various styles?

6 What is the primary object of describing speech variation: the *idiolect* (individually different speech behaviour; individual competence) or the *sociolect* (speech behaviour specific to social groups; group-specific competence)?

These questions give an idea of the range of problems involved in the theoretical perspectives, which are of course, as is customary in linguistics, manifested in proposals as to how linguistic data can be represented in grammars. Together with Labov (1969, 760), we can formulate five points which must be accounted for by rules of a grammar, which should themselves adequately describe linguistic variation:

'(i) What is the most general form of linguistic rule? That is, what notations, conventions, schemata and interpretations allow us to account for the productive and regular patterns of linguistic behavior?

(ii) What relations hold between rules in a system? . . .

(iii) How are systems of rules related? What is the range of possible differences between mutually intelligible dialects? How do languages, originally diverse, combine within a bilingual community?

(iv) How do systems of rules change and evolve? This historical question is of course closely related to the last point:

(v) How are rule systems acquired? How does the individual's system of rules change and develop as he acquires the norms of the speech community?'

The variable rules are *one* of the possible answers to the questions raised.

5.2.1 Variable rules

Labov developed the concept of the variable rule in order to describe the internal and socially-determined variation of linguistic data as they occur in concrete speech situations.

The first consistent descriptions of linguistic variation as constant, regulated heterogeneity are given in Labov *et al.* 1968 and Labov 1969. More recently, the theoretical and technical aspects of the concept of the variable rule have been developed further by Cedergren, D. Sankoff and G. Sankoff. At present, the variable rule counts as the most practicable descriptive instrument available for linguistic variation. For an adequate understanding of the formal aspects of variable rules, some elementary knowledge of probability theory is indispensable. Since a full exposé of probability theory would go far beyond the limits of this work, the reader is referred to some publications which contain all necessary information: Stegmüller 1973 (theoretical foundations of probability theory), Runyon and Haber 1973 (introduction to statistics), Kreyszig 1973 (extensive exposé of the foundations and methods of statistics), Smith 1973 (introduction to probabilistic performance models in language) and Klein 1974 (description of linguistic variation based on probability theory).

To begin with, the concept 'variable rule' is to be distinguished (Labov *et al.* 1968, I, 88–90) from two other types of rule which are used for the description of linguistic data. Three rule-types are given: categorical rules (type I), semi-categorical rules (type II) and variable rules (type III). A rule is assigned to one of these three types on grounds of speakers' social perception of linguistic rules.

Categorical rules. The majority of rules are of type I. They are difficult to define as they are never broken. They are 'invisible' to speakers. When speakers hear sentences which offend against their categorical speech form, they do not know how to explain 'what talking like that means.' Their reaction tends to be, 'you just can't say that in English.'

Semicategorical rules. Contraventions of rules of type II are perceived, interpreted and 'can be expressed'. Although they are not frequent (expressiveness, emotionality, literary emphasis, etc.), they are reckoned to fall under a language's potential range of expression. They occur frequently enough to attract attention and to be reported; the appropriate reply to such reports is: 'Really, did he talk like that? Is that what he said?'

Variable rules. Rules of type III cannot be broken by individual utterances. They are known to the analyst as a result of his investigation. They are only subconsciously perceived by hearers, and provide information about the speaker (sex, education, origin, etc.). Normally, speakers cannot make any direct pronouncements about these rules.

In the following we shall deal exclusively with rule-type III. If, as we should (Labov 1969, 728), we aim at a quantitative analysis of linguistic variation, we see the variable rule characteristically as a function of certain selected extralinguistic and intralinguistic parameters (see below). The notion of variable rules is meant to provide an argument against the idea that linguistic rules must necessarily be of a *categorical* nature. This concept is based on the conviction that language displays regular variation and that no communication would be possible without linguistic and stylistic shifts. 'We argue that it is the absence of style-shifting and multi-layered communication systems which would be dysfunctional' (Labov 1970a, quoted in Fishman 1971b, 166).

In broadening the concept of conventional generative rules through the addition of quantitative measure scales which specify the application of a rule in relation to linguistic environment and extralinguistic content, Labov seeks 'to connect theoretical questions with a large body of intersubjective evidence which can provide decisive answers to those questions' (1969, 757). Generative grammar can be blamed for its total concentration on the 'intuitionist' description of what are usually called 'idiolects' (the linguist as his own 'native speaker'), and its neglect of group-specific linguistic behaviour in correlation with social norms. The theory thus runs the risk of becoming too self-contained and losing contact with empirical reality. This reality is to be found in empirical speech material which can be observed through careful techniques of elicitation and a strict definition of the corpus under analysis. In introducing the notion of variable rule, Labov claims to be able to clear up controversial questions of empirical theory and description.

What form does a grammatical rule take that should describe variation of linguistic data? First of all it must be clear that Labov's variable rule is based on the model of generative transformational grammar as found in Chomsky 1965. In this model, every sentence of a language has at least one deep structure, which is transformed by successive stages into the surface structure. Some of these transformational rules are considered to be optional: they may or may not apply when the conditions for their applications are fulfilled.

Let us consider an example, without going into too much technical detail (we shall not, for example, discuss the question of the general justifiabilty of the distinction between obligatory and optional rules in a transformational grammar). In the sentence:

John *run runs* every day

(cf. Fraser 1973), there is obligatory number agreement, through a number agreement rule, in certain forms of English (*runs*), whereas other varieties of the language allow for either *run* or *runs* in these varieties the number agreement rule is optional. The application or non-application of this rule, in these varieties ('dialects') of English, is, however, not a matter of pure chance. On the contrary, it appears that the application, and the frequency of application, of a rule are to a very great extent a function of the linguistic context of the variable (number agreement) on the one hand, and the speech situation, as well as the regional and social origin of the speaker, on the other. Thus one will find that of two contexts, whenever the necessary conditions for the application of an optional rule (e.g. number agreement) are fulfilled, the rule in question tends to be applied in, say, 75 per cent of all cases in one context, but only in 10 per cent of all similar cases in the other. This implies that these tendencies to apply an optional rule should be incorporated into the formal notation of the rule, since it is part of the speaker-hearer's knowledge (competence) of his language that he 'knows' (implicitly, that is) what frequencies are appropriate in what contexts.

For each category of contexts a real number between 0 and 1 can be associated with each optional rule in the grammar. This number indicates the probability of application of the rule in this context. This probability is a well-defined function of the structural properties of the linguistic environment of a linguistic variable on the one hand, and extralinguistic parameters (e.g. age, social status of the speaker, speech situation) on the other.

In view, however, of the very considerable number of linguistic variables and of the contexts or situations involved, it seems unrealistic and practically impossible to associate probability values with each optional rule for each class of contexts. Labov, therefore, proposed to investigate only a very limited number of variables, both linguistic and extralinguistic, and to see what effect the value of each variable had on the frequency of application of a particular optional rule. This method was adopted in Labov's analysis of the contraction and deletion of the copula in Standard English and Non-Standard English (Labov 1969). The formal structure of variable rules developed and proposed there, and also presented in the German edition of the present book (1973, 168–76), has meanwhile been withdrawn by Labov because of various notational defects, and has been replaced by the notation of Cedergren and Sankoff (1974; cf. Labov 1972c, 93–101).

The type of rule developed by Labov specified, essentially, only the output frequency of rules in a given corpus and did not distinguish between theoretical probability and frequency of application. Whereas Labov formulated the probability value of each variable according to an 'additive model' as it is known in statistics, Cedergren and Sankoff (1974) adopted a 'multiplicative model'. Since both the additive model and the multiplicative model can be adopted for the description of linguistic variation (where both models have their advantages and disadvantages), both descriptive methods will be presented briefly below.[2]

It is, in any case, assumed that a structural description is given of the sentence which contains an optional rule that is more or less frequently applied according to the linguistic and extralinguistic context. This structural description will follow the principles of transformational grammar. We shall now sketch the additional formalism containing the quantitative specification of the linguistic and extralinguistic constraints on the application of an optional rule.

The notation of variable rules in terms of the additive model
Let p be the probability of application of a rule in a certain linguistic environment. Then:

$$p = p_0 + \alpha + \beta + , \ldots , + \omega \qquad\qquad 1$$

where p_0 represents the probability value resulting from the individual characteristics of the speaker in question (regional, social, contextual, stylistic etc.), and α, β,..., ω are quantitative values indicating the influence of single features in the linguistic environment of the variable. If these features are symbolized as A, B,..., Z, then p in:

$$p = p_0 + \alpha(A) + \beta(B) + , \ldots , + \omega(Z) \qquad\qquad 2$$

[2] The following account is based on Cedergren 1973a; Labov 1972c; Sankoff 1973; Cedergren and Sankoff 1974; Sankoff 1974.

is the probability of application of the rule as it results from the quantitative contributions of the parameters α, β,..... ω in relation to the features A, B,..., Z. The quantitative values symbolized as Greek characters are specified in the formula only when the corresponding linguistic features are present, irrespective of the presence or absence of other features.

As the statistical values indicating favourable or disfavourable factors for the application of a rule are to be real numbers between 0 and 1, the applicational probability of the rule is (artificially) considered to be given as 1 when the value resulting from the formula is greater than 1. When the resulting value is smaller than 0, the probability value is taken to be 0. (As regards this last point, it should be noted that this 'rounding-off' procedure is untenable from a point of view of probability theory. For an extensive discussion of the foundations of the variable rule in probability theory, see Klein 1974.)

In order to prevent the additive model from yielding probability values outside the interval 0–1, Labov postulated (1969, 740 f.; Labov *et al.* 1968, I, 84) the 'principle of geometric ordering', which was meant to help establishing the relative quantitative size of each feature. The principle implies that the coefficient β is half the coefficient α but double the coefficient γ. The principle of geometric ordering proved, however, to do insufficient justice to Labov's data. For examples of analyses of variation carried out in terms of the additive model, see Labov *et al.* 1968, I, and Labov 1969.

If the following conditions are imposed on variable rules:

1   they must predict rule frequencies in accordance with the observed data;
2   they must have a maximal range of application;
3   they must permit sensible and defensible statements about the linguistic competence of speaker-hearers;

then a formulation in terms of the multiplicative model seems to be more appropriate (see points 1 and 2 below).

The formulation of variable rules in terms of the multiplicative model
In the multiplicative model, as in the additive one, a quantitative value is associated with each feature in the linguistic environment that constrains the application of the rule in question. When these independent factors are multiplied, the product is the applicational probability of a certain rule in a certain environment. The advantages of the multiplicative model over the additive model are mainly the following:

1   It yields only value values between 0 and 1, whereas the additive model needs to be adapted to achieve this.
2   The multiplicative model provides better possibilities of interpretation in relation to the probabilistic component of the linguistic competence of speakers.

On the other hand, the multiplicative model is more complex in the sense that the probability of the non-application of a rule must be distinguished from that of its application: these respective values are calculated in different ways.

We shall first present the multiplicative model which specifies the probability of non-application of rules (the 'non-application probability model'). Let p stand for the application probability of a rule, then $1 - p$ is the probability that the rule is not applied. If, as in (2), $\alpha, \beta, \ldots, \omega$ stand for quantitative measures and $A, B, \ldots, Z$ stand for features of the linguistic context related to $\alpha, \beta, \ldots, \omega$ in that order, then the formula for the non-application of the rule is:

$$1 - p = (1 - p_o) \times (1 - \alpha(A)) \times (1 - \beta(B)) \times \ldots \times (1 - \omega(Z)) \qquad \textbf{3}$$

In this model the parameters $\alpha, \beta, \ldots, \omega$ take values between 0 and 1. The feature B, associated with the parameter β, can be interpreted in such a way that it *causes* the application of the rule with the probability β, irrespective of the presence or absence of other features. Formula 3 enables one to calculate the effect of any particular feature on the application of the rule. It is to be noted that the mutual independence of the features is an *assumption*, which is not always in agreement with the facts.

The multiplicative model for the probability of application of a rule (the 'application probability model') has the following structure:

$$p = p_o \times \alpha(A) \times \beta(B) \times \ldots \times \omega(Z) \qquad \textbf{4}$$

Instead of 'causation' of rule application, as in formula 3, it is more appropriate here to say that each feature makes its own contribution towards the application of the rule.

The structure of variable rules
The structure of variable rules (as they are used in Labov 1972b, Cedergren 1973b, and G. Sankoff 1973, amongst others) will be exemplified here for phonology. It should be understood, however, that the notion of variable rule is not limited to phonology, but has also been applied to syntax (see Sankoff 1973). The structure of variable rules is given in formula 5:

$$X \to \langle Y \rangle \Big/ \left\langle \begin{matrix} [\text{feat. A}] \\ [\text{feat. B}] \\ \vdots \end{matrix} \right\rangle \Big/ \underline{\quad} \left\langle \begin{matrix} [\text{feat. I}] \\ [\text{feat. J}] \\ \vdots \end{matrix} \right\rangle \left\langle \begin{matrix} [\text{feat. P}] \\ [\text{feat. Q}] \\ \vdots \end{matrix} \right\rangle [\text{feat. Z}] \qquad \textbf{5}$$

where X is replaced by Y in accordance with the quantitative weighting through variable constraints, and each pair of angled brackets contains a list of features (bundles of features or also subcategories) that can occupy a certain position in the structural description. In analogy to 'more' and 'less' relations ('$>$' and '$<$'), variable constraints are given between angled brackets, whereas the feature Z, which occurs only between square brackets, stands for an obligatory feature, which makes the application of the rule obligatory.[3]

For each position in the environment (preceding or following) characterized by angled brackets, precisely one of the features of the list must be present in the

---

[3] Labov (1972b, 98f.) discusses at some length the case that variable features of the linguistic environment can become categorical so that they require obligatory application of the rule. He also shows there the computing steps necessary to change a variable feature into an obligatory one.

input string. The features of these lists are thus mutually exclusive: each feature exhausts the possibilities for each position given.

Probability values are associated with the variable constraints enclosed in angled brackets. These values are not given directly in the rule, but are added in a separate table, which also contains the input probability p_o, whose value is determined jointly by linguistic factors and such factors as social class, contextual style, sex, ethnic group etc. As a function of such sociolinguistic factors, this parameter indicates, in the multiplicative model (formula 3), the probability with which the rule will be applied in the least favourable environment (so that often $p_o = 0$). In the multiplicative model (formula 4), p_o is the probability of application in the most favourable environment.

Example of model 3

In order to illustrate how formula 3 can be used for the description of linguistic data involving systematic variation, we shall now present some data for the contraction of the English copula as they were elicited by Labov in interviews with Black and White speakers (see Labov *et al.* 1968; Labov 1972b; and 6.2.6 below). The analysis deals with utterances produced by Black youths and containing contracted forms of the copula in cases where White speakers do not use such forms. Examples are given in Labov 1969 and Labov *et al.* 1968.

What steps are to be taken to account for the variation of the data in the form of a rule? It must first be established in what linguistic environments the copula is contracted and in what environments it is not. Any element of the linguistic environment that can be shown to have an effect on the application or non-application of the contraction rule will have to be listed as a feature. These effects are called 'variable constraints'. The calculation of the probability coefficient of each variable constraint of the rule is based on the frequency with which the rule was applied in relation to the total number of observed cases where the rule was applicable. The so-called 'maximum likelihood method' is used to compute the probability values. This method yields those coefficient values that maximize the probability of production of the observed data in terms of the model given (for this method see Kreyszig 1973, 177–81).

This method also makes it possible to validate the hypothesis that the single variable constraints function independently of each other, in that the predicted frequencies of rule application can be computed and then compared with the actually observed distribution of data. How well the model accounts for the data can then be established by means of a χ^2-test.

Figure 5.1, which summarizes the data of copula contraction collected by Labov (1969, 748), gives the frequencies of the non-contracted copula in relation to the total number of cases according to the influence exerted by certain features of the preceding and following environments.

The variable rule that is affected by the constraints appearing from these data can be formulated as follows:

$$\begin{bmatrix} +\text{voc} \\ -\text{str} \\ +\text{cen} \end{bmatrix} \rightarrow \langle\emptyset\rangle \Big/ \begin{matrix} \langle\text{Pro}\rangle \\ \langle[-\text{cons}]\rangle \end{matrix} \ \#\ \#\ \underline{}_{[+\text{T}]} C_0^1 \ \#\ \#\ \left\langle \begin{matrix} \text{Vb} \\ \text{gn} \\ \text{NP} \\ \text{PA-Loc} \end{matrix} \right\rangle \quad 6$$

Preceding environments	Following environments			
	——NP	——PA-Loc	——Vb	——gn
Pro—— [−cons]	2/32	1/65	1/32	0/23
other NP—— [+cons]	22/35	24/32	5/14	1/9
[−cons]	13/64	7/23	2/14	0/6

Fig. 5.1. Frequencies of non-contracted copula forms in certain preceding and following environments.
(Source: Labov 1969, 748. Cf. also Cedergren and Sankoff 1974.)

Formula 6 states that the contraction of the copula after a pronoun and before *NP* (noun phrase), *Vb* (verb). *PA-Loc* (adjective, adjunct of place) and *gn* (*gonna*, future) is virtually obligatory when the pronoun does not end in a consonant. After an *NP* ending in a consonant and before the same set of environments as above, however, the rule is applied variably, with differing frequencies.

The probability of contraction in an environment:

$$A \quad \# \quad \# \quad \underset{[+T]}{\underline{\quad\quad}} \quad C_0^1 \quad \# \quad \# \quad B$$

is computed according to formula 3:

$$1 - p = (1 - p_o) \times (1 - \alpha(A)) \times (1 - \beta(A)) \times (1 - \gamma(B))$$

where p_o is the input probability resulting from linguistic and extralinguistic factors and common to all environments, and where the coefficient α depends on whether A is a pronoun or not, the coefficient β on whether the last segment in A is or is not [-cons], and the coefficient γ depends on the nature of the grammatical constituent in B.

The maximum likelihood method, used by Cedergren and Sankoff (1974), now yields the following values:

$$p_0 = 0{\cdot}25$$

$\alpha(\text{Pro}) = 0{\cdot}86;$ $\alpha(-\text{Pro}) = 0$
$\beta([+\text{cons}]) = 0;$ $\beta([-\text{cons}]) = 0{\cdot}65$
$\gamma(\text{——NP}) = 0{\cdot}16;$ $\gamma(\text{——PA-Loc}) = 0;$ $\gamma(\text{——Vb}) = 0{\cdot}49;$
$\gamma(\text{——gn}) = 0{\cdot}89$

These estimates predict, instead of the values given in figure 5.1, the following realizations:

Preceding environments	Following environments			
	——NP	——PA-Loc	——Vb	——gn
Pro—— [–cons]	1/32	2·3/65	0·1/32	0·1/23
other NP—— [+cons]	21·9/35	24/32	5·3/14	0·8/9
[–cons]	14/64	6/23	1·9/14	0·2/6

Fig. 5.2. Frequency predictions of the non-contracted copula after estimates of the parameters p_o, α, β, and γ.

It thus appears that there is a good correlation between the frequencies of the observed data and those predicted and computed in terms of the model. This correlation stands in support of the multiplicative model.

The status of variable rules in the theory of grammar
What is the status of variable rules in the theory of grammar? According to Labov (1969, 759) they are 'part of the speaker's knowledge'. They do not describe idiolects ('the construction of complete grammars for "idiolects" ... is a fruitless ... task'), but sociolects or dialects, in any case group-specific linguistic behaviour. They are neither mere statistic statements nor in any way approximations to an 'ideal' grammar: rather, they represent a *set of quantitative relations that constitute for themselves the form of the grammar*. While discussing the question of whether the variable rules belong to the realm of competence or to that of performance, Labov writes:

'I am not sure whether this is a useful distinction [competence v. performance] in the long run. There seem to be some limitations of speakers which have to do with memory span, or difficulties in articulation, which are outside the linguistic system proper. Surely no one would use the notion of performance as a waste-basket category, in which all convenient data on variation and change can be deposited; we have any number of labels such as "free variation" or "dialect mixture", which are readily available for this purpose. Are the variable constraints ... limitations on performance rather than competence? ... The variable rules themselves require at so many points the recognition of grammatical categories, of distinctions between grammatical boundaries, and are so closely interwoven with basic categorical rules, that it is hard to see what would be gained by extracting a grain of performance from this complex system.' (Labov 1969, 759)

The variable rules, therefore, describe capabilities of speakers, which are anyway inadequately represented in the simplifying dichotomy 'competence-performance'. Their application (as we shall see in chapter 6) ranges over the whole of grammar, including phonology.

The concept of the variable rule has been criticized from various quarters. According to Wunderlich, this concept shows

> 'that in grammar nothing alters; there is, rather a secondary grammar application model in the background which is reduced to mere frequency counts; in these it remains obscure whether they are actually meant as statistical figures, or whether the applicability or non-applicability of the rule could still be determined by additional conditions.' (Wunderlich 1971b, 319)

Decamp (1969, 1971a) and Bickerton (1971), however, have criticized the variable rule from a more orthodox transformational point of view (Chomsky 1965). The arguments can be summarized in the following way:

1   The variable rule destroys the fundamental distinction between competence and performance. But as this distinction has achieved so much for linguistics, variable rules would bring 'drastic and undesirable changes in current theories' in their wake (Bickerton 1971, 460).
     According to Decamp (1971a, 35), 'frequency analyses' belong to the 'world of inductive theories' and thus to a 'theory of linguistic performance'.
2   Since there is no adequate sociological theory, and since, moreover, sociological categories are, in contrast to the binary and discrete linguistic data, more likely to be nondiscrete, there is no reason why sociological categories should be treated as 'discrete', whereby the originally binary linguistic oppositions should be turned into 'continuous features' (Decamp 1971a, 37–9; cf. 5.2.4 below).
3   If, in addition to categorical rules, there should also be variable rules, then a speaker must not only have the ability to acquire these two different rule types, but must also have some kind of 'recognition device' which will tell him whether to interpret a particular set of linguistic data as 'rule-plus-exceptions' or as 'areas-of-variability' (Bickerton 1971, 460).
4   Labov's variable rules are related to *groups* of speakers and not to individuals; if they were to appertain to speakers' competence, the latter would have to check constantly whether they were using the frequencies laid down for particular environments, and whether they were doing so in conformity with those defined for groups. In the end this would lead to the absurd conclusion that they would have to continue to check their speech even in the absence of all other group members (Bickerton 1971, 460f.).

To some extent this criticism becomes superfluous as a result of Labov's and Cedergren and Sankoff's (1974) specification of the status of variable rules. Labov writes: 'There is no question but that variable rules are rules of production. . . . They involve a fundamental asymmetry between production and perception' (Labov 1970a, 59).

The assumption of the asymmetry between production and perception of utterances is based on various empirical results. Labov *et al.* (1968, I, 310–34; 1970b, 23f.) demonstrate that in sentence-repetition tests Black boys repeated Standard sentences, which had been spoken to them, with the phonological and grammatical peculiarities of the Non-Standard. They were able to perceive both Standard and Non-Standard, but to produce only Non-Standard. The same results were reported by Shuy, Baratz and Wolfram (1969) and Troike (1970).

Cedergren and Sankoff (1974), moreover, introduced the multiplicative probability model mainly in order to justify Chomsky's distinction between competence and performance also for the probabilistic analysis of speech occurrences:

> 'The power of this approach lies in the uniquely well-defined and economical relationship it posits between competence and linguistic performance, analogous to that between a probability distribution and a sample, or between a model and a simulation. This relationship . . . integrates generative and behavioral aspects in an elegant way. . . . We distinguish rule probabilities from rule frequencies, assigning the former to competence and the latter to performance.' (Cedergren and Sankoff 1974, 353).

It should also be pointed out that Bickerton supports his objections with arguments from a mentalist-transformationalist tradition: he prefers the analysis of idiolects to the investigation of sociolects (speech behaviour of groups). Yet it does seem that sociolects are more appropriate as objects of variation analysis than idiolects. Later we shall come back repeatedly to the fundamental discussion centring on the nature and form of sociolinguistic rules.

5.2.2 Contingency grammar

Houston (1969; cf. the 20 phonological rules for Non-Standard, 605f.) bases her proposal for a *contingency grammar* (1970) on empirical investigations into the speech behaviour of Negroes in Florida. It is divided into three parts: competence (*C*), systematic performance (*SP*) and actualized performance (*AP*) (Houston 1970, 10f.).

Houston does not question the symmetry between production and perception, but she does subdivide the performance level into two types of description: the *SP* should embrace stylistic variation ('register'), as well as regional and social varieties. According to Houston (1970, 10), speakers who shift between styles and varieties share a common basic competence. Any marked differences that may still exist in their speech behaviour (Standard v. Non-Standard) cannot be ascribed to differences in competence, nor can they be disposed of as chance phenomena in performance. As systematic variations they belong to the sphere of *SP* and affect its description levels (phonology, syntax, semantics) to different extents.

The model of contingency grammar provides for categorical and variable rules. Whereas the former appertain to the sphere of *C*, the latter can only appear on the level of *SP* and *AP*. Description by contingency grammar is effected on all three grammar levels: *C* and *SP* have a phonological, syntactic and (probably also) semantic component (Houston 1970, 11). The output of one grammar level is the input for the following one. In contrast to this, the *AP* is 'neither a set of rules nor a set of sentences. It is actual sound realization, which completes well-formed

'The lion he was UH he was trai—he was tame'

I   COMPETENCE

1   Tree:

2   Surface structure:

$$\left[_S \left[_{NP} \left[_{Art}{}^{\#\,the\,\#}\right] {}_{Art} \left[_N{}^{\#\,lion\,\#}\right]_N\right]_{NP} \left[_{VP} \left[_V{}^{\#\,be\,\#}\right] \left[{}^{\#\,Past\,\#}\right]\right]_V\right.$$

$$\left.\left[_{Adj}{}^{\#\,trained\,\#}\right]_{Adj}\right]_{VP}\right]_S$$

3   Phonetics: ðělàyĕn-wêztrĕynd

II   SYSTEMATIC PERFORMANCE

1   SD: Art # $\begin{bmatrix} + \text{N} \\ + \text{animate} \\ + \text{masc} \\ - \text{fem} \end{bmatrix}$ #V

          1   2   3

   SC:

       2 →[2] # $\begin{bmatrix} + \text{Pro} \\ + \text{animate} \\ + \text{masc} \\ - \text{fem} \end{bmatrix}$

2   (Phonology)

3   Phonetics: ðěla: -hîywěztrě́

III   FROM SYSTEMATIC PERFORMANCE TO ACTUALIZED PERFORMANCE

1 $[_* W_1 \# W_2]_* \# W_3 \rightarrow [_* W_1 \# W_2]_* \text{ pause} \# W_4$[3]

where $\#$ = word boundary (insignificant boundaries were omitted here), and $[_*\ ]_*$ includes units that belong to the same phonological phrase.

Specific output: $\# he \# was \# pause \# trained \#$

2 $(C_0\ V_0)\ C_1\ VC_0 \rightarrow (C_0\ V_0)\ C_1\ V\ (C_0) \# pause \#$

Specific output: $\# he \# was \# trai \# pause \#$

3   SD: $W_1 \# W_2 \# W_3{}^* \# pause\ (\# W_4 \#)$

SC: pause $\rightarrow ((UH)\alpha\ (\ (W_1 \#)\ W_2)\ )\beta$

Condition: either α or β or both.

SC: $W_3{}^* \rightarrow \begin{Bmatrix} W_3 \\ W_4{}^1 \end{Bmatrix}$

Output: $\# trai \# he \# was \# tame \#$

4   Phonetic end form of the actualized performance:

$$\text{ðə̆là: -hîywə̆z-}\check{\gamma}\text{-hìywə̆z-trĕ́-hìywə̆z-tĕ́:}$$

Note: W_K is defined as $\begin{bmatrix} + \text{ word} \\ \Sigma pK \\ \Sigma sK \end{bmatrix}$

and $W_{K'}$ is defined as $\begin{bmatrix} + \text{ word} \\ \Sigma pK' \neq \Sigma pK \\ \Sigma sK' \simeq \Sigma sK \end{bmatrix}$

W^* is an interrupted word output from rule III-2 above.

Key: $\#$ approximately denotes a word boundary
       — phonological phrase boundary
    SD structural description
    SC structural change

Fig. 5.3 Origin of an utterance: synthesis of a sentence.
(Source: Houston 1970)

sentences with hesitation pauses, repetitions, ungrammatical sequences, anacolutha etc.' (Houston 1970).

As opposed to this level, which describes speakers' errors and the like, the *SP* describes differences in style, dialect and idiolect; it is also here that the variable rules developed by Labov find their application.

The rules on the three levels of grammar can be assigned so-called *contingency indices* P_0, P_1 and P_2. The index P_0 means that a rule is categorical on all three levels of grammar; P_1 signifies that it is invariant only in the sphere of *SP*, whilst P_2 denotes rules that are applied on the levels of *SP* and *AP* with less probability than 1 (variable rule).

Houston demonstrates the ability of contingency grammar to achieve integrated linguistic description (synthesis) by the example of phonological rules of BEV in Florida (loss of nasals, 'cluster simplification', loss of liquids), and also by that of a short utterance containing a speech error (hesitation); the description is given in all its details from *C* via *SP* to *AP*. The synthesis of this utterance is given in figure 5.3.

Houston emphasizes that the conception of contingency grammar is still very tentative; nevertheless she believes that with this model she has bridged the gap between competence and performance.

The term 'contingency grammar' is not explicitly introduced in the essay, nor is it explained. We can interpret it as a system which contains side by side categorical rules, variable rules, and so-called 'editing rules' (to recast incomplete sentences into well-formed ones).

Butters (1972) has criticized this form of contingency grammar. First, he rejects present notations of the variable rule, which in his view violate three principles of transformational grammar:

1   Linguistic rules represent linguistic knowledge, not linguistic data.
2   A grammar is the theory of the linguistic knowledge of an idealized individual, not of a group.
3   The relationship between linguistic knowledge (competence) and its application (performance) is far too complex to be expressed in variable rules (Butters 1972, 29).

Yet, compared with Labov's concept of variable rules, Houston's approach still has, in Butter's view, the advantage that it assigns these rules to performance: 'the attempt at analysing variable rules as performance rules represents a significant advance over most previous theories, which in general have treated them purely as rules of grammar' (Butters 1972, 30). Nevertheless Butters formulates three points which make contingency grammar appear unrealistic as a model of linguistic competence and performance:

1   Attaching variable rules to the *SP* is not much more meaningful than assigning them to competence. In any case they represent data and not linguistic ability. There is no reason why frequency indices should appear in a performance model.
2   What is even more suspect is that the dichotomous performance model disregards the neutrality of grammar as between speaker and hearer, as

demanded by Chomsky, in that it represents a set of rules which produce *deviant* utterances on the basis of *well-formed* sentences generated by the grammar.

3   The most significant aspect, however, is that of regarding linguistic variation as associated with performance. On the contrary, the capacity for speech variation is often part of the speaker's competence. For, if Houston asserts that 'linguistic competence is identical for all speakers of a language', this would lead to the astonishing declaration that languages do not change (Butters 1972, 30).

Butters reaches the conclusion that speakers of different speech varieties have different forms of competence. As groups always consist of individual speakers 'who have internalized different analyses of the details of their language' (31), *idiolects* are the objects of analysis of speech variation.

5.2.3   Coexistent grammars

Loflin (1969: 1970) and Kanngiesser (1972a and b) propose that the construction of a theory of speech variation is only meaningful in the frame of the competence theory developed by Chomsky; yet they also stress that it can only succeed when his postulate of the homogeneity of the language community is abandoned in favour of an assumption of heterogeneity. Whereas Kanngiesser seeks a means of describing linguistic change, Loflin is concerned with dialects and Non-Standard Negro English (or BEV) in particular.

According to Loflin, regional varieties of a language can be described by coexistent grammars:

'Two or more language varieties V_1, V_2, V_3,..., V_n are *dialects* of the set L_1 if and only if the categorical subcomponents of the bases of the grammars postulated for V_1, V_2, V_3,..., V_n are identical. Identity of categorical subcomponents is necessary to define the membership of language varieties, V_1, V_2, V_3,..., V_n in the set L_1: language varieties which have identical categorical subcomponents also, of necessity, have identical deep structures.' (Loflin 1970, 27).

Loflin adduces the example of the auxiliary verb 'be' in BEV to show that the realization of 'be', which is deviant from Standard English and varies with the syntactic environments, can be described not by 'low-level rules' (phonological rules of the surface structure: cf. Labov 1969), but only by 'high-level rules' (differences in the deep structure). Differences between linguistic varieties can only be described in the surface structure if both varieties exhibit similar symbol sets in the deep structure. For any linguistic variety, only that set of symbols in the deep structure which generates all its sentences as economically as possible can be considered adequate. Loflin sees a chance of testing empirically 'whether or not two or more utterances are the same or different at some explicit structural level' in the 'grammatical taxonomy' of a 'transformation test' (Loflin 1969, 78), which was employed for the first time by Chomsky, and further developed by Lakoff. The form taken by a *transformation test* is, for example, to apply a nominalization transformation to two sentences, (1) *John is easy to please* and (2) *John is eager to please*, which look as though they might have the same deep structure; the application of the nominalization transformation to (1) and (2) reveals that the two sentences differ in their deep structure.

Loflin carries out similar transformation tests on a series of utterances with the copula 'be' in SE and BEV. Finally, he postulates a grammar of the copula in BEV, consisting of four rules, where the deep structure differs in number and type of symbols from that of the auxiliary verb in SE. It demonstrates that the copula can only be adequately described by 'high-level rules'.

Loflin summarizes thus:

'In order to test the hypothesis that any two language varieties have the same deep structure it is obvious that we must construct grammars of the two language varieties which are the objects of the test. In the process of constructing grammars about which there is a question of deep structure identity, we must justify each relational entity in the categorial sub-component of each grammar. In other words, we must move away from the non-empirical approach wherein there is an *a priori* assumption of deep structure identity between two language varieties.' (Loflin 1970, 26)

Kanngiesser (1972a and b) has taken Loflin's deliberations a stage further, by attempting to formulate both the formal aspects and the actual contents of the requirements for constructing a linguistic theory which will account for linguistic variation and change. Here we can give only an informal and inadequate outline of some of these conditions:

1   The language community consists of a set 'of a finite number of disjunctive speaker-hearer groups'. The scope of a competence theory embraces (a) 'the different forms . . . of linguistic knowledge possessed by a finite number of internally homogeneous groups . . . of speaker-hearers' in a language community and (b) 'the processes of grammatical interaction' between these groups. Disjunctive generative grammars are then constructed for the sets of data obtained from these speaker-hearer groups on the lines laid down by Loflin. They are meant to describe a system of coexistent and group-specific forms of linguistic knowledge, which can be termed a 'coexistence model' (Kanngiesser 1972b, 98–101).

2   The coexistence model makes for integration of the synchronic and diachronic approaches by ascribing to the groups of speaker-hearers a competence that is *capable of innovation*. In this sense it can be said that there are different 'levels of grammaticality'. This is connected with a 'relative concept of grammaticality' which accounts for the fact 'that in certain communication situations the speaker-hearers . . . can be confronted with sentences' which are for them to a certain degree semigrammatical (i.e. do not correspond completely to their linguistic knowledge), but which are 'unquestionably sentences of the language spoken by them'.

The formulation of a condition of semigrammaticality is linked to the 'principle of *grammatical tolerance*', which explains 'why it is possible for groups with different forms of competence to be able to coexist at all in a language community. The tolerance principle is based on the assertion that in verbal interaction

speaker-hearers 'exercise grammatical tolerance without reflecting on it or being conscious of it' (cf. Kanngiesser 1972b, 101ff.).
3   Speaker-hearers have the ability to make innovations to their grammars. Innovation processes can be rendered in a coexistence model by 'extension rules'. In so doing, 'two essentially different types of innovation should be kept distinct from one another': (a) the conservative and (b) the non-conservative innovation. In (a), only a 're-ordering' of the varieties of linguistic knowledge takes place amongst the groups; that is, the speaker-hearers assimilate reciprocally linguistic knowledge from one another. In (b), new linguistic developments are brought about which collectively change the different varieties that make up the language of the language community (103ff.).

The assumption of heterogeneity is the basis of Kanngiesser's reflections on a new competence theory, which would have to take account of social parameters. It also leads him to outline the conditions for a sociolinguistic theory. As we have already shown in 1.2.2, he poses the precondition that concepts of one system (linguistics) are formulated independently of those of the other system (sociology). Correlations between elements of the two systems are only meaningful when this condition is fulfilled.

This precondition, however, necessitates the construction of a theory which will go beyond the bounds of both linguistics and sociology, so as to be able to explain those data which cannot be explained in either of the two disciplines (Kanngiesser 1972b, 88).

We shall make two observations on the conception of coexistent grammatical systems. The first concerns the meaning of the term 'methodology' in linguistics, and the second the term 'system'.

Loflin (1970, 26) justifies his plea for the construction of coexistent grammars by urging that 'we must move away from the *non-empirical* approach' [italics mine]. 'Empirical' means here: making deductions according to the principles of generative transformational theory; 'evidence' exists for Loflin when test principles that have been determined *a priori* yield conclusive results relatively independently of the existing 'empirical' reality. It should be pointed out here that in adducing only *one* BEV subject to support his arguments (cf. Loflin 1969, 14 n. 1), Loflin is employing the purely intuitionistic principle of transformational grammar.

There is, however, also a broader concept of empirical method in linguistics which differs from that of Loflin. By 'empirical method' Labov understands a theory-oriented description, which relates to data that has, from an experimental and sociological point of view, been reliably obtained. Thus his primary concern is 'urging people to drop speculation and to base their theories upon *empirical* studies' (personal communication). 'Evidence' exists for Labov when theoretical problems can be resolved by the description of valid sets of data (cf. 6.1.1).

There is an urgent need for deeper and more systematic investigations into the problems raised by the concept of empirical method in linguistics. It is, after all, still unclear (and to explain this is a considerable task for linguistics) where grammars should end. Loflin does not discuss this question at all.

The concept of 'system' is a second element which needs to be considered in linguistics. Models of ordered heterogeneity can be conceived on the lines of cooccurrent or covariant systems. The latter assumption has led Labov (1971b) to devote some space to a discussion of the term 'system', which in linguistics has often been understood as a set of elements so tightly organized that the position of one element cannot be altered without altering the positions of them all. Structure (configurations of elements and categories) and system (principles specifying possible structures) are identified with homogeneity. This concept of system can be questioned, however, in the light of facts of Pidgin and Creole languages:

1   Pidgin languages display a fluctuating and unsystematic character, which makes it difficult to present them as a system in the sense described above.
2   In their historical sources, Creole languages reveal overlaps in their central sub-systems; these show that no component of their linguistic structure is immune to hybridization and external influences.
3   The complex 'continuum' in post-Creole language communities leads to difficult questions as to whether one can speak of a variable system or whether there are various coexistent systems.

It is true that speech variants in the sense of coexistent grammars can be assigned to various separate systems, yet such an analysis cannot solve questions concerning the interaction of systems. A corpus of natural speech would be needed, in which actual linguistically-mixed sequences occur, to achieve a separation of the systems and make it possible to explain according to which rules and under which conditions and constraints speakers shift from one style to another.

The central factor in the study of languages in contact, which calls into question the traditional monolithic concept of system, is that of *variation* (a factor which is of course equally active in monolingual communities). We can only hope to reduce our ignorance (expressed by such labels for linguistic variation as 'free variation', 'social or expressive variants', or 'variphone') if we are prepared and able to come to terms with a notion of linguistic competence which involves *inherent variability*. Variation cannot be understood as strict cooccurrence, but should be taken to correspond more closely to the notion of covariation, i.e., an irreducible and regular variation within one comprehensive system. Many traditional problems can be seen in a new light as a result of Gumperz's assumption of a single verbal repertoire forming the total competence of a bilingual speaker, in which variation occurs as alternation between varieties. This, according to Labov (1971b, 461–70), quashes the concept of coexistent systems. Yet it has to be admitted that, at the moment, no empirically and theoretically satisfactory answer seems available to the question of the precise formal properties and the internal structure of a comprehensive, internally pluriform system of linguistic competence.

If two subsystems are given (for what follows, cf. Labov's comments on Gumperz in Kelly 1969, 250–55):

$$A_1 \updownarrow A_2 \qquad\qquad B_1 \updownarrow B_2 \qquad\qquad C_1 \updownarrow C_2$$

then formulating strict cooccurrence relations—implying that only forms such as A_1, B_1, C_1, or A_2, B_2, C_2 ever occur, and never for example A_1, B_2, C_1—would not be an adequate way of representing Gumperz's notion of *one* single repertoire: it has been revealed in various inquiries that many (bilingual or bidialectal) code-shifting situations do not have this categorical character. The systematic interrelation of A_1, B_1, C_1 is produced rather by the uniform direction of the code shifting under identical conditions, by its relation to the same independent variables and by the possibility of its description in terms of the same quantitative functions.

It is easy to show that many systematic generalizations of change do not correspond to pure processes that actually take place at a stroke. Demanding an all-or-nothing alternation between the systems of a bilingual or bidialectal situation, otherwise considering only non-structured systems, is merely the result of an over-restricted theoretical model. The systematic character of the two poles A_1, B_1, C_1 and A_2, B_2, C_2 can be established if it is demonstrated in what ways the variables A, B and C covary. Such a concept can serve as the starting point for studies concerned with long-term interaction of languages in contact.

5.2.4 Implicational analysis

Decamp (1969; 1970; 1971a and c) proposes an *implicational scale* as an extension to generative transformational grammar; this does not, however, cause any radical modifications, but only requires the technical inclusion of a supplementary apparatus. Before describing this analytical instrument in more detail, we shall list some basic definitions of grammar and code shifting from Decamp (1969). The assumption underlying these definitions is that the form of grammar proposed by Chomsky (1965) should be retained as far as possible; it need only be supplemented by a number of discrete configurations which are describable by simple mathematical functions and represent the infinite number of interidiolectal linguistic shiftings between speakers.

Definitions

1   An *idiolect* is an infinite set of sentences which are all generated by an idiolectal grammar.
2   An *idiolectal grammar* is a specific finite set of rules of an individual speaker-hearer's linguistic competence.
3   A *language* is an intersecting set of idiolects which are all generated by a grammar.
4   A *grammar* is an individual finite set of rules which represents the idealized competence of a language community. From this it follows that a grammar has to generate:
    a   all idiolects of this language and only these, and
    b   all interidiolectal code shiftings (*ICS*) within the idealized competence of a language community, and only these.
5   Both an idiolectal grammar and a grammar possess *strong* and *weak* *generative capacity*.

a   Weak generative capacity requires of an *idiolectal* grammar that it should generate all sentences of an idiolect, and only these.

b   Weak generative capacity requires of a *grammar* two different things: (i) to generate the infinite set of grammatical strings, which represent the idiolects of the grammar, and only these; (ii) to produce the infinite set of ICS's in the language community, and only these.

c   Strong generative capacity requires of the *idiolectal* grammar that it should aim at giving an adequate account of the speaker's mental structures associated with every grammatical string of an idiolect.

d   Strong generative capacity imposes two requirements on a grammar: (i) to give as adequate an account as can be achieved of the (idealized) mental structures associated with every grammatical string of each idiolect of the language; and (ii) to yield a maximally faithful picture of the (idealized) mental structures underlying every ICS in the language. For this the psychological, ethnological and socioeconomic covariables, in particular, of each ICS should be specified. (Decamp 1969, 18)

In other words, a speaker, through his competence, has control over not only an unlimited number of sentences, but over innumerable variants of these sentences, which correspond to his social experience. The styles specific to situations and roles of which a speaker must have a command are too numerous for them not to be governed by some form of competence: every speaker acquires a *sociolinguistic competence*, which it is necessary to describe and explain (Decamp 1971a, 30).

How can a grammar take account of sociolinguistic competence? Decamp sets up abstract units in the grammar to correspond to style shiftings; these units are represented in deep structure and control the conveyance of syntactic and semantic features to the surface structure. A rule of the form $[+M_1] \rightarrow [\pm M_2]$ is made to mark a segment of the deep structure as $[+M_2]$ or $[-M_2]$. All further rules can be produced or blocked by these two features (Decamp 1971a, 31). All derivations, transformations and lexical selections, as well as the phonological, syntactic and semantic rules can be controlled by such a feature. Theoretically, it is thought possible for a speaker to effect an unlimited number of shifts between styles and linguistic varieties; in practice, however, every one of these shifts is connected with the control of numerous linguistic variants, and this control is exercised unconsciously. The exertion of this control is only thought possible because of the *hierarchical* ordering of style features, which is formally governed by the 'redundancy rules'; they specify, for example, 'that any segment marked $[+\text{pompous}]$ would also be $[+\text{formal}]$ and $[-\text{casual}]$. In other words, the speaker directly controls some of the control features and the rest are filled in without the necessity of conscious decision' (Decamp 1971a, 32).

In order to give a formal illustration of this mechanism it is necessary to have a pattern of features from which one can see how features control other features that are hierarchically subordinated.

Precisely this is achieved by the *implicational scale*, which was introduced by Guttman (1944: see commentary in the appendix) under the name of 'scalogram analysis', and employed by Decamp (1971a) independently of the earlier work by Guttman.

> 'An implicational analysis is a binary relation between linguistic features and language varieties (dialects, styles etc.) so selected and so arrayed in order, as to result in a triangular matrix.' (1971a, 33)

This principle of implicational analysis is made clear in the following diagram:

Features

M_1	M_2	M_3	M_4	M_5		
1	1	1	1	1	V_1	
1	1	1	1	0	V_2	
1	1	1	0	0	V_3	*Varieties*
1	1	0	0	0	V_4	
1	0	0	0	0	V_5	
0	0	0	0	0	V_6	

Fig. 5.4 The principle of implicational analysis.

If the value of any desired point of intersection of the matrix, the product of $M \times V$, is 1, then this implies that any value *above* or to the *left* of this value is also 1. A value of 0 implies that every value *below* or to the *right* of it is likewise 0.

> 'Such a triangular matrix obviously does not accommodate just any random set of features. Every pair of features implies an empty cell, i.e. for any pair of features M_i, M_j $(i > j)$, only three of the four possible combinations occur.' (33)

Thus for every pair of features there are, as figure 5.5 shows, only three combinations, i.e. one field remains blank:

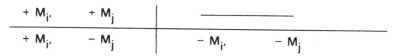

$+ M_{i'}$	$+ M_j$		
$+ M_{i'}$	$- M_j$	$- M_{i'}$	$- M_j$

Fig. 5.5 Combinations of a pair of features with a blank field.

The combination $- M_i, + M_j$ does not occur, as $- M_i$ implies a $- M_j$. The same pattern with the same value combinations (likewise with a blank field) can be drawn up for the values V_i and V_j.

Implicational scales approach a *continuum*, which extends from the extreme of purely positive values to that of purely negative values. Figure 5.6 shows the ordering of 11 speakers on the basis of 10 features. See p. 154.

Figure 5.6 shows how a group of speakers realizing various linguistic features can be ordered on an implicational scale in such a way that the use of the 10 features describes a continuum between speaker 5, who uses *all* the features, and speaker 3, who uses none. Such a continuum represents a hierarchy of variants which are based solely on the cooccurrence of features. Thus from one

Feature		speaker	A	B	C	D	E	F	G	H	I	J
+ A	it is I	1	−	+	−	−	−	−	−	+	+	+
+ B	may I	2	+	+	−	−	+	−	+	+	+	+
+ C	vahz	3	−	−	−	−	−	−	−	−	−	−
+ D	may he	4	−	−	−	−	−	−	−	+	−	+
+ E	the man whom I	5	+	+	+	+	+	+	+	+	+	+
+ F	shan't	6	+	+	+	−	+	−	+	+	+	+
+ G	needn't	7	+	+	−	−	−	−	−	+	+	+
+ H	eyether	8	+	+	+	−	+	+	+	+	+	+
+ I	tomahto	9	−	+	−	−	−	−	−	+	−	+
+ J	I shall	10	+	+	−	−	+	−	−	+	+	+
		11	−	−	−	−	−	−	−	+	−	−

(1)

	+ A	− A
	2, 5, 6, 7, 8, 10	1, 3, 4, 9, 11

(2)

	+ A	− A	+ B	− B
	2, 5, 6, 7, 8, 10	1, 9	3, 4, 11	

(3)

+ C	− C	+ A	− A	+ B	− B
5, 6, 8	2, 7, 10	1, 9	3, 4, 11		

(4)

+ D	− D + F	− F + C	− C + G	− G + E	− E+ A
5	3	6	2	10	7

	− A + I	− I + B	− B + J	− J + H	− H
	1	9	4	11	3

(5)

	H	J	B	I	A	E	G	C	F	D
5	+	+	+	+	+	+	+	+	+	+
8	+	+	+	+	+	+	+	+	+	−
6	+	+	+	+	+	+	+	+	−	−
2	+	+	+	+	+	+	+	−	−	−
10	+	+	+	+	+	+	−	−	−	−
7	+	+	+	+	+	−	−	−	−	−
1	+	+	+	+	−	−	−	−	−	−
9	+	+	+	−	−	−	−	−	−	−
4	+	+	−	−	−	−	−	−	−	−
11	+	−	−	−	−	−	−	−	−	−
3	−	−	−	−	−	−	−	−	−	−

Fig. 5.6 Ordering of 11 speakers by 10 linguistic features on an implicational scale. (Source: Decamp 1969, 4)

intersection on the scale the other points of intersection can be predicted:

> 'The scales then automatically generate all the code switches, the features necessary to the generation of a sociolinguistically appropriate sentence. Note that then a whole new dimension of explanatory power is thus given to a grammar without increasing its complexity.' (Decamp 1971a, 36)

The implicational scale has the advantage that speakers can be classified by purely linguistic features, and only then be correlated with extraverbal parameters.

Decamp criticizes Labov and other sociolinguists for assuming discrete sociological categories, and obtaining in correlation with them nondiscrete linguistic features (e.g. the values for phonological variables). Instead he argues that they should proceed the other way round, taking as their basis the essentially discrete linguistic features before obtaining intrinsically nondiscrete (continuous) extraverbal values. The implicational scale makes this method feasible: the linguistic features which have been subjected to linear and implicational ordering can serve as discrete categories and the social data as dependent variables (Decamp 1971a, 37ff.).

Decamp also discusses the variable rule or frequency analysis of Labov. 'Frequency and implicational analyses are not rival procedures, for they involve entirely different conceptions of what a theory should be and do' (*ibid.*, 34). Frequency analysis generalizes an empirical description and belongs to the sphere of performance. On the implicational scale it is not individual speech acts but the idealized competence of speakers which is described. Thus the latter belongs to the 'ideal world of theoretical models', and the former to inductive theories (*ibid.*, 35). Finally, Decamp regards implicational analysis as a technique which can find general application in sociolinguistics: 'Most, perhaps all, sociolinguistic variables belong to one or more implicational scales and . . . each scale is a linear generative device' (*ibid.*, 39). This 'linear device' does not have to be a straight line, but can also form a loop, where the two extremes have the same values. Thus figure 5.7 shows, with regard to age-specific speech behaviour, that 5- and 80-year-olds, as well as 10- and 70-year-olds, exhibit the same speech attributes, whereas all the other age groups differ from these.

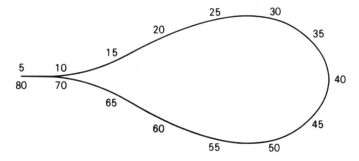

Fig. 5.7 Graph of age-specific speech behaviour: 5- and 80-year-olds, and 10- and 70-year-olds, show identical speech attributes.
(Source: Decamp, 1971a)

Likewise, discrete linguistic features can have the same values on a socioeconomic scale and on a scale of 'education'. It is even possible to represent regional dialects on a linear implicational scale. In dialectology a problem is posed by the way in which linguistic features can spread, when favoured or inhibited by extralinguistic conditions: 'The extent of acceptance of a linguistic innovation is a function of linear distance from a cultural center' (Decamp 1971a, 41). According to Decamp the regional spread of discrete linguistic features can also be understood by means of implicational analysis or, to be more precise, in an implicational *wave model*. In many respects it may be said that 'linear representation of complex events is thus basic to the very idea of language' (*ibid.*, 43).

By means of the implicational scale Bailey (1969; 1971) attempts to formulate a model of the 'panlectal'[4] competence of speakers, which does away with the traditional linguistic distinction between synchronic and diachronic, in favour of a *dynamic* speech model. Bailey's model is three-dimensional, i.e. it includes in the analysis the dimensions of the *language*, which is heterogeneously structured, of the *space* in which it spreads and of the *time* in which it changes. Seen from the angle of space and time, linguistic features have a hierarchical implicational ordering. This principle is illustrated in figure 5.8.

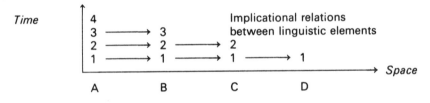

Fig. 5.8 A Bailey three-dimensional speech model.

Bailey explains that 'A, B, C, D are idioms progressively more remote from the origin. The numbers represent points on an implicational scale (e.g. more likely environments) implied by the points higher up the scale (e.g. less likely environments). The arrays represent the spread . . . of the change' (Bailey 1969, 123). Bailey demonstrates the implicational spatial and temporal change for a series of English phonemes. The data which have been hierarchically ordered in this way can be transferred from the scale to a wave model, which corresponds to certain regional conditions. A further advantage of Bailey's model is that it can assimilate categorical, optional and variable rules.

The value of this all-embracing dynamic speech model is demonstrated by Bickerton (1971), who employs an empirical test to analyse models describing inherent speech variation. Bickerton bases his work on data obtained from 28 speakers of the Creole speech continuum in Guyana; he describes the variation in their use of various pre-infinitival complementizers (*fi, fu, tu, a, φ*), in particular the opposition F/T (*fi, fu, tu*). He analyses their realizations in three different sentence constructions, which can be derived from different deep structures. On

---

[4] Bailey's basic term for all varieties open to speakers is the 'lect'. 'Panlectual' competence should include the ability of speakers to use different varieties in different contexts.

the basis of various models of linguistic variation, predictions can now be made about the series of the possible grammars which embrace the variable T/F use of the speakers. When a model accurately predicts the distribution of the T/F grammars, i.e. when none of a speaker's grammars lies outside the model, this proves first the correct choice of the descriptive categories, and secondly the superiority of the model in question over other models.

Model 1: Labov variable-constraint model
In addition to the two 100 per cent cases of grammars like $T T T$ and $F F F$ there are various possibilities:

1   Each of the three categories acts as a variable constraint: the remaining speakers would then have the grammars T/F, T/F, T/F.
2   One category per grammar represents a 'knockout' feature (i.e. produces a categorical rule); with the 3 grammars mentioned above and the 6 in figure 5.9, this gives 9 grammars in all.

	I	II	III
4	T	T/F	T/F
5	T/F	T	T/F
6	T/F	T/F	T
7	F	T/F	T/F
8	T/F	F	T/F
9	T/F	T/F	F

Fig. 5.9   Possible grammars for a Variable-Constraint Model.

3   For *two* possible knockout features there is a total of 21 possible grammars.

Model 2: modified model of obligatory rules
The majority of rules are obligatory, a few are optional: there is no variable rule which gives T/F. As is shown in figure 5.10, this model embraces 8 possible grammars.

	I	II	III		I	II	III
1	F	F	F	5	T	T	T
2	T	F	F	6	F	T	T
3	F	T	F	7	T	F	T
4	F	F	T	8	T	T	F

Fig. 5.10   Possible grammars for a modified model of obligatory rules.

Model 3: model of obligatory-cum-optional rules
Model 3 can comprise periods of variable speech (linguistic change), in which the transition is effected from one obligatory rule to another. For this there are several possibilities:

1   Variable speech is assumed for exactly one category per grammar, giving 14 possible grammars (figure 5.11 does not list the grammars *T T F* and *FFF* separately).

	I	II	III		I	II	III
3	T/F	F	F	9	T/F	F	T
4	F	T/F	F	10	T/F	T	F
5	F	F	T/F	11	F	T/F	T
6	T/F	T	T	12	T	T/F	F
7	T	T/F	T	13	F	T	T/F
8	T	T	T/F	14	T	F	T/F

Fig. 5.11   Possible grammars for obligatory-cum-optional rules model.

2   If in-change and static grammars are assumed to exist side by side, grammars 2–4 and 6–8 from model 2 must be added, giving 20 possible grammars.

3   If only in-change grammars are assumed, but changes allowed in up to *two* categories, six further grammars of the type *T/F, T/F, T* must be added, giving again 20 possible grammars.

4   If both static and in-change grammars of type 4 are assumed, the 6 further grammars of type 3 must be added to those of type 2, giving a possible 26 grammars.

Model 4: Bailey wave model

This model contains categorical and optional elements, which are implicationally ordered (see Decamp and Bailey above). Speech change spreads implicationally in the form of waves, as a motion in time and space which has reached some speakers, but not others. For this model, as for the previous ones, there are two possibilities: static grammars and in-change grammars. In order to preserve the implicational relation, an element which appears on the left in the table may not appear later to the right of its alternating form, and vice versa. According to figure 5.12, there are 7 possible grammars for the wave model:

	I	II	III
1	F	F	F
2	T/F	F	F
3	T	F	F
4	T	T/F	F
5	T	T	F
6	T	T	T/F
7	T	T	T

Fig. 5.12   Possible grammars for the Bailey wave model.

A comparison with the empirical data reveals that all grammars—except for those of two speakers—correspond with Bailey's model 4. Altogether the speakers have 6 grammars, structured as follows: *TTT, TT T/F, TTF, T T/F F, TFF, FFF*. Bickerton considers that on criteria of simplicity and completeness the Bailey model is unquestionably superior, since the question is not to predict the maximum number of grammars, but only those which are realized, and, as far as possible, all of those (for the above arguments cf. in particular Bickerton 1971, 474–9).

5.2.5   Speech acts

In recent years 'ordinary language philosophy' has stimulated discussion in linguistics of the pragmatic functions of utterances or speech acts. Speech-act analysis is both an attempt at including semantic and pragmatic questions in generative theory (cf. amongst others Wunderlich 1970 and 1971a; Gordon and Lakoff 1971) and the initial stage of founding a general theory of linguistic behaviour (Schegloff 1968; Searle 1969; Labov 1970a and 1972a; Sacks 1972a and b; Maas and Wunderlich 1972). We shall now give a rough characterization of the three lines of thought which are at present beginning to develop:

1   *Generative trend*
    Attempts are made to classify performative verbs according to their function, and to bring into the description as parameters the speaker-hearer roles which imply them. The parameter appears in the deep structure and controls the derivations.

    Greatly simplified and idealized parameters are assumed, such as *speaker roles* (which should be understood grammatically, e.g. assignment of roles by pronouns), *place* (deictic particles), *time* (e.g. temporal adverbs).

    The linguistic description remains, moreover, purely intuitionistic (cf. Ross 1970; Wunderlich 1971a; Joas and Leist 1971).

2   *Philosophical trend*
    Here the concern is chiefly with true and false sentences in everyday speech, and with their logical and colloquial significance. Conditions are laid down which relate to the situations and circumstances in which utterances are or are not valid. Here, too, it is a matter of verbs of requesting, demanding, commanding etc. The 'conditions' for the validity of speech acts are formulated without taking into account the social reality (Austin 1962; Wittgenstein 1969; Searle 1969).

3   *Empirical trend*
    This is based on the principle that speech acts can only be described and explained if the social situation in which the speech takes place is known, as well as the social roles of the speakers. The dependency of the function of speech acts is precisely specified with relation to the social parameters. The correlation between speech act and behaviour is illustrated by examples from empirical reality (Labov *et al.* 1968; Labov 1970a and 1972a).

Speech-act analysis is in any case still at the speculative stage. The somewhat better-established theoretical development of the generative trend is still too restricted for the complex pragmatic questions under discussion. On the other hand, the empirical trend is as yet underdeveloped from the theoretical point of view. Its highly promising analyses, however, which are of interest precisely for sociolinguistics, will be treated in the empirical section (6.3) in the context of investigations into communicative competence. It should be emphasized here that speech-act analysis will be extremely important for the development of a social pragmatics.

5.2.6 Marxist sociolinguistics

Apart from some significant Marxist analyses of bourgeois linguistics or sociolinguistics (Neubert 1962; Ehlich *et al.* 1971a; Maas 1972a; Eisenberg and Haberland 1972), few approaches seem to have been made as yet on the lines of Marxist linguistic theory or sociolinguistics (for a promising start, however, cf. Maas in Maas and Wunderlich 1972). Some of the more recent work of Šaumjan in the Soviet Union does not yet seem to have taken speech variation into consideration. There are of course programmatic demands, for example that a Marxist linguistic theory should investigate the 'relation between language, thinking and reality, with special consideration of the Marxist theory of reflection' (Ehlich, Müller and Wiehle 1971b, 109). Grosse and Neubert (1970) stress that sociolinguistics should be developed as part of Marxist-Leninist social theory, although the terms that they then choose for sociolinguistic analysis show that they are following more or less the lines of traditional linguistic theories. The essential difference between the Marxist concept and bourgeois sociolinguistics is that the former rejects the categories of bourgeois sociology such as class and role, to mention but a few (cf. 3.5) and argues in support of a *dynamic contextual* theory. According to Slama-Cazacu (1971, 41–54), this method should be conceived as one in which all data and interpretations of speech behaviour are to be related to the course of action which is in constant development during speech.

Whilst there does not as yet seem to be any palpable Marxist linguistic theory of general relevance, theoretical notions do exist in restricted areas of Marxist linguistics. Those concerning linguistic change have been evolved by Mučnik *et al.* (1968); what follows is taken from Lencek 1971. The theoretical outline derives from a description of the linguistic change of the Russian Standard in the last 50 years, which is itself based on a large quantity of data relating to lexicon, phonetics, morphology, word formation and syntax. The theory is based upon the Marxist-Leninist dialectic principle, which postulates the unity of opposites. Language is in a continuous process of change, all linguistic elements contain contradictory aspects, and the tension or conflict between them impels change. Linguistic development is effected under the pressure of the dynamism exerted by these opposites. Every individual concrete solution of the antagonism produces new conflicts and new contradictions, whose solution in the end is impossible. The opposites thus continuously give impetus to the evolution of lanuage.

The theory formulates five such contradictions as *linguistic antinomies* (this term originates from Jakobson):

1   Antinomy between transmitter and receiver, or incompatibility between the speaker's tendency to simplify the message and the hearer's tendency to simplify the perception.

2   Antinomy between speech form and the possibilities of the linguistic system, or conflict between the tendency to restrict use of linguistic constructions and the possibilities afforded by a linguistic system.
3   Antinomy between code and text, or conflict between the tendency to reduce the code and that to extend the text, and vice versa.
4   Antinomies inherent in the asymmetrical character of the linguistic sign, or conflict between the signifier and the signified of the linguistic sign, whereby the signifier tends to assume new meanings, and the signified tends to produce new means of expression. (The terms 'signifier' and 'signified' derive from Saussure 1949.)
5   Antinomy between informative and expressive functions of language, or contradiction between regularity or uniformity and heterogeneity of language (Lencek 1971, 282).

An analysis of these antinomies cannot leave out of account the continuous processes of social change. Although they can be traced back to social factors, their relation to social reality is still by no means clear. The way in which inherently linguistic antinomies and extralinguistic factors interact to impel the evolution of languages is elucidated by the theory as follows:

1   Sudden fundamental change in the social structure exposes the latent antinomies to external tension and forces them to neutralize these tensions.
2   Sociostructural change can accelerate language development. In both cases, in (1) as well as in (2), linguistic change is only indirectly caused by external social factors, in so far as the social structure merely stimulates solution of the antinomies.
3   In some cases social factors can impede the development of one or the other tendency in linguistic evolution.
     The latter two processes (stimulating or protracting linguistic change through the influence of social factors) are particularly typical for linguistic evolution (cf. Lencek 1971, 283).

These three types of interaction are considered universally valid; they bring about some form of quantitative and qualitative linguistic change independently of the form of society in which they exist.

5.3 Functional and interactional approach

The abandonment of a narrow grammatical perspective, restricted to phonology and syntax (cf. 5.2), in favour of an analysis of the pragmatic and communicative function of language in verbal interactions can be attributed to different recent developments both within and outside the field of linguistics: anthropological approaches ('the ethnography of speaking', Hymes 1962), studies of verbal interaction (cf. Gumperz and Hymes 1972; Sudnow 1972), and situation-oriented analysis of speech acts (Maas and Wunderlich 1972). A characteristic background to the latter analysis is as follows: (1) certain descriptive problems of syntax cannot be solved without semantics, and again problems of semantics cannot be solved without pragmatics (Wunderlich 1970); (2) the reduction of the scope of 'language' to static formal description excludes the *procedural* aspects of all communication (Ungeheuer 1972); (3) language should only be comprehended in the context of social behaviour (Maas and Wunderlich 1972).

Wunderlich (1970) lists seven difficulties that arise for a linguistic theory concerned solely with the grammatical competence of speakers, and which leaves out of account 'pragmatic' aspects; at the same time these points are arguments for the extension of the traditional concept of competence:

1   According to recent results of psycholinguistic research, the picture of what happens in the speaker's mind when he formulates utterances is different from the simplified assumption of the generative grammar model.
2   Linguistic rules are learned in correlation with situations and contexts.
3   Speakers acquire the ability to create completely new verbal interaction situations (dialectic competence).
4   Deictic expressions of person, time and place, forms of establishing contact and reverting to previous conversation, as well as certain modal adverbs, cannot be meaningfully explained without recourse to circumstances of the speech situation.
5   Speech that is frequently described as ungrammatical does not impair the understanding so long as the meanings are clearly derivable from the situation.
6   The correct interpretation of an utterance's meaning often cannot be deduced from its grammatical structure (speech acts which can be interpreted as requests, commands, demands etc., according to context).
7   It is part of a speaker's pragmatic competence to be able to examine utterances for their underlying intentions, to recognize their contradictions and to reject them if necessary (cf. Wunderlich 1970, 12–8).

Those aspects which make it necessary to expand the over-restricted scope of existing linguistic theory suggest the development of a functional, context-specific linguistic analysis, whose theoretical aim would be the investigation of speakers' *communicative competence*.

5.3.1 Communicative competence

Broadly speaking, 'communicative competence' describes the ability of individuals to communicate with one another under situationally and normatively defined conditions (linguistic, psychological, social and pragmatic in nature). In defining this notion it must be taken into account that communicative behaviour ranges from mutual agreement between speakers to the solution of serious conflicts. Stylistic features reflect such differences through a whole repertoire of different strategies.

A sociolinguistic theory, which is based on the concept of communicative competence, is founded partly on a 'linguistic (syntactic and phonological) theory which incorporates appropriate sociological parameters, and partly on a *theory of speech in situation*; in this, linguistic elements are not only correlated with extra-linguistic elements, but also seen as factors which presuppose, as well as alter, a situational context' (Wunderlich 1971b, 298).

Hymes (1968a) was the first to coin the term 'communicative competence' with his demand for qualitative extension of linguistic theory by the incorporation of aspects of functional communication. Hymes criticizes Chomsky's postulate of the ideal speaker-hearer for excluding social aspects of communication, which the latter had assigned to the sphere of performance. Chomsky's concept of performance, however, is of little use, as it relates to psychological factors of actual speech (incompleteness of natural utterances, restrictedness of memory etc.), and does not consider speech as action related to situation. Performance rules are thus seen solely in a psychological dimension.

Grammatical and psychological aspects, however, are only some of those covered by the concept of communicative competence. This broader perspective shows that Chomsky's dichotomous judgement of utterances according to *grammaticality* and *acceptability* (a pair of terms analogous to competence and performance) is also oversimplified. Utterances are not only grammatical or acceptable, but must also be assessed by the extent to which they are successful and appropriate to the context, by the way in which they are effected as actions, and with what results. In other words, the analysis must include those aspects which, in a theory of communicative competence, should decide the way in which sentences of a particular phonological and syntactic structure are regarded as functional for a given situation. This is where the concept of speech acts comes into its own. Sentences that are identical in their formal grammatical structure can, according to the situational context, be commands, requests, demands or apologies. Conversely, two grammatically different sentences can be understood as one and the same speech act. Furthermore, speech acts have immediate pragmatic consequences: a person who makes a promise or apologizes for something is performing an action which has consequences both for himself and for others. It is obvious that traditional grammatical categories are not adequate for describing distinctions of this kind.

In fact, the pragmatic dimension of speech acts is connected with a broader problem: how speakers interact with one another by means of the speech they employ, i.e. how a speech act that has been uttered is correctly understood and transformed into a new speech act. With regard to the concrete process of communication, the verbal interaction of two speakers is a question of interpreting utterances. This interaction process should be described by the concept of *sociolinguistic interference*, which is borrowed from Weinreich. The concept of sociolinguistic interference embraces 'problems of the interpretation of manifestations of *one* system [e.g. transmitter] in terms of *another* [e.g. receiver]' (Hymes 1968a, 25). Sociolinguistic interference involves the interaction of reception and production, of competence and performance, of production and interpretation strategies. As distinct from the theoretical concept of grammar with which we have been concerned up till now, it can only be described adequately by an integrated theory of sociolinguistic description, whose scope should incorporate primarily the function and secondarily the structure of language.

According to Hymes, such a theory is centred on three concepts: (1) the *verbal repertoire* of speakers (context-specific range of speech and styles; cf. Gumperz 1968); (2) the *linguistic habits* or 'linguistic routines' (everyday sequential organization of utterances in narratives, verbal interactions etc.); (3) *social spheres* of linguistic behaviour (context-specific use of linguistic varieties, e.g. variety *A* in the family, variety *B* in certain institutions etc.; cf. Fishman *et al.* 1968, and above 5.4).

With the aid of these concepts the communicative or sociolinguistic competence of speakers can be measured on a two-dimensional scale, whose horizontal dimensions (concepts 1 to 3 above) are graded vertically according to the three degrees of linguistic command (restricted, flexible and versatile). (This scale was only tentatively proposed by Hymes; we shall not reproduce it in diagram form.) On such a scale it should be possible to indicate roughly three different degrees of communicative competence:

1   *Minimal competence:* speakers are characterized by a single speech habit in a single social sphere without any shifting of repertoire or code (*restricted*).
2   *Average competence:* speakers have a command of a set of speech habits which is neither large nor small, they use these in a limited range of different social spheres, and shift their verbal repertoire accordingly (*flexible*).
3   *Maximal competence:* speakers have versatile speech habits in many social spheres, and shift their verbal repertoire with ease (*versatile*) (Hymes 1968a).[5]

Hymes does not clarify the question of the theoretical definition of this concept, i.e. with what theoretical apparatus communicative competence should be described and explained. It is true that he says that a 'taxonomy of sociolinguistic systems' should be drawn up (Hymes 1967a), or that speech occurrences should be recorded by 'rewriting rules'; but it is not made clear in what form this should take place.

The theoretical concepts of communicative competence are still vague, a fact which is understandable in the light of the complexity of the subject. Wunderlich (1971b) has made an attempt—roughly on the lines of the notion of verbal repertoire—to link speech behaviour to role behaviour. In his model, the 'speech code as a system of strategies of rhetoric and hermeneutic' (313) is a representation of role structures, which themselves depend on material social conditions and their superstructure (ideological norms, value systems, manipulations etc.). *Rhetoric* and *hermeneutic* (a set of subsequent hypotheses which speakers construct in the course of communication) are functions of role behaviour . What communicative competence should then mean is described by Wunderlich as follows:

'If *R* is a set of role structures r_i (each r_i being a function of extralinguistic variables) and *S* is a set of speech (behaviour) forms s_j (each s_j being a selective function from the union set of the repertoires of linguistic—i.e. phonological, syntactic and semantic—variables, and of variables of extraverbal situational factors), then a particular code is a mapping from *R* into *S*. The set in *S* of the rhetorical code is in general a subset of the set in *S* of the hermeneutic code; at any rate it is more limited in range. This means that there may well be speech behaviour forms in *S* which can be interpreted (e.g. when the reciprocal role is

[5] The value and meaning of this scale must be measured according to the norms by which 'minimal' and 'maximal' competence are defined.

filled by a member of another social group), but which cannot or may carried out.' (Wunderlich 1971b, 319f.)

The theoretical implications of linking speech behaviour to role behaviour have since been discussed by various authors. Following the lead taken by Habermas (1971), Joas and Leist (1971) sought to represent roles expressed in speech acts (which are correlated with performative verbs such as 'promise', 'apologize' etc.) in the deep structure of sentences. They base their work on a sociological analysis of the functions of speech acts (Scott and Lyman 1968), which is pledged to the tradition of symbolic interaction.

In the next section we shall deal with some of the components in speech which are specific to situations and roles, and which should be considered in a theory of communicative competence.

5.3.2 Components of situational and interactional speech behaviour

All speech in verbal interaction (face-to-face communication) takes place in a physical environment, is situated in a particular speech context and is concerned with a particular topic, which depends on the prevailing psychological circumstances (intentions, attitudes) and on social features of those taking part in the conversation (position in the production process, roles). Limiting herself to those extralinguistic factors which are relevant for the linguistic organization of interaction processes (they may either affect these or be affected by them), Ervin-Tripp (1969) puts forward the following components of speech as essential for communication: (1) participants, (2) situation, (3) form of communication, (4) speech act, topic and message, and (5) functions of interaction. These components can be regarded as variables which systematically determine the style-shifting and variations of speakers (cf. Ervin-Tripp 1969, 121–39).

1   *Participants*
Every act of communication involves at least a transmitter and a receiver, and possibly also listeners in particular, Grimshaw (1966) has pointed out the influence of listeners on speech behaviour; (cf. 6.4.3 below). It is rare for the speaker role, i.e. speech frequency in interactions, to be evenly distributed: it depends on the situation (formal or informal conversation), the types of speech act (question, request, demand etc.) and the social roles of the participants (in the group, at work, in the family etc.). The most important sociological attributes of the participants are sex, age, occupation and position in the production process; these determine their rights, duties and privileges. It is particularly in the forms of address that the roles specific to situations and contexts are manifested. (Systems of address in different societies have been a favourite object of investigation for anthropologists.) Social features such as respect, familiarity, obsequiousness, aversion etc., which characterize the relationship of speakers to one another, are a crucial factor in determining speech behaviour (polite forms, standard v. dialect, insults, ellipses, metaphors etc.); what should also be noted, however, is the assimilation of speech behaviour to that of the partner (this is particularly striking in adults' assimilation to child language in interactions with children).

2   *Situation*

'Situation' relates to a physical environment and to a period of time determining the framework for role interactions. The three factors of physical environment, period of time and role constellation produce certain patterns of behaviour and exclude others. Situations differ in the degree of restriction imposed on behaviour and in the amount of variation they allow. They are moulded by the conditions prevailing in a society, and standardized accordingly.

As Ehlich and Rehbein (1972) have shown, the situation of diners in a restaurant is determined by the sphere of material production and consumption, which is again rooted in a system of market-oriented production and of ideological norms. The authors establish that in a bourgeois restaurant speech acts are restricted by the reciprocal expectations which are determined by roles of both the production and the consumption spheres.

3   *Form of communication*

This is determined by the following types:

a   *Channel:* communication can be effected by written or spoken language, by gestures or by media that convey information symbolically.
b   *Code* or *variety:* the code is an ordered set of linguistic signs of the verbal repertoire which cooccur in social situations according to certain rules.
c   *Variants* within a code, which are selected according to situation and interlocutors.
d   *Paralinguistic features* (cf. the commentary on Trager 1964 in the bibliography).

4   *Speech act, topic and message*

According to Ervin-Tripp, 'speech acts' are functional segments of interaction which can be interpreted as greetings, invitations, requests, demands, commands, apologies etc. (cf. Maas and Wunderlich 1972 for a comprehensive analysis). Grammatically identical speech acts can be different in function, and functionally identical speech acts can have different grammatical structures. Successions of speech acts can be notated in terms of sequence rules, and this can be done most effectively when they are strictly normalized, such as when ordering and paying in a restaurant (see Ehlich and Rehbein 1972), or when extending or declining invitations, etc.

According to Ervin-Tripp, 'topic' describes the informational content of conversations. It intervenes as a variable when, for example, newcomers' participation in a conversation is invited or refused. Continuity rules can underlie topics, and their influence is revealed by apologies for getting off the subject ('but to come back to your question . . .'). The topic is a fundamental variable in interaction, as for speakers a change of topic often coincides with a change of code (characteristic of bilingual persons; cf. Ervin-Tripp 1964).

The term 'message' incorporates two aspects: the explicit or manifest, and the implicit message. The latter relates to the intention, which is part of the whole constellation of social features from which the interaction arises in the first place. It can be realized in different ways, and verbal interaction is only one of the possibilities. On the other hand, the explicit or manifest message is a product of the social features of the specific interaction situation *and* of the speech intention; it is therefore inseparable from the result and effect of the interaction. (Cf. Ducrot 1972, in particular 131–41.)

5   *Function of the interaction*

There are two possible means of identifying the function of interactions: by equating it with the social value of the speech act and its effect, which are different for speaker and hearer; or by analysing speech acts in order to deduce from them whether the hearer's answer satisfies the speaker or not.

In the latter case, on which Ervin-Tripp (1969, 132) concentrates, the function is identified with types of satisfactory answer given by the hearer. In order to draw up these types, categories of functions must be found which relate to the setting in motion of dyadic interactions.

Ervin-Tripp's criterion for classifying interaction functions is the hearer's answer which concludes the interaction to the satisfaction of the speaker; as a first approximation, they can be categorized thus:

a   requesting/demanding goods, services, information;
b   implicit invitation/request to give social replies, such as applause, sympathy, laughter etc.;
c   conveying or proffering information;
d   expressive monologues;
e   routines.

These functions can be expressed in different explicit or implicit ways; speech acts can be functionally ambiguous when seen in isolation from the social context.

Many of these aspects discussed by Ervin-Tripp in her five components of verbal interaction have been incorporated by Wunderlich (1970, 18–24) into a model which is designed to provide the terms for a kind of integrated description of speech behaviour. This should take into consideration the factors which we list here in abbreviated form: (i) the person speaking at the time in question, (ii) the person spoken to, (iii) the time of the utterance, (iv) the place of the speaker, (v) the speaker's field of perception, (vi) the phonological and syntactic attributes of the verbal utterance, (vii) the phonetic attributes of the paralinguistic concomitant phenomena, (viii) the structural attributes of the extraverbal forms of expression, (ix) the structural attributes of the speaker's accompanying actions, (x) the cognitive content of the utterance as intended by the speaker, (xi) the speaker's intention (with regard to orientation towards topic, action and expression), (xii) the presuppositions associated with the speaker (general presuppositions such as knowledge and capabilities and special presuppositions such as assumptions about the person spoken to, understanding of the preceding utterances and actions, understanding of his own role, emotional state, attentiveness etc.), and (xiii) the interrelation established with the utterance between speaker and person spoken to (functions of the interaction). According to Wunderlich, this model should provide the frame for a dynamic description.

5.3.3   Sociolinguistic rules

Ervin-Tripp (1969) lists three types of sociolinguistic rules: alternation rules, sequence rules and cooccurrence rules. As we have already discussed the latter in 5.2.3, we shall treat here only the first two types of rules. They are typical of anthropological methods of inquiry.

Alternation rules
The customary forms of address in a language community can be incorporated into a rule system whereby a particular form (title and surname, Mr/Mrs/Miss and surname, appellation denoting kinship and first (Christian) name, or simply first (Christian) name) is determined by

1   characteristics of the person addressed (e.g. adult, male or female, married or single, titled);
3   features that characterize the relationship between speaker and person addressed (e.g. role, age, blood relationship);
3   attributes of the situation (e.g. intimate, formal or informal).

The forms of address can be represented in a flow diagram whose structure is a sequence of decision processes (binary decisions +, −), which ultimately lead to

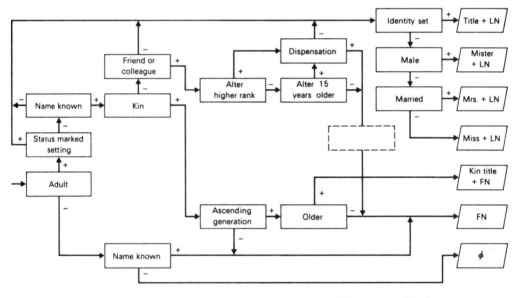

LN = surname.   FN = forename

Fig. 5.13 Ervin-Tripp's system of American forms of address.
(Source: Ervin-Tripp 1969, 95)

alternative forms of address. These decision processes, which are represented by a set of paths, correspond to a formal grammar intended to be a *logical*, descriptive model and not a model of *actual* (psychological) decision processes. The American system of address is constructed (figure 5.13) on the principle of binary paths.

Ervin-Tripp observes that the formulation of address forms in such a system permits a comparison of different sociolinguistic address systems. One will have to beware, however, of regarding a flow diagram such as that in figure 5.13 as an adequate description of American address forms. It is oriented towards superficial categories ('status-marked setting' or 'dispensation'), which do not explain the actual conditions reflected in address forms. These can only be elucidated by a more penetrating analysis that brings to light the ultimate and most general social causes determining forms of address, and also covers the sociohistorical genesis and transmission of the conventions concerning address forms (cf. Ammon 1972b).

Sequencing rules.
Sequencing rules are meant to describe sequences of utterances in abstract form. Thus according to Schegloff (1968), the normalized sequences contained in the opening stages of telephone conversations can be written in the form of five replacement rules (which are vaguely borrowed from generative grammar; they are the result of a larger empirical investigation). The speech occurrences, which are characterized below by means of conceptual labels, can be realized linguistically in different ways, but this does not affect the structure of the rules (cf. Ervin-Tripp 1969, 108).

1 Summons sequence $\longrightarrow \left\{ \begin{array}{l} \text{summons} \quad \text{answer} \\ \text{continuation response} \end{array} \right\}$

2 Summons $\longrightarrow \left\{ \begin{array}{l} \text{courtesy phrase [to stranger]} \\ \text{attention-call [to non-stranger]} \\ \text{telephone bell} \ldots \end{array} \right\}$

3 Answer [phone] $\longrightarrow$ greeting 1 (+ identification [office])

4 Continuation $\longrightarrow$ (greeting 2) + (identification) + message

5 Response $\longrightarrow$ (deferral +) reply to message

Labov (1970a, 78–84) formulates some rules for the dialectic interaction of a mother with her schizophrenic daughter; they concern requests and demands for action or information. Only when more is known about the social roles of the two speakers can any formulation be made of the rules for which, in accordance with the principle in Searle (1969), conditions of application are specified. Labov demonstrates, by means of examples of Yes/No replies and of questions (in the first case a therapeutic interview, and in the second mother-daughter interaction), that the communicative function of a given linguistic form must be inferred from the context and the social conditions, if one is to be able to determine and describe it adequately.

'First there is the distinction between utterances and actions, and the hierarchical relations of actions whereby a question may be seen as a request for information, which is in turn interpreted as a request for action, which may appear on a higher level as a challenge.' (Labov 1970a, 83).

A résumé of the 'overall pattern of discourse analysis' (Labov 1970a, 80) on which the rules are based is given in figure 5.14.

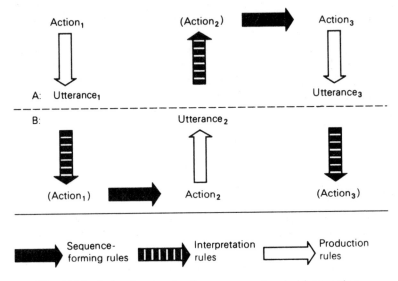

Fig. 5.14   Labov's rules for the process of verbal interaction

We shall come back to questions concerning the description of verbal interactions and continuous narratives in the section dealing with empirical works.

5.4 Special descriptive problems: bilingualism and multilingualism

'Bilingualism' or 'multilingualism' is the term given to the linguistic situation where two or more languages coexist within the bounds of one society, or are kept in constant contact by politically and economically determined interests.

Up till now inquiry into bilingualism has been centred on four questions:

1   To what extent are speakers bilingual? How good is their command of each of the two languages they use?
2   In what functions do speakers use two languages? For what occasion do they use one language, and for what occasion the other?
3   To what extent do bilingual speakers shift languages? Under what conditions do they alternate between the two?
4   To what extent do bilingual speakers employ the two languages *separately*, of as *one* integrated system? What interference phenomena are manifested in the interchangeable use of the two languages? How does the use of one language influence that of the other?

These points were discussed by Mackey (1962, quoted in Fishman 1968b, 555); they characterize lines of inquiry which, since Weinreich (1953), have been followed in linguistics and psychology. They are connected with the question of how and in what circumstances bilingual speakers acquire languages; whether they are socialized in both languages and learn to use them side by side in many functions (this type of bilingual speaker is called 'independent' or 'coordinated'), or whether they do not learn the second language until after the primary socialization phase, on the basis of the system of their first language (this type of speaker is described as 'compound' or 'interdependent').

On the other hand we should ask, in connection with the origin of bilingualism: how does a bilingual language situation come about? What social factors produce it? Here questions of colonialization, industrialization and trade relations come into play, which force speakers of a certain language to use another language. This will then give rise to problems of bilingual education (cf. Grimshaw 1971b).

Although descriptive problems of bilingual language use are generally not different from those of speech-variation description (theoretically it is also a question of describing cooccurrence and covariation; cf. 5.2.3), special problems do arise, and these have been approached by linguistics, psychology and sociology in different ways.

This will become clear in the following section when we examine traditional ways of dealing with bilingualism phenomena followed in different disciplines.

5.4.1 Isolated disciplinary approach v. interdisciplinary theory

Fishman (1968a) states that if one wants to arrive at an integrated sociolinguistic theory of bilingualism one must first of all ask what the individual disciplines of psychology, linguistics and sociology have hitherto achieved, and how much of this can be integrated into a perspective that goes beyond the separate disciplines. What follows is based on his critical account of the three disciplines.

Psychology
Psychological inquiries were carried out primarily to test the intelligence, educability and school success of bilingual children. A result of these efforts was the unproved assertion that early bilingual education is damaging for the intellectual development of the child (Fishman 1968a, 3). This argument is wrong for two reasons: first because it does not distinguish between bilingualism in itself and the socioeconomic handicaps suffered by bilingual members of the working class (e.g. foreign workers in the Federal Republic of Germany); secondly because, according to MacNamara (1970), there is no correlation at all between bilingualism and intelligence. MacNamara reaches the conclusion that the distinction between 'coordinate' and 'compound' is as devoid of meaning as is the theory that learning two languages at the same time influences intelligence and creativity; one should rather direct all efforts at the semantic problems of bilingual speakers, which are again connected with context-specific language use.

Psychology has never been able to outline a model of bilingual speech behaviour, nor make any progress with regard to a theory. On the strength of traditional but now outdated psychological research, it was assumed that bilingual speakers have an individual, uniform, context-invariant 'language capacity', which can be differentiated by context-independent measures such as range of word associations in the two languages or speed of speaking to establish degrees of realized competence. But if one seriously takes speed of speaking to be a measure of competence, it can only be on the view that the more automatic a speaker's use of a language the greater his competence in it. Although a great deal of data has been obtained for the speaking speed of bilingual people, no explicit theory has ever been developed on the significance of speed measurements as an index for bilingual fluency.

Characteristics of psychological models are that (1) they are context-independent (i.e. they take no account of circumstances affecting performance, such as motivation, social class, education, interactive relation); (2) they concentrate on measures that are specific to speech (speed of translation and speaking, word-naming and word-association tests, although in cases of socially-structured intragroup communication these can be totally irrelevant); (3) they draw conclusions from measurements of 'pure' linguistic skill about the 'dominance' of one language or the 'balance' between two languages (a person who speaks both languages equally well, frequently and fast is 'balanced'; a bilingual person who speaks more often and faster in language X than in language Y is X-dominant). As regards this last point, we should point out that it reflects an unrealistic view, in that 'dominance' v. 'balance' must be regarded as relating to specific contexts. Other than this there are difficulties when 'skill' and 'dominance' do not coincide.

The psychological concepts are inadequate, as bilingualism can only exist as a stable phenomenon if the two languages are differentiated according to their functions, and not described by means of the global notions of dominance v. balance.

Linguistics

Linguistic inquiry is restricted in the same way as that of psychology. The study of languages in contact, as promoted by Weinreich, is concerned with discovering the interference between two *pure* languages, and as such takes no account of the context-specific reality of language use. Thus the linguist inquires as to what structures (lexical, phonological, grammatical) of language X are transferred to language Y, and vice versa, despite the fact that the inadequacy of such a method has not gone unnoticed (cf. formulation of problems raised in Diebold 1964 and Mackey 1962).

This procedure is also visible in Mackey (1970), who investigates the integration of lexical units of one language into those of another. Mackey tries to describe the integration by means of a two-dimensional continuum, which relates to elements of language use (message) and to the incorporation of elements of one language system into another (code). The integration can now be measured (1) in the sphere of the message (frequency of the elements, area in which they appear) and (2) in the sphere of the code (level of command of semantic fields, ability to translate).

From the sociolinguistic point of view, however, we should ask whether the use of two languages ought not to be regarded as a functionally-structured *intragroup* (interaction within a group), rather than as mere *intergroup* communication (interaction between groups). If there is intragroup communication, the question arises whether there are two separate grammars or one grammar with internal variation.

Traditionally, linguists have taken it for granted that the conditions of language use in bilingual communities are well known, i.e. that the task of linguistics is to analyse the interferences between X and Y. Yet in so limiting themselves they overlook the conditions for different language behaviour of speakers and their attitude towards the use of varieties. It must also be realized that the speaker does not necessarily think in discrete terms: 'now X, now Y', or 'partly X, partly Y', or 'X and Y', but that he may use what he speaks in a certain situation (e.g. a certain mixing of X and Y) as a coherent system, i.e. as an independent variety (cf. the discussion in 5.2.3).

Sociology
Up till now sociological inquiries have concentrated chiefly on data of the macro-level: they have carried out census surveys, examined school systems with regard to bilingual education, or they have investigated sociopolitical reasons for bilingual situations.

One result of the concentration on large social groupings, including social institutions, is that sociological inquiry into bilingualism is oriented almost completely towards statistics; in compiling these it relies heavily on bilingual speakers' own accounts of themselves and classifies these on the basis of larger sociological categories (in any case not of categories of interaction in small groups). No discussion is included of, for example, the problem of the relation between personal accounts of bilingual behaviour and actual measured behaviour. Census data, moreover, prove to be problematic in that they often originate from government surveys, which in most cases simply provide bad data.

As far as the traditional social categories are concerned, such as social class and membership of ethnic and religious groups, it must be pointed out that these are too crude a basis for the analysis of group behaviour; social behaviour in groups takes place according to parameters that often cut across these broad categories. The conclusion we can draw for a sociological approach to bilingualism is that the categories of higher ordering (social class etc.) should be founded on those of a lower ordering of interactional group behaviour.

Psychological, linguistic and sociological inquiries are subject to limitations specific to the discipline concerned. As none of the disciplines goes deep enough in the case of bilingualism, it is necessary to evolve an interdisciplinary perspective.

Outline of an interdisciplinary theory of bilingualism
According to Fishman *et al.* (1968), inquiry into bilingualism can only be carried out adequately from a broadly sociolinguistic perspective. Yet every theoretical approach should be based on data from empirical inquiries, which are usually conducted with different methods:

'It would be foolhardy to demand that one and the same method of data collection and data analysis be utilized for such a variety of problems and purposes. It is one of the hallmarks of scientific social inquiry that methods are selected as a *result* of problem specifications rather than independently of them. Sociolinguistics is neither methodologically nor theoretically uniform.' (Fishman *et al.* 1968, 1023)

Fishman argues for an inductive theory which should start from constructs of a higher ordering, and descend successively to constructs of a lower rank, i.e., in concrete terms: starting from the language community (1), domains of social behaviour should be isolated (2), in which the dimensions of social relations (3) and the types of interaction found in them (4) should be identified.

1   *Language community.* In every language community in which two languages coexist in more or less stable contact, each of them must be connected with a specific subset of complementary values. As an example of a stable situation of language contact, Ferguson (1959) mentioned *diglossia* (which implies the coexistence of two language varieties, of which one is used in specific spheres that are complementary to those for the other: cf. 4.3.3 above).

Fishman stresses that diglossia and bilingualism need not coincide in their distribution over members of societies, and distinguishes four possible configurations: (a) diglossia with bilingualism, (b) bilingualism without diglossia, (c) diglossia without bilingualism and (d) neither diglossia nor bilingualism. These notions and this scheme will be discussed in more detail in 5.4.2.

It is possible to find out whether the clusters of values or norms underlying the two language varieties complement or mutually exclude one another, by means of sympathetic (participant) observation, skilful indirect interviews and direct questions (depending on the speakers' ability to assess correctly their own behaviour and normative judgements). These methods permit the analysis of the nature of the speakers' behaviour and their attitudes towards the varieties, so that reliable parameters can be derived on the micro-level.

2   *Domains.* Although the identification of speakers with particular value clusters is derived from concrete observations of behaviour, this derivation must nevertheless be made with a relatively high degree of abstraction. The domains are parameters for the identification of value clusters; they specify institutional contexts in which certain identifications take place. Domains originate in the 'integrative intuition' of the inquirer, and are defined as

'institutional contexts and their congruent behavioral cooccurrences. They attempt to summate the major clusters of interaction that occur in clusters of multilingual settings and involving clusters of interlocutors. Domains enable us to understand that *language choice* and *topic* ... are ... related to widespread sociocultural norms and expectations.' (Fishman *et al.* 1968, 1006f.)

Domains relate to gross, norm-bound and institutionalized behavioural activities, for which the decisive factor is situational congruence: 'a particular set of domain-appropriate people interact with each other in domain-appropriate locales and during domain-appropriate hours' (Fishman *et al.* 1968, 975). In other words, for a given context X with the roles $x_1, x_2, \ldots, x_n$, the speech forms of the roles $y_{x_1}, y_{x_2}, \ldots y_{x_n}$ should be predictable, assuming situational congruence for a certain time T.

For the analysis of bilingualism, Fishman tentatively assumes five domains: family, friends, religion, education and occupation. Domain-appropriate roles, place and topic of conversation are hypothetically defined for each of these spheres. The construction of the domains is based on the following (macro-level) consideration: if the stability of two language varieties depends on two complementary value systems being kept stable, then the latter must themselves be manifested in two complementary sets of domains in which one or other variety is clearly predominant.

3   *Dimensions of social relations.* The next level of analysis lower down the scale relates to the reciprocal relations between individuals, which can be organized in *closed* and *open* networks (cf. Gumperz 1966). In closed networks a specific variety is used with specific rules, whereas in open networks alternating, variable language forms are possible as a result of different values and interests. Whereas the domains are recognizable only in concrete situations, networks can only be abstracted from the concrete role relations.

4   *Types of interaction.* The types of interaction are more concrete still than the social networks. Again in keeping with Gumperz (1966), *personal* and *transactional* interactions are distinguished: the first type refers to formal speech situations, where social status is dominant; the second denotes casual intragroup communication in informal situations. Both types can give rise to linguistic and stylistic shifting. In the case of transactional interaction, such a shifting between varieties can be sparked off by a change in the situation or the person constellation, and in the case of personal interaction it usually coincides with a change of topic. The individual speech occurrences and speech acts are decisive for the types of interaction.

Fishman sees this hierarchy, composed of constructs of higher ordering right down to those of the smallest analytic segments, as yielding a possible theoretical and methodical framework for the integrated description of bilingualism. Essentially this should embrace bilingual speakers' functional repertoire of competences.

Without going into great detail, we shall now make a few observations on Fishman's conception:

i   Language communities are societies with a particular economic structure and particular conditions of authority and power.

ii   Values and norms do not suddenly 'appear' mysteriously and inexplicably in a society, but exist analogously to these structures.

iii   'Domains', for which different social roles and situations are assumed, differentiate arbitrarily between distinct spheres of life, i.e. this notion tends to obscure the overlap relations between these spheres. This isolation of the spheres (the 'hearth' has nothing to do with the 'work sphere') is a characteristic feature of a shallow sociology.

iv   Fishman does not seem to deal at all with the question of why, in what way and in what type of society language behaviour is differentiated according to domains. Here, in this concrete instance, reference should be made to the historical and social causes which give rise to such differentiations.

5.4.2 Bilingualism and diglossia

Ferguson (cf. 4.3.3 above) has described the concept of diglossia as a stable situation of two varieties of the same language in contact, whereby the H variety prevails in all public spheres, and the L variety is the uncodified variant for the informal sphere of families and friends. Fishman (1971a; 1971b, 286ff.) maintains that this concept is a suitable criterion for classifying bilingual communities. For him, however, diglossia is that form of coexistence of two (or more) language varieties or languages where the values of *social class* and *class-bound functions* are complementary to one another: 'This separation was most often along the lines of an H(igh) language, on the one hand, utilized in conjunction with religion, education, and other aspects of High Culture, and an L(ow) language, on the other hand, utilized in conjunction with everyday pursuits of hearth, home, and lower work sphere' (Fishman 1971a, 74; 1971b, 287).

It should be noted that for Fishman the notion 'diglossia' is no longer restricted (as it was for Ferguson) by the condition that two varieties of the *same* language are involved. In Fishman's sense, 'diglossia' is the term to denote any situation where clearcut differences between linguistic systems correlate strictly with social class and/or class-governed social functions, whereby this strict correlation is explicitly known and respected by at least large sections of the society in question. (He agrees with Ferguson that the H variety (or language) is normally not acquired at home as a part of the primary processes of language acquisition and socialization, but rather as a result of education at school.)

The difference with Ferguson's concept of diglossia is not as slight as it might seem: there are significant differences between societies where an H variety of the same language is used and taught and those where the H system is a completely different language, without the correspondences with the L variety pointed out in 4.3.3. Factors of national and historical coherence play an important part in the attitudes held by members of such societies with regard to the H and L varieties of *their* language.

Theoretical general linguistics has so far been unable to define in any clear sense the distinction between varieties within the same language on the one hand and different languages on the other, due mainly to the widespread acceptance of Chomsky's (1965, 3) abstraction of an ideal speaker-listener in a homogeneous linguistic community, and hence the lack of any coherent notion of pluriform linguistic competence; even so, one should not be tempted to think that, therefore, no such distinction exists. The historical accident of the present-day state of linguistics does not make the distinction less real. From a purely grammatical point of view, there does not have to be a clearcut dichotomy between the notions 'variety' and 'language': there may well be a sliding scale. It may also be that the ultimate decision in applying the label 'language' or 'variety' ('dialect') rests with the members of a linguistic community and is determined by sociopolitical factors. In that case one would wish to establish what constraints are imposed by the sliding grammatical scale on the choice of such labels, and what are the causes as well as the consequences of their application.

In Fishman's terminology, bilingualism is distinguished from diglossia, not so much by the criterion of a subject's having competence in two different languages rather than in two varieties of the same language, as by the fact that linguistic differences (of any kind) are not closely correlated to institutionalized class distinctions: 'Here we see ... that bilingualism is essentially a characterization of *individual* linguistic versatility whereas *diglossia is a characterization of the social allocation of functions* to different languages or varieties' (Fishman 1971b, 295).

On the whole, Fishman's use of the term 'language' is wide and unspecific, and to some extent metaphorical. Thus we read: 'Ultimately, the language of school and government replaces the language of home and neighborhood, precisely because it comes to provide status in the latter domain as well as in the former' (*ibid.*, 297), where it is left unclear whether the term 'language' refers to a variety (code, speech form, register, or the like) or to a grammatically-defined distinct system of communication. When Fishman continues: 'Many studies of bilingualism and intelligence or of bilingualism and school achievement have been conducted within the context of bilingualism without diglossia' (*ibid.*, 297), he lays himself open to the very same criticisms that have been formulated earlier (chapters 1 and 2 above) with regard to Bernstein's lack of conceptual clarity in this respect.

It is in this context that Fishman's scheme of the cooccurrence relations of diglossia and bilingualism within a given society should be understood. These relations are represented in a matrix, which is shown in figure 5.15.

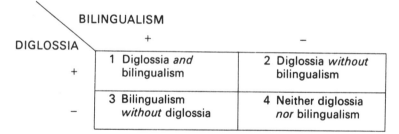

Fig. 5.15 Relations between bilingualism and diglossia.
(Source: Fishman 1971a, 75; corrected version in 1971b, 288)

1   *Diglossia and bilingualism.* The coexistence of both forms (stable distribution of language varieties strictly according to social functions, and a more flexible form of coexistence of two 'languages') is to be found mainly in large societies. There are few language communities in which bilingual and diglossia-specific behaviour is fully developed (e.g. USA, India, Paraguay, Switzerland).

2   *Diglossia without bilingualism.* In language communities of this type there is a strict functional separation of language varieties according to *H* and *L* variants.
      It is mostly a question of intragroup-specific behaviour of elite ruling forces (*H*

variety), who not only live apart from the ordinary people but intentionally contrast their language with that of the masses (authoritarian dissociation from the *L* variety symbolized in use of language, e.g. French at German and Slavonic courts in the nineteenth century; even today in north African states, amongst others). This type of diglossia is often found in societies that have been colonized.

3   *Bilingualism without diglossia.* In a language situation, where, in Fishman's scheme, bilingualism exists, but generally not diglossia, there is a marked difference between the two: diglossia is characterized by a rigid social distribution of its functions, whereas bilingualism can occur in different ways, according to individual and social circumstances. Thus, as in 5.4.1, the occurrence of bilingual behaviour varies with the situation, roles, topics and aims of communication; bilingualism without diglossia is found in most societies. Such a situation is by no means stable, but rather subject to rapid change as a result of its correlation with extremely varied social parameters (resettlement, immigration, movement of foreign workers etc.).

4   *Neither bilingualism nor diglossia.* This type applies to isolated, undifferentiated language communities that have little contact with the outside world; it is, says Fishman, now only rarely found, and is slowly dying out.

According to Fishman, the relationship between diglossia and bilingualism is a central criterion for the classification of language communities. However, these classifications are superficial: they make it look as if language were originally bilingual or diglossic in nature, or both at the same time. In any case, the reasons for the observed phenomena are not explained, although in the case of Fishman's or Ferguson's notion of diglossia, they can certainly be partly accounted for by prevailing economic and political conditions. Apart from the shallowness of the classification proposed, a general lack of conceptual clarity is apparent, as well as the occasional contradiction.[6]

5.4.3 Language retention v. language loss

The retention or loss of a language variety is attributable to various factors. One way of determining whether a variety has a stable or in-change state is by means of the domain-related *dominance configuration*; this frequently has its origins in sociopolitical conditions, or else depends on certain factors of prestige connected with a language variety.

The dominance configuration can generally be inferred by observing whether a language increases its domain from one sphere to another, or whether, conversely, its use decreases. Usually, a language (variety) that is not used in the family has less chance of being retained than one which is. Furthermore, an important factor for the stability of a bilingual language situation is whether its speakers have learned the two languages interdependently ('compound') or independently of one another ('coordinated').

[6] Thus, for example, when discussing diglossia, Fishman (1971b, 295) speaks of 'interaction that does occur between servants and masters who differ in mother tongue', although on p. 287 he has agreed with Ferguson that the *H* system is 'learned later and in a more formal setting than *L* and is, thereby, superimposed upon it.'

Using the example of the acculturation of American immigrants in the USA at the turn of the century, Fishman (1971b, 306) has shown how a dominance configuration changed, which was related to domains where strictly only one language was spoken (non-overlapping domains), as well as to domains where both languages were used side by side (overlapping domains). As can be seen from figure 5.16, the change in the dominance configuration takes place in four stages, the first of which consists in learning a new language at work, and the last in using this newly-learned language in the family sphere.

Bilingual functioning type	Domain overlap type	
	Overlapping domains	Non-overlapping domains
Compound ('Interdependent' or fused)	2 *Second stage:* more immigrants know more English and therefore can speak to each other either in mother tongue or in English (still mediated by the mother tongue) in several domains of behaviour. Increased interference.	1 *Initial stage:* the immigrant learns English via his mother tongue. English is used only in those few domains (work sphere, governmental sphere) in which mother tongue cannot be used. Minimal interference. Only a few immigrants know a little English.
Coordinate ('Independent')	3 *Third stage:* the languages function independently of each other. The number of bilinguals is at its maximum. Domain overlap is at its maximum. The second generation during childhood. Stabilized interference.	4 *Fourth stage:* English has displaced the mother tongue from all but the most private or restricted domains. Interference declines. In most cases both languages function independently; in others the mother tongue is mediated by English (reverse direction of initial stage, but same type).

Fig. 5.16 Type of bilingual functioning and domain overlap during successive stages of immigrant acculturation.
(Source: Fishman 1971b, 306)

It is chiefly sociopsychological and sociopolitical conditions that are responsible for the actual profile of the dominance configuration. We shall not go into details here, but merely list three aspects of language shifting, which are however considered by Fishman (1971b, 310–24) as problematic generalizations:

1   Language preservation is a function of the intactness of groups, especially
     of ideological manifestations of group loyalty in nationalist contexts.
2   Urban inhabitants tend more than rural inhabitants towards language
     shifting.
3   The language with greater prestige displaces that with lesser prestige.

Before going into theoretical questions connected with measurements of
language attitudes, we shall mention another assessment of language retention v.
loss, which refers to underlying economic and political conditions as the
explanation for such processes.

With regard to the situations in which Creole (*C*) and Pidgin (*P*) languages
come into contact, Grimshaw (1971b) discusses the taxonomy of some social variables that reflect the development of language varieties and their historical
prerequisites. A consideration of the political, economic and social situation of *C*
and *P* in connection with their development should include these points: (i)
whether a mercantile system, or one of latifundia prevails; (ii) whether there is
colonial rule or cultural conact on a more equal footing; (iii) in what way the
factors mentioned in (i) and (ii) overlap one another; (iv) whether *C* and *P* are
efficient or inefficient in respect of the industrial situation of the workers. Three
sets of variables can be adopted in order to analyse the different ways in which
language contact is manifested for speakers of the *C* and *P* varieties:

1   The types of conflict (i) between the ruling group of prestige speakers and
     the oppressed population and (ii) between individual groups of the
     oppressed population.
2   The industrial and commercial situation which brings about language
     contact (trade v. agriculture, farm v. plantation etc.). This variable includes
     the social organization of work: apprenticeship, slavery, hired labour,
     contract, freelance occupation etc.
3   Demographic variables.

A combination of demographic, social and political variables then determines
whether, in the process of standardization, for example, a Creole language
emerges as a new Standard language (as in Australian New Guinea), or as a
dialect of the Standard, or whether it simply mingles with the latter.

Variables 1 to 3 are, moreover, dependent on the degree of industrialization
and the extent to which immigrants' work is voluntary.

As regards the correlation between social structure and language structure,
Grimshaw posits that one should try to discover the way in which language and
speech function as devices for maintaining and increasing prestige, as agents of
social control, or as weapons in social conflicts. In all multilingual contact every
choice of language is connected with considerations of prestige and social
interaction. Newly-emerging languages gaining in prestige can be regarded as
vehicles of social cohesion, which causes the initially varied language of groups to
evolve in an increasingly more unified form, and to become the symbolic
expression of national identity (e.g. the gain in prestige of BEV in the USA as an
expression of the struggle for equality and independence).

5.4.4 Language attitudes

Attitudes to language varieties have a bearing on a number of different questions: the choice of language in multilingual communities, the distribution of verbal repertoires, dialectal differences and problems of mutual understanding between individuals. Measurements of language attitudes are based on two different theoretical standpoints (cf. Fishman and Agheyisi 1970, 138ff.): the mentalist and the behaviourist position.

For the distinction between these two positions, Fishman and Agheyisi rely on pre-war sources, which are to be interpreted in terms of the intellectual discussions of those days. In that concept of mentalism, attitudes are 'a mental and neural state of readiness' (138). They cannot be observed directly, but must be inferred from the subject's introspection. This definition, they say, has given rise to two difficulties: from what data can attitudes be derived, and in what way are these quantifiable? One solution to the problem is to regard attitudes as a 'hypothetical construct' that can be validated by verbal responses to a given set of stimuli. The advantage of this concept is that attitudes represent an independent variable in the form of a latent psychological constant that is not bound to specific external situations, in which behavioural reactions are manifested. Attitudes can thus be used to explain other forms of behaviour by the same 'organism'.

In contrast to this, the behaviourist notion regards attitudes (or 'dispositions') as a dependent variable. They can be determined statistically by observing actual behaviour in social situations. 'The extreme *behaviorist* definition locates attitudes in actual overt behavior or responses. Such an approach therefore faces few or no problems at the level of analysis because attitudes have been defined entirely in terms of the observable data' (Fishman and Agheyisi 1970, 138). To this staunch form of behaviourism two main objections can be raised. First, it should be recognized that attitudes cannot be regarded as independent of the 'stimulus situation' (the actual test) in which the 'reactions' that make them manifest are observed: the test situation itself may well influence the responses given by the test-subject. Secondly, results of behaviouristic measurements cannot, in principle, be extrapolated to other forms of behaviour of similar organisms. Generally, introspection, or even any reliance upon one's recognition or understanding of the processes involved, is banned.

The practical difference between these two approaches is manifest, for example, in the fact that the mentalists assign to attitudes a 'multi-layered componential structure' (*ibid.*, 139) (e.g. Lambert 1967), whereas the behaviourists regard them as 'unicomponential' (e.g. Osgood, Suci and Tannenbaum 1957). The different views on the structure of attitudes (multicomponential v. unicomponential) are summarized in figure 5.17. According to Lambert, attitudes consist of three components: the cognitive (knowledge), affective (evaluation) and conative (action) components. Rokeach (1968), however, maintains that they are composed primarily of beliefs, from which cognitive, affective and behavioural attitude types can then be formed. On the other hand, Osgood's definition allows of only one component, the affective one. Fishbein (1965) modified this by asserting that both attitudes and beliefs can crystallize with respect to an object: whilst the former are affective, the latter have a cognitive and an action-oriented dimension (139f.).

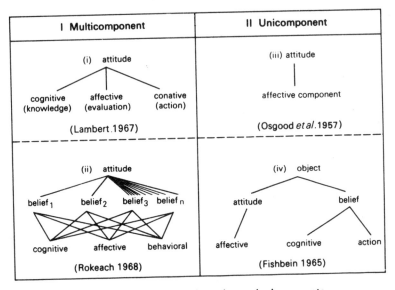

Fig. 5.17 Structure of attitudes: four theoretical concepts.
(Source: Fishman and Agheyisi 1970, 140)

There are various empirical studies connected with these different theories, and these have been classified in a large table by Fishman and Agheyisi (1970, 142f.), according to the methods employed in each case (survey and eliciting techniques). (This table is a good general review of all the attitude measurements carried out up till now, and the methods underlying them.) We shall now briefly discuss the two most important methods, the 'commitment measure' and the 'matched guise technique'.

The *commitment measure* measures a person's readiness or inclination to behave in a certain way, without actually displaying this behaviour openly. The individual questions are constructed on the lines of a Guttmann scale, with every question on the pattern, 'Would you agree that...?' The commitment measure is based not only on written responses but also on oral answers, which are recorded on tape. Measurements were taken chiefly for bilingual speakers (Fishman *et al.*, 1968).

The *matched guise technique*, which was developed by Lambert *et al.* (1960), measures group-specific evaluative reactions to individual languages (or language varieties) spoken by representative speakers. Measurements were carried out for numerous languages (French, Hebrew, Arabic, English, amongst others) as well as for dialects (Canadian and European French, various American Non-Standard dialects). The method implies that selected judging groups assess the characteristics of speakers' personalities whose taped voices were played back to them. The voices were those of bilingual speakers who were equally fluent in both varieties, and who all read the same text. In addition to the assessments of personality features, other variables were measured, such as prejudices, personal attitudes, group preferences and degree of bilingualism. The values of these variables were later correlated with the results from the valuation reactions.

The majority of measurements of language attitudes have been carried with the matched guise technique, and we shall come back to the results of these in the empirical section.

The methods which have been described here are superficial and inadequate to the extent that they cannot explain how these language attitudes have come about. This could be clarified in the framework of an historical analysis.

5.4.5 Multilingualism

We have already shown (5.4.2) certain ways of classifying multilingual societies. We shall now complement this with an effort made by Stewart (1968), which is still relevant today.

Stewart classifies multilingual societies according to four variables for each language concerned: (1) degree of standardization, (2) degree of autonomy, (3) language tradition (historicity), and (4) vitality (as a spoken language); from combinations of their values ('+' and '−' values) it is possible to deduce whether the language in question is a Standard, a dialect, a Creole or Pidgin language. The possible combinations are given in figure 5.18.

Attributes*				Type	Symbol
1	2	3	4		
+	+	+	+	standard	S
+	+	+	−	classic	C
+	+	−	−	artificial	A
−	+	+	+	'vernacular'	V
−	−	+	+	dialect	D
−	−	−	+	'creole'	K
−	−	−	−	'pidgin'	P

* 1 = standardization, 2 = autonomy, 3 = historicity, 4 = vitality.

Fig. 5.18 Stewart's classification of language types. (Source: Stewart 1968, 537)

The language types described by capital letters must be further specified according to their functions, which are denoted by small letters; attributes that can be assigned to the types are: (i) official (*o*), (ii) provincial (*p*), (iii) wider communication (*w*), (iv) international (*i*), (v) capital city (*c*), (vi) group (*g*), (vii) education (*e*), (viii) school subject (*s*), (ix) literary (*l*), (x) religion (*r*). With the help of the language types and language functions, 'profiles' can then be constructed for multilingual communities.

This is only meaningful if the degree of use is given as a percentage for each language type. The degree of use can be specified in terms of the following six classes: class I = 75 per cent, class II = 50, class III = 25, class IV = 10, class V = 5, class VI = under 5.

A sociolinguistic profile can be given for the Curaçao group of islands in the Dutch Antilles on these lines (after Stewart 1968, in Fishman 1968b, 544):

Class I	Papiamentu	*K* (diglossia: *H* variety Spanish)
Class IV	Dutch	*So*
	English	*Sigs*
Class V	Spanish	*Sisl* (diglossia: *L* variety Papiamentu)
Class VI	Hebrew	*Cr*
	Latin	*Crs*

5.5 Summary

The discussion of theoretical concepts in sociolinguistics led us from the more particular perspective of linguistic inquiry to the more general perspective of predominantly sociological descriptive problems. In the process we assumed that sociolinguistics can be pursued either as an interdisciplinary theory or as an extension of the traditional disciplines of sociology and linguistics. By referring to the USA as an example we showed briefly how closely the evolution of sociolinguistics in each of the two cases is linked to sociopolitical problems.

We shall combine our résumé or the theoretical concepts with some remarks on their explanatory power and their respective merits.

Attempts to attach sociolinguistic data to transformational theory seem viable only with respect to the grammatical components of phonology and syntax. Depending on the theoretical position taken, the extension of these components is either insignificant or far-reaching. The coexistence model is founded on an assumption of heterogeneity, but it is still conservative in that it fails to take sufficient account of the empirical validity of linguistic data in correlation with extralinguistic parameters. In this respect the implicational analysis goes a step further: it enables speakers to be classified according to implicationally-ordered intralinguistic features, which can then be correlated with social parameters. The starting point of both approaches reinforces an old linguistic tradition, namely that rules have to be categorical in nature. On the other hand, Labov's concept, in which linguistic data are quantified in ways that depend crucially on social parameters, implies that in addition to categorical rules there are also variable rules which, through quantitative weightings of intralinguistic and extralinguistic variable constraints, are particularly suited to rendering a differentiated account of the complex processes of linguistic variation and change. The status of these rules in a grammar is, however, still problematic: it is not clear whether they reflect speakers' basic capabilities or merely temporary manifestations of their speech behaviour.

Even though it is a commonly shared view, with regard to describing linguistic variation, that assertions made in two systems (linguistics and sociology) can only be correlated when these systems are defined independently of one another, there is still no agreement on the question of

1   whether idiolects or sociolects should be the subject of description;

2   whether the linguistic data should be treated as discrete categories and the sociological as nondiscrete, or vice versa;

3   whether the whole sphere of intuitionist speech description can be regarded as empirical, or whether linguistic descriptions should not rather be founded on sets of data that have been reliably obtained and elicited.

In our opinion it is precisely this last point which deserves a great deal more consideration in linguistics.

The grammatical concepts of description only explain language acquisition and linguistic change to a limited extent, since they take no account of semantic and pragmatic aspects. As the latter play a decisive part in any inquiry into the communicative competence of speakers, it seems that a simple extension of traditional syntax and phonology by social parameters must be less than adequate. Rather, a *qualitative* change in grammatical and semantic theory, more in keeping with anthropological and interactional linguistics, should lead to a consideration of the pragmatic conditions of speech acts, which are uttered in certain situations, at a certain time, in a certain place and under certain dynamic conditions of interaction. The grammatical categories are insufficient for a description of verbal interaction through speech acts, and for an adequate understanding of the processes by which speaker-hearers understand one another. The description of speech acts requires a comprehensive model of speech behaviour that includes the psychological and social configurations of interaction, as well as containing, amongst others, rules of interaction, interpretation and production specific to speaker-hearers. The concept of communicative competence seems the most promising for the foundation of a pragmatic model of social communication. On the basis of such a model it will also be possible to explain in greater depth the phonological and syntactic descriptions of speech variation.

In principle, analyses of bilingual language behaviour are dependent on the available means of describing speech variation and the pragmatic functions of utterances. Nevertheless they do involve special problems, which require an interdisciplinary approach, for example the determination of the degree to which bilingual speakers have a command of two languages, or of the degree of interference occurring as a result of constant shifting between two varieties. A possible solution is presented by Fishman's integrated sociolinguistic concept, which proceeds from constructs of a higher ordering (norm systems in language communities, domains of language behaviour) to constructs of a lower ordering (types of interaction, role relations, social networks, speech acts). The changes in the constellation of these constructs (e.g. in the sphere of the domains) show how languages change, in the context of what social dimensions and in what temporal stages. In terms of such a construct, language retention and loss depend essentially on the dominance configuration, which results from bilingual speakers' functional use of language, and on the positive or negative attitude towards varieties; measurement of such attitudes can yield information on linguistic norms.

The treatment of bilingualism led finally to the description of multilingual societies. Two criteria have been proposed to classify these: the extent to which bilingual and diglossic situations coocur in them, or reciprocally exclude one another; and the degree of standardization, autonomy, historicity and vitality of their language varieties.

Yet it was with regard to precisely these bilingual and multilingual societies that we noticed the superficiality of the descriptive concepts concerned. They relate, for example, certain types of language contact and change to norms that are not further specified, whereas their explanation requires an analysis of the underlying social conditions. An adequate explanation of the functional distribution of H and L varieties of bilingual and multilingual speaker-groups will only be achieved by an analysis of the historical development of societies which includes a specification of the social classes to which the various speakers belong.

⑥ Sociolinguistic competence of speakers: correlative and functional studies

This chapter is concerned chiefly with the application of theoretical concepts in empirical investigations. First, we shall describe the difficulties that arise in obtaining valid linguistic data, and outline some possible approaches of empirical methodology. In 6.2 and 6.3 we discuss results of American investigations into the grammatical and communicative competence of speakers, and it is the general significance of their findings which will enable us to formulate some typical aspects of the relationship between linguistic and social structures in 6.4.

6.1 Methodology of empirical linguistic investigations

The traditional disciplines of linguistics and sociology have followed different lines of empirical inquiry. This can be seen from the simple fact that sociology could only justify its status as a science by undertaking to investigate the multiplicity of social phenomena by means of inductive empirical methods (but on the problems raised by empirical inquiry, cf. Hahn 1968 and Topitsch 1968). Linguists, on the other hand, have always been able to fall back on their intuition to describe linguistic structure, and, for the last couple of decades, on a deductive linguistic theory with empirical predictive power, as well. As sociolinguistics is concerned with analysing and explaining linguistic behaviour in social environments, it shares the problems of all sociological inquiry: the justification and precise formulation of the problem; the representative selection of informants; the problems of obtaining and eliciting data; the choice of descriptive categories; and the explanation of social behaviour.

It is well known that these problems—which are only a few among many— can be approached in very different ways. In connection with the choice of method and subject for an investigation, sociology has emphasized in recent years (cf. Habermas 1967 and 1968) that the choice of categories and methods is largely determined by the analyst's own values, which can have a considerable influence on the results of the investigation. Sociological analysis is bounded by the incidental social experience of the analysts, who are themselves pursuing their inquiry from a concrete historical situation in society. Whether sociologists attribute a certain type of linguistic variation to different social values or norms, without further specifying these, or to deeper-lying elements of the social structure (e.g. economic conditions and the power structure), in both cases we have a manifestation of their academic interest, which is determined by their position and interests in this society. However successful their description of certain social conditions may be, it is the explanation which is crucial for theory and practice alike, since only this enables the knowledge gained to be applied meaningfully to the task of improving social conditions.

Empirical inquiry into speech behaviour is not a value-free academic activity. This has already been shown in respect of Bernstein's inquiries, and at the beginning of the last chapter by reference to examples in the USA,[1] where interest in sociolinguistic research is connected with political problems raised by ethnic minorities. We shall have to postpone, however, any demonstration of a correlation between the choice of analytical categories and the explanation advanced until we have elucidated the techniques of modern inquiry into speech behaviour and have presented their results.

We shall, therefore, within the context of general sociological inquiry, use the terminology associated with each particular study that is discussed and presented.

When considering the function of language studies from what until recently was taken to be a more linguistically-oriented perspective, one will, as a result of the history of this predominantly theoretical subject, pay relatively little attention to sociological aspects and problems. One of these problems is the relationship between theory and empirical requirements in the investigation of language; a further (sociological) problem is that of obtaining and eliciting linguistic material. First of all, we must establish why empirical language studies are necessary.

6.1.1 Relation between theory and methodology in linguistics

In the course of this work various references have been made to the general benefits to be gained from investigations into speech behaviour: as our knowledge of linguistic behaviour increases, our descriptions and explanations of language will become more precise; as language description becomes more precise, so it becomes easier to avoid, or at least to become aware of, communicative conflicts between people. Although the most recent formalization procedures in linguistics have proved to be a great step forward, in that sentences of a natural language can be generated as well as analysed, linguistics has, to its disadvantage, dissociated itself from the actual linguistic behaviour of speakers on the following points:

1   it is not possible to determine the correctness of descriptions to the extent that linguists describe solely their linguistic intuitions;
2   in analysing *possible* sentences, an analysis of sentences that actually *do* occur is often neglected;
3   the grammaticality and acceptability of utterances cannot be satisfactorily ascertained by questioning.

The Saussurean paradox—the social aspect of language can only be studied through the intuitions of any individual, whereas the individual aspect can only be investigated by examining an entire population (cf. 4.3.1) has given rise to the assumptions among generative grammarians that language is homogeneous, and that speakers have access to their competence by way of their intuitive judgements. The last point has led to the view that in order to verify the

---

[1] It will be a necessary and rewarding task to corroborate the viewpoints mentioned there on the basis of numerical material.

correctness of linguistic descriptions, speakers' utterances should be tested for grammaticality and acceptability. The initial straightforward dichotomy of 'grammatical-ungrammatical' was soon replaced by the proposal of a scale of grammaticality (Chomsky 1961), which in practice was limited to three types: * = ungrammatical, ? = questionable, ?* = questionable, but close to ungrammatical. At the same time, the class of data was extended to include judgements on ambiguity and correct paraphrasing, judgements on the formal identity or distinctness of sentence types, as well as on proper pronunciation. When two (or more) theories are in competition with regard to the explanation of the data (i.e. the judgements) gathered, and none of these theories makes factually false predictions (to the extent that this has been investigated), then the *simplest* theory is preferred. This criterion of simplicity is applied in two steps: (1) within the terms of the language under description, that theory (grammar) is preferred which makes more predictions with fewer rules; (2) if there are still competitors left, that theory is preferred which agrees best with what is known about reliable grammars of other languages. The second step ensures the most specific set of linguistic universals.

In all this, the empirical reliability of the data has always been a problem: linguists differ considerably in their syntactic and semantic judgements. Therefore, the problem arises of how this difficult passage from data to theory is to be negotiated. Dissatisfied with the fact that linguists often fail to come to an agreement as a result of conflicting intuitions, Elliot, Legum and Thompson (1969) presented a set of linguists with four gradually differing sentences, which they were then asked to judge with regard to their acceptability on a scale of four marks. The results could be described on an implicational scale as ordered variation.

Although this example shows that speakers can, according to their judgements, be ordered in group-specific formation, speakers' judgements should nevertheless be treated with scepticism. Judgements are often just reports of what one thinks one's own speech behaviour is like; they vary from one situation to another, and do not always reflect the actual speech used (cf. the self-evaluation tests in Labov 1966a, 455–80; see also Labov 1972d, 213). In fact, descriptive problems can often be resolved more satisfactorily by means of systematic observation of natural speech behaviour (cf., for example, the description of the English copula by Labov 1969; 1972d, 226–34) than by intuitive judgements. The more restricted data set of generative grammarians can be enriched by better methods of observation: 'The more that is known about a language, the more we can find out about it' (Labov, in Klein and Wunderlich 1971, 128). Better quality data have the great advantage of providing a first criterion for deciding between competing descriptions (theories): observational inadequacy will be spotted more quickly and with greater precision. We will thus have better tools for the elimination of bad theories, and our chances of being on the right track will be improved.

6.1.2 Social categories and collection of linguistic data

A fundamental problem is to ascertain what information on what type of speech behaviour should be obtained from what speakers, and in what way. Currently, there are two methods used to solve this problem: the correlative and the functional approaches.

The *correlative approach* regards the relation between linguistic and social categories as one of closely-connected but independent systems. Verbal means are used to convey information about the material environment of individuals (in surveys using questionnaires, interviews, particular tests). Social categories are considered to be part of this material environment; they are measured by social characteristics that are independent of the process of communication. The empirical premise is that systematic changes in the social and linguistic structure can be revealed by correlating the two sets of variables which have been measured independently of one another. Categories such as socioeconomic status (which is generally determined by income, education and occupation), place of birth, membership of groups, age, certain attitudes in evaluation tests etc. serve as social indices. In the correlation, the social categories are usually treated as *independent* variables, and the linguistic ones as *dependent* variables (cf. 6.2).

The principle is explained by an example from an investigation by Labov (1966a; 1972d), in which (r) is used as a variable indicating social status: '... if any two sub-groups of New York City speakers are ranked in a scale of social stratification, then they will be ranked in the same order by their differential use of (r)' (Labov 1972d, 44).

Functional or ethnomethodological approach. In sociology, correlative approaches have been criticized by Garfinkel (1967) and Cicourel (1970), among others; as regards sociolinguistic inquiry, it is chiefly Gumperz who has objected to this method. According to Gumperz (1967, 131ff.), correlations can only provide inadequate explanations for variations in speech behaviour. In the first place, they do not explain why it is that speech behaviour varies in different societies with social categories that are based on very different criteria; secondly (and this is the main objection) correlations do not enable us to understand the different social norms and rules underlying the actual communicative behaviour of subjects, or to know the differences in their perception of social relations.

Gumperz maintains that the inadequacy of correlative measurements is overcome by the interactionist approach (e.g. Garfinkel, Cicourel), which rejects the parallel between social and 'physical' measurements. Its point of departure is rather that information about social categories can be obtained only from linguistic data. Thus sociological measurement always entails the perception of the categories to be measured, both by the informants and by the interviewer:

> 'Just as the meaning of words is always affected by context, social categories must be interpreted in terms of situational constraints. Concepts such as status and role are thus not permanent qualities of speakers: instead they become abstract communicative symbols, somewhat like phonemes and morphemes. Like the latter they can be isolated in the analyst's abstract model, but they are always perceived in particular contexts. The division between linguistic and social categories is thus obliterated.' (Gumperz 1967, 132)

Communication is thus regarded as a unique process, in the course of which speakers modify stimuli from the external environment in accordance with their cultural background, and derive from these the communicative norms for the situation concerned. Figure 6.1 illustrates the way in which the norms govern the selection of verbal signals. The double line represents the distinction between the actual communication process and the external stimuli, which are transformed by cognitive categorization into communicative symbols. After this first categorization, every piece of information that the speaker wants to communicate is remoulded by social and situational restrictions (tree diagram). These restrictions determine the social identity of the speaker, his rights and duties at certain social events in certain environments. From this process is then derived, via the behavioural norms, the selection of an appropriate code (speech variety), which further determines the type of transmission channel (oral, written etc.) and the phonological and syntactic rules by which the concrete utterances are produced.

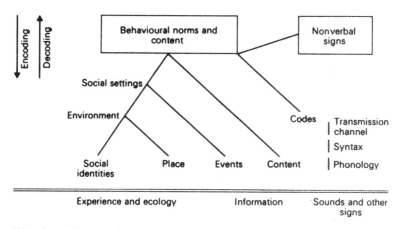

Fig. 6.1 Communication process.
(Source: Gumperz 1967, 133)

The components of communication which Ervin-Tripp adduces as independent variables (cf. 5.3.2) are conceived by Gumperz as hierarchical stages in the communicative process.

From the point of view of obtaining and eliciting data, the interactionist view (see 5.4.1 (4)) means that social relations become the most important determinants of speech behaviour. 'Outside factors such as ecology, rank, educational background significantly affect verbal behaviour only to the extent that they influence speakers' perception of their social relationships' (Gumperz 1967, 134). The sociolinguist, who is aiming at an adequate description of speech variation, must try to grasp the normative rules underlying performance. The only possible ways for him to achieve this are participant observation, unstructured interviews and protocols or records of conversations.

6.1.3 The Observer's Paradox and its solution

The reliable observation of linguistic facts, a task most intensively pursued by William Labov with his combination of correlative and functional techniques (cf. Labov *et al.* 1968), is affected by four difficulties, which experience has shown to handicap the systematic investigation of everyday language (Labov 1970a, quoted in Fishman 1971b, 156–9): (1) the ungrammaticality of actual speech (asserted by Chomsky and others); (2) variations in speech behaviour and in the speech community (the often inexplicable shifting of speakers between different stylistic variants); (3) difficulties in hearing and recording (the analysis of speech sounds uttered in the social context is frequently complicated by noise interference); (4) the rarity of certain syntactic forms (certain constructions that play an important part in solving questions of description only appear rarely in the data, or not at all).

These difficulties are not all equally serious, and they can be partly reduced. According to Labov (in Fishman 1971b, 165ff.), (1) proves to be of very limited impact: in his surveys 75 per cent of sentences were well formed; if ellipse and 'editing' rules are applied to incomplete utterances that are attributable to stammering or speech errors, then the number of ungrammatical sentences drops to 2 per cent. As far as (2) is concerned, we have already made sufficient reference to the ordered heterogeneity of speech variation. Systematic variation parallel to social parameters can be demonstrated with a random sample of only 25 speakers (Labov *et al.* 1968), sometimes even for an extremely small group of five speakers (Labov 1966a). The development of taperecorders that could be fitted with various refinements[2] played a decisive part in overcoming the problems mentioned in (3) by producing speech recordings, sometimes of excellent quality. Finally, the problem of the rarity of certain linguistic constructions can be reduced, to some extent at least, if, on the lines of participant observation, speakers are drawn into normal conversations where forms of a certain rarity can be unobtrusively elicited (cf. Labov and Waletzky 1967).

The way is now clear for a discussion of the methods of obtaining valid speech data. This task imposes various demands on the inquirer: the suitable selection of speakers, establishing an appropriate rapport with them, arranging the techniques necessary for eliciting and recording data, and defining social and linguistic parameters. Five methodological principles or hypotheses can be formulated for empirical linguistic research (Labov calls them 'methodological axioms'), which are based on past 'fieldwork' projects (Labov 1966a and Labov *et al.* 1968) and lead to a methodological paradox, the solution of which is central for empirical inquiry (Labov 1972d, 208f.). They are as follows:

1   *Style shifting.* As the social context and topic change, speakers shift between styles, which are characterized by particular linguistic features.
2   *Attention.* 'Attention' is a criterion by which different styles can be defined: '. . . *styles can be ranged along a single dimension, measured by the amount of attention paid to speech*' (Labov, *ibid.*). This hypothesis is based partly on the observation that speakers use the same linguistic variables in informal as well as in highly emotional speech. The common factor for both styles is that minimum attention is paid to one's own speech.

[2] Cf. the informative description of types of recorder and all the accessories necessary for fieldwork given by Stross (in Slobin 1967, 71–83), who also discusses questions of recording techniques, transcription, tape indexing and care of tapes.

3   *Vernacular.* As the vernacular is the natural means of communication between speakers and is hardly subject to their monitoring, it provides a good basis for data of natural speech behaviour.

4   *Formality.* This axiom reflects the interview situation as a formal speech situation: '*Any systematic observation of a speaker defines a formal context in which more than the minimum attention is paid to speech.*' Even if the interview situation appears natural and relaxed, it must nevertheless be assumed that speakers have a command of a style other than that which is manifest in the interview situation.

5   *Good data.* In spite of objections and granting the merits of other methods (group sessions, anonymous observation), the individual, taperecorded interview must be said to offer the most reliable method for systematically obtaining speech data.

Analysing speech behaviour on the lines of these five 'axioms' would not present any great difficulties if it were not for the '*Observer's Paradox:* the aim of linguistic research in the community must be to find out how people talk when they are not being systematically observed; yet we can only obtain this data by systematic observation' (Labov 1972d, 209).

The success of empirical data collection depends on how this paradox can best be solved. Some approaches concentrate essentially on altering the interview situation and supplementing the interview data with other data. The main techniques, however, proposed for overcoming the observer's paradox are as follows (cf. Labov 1972d, 209–12):

1   *Adapting the interview situation.* Various devices may be employed to divert the interviewee's attention from the formality of the situation and to induce him to speak in the vernacular. Some of these are: allowing the informant to digress, or to talk about his childhood, asking him to recount an unusual event ('have you ever been in a situation where you were in serious danger of being killed?'), inserting a break in the interview, during which other things are discussed.

2   *Group sessions.* Speakers often display their 'normal' speech behaviour in natural interactions with friends. In group sessions the effect of systematic observation is reduced to a minimum. (Such sessions, combined with individual interviews, were carried out in the studies of Gumperz (1966) and Labov *et al.* (1968)).

3   *Rapid and anonymous interviews.* Whereas in (1) and (2) the demographic data of every individual person are known, this is dispensed with in anonymous interviews. They serve, among other things, to verify whether a chosen variable actually is a social indicator. For this it is important that the situation should be informal. In his preliminary investigation into class-specific speech forms in New York City, Labov (1966a, 63–87) tested the variable (r) in three New York department stores, which he stratified according to the class to which their customers belonged.

4   *Unsystematic observations.* They are intended to verify whether the speech data obtained in interviews, group sessions etc. actually are representative of the vernacular. It is possible to test a number of constant and variable linguistic features in conversations with speakers or by observing them in public places such as stations, bus stops etc. They can be a corrective of the results of systematic observation.

5   *Mass media.* Linguistic data can also be obtained from radio and television broadcasts, although here the speakers do not vary much in status and verbal repertoire. The most formal speech style can be observed in these broadcasts.

6   *Stylistic range.* Informants vary their verbal expression according to the degree of attention with which they monitor their speech. When reading individual, unconnected words they will pay more attention to the pronunciation of individual sounds than in informal conversations. In his New York City study Labov (1966a, 90–135) distinguished five styles: (a) *casual speech* (in the family, with friends), (b) *careful speech* (semi-formal; normal case in interviews), (c) *reading*, (d) *word lists* and (e) *minimal pairs* ((c)–(e) are monitored reading styles whose degree of formality increases from (c) to (e)).

Levine and Crockett (1967) discovered how to elicit the less well monitored style by embedding (r), the variable to be tested, in certain sentences; they diverted the subjects' attention from the variable by asking them to insert lexical units into gaps that had been left in the sentences. The subjects devoted all their concentration to this task and produced the (r) as naturally as in conversations.

Tests are to be carried out to provide further information on speech behaviour. They are an important means of checking the validity of data that have been obtained. Examples are (cf. Labov 1972d, 212–4):

Repetition tests. These test the degree to which speakers adhere to the variety they use in everyday speech. Blacks, who normally spoke in Non-Standard, repeated Standard sentences in the Non-Standard form to which they were accustomed. This proved how regular and spontaneous their command of Non-Standard was.

Language attitude tests. As pointed out in 5.4.4, informants evaluate speech samples played back to them, which contain variants that have been stigmatized to varying degrees. They then arrange the speakers of these samples on a scale, perhaps in response to the question, 'What is the highest position that the speaker could occupy with his type of speech and manner of speaking?' Subjective reaction tests make it possible to separate linguistic variables from factors relating to personality.

Self-evaluation tests. These are a means of finding out the speaker's assessment of his own speech behaviour. They often reveal a discrepancy between actual speech and the speaker's own idea of it.

'*Classroom correction tests*' (correction tests based on scholastic norms). These give an insight into the speaker's consciousness of stigmatized speech variants.

The subjects correct sentences in which taboo expressions occur that are normally subject to sanction by teachers. The speaker's knowledge of stigmatized forms can be inferred from the degree of accuracy and the completeness of the corrections he makes (in connection with this cf. the revealing study on teacher behaviour vis-à-vis pupils made by Seligman, Tucker and Lambert (1972)).

Such tests should be seen as yielding secondary data of further (dis)confirmation. They are only of importance when an assessment of what constitutes the speakers' natural behaviour has been hypothetically derived from interviews and participant observation. In connection with the repetition tests, Labov writes: 'Despite the many advantages of repetition tests, we feel it necessary to enter a strong warning against the adoption of such methods by those who wish to study the linguistic competence of Negro children without an accompanying study of the actual use of language by these children in favorable environments.' (Labov *et al.* 1968, I, 310)

6.2 Correlative studies

The correlative studies described in this section relate exclusively to phonology and syntax. Apart from the early investigations and one analysis using the implicational scale, the instrument of analysis is predominantly the linguistic variable (cf. 5.2.1).

6.2.1 First empirical investigations into speech variation

The systematic covariation of linguistic and sociological features was demonstrated for the first time in the course of the 1950s by three studies. Putnam and O'Hern (1955) reveal, by means of subjective evaluation tests, the significance of status marks in speech, using the example of an extremely low status group; Fischer (1958) proves the significant use of a linguistic variant as specific to sex and context; and Reichstein (1960) investigates the linguistic change of some phoneme variants in Paris.

Putnam and O'Hern selected a socially isolated group of Blacks from Washington with an extremely low status, whose family organization was matriarchal and whose social values were opposed to the surrounding society. Interviews (formal) and conversations (informal) were carried out with 74 people, taperecorded and then transcribed phonetically. The first part of the investigation is the grammatical description of the BEV dialect, the second part is concerned with its social evaluation.

The phonemic structure was divided into segments and suprasegments. The former were specified according to vowels, consonants and diphthongs, the latter related to stress and intonation, which were represented on spectrograms and oscillograms. In grammar, deviations from the Standard were found in *verb morphology* (an -*s* suffix was used for all forms except the third person; 'be' was used as a full verb) and in *word order* (e.g. in interrogative sentences there was no inversion). The double negative was recorded as a special syntactic marker.

Together with nine speech samples of speakers with a higher social status (status criteria: income, occupation, type of house, area of residence), three samples of this analysed BEV dialect were played back to three groups of subjects, who were asked to judge the social status of the recorded speakers (first group: men v. women; second group: Whites v. Blacks; third group: students v. teachers). The evaluations were marked up on a measuring scale with a high-low continuum.

All the subjects were able to identify the speakers' status with the help of the samples. The low status was recognized with the highest degree of reliability.

This investigation described for the first time language attitudes and the BEV dialect. Labov (1966a, 19) criticizes it in two respects: first, the selection of the subjects was relatively unsystematic; secondly, it is not clear precisely what the linguistic variables were to which the subjects reacted in the evaluations.

Fischer (1958) investigates the social significance of the variants *-in* and *-ing* of the present participle ending. His sample comprises 24 children from a village in New England (two age groups: 3–6 and 7–10, an equal number of boys and girls). All the children had to tell a story, and this served as material for analysis; some of the older children had to answer a questionnaire, others were given an interview. The most important results were:

1. *Differences specific to sex:* more girls than boys used *-ing*. Fischer considers *-ing* to be the characteristic of female speech, and *-in* that of male speech.
2. *Status:* children with higher status used more *-ings*; these results were, however, not significant.
3. *Situation:* the variants are good indicators of the degree of formality; the frequency of the *-ing* forms decreases as the situation becomes more informal.

Fischer sees his results as confirming two hypotheses: linguistic variants are socially conditioned; investigations of this type contribute to the explanation of linguistic change.

The first large-scale analysis of speech forms in cities was carried out by Ruth Reichstein (1960) in Paris. Five hundred and seventy Parisian schoolchildren from three socially different types of school were examined on their use of three phonemic contrasts, which were supposed to indicate the phonetic change from the older to the younger generation: (1) /a–ɑ/(e.g. in *patte/pâte*);(2) /ɛ–ɛ:/ (e.g. in *belle/bêle*); (3) /ɛ̃–œ̃/ e.g. in *brin/brun*). The quantitative analysis reveals that the phonemic contrasts disappear relatively rapidly, this development being promoted by the working class districts near the centre of the city. This result suggests an explanation of linguistic change as a result of the pressure exerted by the lower social classes. The quantification of the linguistic units was related to the following extralinguistic variables: (1) type of school, (2) *arrondissement*, (3) parental occupation (middle-class or lower-class), (4) origin of the parents (Paris or the provinces).

As Paris is the source of linguistic prestige in France, the results are, to some extent, typical of the whole country.

The main weaknesses of this investigation are that only female subjects were selected, and that the interviews were carried out in a formal situation at school. Nevertheless, in this study linguistic change is approached, for the first time, in relation to extralinguistic parameters.

6.2.2   Class-specific speech forms in New York City

Labov's investigation (1966a) was the first accurate, empirically-founded analysis of speech behaviour, introducing new methods in linguistics and offering new explanations for linguistic variation and change.

The most important features of this study are: the selection of speakers according to well-defined social categories, the distinction of context-specific speech styles and the correlation of linguistic variables with extralinguistic parameters.

Sample. 155 speakers from New York's 'Lower East Side' were selected on the basis of a sociological investigation that had been carried out earlier. The speakers represented various ethnic groups (New Yorkers, Italians, Jews, Blacks) and different social classes (upper middle class (UMC), lower middle class (LMC), upper working class (UWC), lower working class (LWC)). The classification into social classes was made on three criteria: income, education and occupation, on a formally constructed scale of 10 marks. The speakers were selected in such a way that they were representative of the different social and ethnic groups. The correlations between linguistic features and extralinguistic parameters were not checked for statistical significance.

Interview. 122 subjects were given interviews in their homes, concerning the following points (Labov 1966a, 589–602):

1   *Social background details:* questions on the speakers' income, occupation, place of birth, age, religion, mother tongue, personal status etc.
2   *Lexicon:* questions on everyday objects (this was designed to record lexical differences).
3   *Social customs:* questions on the environment in which the speaker grew up, and on general social activities.
4   *Syntax and semantics:* specific questions on speech form; speakers were induced to tell a story, which was used for grammatical analysis.
5   *Pronunciation:* reading a story aloud, reading a list of words, reading selected word pairs containing minimal phonemic oppositions (*god/guard*).
6   *Questions on the linguistic norm:* speakers had to establish which of two linguistic variants represented, in their opinion, the correct pronunciation.
7   *Speech reaction tests:* reaction tests to samples of speech from New York speakers; self-evaluation tests in respect of the assessment of one's own speech.
8   *Linguistic attitude:* questions on the assessment and evaluation of speakers of linguistic varieties other than that of New York.

Each interview was taperecorded in full. If other members of the family were met during the interview, they were if possible also included in the interview, especially children.

For technical reasons 33 subjects could only be given brief interviews, but these were so designed that they were able to answer satisfactorily the questions important for the investigation as a whole.

Context-specific styles. Four contexts were isolated, in accordance with 6.1.3 (axioms 1 and 4; point 6 for overcoming the observer's paradox), for which a total of five different styles were assumed (91–8): *A*, casual speech; *B*, careful speech; *C*, reading style (reading a longer passage); *D*, word lists (individual words with different variables acting as social markers); *D'*, minimal pairs (phonemic oppositions). It proved problematic to establish the nature of casual speech (Labov 1972c, 94–9). Normally this is not to be found in the interview situation unless it is skilfully provoked. Section 6.1.3 shows how this can be achieved, under the heading *interrupting the interview situation*. In order to distinguish between careful and natural speech, Labov (1966a, 110) lists formal criteria, which relate to actual characteristics of speech: changes in speech rhythm, in pitch range and in the rate of breathing. Laughter in particular was regarded as a sign of natural speech behaviour. Wolfram (1969, 58f.) and Bickerton (1971, 467) have criticized these 'channel cues' as formal indicators of casual speech, describing them as unsuitable criteria.

Labov sees the five styles as a continuum between an informal and a formal end.

Linguistic variables. Linguistic variables are selected on the basis of four criteria (Labov 1966a, 166): the variable should (1) have a high frequency, (2) be as immune as possible to conscious suppression, (3) be an integrated component of a larger structure and (4) be easily quantifiable on a linear scale. These conditions are fulfilled by the phonological variables *(oh)*, *(eh)*, *(r)*, *(th)* and *(dh)*, whose quantification is intended to indicate social, ethnic and stylistic differentiation. The social significance of the variable *(r)* was successfully tested in a preliminary investigation (*ibid.*, 63–89). The five variables were subdivided, according to articulatory phonetic qualities, into a number of variants. The differentiation of the variable *(eh)* is given in figure 6.2:

No. of the variable	Phonetic quality	Examples
*(eh-*1)	$[\text{I}^{<:\theta}]$	NYC *beer, beard*
*(eh-*2)	$[\text{e}^{<:\theta}]$ $[\varepsilon^{<:\theta}]$	NYC *bear, bared*
*(eh-*3)	$[\text{ae}^{\wedge}{:}]$	
*(eh-*4)	$[\text{ae}{:}]$	NYC *bat, batch*
*(eh-*5)	$[\text{a}{:}]$	Eastern New England *pass, aunt*

Fig. 6.2 Index of the variables *(eh)*.
(Source: Labov 1972d, 75)

The correlation of extralinguistic parameters with the phonological variables shows that the latter discriminate regularly with respect to both social status and stylistic variation. If we interpret the fact that speakers belong to different classes as meaning that they adapt differently to social norms, and if we regard stylistic differentiation as reflecting degrees of speech monitoring. then the linguistic variable differentiates along both dimensions, as is shown in figure 6.3.

Thus the variable discriminates factors that are founded in the social history of

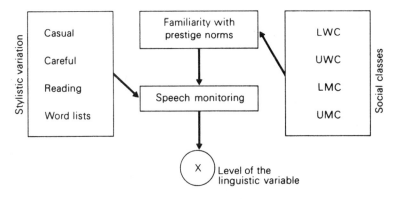

Fig. 6.3 Level of the intervening linguistic variable.
(Source: Labov 1971a, 203)

the individual as well as those that determine his social relations with the hearer, the speech context and the topic of conversation. Linguistic variables differentiate two-dimensionally the *social distance* and the *stylistic function*.

This can be demonstrated by the example of the variable (*th*), whose index ((*th*–0) denotes the fricative [θ], (*th*–1) the affricate [tθ], and (*th*–2) the plosive [*t*]) varies with regular variation of style and socioeconomic status.

The other variables also indicate like the variable (*th*), differences in social status, style, sex, age and ethnic group.

On the basis of the results quantified, linguistic features can be either indicators or markers.

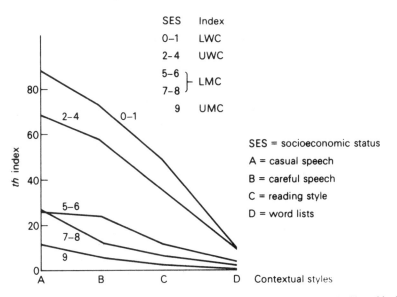

Fig. 6.4 Stratification of the variable (*th*) for adult speakers born in New York.
(Source: Labov 1966a, 260; also 1972d, 113, 125)

Indicators are evenly distributed for socioeconomic, ethnic and age groups alike; they are used in a relatively similar way by every individual in every context. The *markers*, which are more highly developed and more sensitive sociolinguistic variables, go beyond systematic social distribution and reveal stylistic differentiation. In figure 6.4 the variable (*th*) shows the interrelationship of social and stylistic stratification. It is a stable sociolinguistic marker (cf. Labov 1970a, 66f.). Prestige form is the fricative; its variants, affricate and plosive, on the other hand, are stigmatized.

Reaction tests. It is possible that the regular distribution of the linguistic variables in correlation with social parameters is coincidental; in order to check the validity of the results, Labov (1966a, 405–54) made informants react to the variables by employing Lambert's 'matched guise technique' (cf. 5.4.4). The reaction tests were designed to solve three problems:

1   'to isolate the subjective reactions to particular values of a single variable;
2   to reduce these reactions to a quantitative measure;
3   to find the overall structure reflected in the pattern of the resulting measurements' (407).

The individual variables were distributed with particularly high frequency in samples of speech that were recorded on tape. Speakers then had to evaluate on a scale of 7 marks what status (specified as different occupations) they would assign to the recorded speaker.[3]

The results obtained from the interviews were completely corroborated by the reaction tests. A general principle may therefore be derived: '*the correlate of regular stratification of a sociolinguistic variable in behavior is uniform agreement in subjective reactions towards that variable*' (Labov 1970a, 74). These features of linguistic expressions that stimulate unconscious and uniform reactions in the speech community can be termed *stereotypes*; they reflect the linguistic norms of a society.

Results and explanations. The diagrams showing the correlation of linguistic variables with social parameters make it possible to explain speakers' modes of behaviour and certain trends of development of the linguistic structure: the history of language acquisition in different age groups (Labov 1964b), the social stratification of the vowel system in New York City (Labov 1966a, 507–75) and general tendencies of linguistic change (Labov 1965 and 1966b) as well as the social mobility of speakers (Labov 1966b and 1966d).

We shall now be concerned solely with the process of linguistic change, to which Labov attaches particular importance in evaluating his results:

'Variability itself is change: but some types of variation are themselves invariant from generation to generation. We are particularly interested in gradual alteration of the linguistic habits of a population through the course of time, which will be referred to here as linguistic change.' (1966a, 318)

---

[3] The speaker was the same in all recordings; he was able to reproduce the different variants so correctly that the subjects thought the speech samples came from different speakers.

The hypercorrect pattern of the LMC for the variable (*r*), as well as the 'fine' stratification of variable (*r*) and the 'sharp' stratification of the variables (*th*) and (*dh*), is particularly suitable for explaining linguistic change.[4]

According to Labov, the phenomenon of *hypercorrection* is a reliable index of linguistic change. The social and stylistic differentiation of the variables (*r*), represented in figure 6.5, shows a sudden, sharp 'crossover' of the lower middle class (LMC) for the end of the stylistic continuum, styles *D* and *D'*.

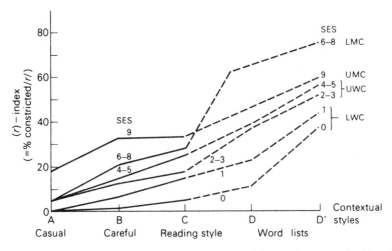

Fig. 6.5 Class-specific distribution of the variables (*r*) guard, car etc. for New York adults.
(Source: Labov 1966a, 240; 1972d, 114)

The same pattern as that in figure 6.5 is also produced for the variables (*eh*) and (*oh*). The LMC's crossover over the UMC reflects a 'change in progress', given that, whereas before the second world war the vernacular in New York was *r*-less, the *r* pronunciation has now become a prestige norm. It is precisely this process that is reflected by the LMC's use of (*r*). They pronounce *r* overcorrectly in their eagerness to establish a link with the prestige norm. This and other linguistic features show that in their social behaviour the LMC is upward mobile (1966d).

The historical dimension, implied in the 'linguistic change' interpretation of the LMC crossover behaviour with respect to (*r*) in more formal styles of speaking, is shown explicitly when the proportions of pronounced *r*'s are plotted over age groups for each social class and for each speaking style (Labov 1970a, 74; and 1972d, 116, 137). Such a plotting for style A (casual) reveals a sudden and dramatic increase (from about 10 per cent to about 40 per cent in the pronunciation of *r* in the UMC age group of 39 years and younger,—which is

---

[4] Sharp stratification for a linguistic variable means that its distribution over social classes is not continuous but discrete: the classes cluster in their use or avoidance of the variable, as in figure 6.4. Fine stratification means that the linguistic variable displays continuously differentiated values: there are 'a great many divisions of the socioeconomic continuum in which stratification is preserved at each stylistic level'; the values of the variable relate closely to the 'continuous network of social and economic factors', as in figure 6.5 (Labov 1966a, 235f. and 1972c, 113–4).

roughly the generation who acquired their language in the years preceding and during world war II. Interestingly, this increase in *r*-pronunciation among UMC speakers is matched by a drop in *r*-pronunciation among the same age group of all other classes, whose *r*-incidence approaches zero. (*r*) has thus become an unmistakable marker of UMC behaviour and norms.

Labov concludes (1972d, 115) that 'the hypercorrect behavior of the lower middle class is . . . a synchronic indicator of linguistic change in progress.' It does seem, however, that it can be no more than a mere indicator: age plotting is necessary to establish the conclusion of 'change in progress'. In general, neither the distinction between fine and sharp stratification, nor an (upward or downward) crossover seems sufficient to predict that a change is taking place for the variable in question. As we shall see below, the (slight) downward crossover for the variable (*th*), as shown in figure 6.4, does not indicate change. It would be of interest to investigate whether an empirical correlation can be established between certain patterns of distribution of a linguistic variable over a speech community and a change in progress, without isolating the factor 'age'. (As for age plotting, the reader is referred to Labov's exemplary analysis for (*r*) in New York City mentioned above, as well as to his chart for the variable (*aw*) in Martha's Vineyard (Labov 1965, 98).)

In the context of linguistic change, Labov distinguishes between *pressures from above* and *pressures from below*:

> 'By *below* is meant "below the level of conscious awareness". Pressures from below operate upon entire linguistic systems, in response to social motivations which are relatively obscure and yet have the greatest significance for the general evolution of language. . . . Social pressures from above . . . represent the overt process of social correction applied to individual linguistic forms. In this process the special role of the lower middle class, or more generally, the role of the second-ranking status group, will be the principal focus of attention.' (Labov 1972d, 123)

Upward crossover of the LMC has traditionally been called *hypercorrection*. It is a clear case of pressures from above.

For a correct understanding of linguistic change it is necessary to distinguish between *real* and *apparent* time. Until recently, linguistic change had only been considered with regard to its taking place in real time, which has the disadvantage that processes of change can only be interpreted retrospectively. On the basis of synchronic analysis, however, change can also be observed in apparent time when linguistic features are plotted over social and age groups. Labov (1966b, 95; 1972d, 133) isolates the following channels of change:

1   Stigmatized feature: a) not in process of change
                                    b) in process of change

2   Prestige feature: a) not in process of change
                                    b) in process of change

3   Change from below: a) early stage
                                    b) later stage with correction from above

There are empirical examples for each of these categories. The variable (*th*) corresponds to the case of the stigmatized feature in (1) which is not involved in change. (*oh*) indicates the early stage of a change as pressure from below ('change from below'), whereas the diagram values of the variables (*eh*) show the later stage of a change to be pressure from below which is taken over and corrected by the upper classes.

6.2.3 Phonological variation of bilingual Puerto Ricans

In the comprehensive study *Bilingualism in the Barrio* (Fishman *et al.* 1968), a team of sociologists, psychologists and linguists investigated the context-specific bilingualism (Spanish, English) of 431 Puerto Ricans living in the New York area. The demographic data were taken from a government survey and supplemented with speakers' own accounts as well as tests in linguistic skill, which took place in interviews and test sessions lasting from two to four hours.

The investigation is subdivided according to the following headings, on the lines of Fishman's interdisciplinary theory, outlined in 5.4.1, whose nucleus is the behavioural domains:

1   *Studies of the social background* (ethnographic relation of the Puerto Ricans (PR) to the New York population; position, capabilities and evaluation of PR intellectuals; attitudes and modes of behaviour of PRs; the press's opinion of PRs).
2   *Sociologically-oriented analyses* (sociolinguistic data from the census; interviews; measurements of the situational speech variations of PRs with regard to person, place and topic).
3   *Psychologically-oriented studies* (tests in reading, writing and linguistic skill, of which the most common are word naming and word association tests (cf. Cooper 1969 and Cooper, Fowler and Givner 1969); comprehension and evaluation tests; measurements of the interaction of language, the behavioural domain and the semantic dimension in bilingual speakers).
4   *Linguistically-oriented studies* (variation of phonological variables; prosodic features, cf. Silverman 1969).

For the rest of this section we shall restrict ourselves to selected aspects of the linguistic analysis of the phonological variation of bilingual PRs (for detailed results cf. Ma and Herasimchuk in Fishman *et al.* 1968, V, 636–928). The techniques employed in the survey and analysis correspond to a great extent with those of Labov (1966a).

Demographic variables. The analysis was based on four demographic variables: sex, age, education and birthplace. Social class was not taken into account as a variable, since PRs must in general be identified with the working class.

Context-specific styles. Five context styles were to be isolated, on the lines of Labov, which would form a formal-informal continuum:

A   casual speech (expressing personal opinions);

B   careful speech (answering certain calculated questions, half of which were in
       Spanish, half in English);
C   'word naming' (the speakers were asked to name as many words as they
       could think of for five domains (home, district lived in, school, work,
       church); this test was carried out separately for Spanish and English);
D   reading four passages, two in Spanish, two in English;
E   word lists (two word lists had to be read, one Spanish and one English).

Only *A*, *B* and *C* were drawn up for the analysis as the data for the other two
contexts were very limited.

Linguistic variables. The speech samples obtained in the interviews were
evaluated independently by two linguists for seven Spanish and ten English
variables. We shall be concerned here with only one Spanish and one English
variable, but these may be regarded as representative for the other variables (for
what follows cf. also Fishman 1971b, 273 80).

The Spanish variant SpC–0 relates to the omission of the plural marker -*s*, when
the next word begins with a consonant (example: (1) for SpC–0; *los muchacho
comen*, contrary to the Standard realization (2) SpC–1: *los muchachos comen* and
to the usual PR variant (3) SpC–2: *los muchachoh comen*). SpC–0 proved to be a
suitable feature for differentiating context-specific styles.

The English variant EH–2 represents the [ae] sound of Standard American in
cat and *bad*. EH–2, as distinct from EH–1 in New York City English (e.g. [kɛ:ˀt],
[bɛˀd] and EH–3 in accentuated English (e.g. *cahn't, bahd*), was suitable as a
variable chiefly because it differentiates clearly between accentuated and
naturally spoken English and is, moreover, not present in the Spanish phonemic
system.

Hypotheses. The general hypothesis for the Spanish variable was that only
contextual, and not demographic, factors were responsible for variation.
Precisely the reverse was postulated for the English variable: it was assumed that
variation was only attributable to demographic, and not context-specific, factors.

Statistical methods. The statistical technique employed was the 'analysis of
variance via multiple regression analysis' (Fishman 1971b, 271). This method was
designed to ascertain any significance that could be ascribed to individual factors,
or to the simultaneous interaction of different effects.

> 'Analyses of variance can tell us whether context, age, education, or birthplace
> are separately significant in explaining variation in the production of a
> particular linguistic variant or whether the interaction between any two of
> them, e.g. between context and birthplace, has explanatory significance.
> Multiple regression analysis is a technique designed to answer questions
> concerning the value of utilizing additional explanatory parameters beyond
> those already utilized at any given stage in the explanatory process.' (Fishman
> 1971b, 271)

Results. The hypotheses were completely confirmed. The realization of the
Spanish variant SpC–0 varies primarily with contextual factors along the formal-

informal continuum, whereas demographic factors either have only secondary significance, or none at all. When the demographic factors are taken into account in the analysis of variance, it becomes quite clear that the norms specific to the language community associated *SpC*–0 with informal rather than formal situations. Other variables corroborate the same tendency. One should therefore assume on the basis of phonological results that the PR district is a homogeneous speech network with substantially uniform linguistic norms.

The reverse applies for the variation of the English variables. *EH*–2 does not show any recognizable specific contextual variation for the PR district. There are thus no commonly shared English linguistic norms. In other words, *EH*–2 varies exclusively with demographic variables. Fishman (1971b, 280) draws two conclusions from the analysis of the phonological variance of bilingual Puerto Ricans:

1   For Spanish, the sample of speakers investigated has commonly shared norms and uniform speech networks, whereas the same is not true for English.
2   Contextual and demographic variance do not always coincide (as, for example, was the case in Labov 1966a).

6.2.4 Speech behaviour of Blacks in Detroit

The investigation carried out by Wolfram (1969) comprises a random sample of 48 Blacks (a subsample from the Urban Language Study of Shuy, Wolfram and Riley 1967). Although it is linked to that of (1966a) it is in many details an even more accurate analysis. Wolfram adopts Labov's interview technique and methods of analysis, but refines and modifies them on the following points:

1   Quantitative measurement is carried out for grammatical variables in addition to phonological ones.
2   The social parameters are more strictly defined.
3   Only two contextual styles are distinguished: interview style and reading style.

Extralinguistic variables. Five social parameters are classed as independent variables: (1) *social status* (classification into upper middle class (UMC), lower middle class (LMC), upper working class (UWC) and lower working class (LWC), using similar criteria to those of Labov, (2) *sex*, (3) *age* (three age groups: 10–12, 14–17 and 30–55), (4) *racial segregation* (contact predominantly with Whites or predominantly with Blacks) and (5) *contextual style* (interview style or reading style).

For variables 1 to 3 the sample was unusually well balanced: 12 speakers belonged to each of the four classes; 24 Blacks were male, 24 female; each age group was represented by 16 persons.

A sample of 12 White SE speakers from the UMC was selected as a pilot group for BEV speakers. This was to make possible an assessment of the influence exerted by the norms of White speakers on the speech behaviour of non-Whites.

Wolfram decided to isolate only two contextual styles when exploratory interviews revealed that casual and careful speech in interview situations could not be differentiated with the criteria given by Labov (1966a: cf. 6.2.2 above). On Labov's criteria for casual speech Wolfram comments: 'any of the paralinguistic channel cues cited as indications of casual speech can also be indications that the informant feels an increased awareness of the artificiality or formality of the interview situation. Can nervous laughter reliably be distinguished from relaxed or casual laughter?' (Wolfram 1969, 58). Wolfram's own differentiation of styles is therefore restricted to the dichotomy *formal* (reading)/*semiformal* (interview).

Linguistic variables. The values for four phonological and four grammatical variables (42–56) were ascertained independently of the social parameters according to the principle x = f (a, b, c, d, e) (cf. 5.2.1).

The four phonological variables are:

1 consonant clusters at the end of a word (monomorphemic, e.g. in te*st*, wa*sp*, le*ft*, co*ld*, and bimorphic—in conjunction with the past suffix -*ed*— e.g. in mi*ssed*, ma*pped*;

2 /th/ in morphemic medial and final position (realization of /th/ as (th–0), (th–1) or (th–2) (cf. 6.2.2) in words such as too*th*, a*th*letic, no*th*ing etc.);

3 -*d* terminating a syllable (realization in, for example, goo*d*, ba*d*, as glottal stop [ʾ], voiceless alveolar plosive [t˥] or as [ø]);

4 postvocalic /r/ (omission of /r/ in siste*r*, fi*r*e etc.; a pronounced sociolinguistic feature).

The variables below were quantified as grammatical features:

1 omission of the copula *be* in a series of syntactic environments in which it is obligatory in SE, e.g. in sentences such as *she nice* (before a predicative adjective), *we going Friday night* (before a verb +*ing*), *it's something you gonna have* (before the intentional future *gonna*);

2 invariant use of *be* (as a finite verb), e.g. in *the problems always be wrong*;

3 omission of the suffix -*Z* as (a) a morpheme of the third person singular present, e.g. in *he stand on his hind legs*, (b) a consonant denoting possession in *my grandfather dog* and (c) a plural marker in *a million dollar*;

4 multiple negation in sentences with (a) an adverb with internal negation, e.g. *I couldn't hardly pick*, (b) an indefinite pronoun, e.g. in *I don't bother nobody* and (c) with an indefinite determiner (which is sometimes realized as ø in SE), e.g. in *they didn't have no gym*.

As in Labov (1966a), the correlations of the linguistic variables with the social parameters display constant patterns. The tendencies of linguistic differentiation described below are specified according to social parameters and qualities of the linguistic variables.

1 *Social status* is the most significant variable with which the linguistic features correlate. The sharpest dividing line runs between LMC and UWC and the smallest difference is between UWC and LWC. The scales best discriminate 'education' and 'occupation'.

2   *Sex* discriminates consistently as a parameter. Women adapt more to the Standard norm than men.

3   The variable *age* shows that adults use fewer stigmatized variants than the youngest and second youngest age groups. The middle-class adults are relatively consistent in their use of the Standard, whereas the two younger age groups deviate considerably from this. The adults of the working classes partly adapt to the Standard and partly tend towards BEV; working class youths speak BEV categorically and systematically.

4   With regard to *contextual styles* there are considerable differences between interview and reading style. The speakers came significantly closer to the Standard norms in the reading style. The stylistic variation as a whole demonstrates that the subjects regard individual variables very much as 'markers of social status' (Labov 1966a, 216). The greater the stylistic variation, the sharper the social marking of the variables.

5   The factor of *racial isolation* is only revealing if one compares the speech behaviour of a number of UMC subjects who have predominantly 'White contacts' with that of other UMC subjects who only have contacts with Blacks. On the whole this variable does not allow any consistent conclusions to be drawn.

6   *Linguistic variables* exhibit three fundamental qualities:

    i   Phonological variables tend towards non-discrete quantitative differentiation, grammatical variables to qualitative differentiation. The stratification of the phonological features is continuous except for the variable (*th*), whose variant [*f*] is categorically absent in middle-class speech. All four grammatical variables, on the other hand, are categorically absent in middle-class speech.

    ii   The relation between phonological and grammatical variables can also be expressed in terms of *fine* and *sharp stratification*. The two terms were first used by Labov (1966a, 236), and are defined by Wolfram on the same lines (cf. 6.2.2 above, n. 4). The stratification of phonological variables is fine, that of grammatical variables sharp.

    iii   A satisfactory understanding of sociolinguistic differentiation is not possible without taking into consideration the intralinguistic constraints of variation. A division should be made between the extent to which variation is influenced by extralinguistic factors and that to which it is affected by intralinguistic factors. Part of Wolfram's results (1969, 214–20) provide an impressive confirmation of the variable rule (cf. 5.2.1 above).

6.2.5 Standard/Non-Standard dimension of English-speaking Texans

Stolz and Bills (1968) investigated grammatical Standard and dialect features of 23 speakers, 14 male and 9 female, from the area surrounding Austin, Texas, on the principle of the implicational scale (cf. 5.2.4). They intended to ascertain differences between the Standard of central Texas and rural Texan. The informants were not selected according to systematic sociological aspects, but could nevertheless be identified with different levels of socioeconomic status. The sample consisted of, among others, four teachers, a student, a chemist and an army officer on the one hand, and four totally uneducated workers, some craftsmen and salesmen, on the other. The speakers were between 17 and 60 years old.

A twenty-minute conversation was held with each of the informants, which was kept informal, when possible, by giving the speakers the opportunity to talk coherently about themselves or to recount an incident.

Linguistic variables. Dichotomous variables are adopted, on the lines of the implicational scale, which assume either the value 0 or 1 for each speaker with regard to a particular stylistic feature. If the speaker uses the Standard variant he is graded with 1 for this variable, and with 0 if the reverse is the case. This coding presupposes that each of the speakers uses one or other feature, in any case not both.

Of the 17 dialect features, which were selected in a relatively unsystematic way, 12 were finally classed as linguistic variables (5 occurred with too little frequency). We shall briefly list these here, according to their left-to-right ordering in figure 6.6:

1   Use of the auxiliary verb construction *ain't* (single use was coded with 1, repeated with 0).

2   *AuxD:* deletion of the copula (*post hoc* coding: more than two omissions were coded with 0).

3   *p-pp:* confusion of the past participle in sentences such as *they done it already,* where it is not clear whether *have* was omitted or whether *done* was confused with *did* (0 was recorded for more than two instances).

4   *DN:* double negation (cf. 6.2.4) (more than single use = 0).

5   *-ing:* reduction of *-ing* to *-in* (two or more *-ing*'s = 1).

6   *s/p:* lack of concordance in number between subject and verb (each occurrence of this feature was registered with 0).

7   *have:* use of *have got* for *have* (*post hoc* coding: more than 30 per cent *have got* was counted as 0).

8   *th → ⊘:* deletion of /th/ in *there* (twice and more = 0).

9   *adj:* substitution of an adjective for an adverb (given the value 0 when it occurred twice).

10   *wadn't:* substitution of *d* for *s* before *-n't* (assigned the value 0 if the informant substituted a /d/ for every /s/).

11   *there's:* use of *there is* in conjunction with a plural nominal phrase, e.g. *there is three of them* (single use = 0).

12   *that:* substitution of *that* for *who* when introducing a relative clause (consistent use of *who* was coded with 1).

As is evident from the remarks in brackets, the coding into 0 and 1 was rather arbitrary: the informants had to be categorically graded, although the forms they used were fairly varied. As Stolz and Bills point out: 'Since the data usually do not come in this all-or-nothing way, the necessity arose for setting a threshold for each feature—that is, to specify a critical number or proportion of occurrences such that if any informant exhibited more than that amount of the standard (or for some features, the Non-Standard variant. he was given a 1 (or a 0). Because of our previous inexperience with the dialect, such thresholds were impossible to set *a priori* without a great deal of arbitrariness. Thus the thresholds were set *post hoc* to give the optimal fit between the data and the scalogram model' (1968. 14).

As is obvious from figure 6.6, it was possible to order the informants (denoted by capital letters) systematically on the basis of implicational hierarchies of features.

Each informant could now be assigned a dialect value, which

	Dialect features											
Infor-mant	*ain't*	*AuxD*	*p-pp*	*DN*	*-ing*	*s/p*	*have*	*th→φ*	*adj*	*wadn't*	*there's*	*that*
AF	1	1	1	1	1	1	1	1	1	1	1	1
MJW	1	1	1	1	1	1	1	1	1	1	1	1
ML	1	1	1	1	1	1	1	1	1	1	1	nd*
JP	1	1	1	1	1	1	1	1	1	1	1	0
RC	1	1	1	1	1	1	1	1	1	0	1	0
NG	1	1	1	1	1	1	1	1	1	1	0	1
GK	1	1	1	1	1	1	1	1	1	1	0	0
DW	1	1	1	1	1	1	1	1	1	0	0	0
MW	1	1	1	1	1	1	1	1	1	nd	nd	0
EW	1	1	1	1	0	1	1	1	1	0	0	0
WF	1	1	1	1	1	1	1	1	1	0	0	0
LB	1	1	1	1	0	1	0	1	1	0	0	0
JM	1	1	1	1	1	1	1	0	0	0	0	0
KF	1	1	1	1	1	1	1	0	0	0	0	1
BH	1	1	1	0	1	0	nd	0	0	0	0	0
GJ	1	1	1	1	0	0	0	0	0	0	0	0
MVW	1	1	0	0	0	0	0	0	0	0	0	0
EH	1	0	0	0	0	0	0	0	0	0	0	0
ENH	1	0	0	0	0	0	0	0	0	0	0	0
GF	0	0	0	0	0	0	0	0	nd	0	0	0
JC	0	0	0	0	0	0	0	0	0	0	0	0
HM	0	0	0	0	0	0	0	0	0	0	0	0
JT	0	0	0	0	0	0	0	0	0	0	0	0

*nd = no data.

Fig. 6.6 Classification of 23 Texan speakers on an implicational scale according to 12 dialect features.
(Source: Stolz and Bills 1968, 16)

corresponded to the number of features that were categorically present or absent. This index, which indicates the degree to which a speaker speaks Standard or Non-Standard, can then be correlated with sociological and other variables. The correlation of indices of dialect value with socioeconomic status shows, amongst other things, that the four uneducated speakers (lowest socioeconomic index) are to be found on the lowest grade of the continuum as categorical dialect speakers (speakers GF, JC, HM and JT); the four teachers and the chemist, on the other hand, are, as representatives of the highest status, graded at the top of the scale as (virtually) categorical speakers of Standard.

6.2.6 Non-Standard English of Blacks and Puerto Ricans in New York

The investigation of groups of Black youths and some Puerto Ricans (aged between 10 and 12 years) in New York ghetto districts made by Labov *et al.* (1968) is 'the largest single body ever gathered on systematic and inherent variation within a speech community' (I, 91). The main aims of this investigation were to find out (1) differences between SE and BEV and (2) differences in the way in which Blacks use their BEV dialect, taking into special consideration the 'speech events, verbal skills and social controls which govern the development of the vernacular' (Preface). Yet the two dominant aims of the inquiry, an analysis of the *structural* and the *functional conflict* (i.e. the conflict between SE and BEV, meant in the broadest sense), do not show solely an academic interest in the 'grammar of a speech community' or mere linguistic norms and change, but also a deeper-lying, sociopolitical interest generally concerned with the disintegration of the Blacks, as symbolized in their dialect:

> 'The problem upon which this research is focused is one part of the general social and economic situation of the non-White population in the urban ghetto areas of the northern United States. . . . The principal groups whose language behaviour is studied here match the descriptions of the most depressed and disadvantaged subgroups. . . . The low educational achievement of this population is the specific part of the socioeconomic problem with which we are concerned. One general index of the educational problem is the relatively low number of non-Whites who finish high school. . . . Reading problems are clearly central to the overall educational problem and the widespread failure of youth in the urban ghetto to learn to read may be an even better index of the relation of education to employment than completion of high school. . . . For the specific peer groups studied intensively in this research, reading may be three, four, or five years behind grade levels. . . . A great many of these Negro youths cannot use reading for other learning; they are functionally illiterate in the full sense of the term. . . . Given these facts, we decided to concentrate our efforts on the reading failure of adolescent and pre-adolescent boys.' (Labov *et al.* 1968, I, 1)

The caustic criticism of the Deficit Hypothesis made by Labov (1970b) on the basis of this investigation is understandable in view of his claim to utilize the implications of his results for 'recommendations for cultural and structural changes within the classroom' (Preface): 'If linguists can contribute . . . toward this end, we will have done a great deal to justify the support that society has given to basic research in our field' (1970b, 42).

This basic research (Labov *et al.* 1968) is divided into two parts: the analysis of the structural conflict and that of the functional conflict (between BEV and SE). In the first case, the phonological and grammatical structure of BEV is described correlatively to SE; in the second, the general verbal capabilities of BEV speakers (structure of verbal interaction, speech games, rhymes, narratives) are analysed functionally. Here it is emphasized that the results of the functional analysis of communicative competence are of greater relevance to educational problems than those of the sphere of grammatical competence.

The analysis of the grammatical competence of BEV speakers comprises:

1 *phonological variables* (those used in Labov 1966a and Wolfram 1969; particular attention was paid to the simplification of consonant clusters and to the contraction and deletion of the copula *be*);
2 *grammatical variables* (concordance in number of nouns and verbs, double and multiple negation, questions and pleonastic forms);
3 *repetition tests* to assess the command of BEV;
4 *'classroom correction tests'* (correctional tests related to instructional norms; cf. 6.1.3 (9));
5 *'vernacular correction tests'* (correction tests related to the norms of the vernacular);
6 *subjective reaction tests* (cf. 6.1.3 (7) and 5.4.4).

Whereas the analytical techniques for (1) to (6) are quantitative, functional methods (based on speech acts and texts) are employed in the study of communicative competence in order to describe:

7 *speech events* in verbal interaction ('toasts' [oral epic poetry] and ritual insults);
8 *accounts* of personal experiences.

These analyses of BEV speakers' verbal capabilities are supplemented by:

9 *a theoretical outline* of formal analysis of speech variation (also contained in Labov 1969);
10 *sociological analyses* of the peer groups studied (structure of the groups and the families of their members; values of the groups, particularly with regard to 'nationalism' and criminality; the relation between peer group behaviour and speech behaviour).

Selection of speakers. The speakers come from central Harlem, a ghetto area in New York inhabited by 200,000 people, 97 per cent Blacks and predominantly working-class. Subjects of the investigation were six groups (peer groups) of youths in the south of central Harlem, who were analysed against the background of a random sample of 100 adults from one middle-class and two working-class districts in the same area and were compared with a random sample of 50 young individuals living without any group contact.

The study was centred on four peer groups: the group of 18 'Thunderbirds' aged between 9 and 13 (the group of 'preadolescents') and the 29 members of three further groups, the 'Jets', the 'Cobras' and the 'Oscar Brothers', aged between 13 and 17. The group values were different: whereas the Cobras were nationalistic in their attitudes ('nationalist . . . and Muslim ideology' (Labov *et al.* 1968, I, 40)), the Jets were completely unaffected by this: they were in fact enemies of the Cobras. In the third group, the Thunderbirds, it could finally be observed how they increasingly adopted the 'nationalist ideology' of the Cobras.

The rapport with the groups varied. Contact was made with them by John Lewis, a Black, and they were observed over a period of two and a half years. During this time there were various interruptions in the observation, some of which were attributable to the fact that groups with 'nationalist ideologies' would no longer tolerate contact with Whites.

Group norms. Here we can only give a few of the many different aspects of the group structure. Rigid organization existed in all the groups: they had group leaders and ordinary members; the Jets, for example, had a president, a vice-president, a 'prime minister' and a 'war lord' (II, 19). A strong sense of solidarity between the members was established in all the groups: 'As far as adolescent culture patterns are concerned, it is clear there is a strong, focal concern with belonging, a sense of solidarity with the group; the importance of group membership cannot be overestimated' (II, 26). The solidarity of the group members resulted from constantly being together, and hard and fast rules were developed from this. Individual activities outside the group were despised and carried penalties.

Labov and his assistants repeatedly point out that the values of the groups are diametrically opposed to those of school and the middle class: 'In fact, the values which the peer group endorses are usually the exact opposite of those which are endorsed by teachers . . .' (II, 35). 'The peer group culture . . . is diametrically opposed to gentlemanly and chivalrous deportment which is upheld as a model in most schoolbooks . . .' (II , 44).

The behaviour of the groups cannot be understood unless one knows about their consciously-cultivated 'bad' values that are in opposition to the generally endorsed 'good' values of the middle class. Six of the most important values that deviate from the middle-class norms and in which the groups particularly distinguish themselves, are: (1) fights ('street fights'), (2) stealing, (3) swearing (cf. ritual insults in 6.3.3), (4) drinking, (5) drugs, (6) sex (II, 36). The contrast between the 'good' middle-class boys and the 'bad' boys from the working class is best illustrated by the following passage:

'The "good" boy does not fight, or stays close to the rules of fair fighting; he does not steal, which is against the law; he does not use obscene language, especially in front of women; he does not drink, or drinks only beer now and then; he does not take drugs, and in particular does not get high on reefer; he takes girls out and engages in heavy petting, but he does not have sexual intercourse with a girl unless he intends to marry her: he respects women.

Someone who is "bad" is a dangerous and effective fighter: he pays no attention to rules of a fair fight: he is a daring and successful thief: he pays no attention to any taboos on language. even in front of older women. and he has a good command of invective; he can handle large amounts of whiskey, and he will drink anything else in sight including port; he gets high on reefer, heroin and cocaine; gets all the women he wants by a bold and direct approach, but has no personal regard for women at all.' (II, 36)

It is not possible to explain the speech behaviour of the youths in Harlem without being aware of these values; yet we should not lose sight of the reasons why such values are held in high regard: 'In the NNE-subculture, there is a great deal of prestige in being "bad"—whether it is in fighting, stealing, or laying a great many girls. The overall pattern may be more highly developed in NNE than in other subcultures, for the obvious reason that the society which is being defied has in fact *repressed this group more severely than any other*' (II, 45; my italics).

Interviews and eliciting. The speakers were given individual interviews in their home environment and observed in their everyday behaviour and their interaction processes during group sessions. Interviews and group sessions were recorded on tape. The essential techniques for eliciting linguistic data and other information were as follows:

1   calculated questions in a 'face-to-face' interview;
2   group interviews;
3   reading of texts and word lists;
4   perception and correction tests;
5   self-evaluation tests;
6   memory or repetition tests (I, 47).

Particular value was attached to the group sessions. They were structured in such a way that the groups could pursue whatever activities they wanted. Additional excursions to surrounding areas of New York were designed to provide an opportunity for spontaneous interactions and to ensure that natural speech behaviour was recorded.

Methods of analysis. They are basically the same as those listed in 6.1.3 (1)–(9). some of which were used in Labov 1966a. All the speakers were classified in social classes, according to their education and socioeconomic position (in the case of the youths, according to their family background), and various contextual styles were provoked in the interviews (cf. 6.2.2).

The most important linguistic principle of analysis is the '*principle of accountable reporting*': 'A report of a linguistic form or rule used in a speech community must include an account of the total population of utterances from which the observation is drawn, and the proportion of the expected environments in which this form did in fact occur' (I, 70).

The principle of accountable recording of linguistic data is not restricted to variable rules (the most important analytical instrument used in the investigation, cf. 5.2.1 for its theoretical status), but also applies to the majority of categorical rules.

The results of the investigation were not checked for statistical significance.

Results. The results are so extensive that we cannot do justice even to selected individual aspects. We shall restrict ourselves here to a few characteristics of the phonological and grammatical analysis in connection with some typical features of the way they were verified in tests. We shall not deal with the functional description of ritual insults and accounts of personal experiences until 6.3.

1   *Simplification of the consonant clusters -t, -d.*

The consonants -*t* and -*d* can be simplified in monomorphemic and bimorphemic consonant clusters depending on extra- and intralinguistic parameters (cf. Wolfram 1969). Quantification of the deletion of this variable in monomorphemic final position reveals that:

i   There are no speakers who always realize it, nor any who never realize it (inherent variation).

ii   In all speakers it is omitted more frequently if the next word begins with a consonant.

Case i may be written as a rule in the following way:

$$[-\text{cont}] \rightarrow \emptyset/[+\text{cons}]\underline{\quad\quad} \# \quad \# \quad [-\text{syl}] \qquad\qquad 1$$

This rule means 'that a stop is optionally deleted after a consonantal segment (liquid or obstruent), at the end of a word, if the next word does not begin with a vowel' (Labov 1972d, 217).

The notation in rule 1 does not, however, take into account case ii, where −*t,d* are deleted more frequently if the next word begins with a consonant. With the help of a variable rule notation this can be written as follows:

$$[-\text{cont}] \rightarrow \langle\emptyset\rangle /[+\text{cons}]\underline{\quad\quad} \# \quad \# \quad \langle-\text{syl}\rangle \qquad\qquad 2$$

where the angled brackets around the element to the immediate right of the arrow indicate that there is a variability value $\emptyset(0 < \emptyset < 1)$ for the output of the rule. The angled brackets around '–syl' indicate that $\emptyset$ is affected by the presence or absence of this feature in the environment, i.e. that this element acts as a *variable constraint.* (Labov 1972d, 218) Rule 2 states 'informally . . . that a stop is variably deleted after a consonantal segment at the end of a word, more often if a vowel does not follow than if a vowel does follow' (*ibid.*).

But consonant simplification also applies to the bimorphemic structure ——— C # C (e.g. in *passed*), where the second consonant represents the past tense morpheme -*ed*. The deletion of −*t,d* in the bimorphemic structure is shown in:

$$[-\text{cont}] \rightarrow \langle\emptyset\rangle /[+\text{cons}](\#)\underline{\quad\quad} \# \quad \# \quad \langle-\text{syl}\rangle \qquad\qquad 3$$

The deletion of the consonant would mean, however, in these cases that the past tense marker for regular verbs (-*ed*) disappears. At this point one should ask whether the morpheme boundary in e.g. *passed* really exists in BEV, i.e. whether BEV speakers mentally interpret the cluster [*st*] as containing a past tense marker. This problem cannot be solved without resorting to sociolinguistic data and this, according to Labov (1972d, 219) shows that the past tense marker does exist as a basic form in BEV. The examination of the sociolinguistic structure of the -*ed* clusters yields this general picture (Labov 1972d, 219):

a   There are no speakers who always delete the *-ed* and no speakers who always retain it.

b   The realization of *-ed* is phonologically conditioned: a following vowel has a strong effect in preserving them.

c   In each phonological environment, bimorphemic clusters are deleted less often than monomorphemic clusters.

d   There is no hypercorrection; the *-ed* ending is not supplied wrongly where the present tense would be expected.

Figure 6.7 illustrates the relation between the deletion of the monomorphemic and the bimorphemic clusters and summarizes (1)–(3) in accordance with the empirical data (Labov *et al.* 1968, I, 77; also 1972d, 219).

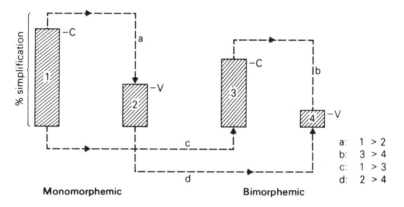

Fig. 6.7 Four relations governing —*t, d* deletion

Figure 6.7 shows that speakers generally simplify the bimorphemic clusters less often than the monomorphemic clusters. This is stated in rule 4:

$$[-\text{cont}] \rightarrow\ <\text{ø}>\ /[+\text{cons}]\ <\text{ø}>\underline{\hspace{1cm}}\ \#\ \#\ <-\text{syl}> \qquad \textbf{4}$$

where 'it is the *absence* of a boundary which favors the rule' (Labov 1972d, 220). Rule 4 can be restated informally 'by saying that a stop is variably deleted after a consonantal segment at the end of a word, more often if it is not a separate inflectional morpheme, and more often if it is not followed by a vowel' (*ibid.*).

2   *Contraction and deletion of the copula 'be'.*
The realization of the copula in **BEV** differs, unlike that in SE, with the varying grammatical environments as well as with extralinguistic parameters, i.e. it is contracted under certain conditions, deleted under others.

The deletion of the copula is illustrated in the following examples (Labov *et al.* 1968, I, 175):

i   *He a eat-and-runner*
ii   *He fast in everything he do*
iii   *We on tape*
iv   *They not caught*

II

In (i) *is* is deleted before a noun phrase [——NP] and in (ii) before the adjectival predicate [——PA], in (iii) *are* is deleted before a locative expression [——Loc] and in (iv) before negation [——Neg]. It could be concluded from these examples that the copula is categorically absent in BEV; in this case its deletion should be described by 'high level rules' (Labov *et al.* 1968, I, 176). But a series of other copula realizations opposes this solution: the appearance of the copula as the preterite *was* in (I, 177–8):

v   *She was likin' me* or in the negative present form *ain't* in:
vi   *It ain't no cat can't get in no coop*

or its contraction from *I am* to *I'm* in:

vii   *I'm not no strong drinker.*

Finally, *be* occurs regularly after auxiliary verbs, in infinitive and imperative constructions (I, 181–2):

viii   *You got to be good, Rednall*
ix   *Each year he will be gettin' worse all the time*
x   *Be cool, brothers!*

Thus we establish initially that forms of the copula are omitted completely in some environments and realized (in contracted or full form) in others. This relation between contraction and deletion which varies with the grammatical environment and the social characteristics of the speakers can only be specified more precisely by sociolinguistic analysis. The discussion of numerous further examples leads Labov to the conclusion that the copula is present in the *deep structure* of BEV grammar, but that its realization is restricted by the phonological and grammatical environment: 'We therefore assume that a copula is originally present in the sentence structure and that it is deleted from the basic declarative constructions by a later rule' (I, 184). The deletion effect by 'later rules' is phonological in nature (I, 184–206). In this regard the following statement may be considered as a general principle with no exceptions: 'whenever SE can contract the copula it can be deleted in BEV, and vice versa; whenever SE cannot contract, the copula cannot be deleted in BEV, and vice versa' (I, 185). On the basis of the data for the four BEV groups, however, the frequency can be specified with which, for example, a pronoun or a vowel impedes deletion or a following verb promotes it.

Contraction and deletion in BEV, two connected processes, can be represented formally by means of variable rules (the notation of the following rules is taken from Labov 1972b, 112; it gives the revised version of the rules formulated in Labov *et al.* 1968, I, 208):

Contraction of the copula: **5**

$$\begin{bmatrix} +\text{voc} \\ -\text{str} \\ +\text{cen} \end{bmatrix} \rightarrow \langle \phi \rangle \Big/ \Big\langle \begin{matrix} +\text{Pro} \\ [-\text{cons}] \end{matrix} \Big\rangle \ \#\# \ \begin{bmatrix} \underline{\quad} \\ +\text{T} \end{bmatrix} \ \text{C}_0^1 \ \#\# \ \Big\langle \begin{matrix} +\text{Vb} \\ +\text{Fut} \\ -\text{NP} \end{matrix} \Big\rangle$$

Deletion of the copula: **6**

$$[+\text{cont}] \;\rightarrow\; \langle\phi\rangle \;\left\langle\begin{bmatrix} +\text{strid} \\ +\text{cons} \\ +\text{Pro} \end{bmatrix}\right\rangle \;\#\,\# \;\begin{bmatrix} \underline{} \\ -\text{nas} \\ +\text{cont} \end{bmatrix} \;\#\,\# \;\left\langle\begin{matrix} +\text{Vb} \\ +\text{Fut} \\ -\text{NP} \end{matrix}\right\rangle$$

Labov explains these rules as follows:

'Rule 5 appears as the removal of a *shwa* which stands before (no more than) a single consonant in a word which incorporates the tense marker. The preceding environment shows two variable constraints: the rule is favored if the subject is a pronoun, and if it ends in a nonconsonantal segment—vowel or glide. The residual case is the least favored: a noun phrase which ends in a consonant. The following environment shows three variable constraints. Most important is whether or not the following element is a verb. Here we find restored in part the distinction between the copula and the *be* of the progressive, and it seems likely that the deletion of that *be* (in its finite forms) is connected with its redundant relation to the following *-ing* form. Instead of showing *gonna* as the most favored form, we abstract its < +Future > feature, the increment which makes it most favored among verbal forms, and show that feature as the second variable constraint. The third is the most problematical: <–NP>, which registers the fact that if the following element is not a noun phrase—i.e. an adjective, locative, etc.—the rule will be favored more than if it is a noun phrase. There are some cases where this constraint is reversed, but they are in the minority, and we tentatively add this constraint subject to further investigation.

The deletion rule (6) appears as the removal of a lone oral continuant between word boundaries. It might well include the deletion of the /d/ from *would* and *had*, but we have not investigated the relatively small number of cases in which this stop disappears. The nasal /m/ of *I'm* is definitely excluded. In addition to the [z] from *is*, the rule also deletes the [v] from *have*, though it is not clear to what extent this deletion obeys the constraints determined for *is*. Turning to the preceding environment, we note that the rule operates categorically when a strident is present. We did not block contraction from operating when the subject ended in a sibilant or strident; but the data shows that if a cluster of two sibilants is formed, the second one is categorically deleted. We also note that the < +Pro > constraint is present. . . . But the consonantal constraint is reversed: whereas contraction is favored by a preceding vowel or glide, deletion is favored by a preceding obstruent or liquid. The configuration of the following environment is the same as for the contraction rule.

Thus the contraction and deletion rules are parallel but distinct rules of the phonological component. They are alike in four variable constraints—all representing the influence of the grammatical environment. They are dissimilar and even opposed in their effect upon the phonetic structure of the phrase, and we find accordingly that the variable phonetic constraints are diametrically opposed. Both the similarities and the differences of the contraction and the deletion rule confirm the view that absence of *is* in BEV is due to the deletion of the lone segment [z] remaining after contraction.

The quantitative data presented in this chapter are suficient to establish the major variable constraints upon these rules—constraints which are independent of each other and which recur regularly in almost all styles and peer groups. It will no doubt be possible to modify this presentation in the future, as more data are accumulated; there are many interesting questions to be investigated concerning the role of various predicate types. But the purpose of this type of analysis is not to explore every conceivable constraint upon a variable rule to the limits of reproducibility, but rather to apply the logic of these converging (and diverging) patterns to establishing the place, form, and order of the deletion and contraction rules of BEV.' (Labov 1972b, 113f.)

3   Negation in BEV.

Of the grammatical variables we shall select negation, which is known to be a feature that distinguishes BEV particularly sharply from SE. If as a normal speaker of English one does not know that double negatives are also used in French, Spanish and Russian, then the following sentences would at first seem quite illogical (Labov *et al.* 1968, I. 267):

xi   *Didn't nobody see it; didn't nobody hear it*
xii   *It ain't no cat can't get in no coop*

One might wonder whether speakers are simply making mistakes or contradicting themselves. Yet double and multiple negatives occur regularly in the speech of all BEV youths.

On closer examination Labov and his assistants discovered that all negative sentences in BEV had three common features: '(a) there were two clauses, and a contradictory negative appeared in the second; (b) there was another negative in the first clause and (c) the first clause also contained an indefinite constituent, such as *one, ever* or *any*' (Labov 1970a, in Fishman 1971b, 190). These three features led Labov and his associates to connect BEV negation with the phenomenon of 'negative concord', by which negatives are attracted to indefinites.

For SE the rule holds that: the negative particle is linked *obligatorily* with the first indefinite pronoun *before* the verb and *optionally* with the first indefinite pronoun *after* the verb.[5] Instead of **Anybody doesn't know it*, we get obligatorily:

[5] Labov relies for this rule on Klima (1964b), which is representative for autonomous syntax ('interpretive semantics') rather than for semantic syntax ('generative semantics') (cf. Seuren 1972). It must be realized that here Labov is not principally concerned with the correct formulation of the rules for negation. To describe the phenomena of negation copying (multiple negation) adequately is in any case a very complex matter (cf. Labov 1972e). An attempt at formulation in terms of semantic syntax (generative semantics) would perhaps let a Neg-copying rule operate post-cyclically. It would copy an original negation for every indefinite element further down in the sentence, and for the auxiliary in the same clause if *Aux* is on the right of *Neg* (so as to get *Nobody don't sit there*). A global condition (Lakoff 1970) would have to be attached to the rule for it to be able to recognize 'indefinite elements'. The rule would, furthermore, have to retrieve deleted original negations, as in the case of the comparative (Seuren 1973, 535) : we see that 'spurious' negations appear in substandard comparatives, as in the Cockney *She did a better job than what I never thought she would*. On the theory that there is an underlying negation in *than*, the negation in *never* can be considered a copy, resulting from 'negative

Nobody knows it; on the other hand, the rule changes *he doesn't sit anywhere* optionally into *He sits nowhere* (*ibid.*). If one now considers various dialects of English, one is led to the conclusion that there are three different rules, 'all operating *after* the negative is placed in its normal preverbal position'.

The first rule, 'negative attraction', is categorical and obligatory for all dialects of English. It moves the negative away from its preverbal position to the position just in front of a *preceding* indefinite:

Negative attraction: **7**

$$Indef \;\_ \; X \;\_ \; Neg$$
$$1 \qquad 2 \qquad 3 \;\; \rightarrow 1 + 3 \quad 2$$

Rule 8a moves the negative to postverbal position (it is optional and only valid for literary Standard English). Rule 8b is also optional, but applies only in Non-Standard dialects. Its function and effect are similar to those of rule 8a for SE, except that it does not delete the negation in preverbal position. The result is a copying of the negation element:

Negative transport: **8a**

$$Neg \;\_ \; X \;\_ \; Indef$$
$$1 \qquad 2 \qquad 3 \;\; \rightarrow 2 \quad 1 + 3$$

SE; movement of the negative to postverbal position

Negative concord: **8b**

$$Neg \;\_ \; X \;\_ \; Indef$$
$$1 \qquad 2 \qquad 3 \;\; \rightarrow 1 \quad 2 \quad 1 + 3$$

Non-Standard; copying of negation before indefinite element

Labov comments:

> 'These two rules are complementary and perform the same emphatic function. Instead of *He doesn't sit anywhere*, the first rule gives us *He sits nowhere*, and the second pleonastic rule yields *He don't sit nowhere*. Rule 8b applies without regard to clause boundaries: thus we can have *He don't like nobody that went to no prep school* = SE *He doesn't like anybody that went to any prep school*. There are also some Non-Standard White dialects [WNS] which can transfer the negative back to preverbal position, so that we have **Anybody doesn't sit there→Nobody sits there→Nobody don't sit there*. NNE shares this property.' (1971a, 191)

Careful analysis of the considerable amount of data shows that rule 8b is both categorical and obligatory for core members of the BEV peer groups when the negative and the indefinite elements are in the same clause ('clause mates'). Whereas corresponding White Non-Standard dialects show inherent variation, with a concomitant emphatic function, there is no variation for rule 8b in BEV when elements 1 and 3 are clause mates, and consequently no emphatic function

concord', but not of an (original) *not* still present in the tree. The copying would be governed by an already deleted element,—which, again, would require a global condition on the applicability of this rule.

is associated with this rule, which thus marks the distinctive norms of SE and BEV in a particularly clear way.

In fact, the domain of this rule is wider than in other negation-copying dialects. We have already seen twice the example *It ain't no cat can't get in no coop*, which was uttered by Speedy, the leader of the Cobras, during a group session where there was a discussion about pigeon coops. It is clear from the context that Speedy's meaning was 'There isn't any cat that can get into any coop' (and not 'There is no cat that can't get into any coop'). Half a dozen similar constructions encountered in the corpus eliminate the possibility of a mistake in Speedy's speech: 'Most convincing is the example from a long epic poem of Negro folklore: speaking of a whore, the narrator says, *There wasn't no trick couldn't shun her*, meaning that she was so good that "there wasn't any trick (customer) that could shun her"' (Labov 1971a, 190).[6] Labov concludes now that the rule should be formulated so as to permit copying the negative in the preverbal position *in a following clause*:[7]

Negative concord: **8b′**

$$Neg \ - \ X \ - \ \left\{ \begin{array}{c} Verb \\ Indef \end{array} \right\}$$

$$1 \qquad 2 \qquad\qquad 3 \qquad \rightarrow \qquad 1 \ \ 2 \ \ 1+3$$

The Standard, two White Non-Standard dialects and BEV can now be classified according to the conditions of application of rule 8b′. Figure 6.8 presents this classification in a table, which is in the form of values of ϕ, where '0' means that the rule never applies, '$\sim$' means that it is a variable rule with $0 < \phi < 1$, and '1' that the rule is obligatory.

Subjective reaction tests. They were carried out on the principles established by Lambert and by Labov (1966a). At the end of the individual interviews a reaction test was conducted with every one of 90 adults from the area where the peer groups lived. The adults belonged to three different classes: LMC, UWC and LWC. Ten sentences were played back to them on a tape recorder which contained stigmatized variants of BEV and prestige features of SE. Each speaker had to evaluate the speech sample on three scales: the *job* scale, the *fight* scale and

---

[6] The full passage of the poem is quoted in Labov (1972e, 787), where the sentence in question runs somewhat differently: *For there wasn't a son of a gun who this whore couldn't shun.* This, apparently, is the authentic version.

[7] Quite clearly, Labov's rule (8b′) is too wide, since it incorrectly predicts the ungrammaticality in BEV of *He don't like nobody that went to no prep school,* quoted above. On the basis of the limited evidence available (see in particular Labov 1972e, 784–91) it looks as though term 3 in the rule should not contain 'Verb' but rather a small set of auxiliary verbal elements, such as '{Modal, *be, do*}'. From the data presented by Labov it appears that this particular form of Neg-copying (only attested in strict BEV) is dominant with forms of *can* (as in the examples quoted above), although it occurs with *be* (once: *Back in them times, there ain't no kid around that ain't—wasn't even thinkin' about smokin' no reefers*) and with *do* (once: *When it rained, nobody don't know it didn't*). The former sentence meant 'There wasn't a kid around that even thought about smoking reefers'; the latter 'Nobody knew that it rained when it did'.

3 =	*Indef.*		*Verb*	
1 and 3 clause mates?	Yes	No	Yes	No
Dialect: SE	0	0	0	0
WNS₁	~	~	0	0
WNS₂	~	~	~	0
BEV	1	~	~	~

Fig. 6.8 Use of·negative concord (8b') for SE, two White Non-Standard dialects and BEV.
(Source: Labov *et al*, 1968, I, 339)

the *friend* scale (Labov *et al.* 1968, II, 217). The scales were divided into eight grades, one extreme of which was 'definitely' and the other 'never'. With the help of the samples the informants had, for example, to determine on the fight scale how probable it was that the speaker of the sample would come out on top in a street fight. The questions were similar for the other two scales. Figure 6.9 shows the reactions to part of the speech samples.

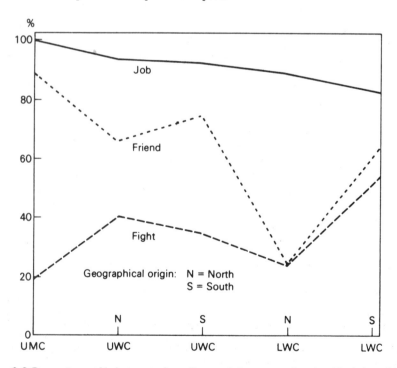

Fig. 6.9 Percentage of informants from five social groups who classified the middle-class speaker higher than the working class speaker on three scales.
(Source: Labov *et al.* 1968, II, 242; also 1972d, 250)

Figure 6.9. shows the following reaction (II, 243):

1   All informants assessed middle-class speakers higher on the *job* scale.
2   The *fight* scale has a contrasting pattern: members of the working class were regarded as better fighters than members of the middle class.
3   The line of the *friend* scale lies in between: it shows, however, that middle-class members were judged to be better friends than members of the working class.

The reaction tests give an insight into the norms of the district studied: they confirm the different values of the lower and middle class that are associated with the speech of their members.

The linguistic sensitivity of the BEV speakers is also evident in the *repetition* and *correction tests*. The main subjects of the tests here were the members of the peer groups. The repetition tests show that the young Blacks repeated sentences spoken to them in SE in the usual form of BEV. In so doing they demonstrated that BEV was for them the everyday means of communication. On the other hand, the conclusion must be drawn from the results that their competence was asymmetrical: they could understand SE, yet produced BEV. The correction tests related to school norms prove, furthermore, that they are aware of the sanctions connected with their speech (II, 4.4). The peer groups had to correct typical BEV sentences from the angle of the teacher. In the vast majority of cases they altered the stigmatized BEV features to SE. Thus they knew precisely which expressions in their speech behaviour would not be accepted by teachers.

Group norms v. individual norms. The differences in speech behaviour between the four peer groups and isolated Black youths ('lames') make it clear just how strong the social control is of group norms (II, 4.3, 159–95). Membership of a group encourages the use of BEV and discredits that of SE forms. In other words, the peer groups speak 'purer' BEV than the lames, who adapt more to the Standard. This statement can be proved by means of the relative frequency with which the groups on the one hand, and the lames on the other, contract or delete the copula:

Figure 6.10 shows the use of complete, contracted and deleted forms of the copula before and after a noun phrase as well as after pronouns. Contraction is

	Thunderbirds			'Lames'		
	FF	C	D	FF	C	D
is						
NP——NP	43	16	3	9	3	1
Pro—	4	46	29	1	8	1
are	6	7	67	0	6	5

FF = full forms; *C* = contraction; *D* = deletion

Fig. 6.10 Contraction and deletion of *is* and *are* by the Thunderbirds and 'lames'. (Source: Labov *et al.* 1968, II, 175)

carried out in both groups with virtually the same frequency: 'it operates only about one third of the time when a noun phrase both precedes and follows the verb' (II, 174). On the other hand, contraction is preponderant for both groups when a pronoun precedes. However, the deletion of the copula *are* produces somewhat different values for both groups: the Thunderbirds delete it with increased frequency, whereas the 'lames' employ it with roughly the same frequency as contraction.

The differences between group members and lames are significant in various respects:

1   It is 'apparent that the influence of SE on the "lames" is pervasive and continuous' (II, 176).
2   BEV is spoken in its purest form in the peer groups, who exert extremely strong social control over positive and negative sanctioning.
3   It is not only the social values of the peer groups (street fights, stealing, swearing, drinking, drugs, sex) that represent a structure totally opposed to the prevalent society, but also their speech behaviour.
4   Whereas the lames are relatively successful at school, the groups are not even capable of minimal school attainments. Nor do they try. The school values mean nothing to them.

This is the essence of their educational problems: the sense of group solidarity prevents a positive attitude towards school and therefore towards society as a whole: 'There is . . . a profound antagonism toward school. . . . From earliest years, NNE youngsters have played the game of defiance of middle-class values, which eventually appear to them as purely negative sanctions against the basic activities of their own peer groups' (II, 346).

Recommendations for integrating Black youths. Labov *et al.* (II, 346–9) gives four recommendations in answer to the question of how the peer groups can be adapted to the Standard and the accepted school values:

1   Reading books for children starting school should be written in the vernacular. The BEV forms can then be rendered progressively in SE forms from one passage to another.
2   The widespread concept of 'teaching Standard English as a foreign language' is misleading and wrong. 'NNE is not a foreign language and SE is not a foreign language to speakers of NNE (II, 347). What ought to be taught should be decided on the basis of the rules formulated in the report.
3   The educational crisis should be overcome by getting teachers to study the language and culture of BEV. Assistant teachers should be trained to carry out the following tasks:

   i   'provide the regular teacher with a continuous flow of matters of local and immediate interest for incorporation into reading materials;
   ii   acquaint the teacher with the peer-group structure that prevails inside and outside of school;
   iii   offer leadership and provide discipline for the boys, especially in sports;

iv   maintain contact with the boys outside of school, and discover what
      success if any school programs have in adding to or changing to their
      thinking' (II. 348).
Since this study shows that young Blacks despise women, only young men
should be trained as assistant teachers.

4   The schools should adhere to their own system of values, but take over the
     socialization of the young Blacks: 'to give them a realistic view of the norms
     and practices of our society; to teach long-range planning for the future; to
     demonstrate the value of a law-governed society; and to advance higher
     educational goals. But in the early grades, the teaching of SE must be linked
     directly to the values that are already there, if it is to succeed. The schools
     have to show the NNE youngster that he can learn Standard English for
     immediate advantage, as a means of getting other people to do what he
     wants them to do. To say that SE means money in the bank is easy, but hard
     to prove in terms of the short-range goals that are clearly visible and
     believable. But it is not too far-fetched to say that SE is useful for making
     excuses, arguments, requests and even insults. Most importantly, there
     must be a strong program for breaking down the identification of Standard
     English with White society' (II; 348f.).

6.3 Functional studies

'Functional', as used in the analyses that follow, should be interpreted as taking
into consideration the situational speech context and relating to this the
description of speech events (cf. 5.3). The studies of Gumperz (1966) and Ervin-
Tripp (1964) are concerned with the influence of verbal interactions on different
phenomena of code shifting. Labov's analysis, on the other hand, deals with new
techniques of analysing speech acts and linguistic texts.

6.3.1 Group interactions of Norwegian speakers

Gumperz (1966) investigates the linguistic variation of a small language
community in Norway (Hemnesberget) from the point of view of social
interaction. The variation occurs in two forms, dialectal or interpersonal
variation and intrapersonal, i.e. style shifting in individual speakers. The
investigation concentrates on these two forms.

The variants in the verbal repertoire of the speakers which are socially
significant can be identified as forms of the local dialect and of one of the two
Standard Norwegian languages. A contrastive analysis reveals certain
phonological and morphological differences between the two varieties.

The speakers' linguistic variation is not analysed on the basis of socioeconomic
status, but is seen as a means of symbolizing different social relations between
speakers. It is therefore investigated with regard to the interactional patterns
which recognize and maintain the existing social relations. This is where the
concept of the *social network* may be employed, which describes groups of
speakers who know each other and are connected with one another in different
ways (e.g. by friendship, religion, politics, occupation, kinship etc.).

Gumperz's analysis is based on friendship networks that include four discussion groups: two open and two closed networks, which comprise people from different social origins.

Method. The groups were observed directly in their interactions to obtain data resulting from a natural speech situation and not from a formal interview.

The situations can be distinguished according to the type of interaction: *transactional* interaction on the one hand, in which the interlocutors act by means of their status (i.e. in accordance with certain norms) and *personal* interaction on the other, in which the interlocutors behave as individuals, i.e. chiefly in the peer group and the family. The two types of interaction correspond to the distinction between formal and informal situations. They are characterized by the linguistic variation of the speakers: transactional and personal 'switching' are connected with shifting between Standard and dialect. This is true for all the groups investigated (cf. Blom and Gumperz. 1972).

Results. The analysis of the four discussion groups (personal interaction) reveals that all speakers use dialect when talking about local topics and sport; in more abstract discussions, however (e.g. about university) the open networks tend to shift unconsciously to the Standard, independently of their attitude to the language. Thus, in the latter case, they break the strict, local cooccurrence restrictions that apply to personal interaction.

Conclusion. The code switching takes place in two dimensions: first, between transactional interaction (formal situation) and personal interaction (informal conversation); and secondly, with changes of topic, whereby the other factors (situation and interlocutors) remain constant.

6.3.2 Code shifting of bilingual speakers

According to Ervin-Tripp (1964, quoted in Fishman 1968b, 192ff.), studies of bilingual speakers are particularly well suited to the investigation of formal linguistic shifting in interactions. Ervin-Tripp conducted an experimental analysis designed to investigate the language behaviour of the Japanese wives of American immigrants. The analytic notions she employs are the same as those described in 5.3.2.

The first step is an ethnographic description of the covariance of topic, interlocutors and language, which is based on interviews given to informants.

1   *Language and content.* The first hypothesis is that a change of language determines a change of content. In order to establish the relevance of the data found, control groups were tested consisting of monolingual American and Japanese women. A Japanese interviewer conversed with each bilingual woman twice in the same situation. The first time only English was spoken, the other only Japanese. Word association tests were carried out during the interview. Furthermore, stories told by the informants were analysed. The change of content could be defined as moving from 'typical Japanese' to 'less Japanese'. It was expected that the relatively abnormal situation of one Japanese woman being compelled to speak English with another Japanese would give rise to a content

more typical for conversations between Americans.

2   *Interlocutors and form.* In a second experiment the listener was varied, but the language was English throughout. The situation was again abnormal, i.e. speaking English with a Japanese. A comparison of the two situations revealed distinct effects on the style. With a Japanese listener it was possible to detect that the syntax was hesitant and the English lexicon punctuated with Japanese forms; moreover, the verbal interaction was briefer.

3   *Topic and form.* The informants had to express an opinion on a series of topics (stimulus words), which were connected with life in the USA as well as in Japan. It was ascertained that the language behaviour was not determined by the listener or topic alone, but by a specific combination of the two. When speaking English the informants had difficulties only with Japanese topics. In a normal situation the combination of 'Japanese listener' and 'Japanese topic' demands Japanese; therefore the syntax was not fluent (many hesitation pauses, transfers of words etc.).

Ervin-Tripp believes that investigations of this kind can also yield information on the psycholinguistic question of, for example, whether a bilingual speaker is like two monolingual speakers with one nervous system.

What is of central interest here, however, is the correlation between language and situation. Although this study differs as an experiment from anthropological investigations that observe language behaviour in natural situations, it nevertheless makes clear (which is of concern to anthropologists) that there is a reciprocal relation between interlocutor and topic which is manifested in the change of language behaviour (code shifting). The result of the investigation confirmed the dependence:

i   of content on language, i.e. the speakers have different experiences in each language ('functional specialization'). This either relates to separate spheres such as 'at home' and 'at work', or, as in this experiment, to different spheres of life and culture (growing up in Japan as against later life in the USA);

ii   of language behaviour on a combination of the factors 'listener' and 'topic' (if natural code shifting is not permitted this leads to hesitation phenomena, difficulties of expression etc.).

6.3.3 Ritual insults

Ritual insults (Labov *et al.* 1968, II, 76–119) are a typical characteristic of Black youths' verbal activities. To these may be added, the 'toasts', long epic poems that have a complicated internal rhythm and are sometimes very artfully rhymed (II, 55–75). There is an indissoluble bond between the singing of songs, epic poetry, verbal rituals and insults, and the social values of the ghetto groups (cf. 6.2.6), the most important of which are: a sense of solidarity between group members and violation at all costs of the middle-class norms. The contents of the rhymes and insults are diametrically opposed to the esthetic feelings of the middle class.

Of all the verbal activities of the peer groups in the ghettos of Harlem it is the ritual insults that best reflect their highly-developed linguistic competence. Ritual insults are speech acts in which speakers summon up all their linguistic capabilities in order to insult one of the other speakers standing round in the group. They are a linguistic game in that the whole point is that each speaker should outdo the other in the coarseness of the insult. The onlookers accompany each insulting speech act with applause or signs of displeasure. Whoever is no longer able to outdo the other is, according to the rules of the game, the loser. 'Since sounding [i.e. in this context, ritual insults] is extremely frequent and is rigorously evaluated by the peer group, we have here an excellent opportunity to study the social control of language, and the emergence of standards of excellence in the vernacular' (II, 76).

In the great majority of cases ritual insults are directed at the mother of the antagonist, roughly on the lines of the following examples, which spark off an escalation of reciprocal insults between two speakers: *Your mother looks like Flipper* (II, 79) or *His mother was so dirty, when she get the rag take a bath, the water went back down the drain* (II, 82).

Labov and his collaborators first determine the syntactic constructions by which the insults are conveyed (e.g. *your mother is like—; your mother eat—*etc.), and then formulate the rules for ritual insults (II, 96ff.). For each speech event there are three kinds of participants: antagonist *A*, antagonist *B* and *listeners*. *A* insults *B*, the listeners evaluate; *B* insults *A* and this insult is again evaluated. The general structure of the speech events is then: *A–1* e *B–1* e *A–2* e *B–2* . . . (e = evaluation). *A–1* refers to *B*'s mother, *B–1* is a direct reply to *A–1*. The more successful *B–1* is as a transformation of *A–1*, the better *B*'s chances of winning. *A–2* may be a new insult; if, however, it is a further transformation of *B–1* it is given an even higher value. While *A–2* may surpass *B–1* if the insult is better, it is also true that *A* has countered well if *A–2* refers explicitly to *B–1*. We shall illustrate this process with an example (II, 96f.), in which Boot and Money are antagonists, while a group including David, Ricky and Roger stands by and evaluates:

A–1	Boot:	His mother go to work without any draws on so that she c'd get a good breeze.
B–1	Money:	Your mother go, your mother go work without any, anythink on, just go neked.
e	David:	That's a lie.
A–2	Boot:	Your mother, when she go to work and she had—you know th– toe shoes, well her stockings reach her be— sweeping the ground.
e	Ricky:	[laughs]
	Roger:	Ho lawd! [laughs]
B–2	Money:	Your mother have holes—potatoes in her shoes.
A–3	Boot:	Your mother got a putty chest [laughs].
B–3	Money:	Arrgh! Aww—you wish you had a putty chest, right?
A–4	Boot:	Your mother got hair growing out her dunkee hole.
C–4	Roger:	Money, your mother got a 45 in her left titty.
	Money:	Awww!
e	Ricky:	[laughs]. . . .

Thus the structure of the insults is such that *A* must either outdo the antagonist B or at least skilfully parry or counter his insults, and vice versa. Occasionally, a third person can also intervene in this process (in the above example Roger, C–4).

Insults can be described by two rules on the lines of basic speech act dyads (here we have not considered a series of further complex factors):

1   When A utters a speech act S in the presence of B and listeners C, which relates to a target, $T(B)$, connected with B in a proposition P, and when
    i B thinks that A thinks that P is not true and
    ii B thinks that A thinks that B knows that P is not true,
    then S is an insult if S is of the form '$T(B)$ *is so X that P*' where X is a pejorative attribute and A is the antagonist who has insulted B (II, 106).

In rule 1, (i) and (ii) are conditions that relate to commonly-shared social knowledge. They are only the first in an infinite series of recursive conditions which state that A and B know that P is not true. 'In the terminology of discourse analysis . . ., an A-event is one known to be known only to A (in A's biography) and a B-event is one known to be known only to B, whereas an AB-event is one known to be known to both. We may summarize conditions a and b as *it is an* AB-*event that* P *is not true*' (II, 107).[8]

The second rule formulates the conditions for the answer to an initial insult:

2   When A has insulted B then B insults A by asserting a new proposition P' which is aimed at a target, $T(A)$, linked to A, in such a way that it is an AB-event that P' is not true (II, 109).

Rule 2 implies, moreover, the condition for P' that when $X' \neq X$, then it is required that $P' \neq P$. In other words, if A says *Your mother so old she fart dust*, B cannot say *Your mother so skinny she fart dust* or *Your mother so black she fart dust*. When, on the other hand, $X' = X$, then it is also allowed that $P' = P$ if the target T is changed (although this type of answer is the weakest).

Rules 1 and 2 are sufficient to 'generate' sequences of insults between two antagonists. Labov cites numerous examples to show the complex syntax and semantics developed by BEV speakers in ritual insults. Sometimes these are rhymed, sometimes they are reduced to a minimum of words which make the insult even more cutting. In any case, the structure of ritual insults shows that BEV speakers have a well-developed verbal competence.

However, Labov does not include an explanation of these speech events that are typical of BEV speakers. Since his work is descriptive, he dissociates himself from psychological investigations which aim at unravelling the psychological function of 'sounding', which possibly consists in the fact that it 'releases the anxiety of Negro youth, and directs aggression against members of their own group instead of against the more dangerous white group' (II, 115). Labov says explicitly: '. . . in this discussion we are not concerned with speculation as to the underlying psychological effects of sounding. We are concerned with the development of rules of discourse and standards of excellence in this verbal activity, as a sharp contrast to the low level of achievement in school by the same speakers' (II, 116).

---

[8] Labov's use of the term *event* seems, perhaps, less appropriate when applied to the truth or falsity of a proposition. A term such as *fact* might well make his analysis clearer.

6.3.4 Stories of personal experiences

In connection with the investigation into the verbal capabilities of BEV speakers in central Harlem, Labov *et al.* (1968, II, 4.8) also analysed stories of peer group members given in response to one of the following three questions: 'Were you ever in serious danger of being killed?' 'What is the best (worst) street fight you've ever seen?' and 'Have you ever been involved in a fight with a boy stronger than you? What happened?' (II, 286)

Labov and Waletzky (1967) developed a theoretical basis for textual analysis in order to give an adequate description of the stories, i.e. to be able to relate the syntactic and narrative qualities to the social characteristics of the speakers; this basis was adopted and put into practice in Labov *et al.* 1968. Labov and Waletzky regard the story as *one* of several methods of recapitulating past experiences: in a story, a chain of events can be reproduced analogously by a sequence of sentences. The following sequence (Labov and Waletzky 1967, 20):

> Well, this person had a little too much to drink
> and he attacked me
> and the friend came in
> and she stopped it

consists of four parts which refer to four events/situations but which, at the same time, have a chronological ordering. This chronological sequence of clauses, which are referentially related to events, is an essential feature in stories. From the principle that the linguistic sequences follow the order of events, it can be deduced that certain independent, chronologically ordered clauses have a particular significance for the framework of the story; others, however (e.g. *S*-embeddings), that are not chronologically ordered, only play a subordinate part in the linguistically-manifested sequence of events.

The embedded or descriptive clauses can be placed anywhere in the account without disturbing the temporal sequence of the narrative or seriously jeopardizing its essential semantic content. Thus, the main principle of functional textual analysis is that the order of the temporal sequence 'cannot be changed without changing the inferred sequence of events in the original semantic interpretation' (Labov and Waletzky 1967, 21).

Clause types and displacement sets. Chronologically-ordered clauses of a story (minimal narrative units) can be isolated from other clauses by using displacement tests to find out whether the clause in question is independent and chronologically ordered, or not. An example will serve to illustrate this:

w and they was catchin' up to me   **1**
x and I crossed the street
y and I tripped, man.

If we test the possible displacements of *w*, *x* and *y* we see that *x* can be placed before *w* but not after *y* without altering the original semantic interpretation of the sequence. Formally we say that for clause *c* the notation $a^c p$ signifies that *c* may be placed before each and every one of the a preceding clauses and after each and every one of the p following clauses (a and p being natural numbers). Then the *displacement set* DS (c) consists of c itself as well as all the clauses that can be placed *before* c and *after* c. Thus for w, x and y the following DS is produced:

0^w2 and they was catchin' up to me	$DS(w) = \{w, x, y\}$	**2**
1^x0 and I crossed the street	$DS(x) = \{w, x\}$	
0^y0 and I tripped, man	$DS(x) = \{y\}$	

Two extreme types of displacement sets result from these operations: (a) 0^c0, and (b) $x-1^cn-x$, where n represents the total number of clauses in the account (Labov and Waletzky 1967, 22). As a clause that cannot be detached from the sequence, c assumes in (a) the function of a simple narrative unit. In the case of (b) the displacement set of c is equivalent to the total number of clauses in the account, so that its chronological position is irrelevant. (a) is a *narrative* and (b) a *freely permutable* clause type. Two further clause types may now be distinguished on the basis of displacement sets: the *coordinated* and the *restricted*.

The coordinated type is permutable with a second clause:

0^y0 (and the rock) came down	**3**
0^y0 and smacked him in the head	
1^u0 and say (slap!)	

In this example t and u have an identical permutation set: $DS(t) = t, u$: $DS(u) = t, u$.

The restricted type has a DS that comprises some subscripts on the left and some subscripts on the right hand side of c. It relates to displacement values which are higher than those of the coordinated clause type and lower than those of the freely permutable type.

The isolation of clause types may be illustrated by the example of story 6 from Labov and Waletzky (1967, 23f.):

		DS
0^a18	yeh I was in the Boy Scouts at the time	(a–s)
1^b17	and we was doing the 50-yard dash	(a–s)
2^c16	racing	(a–s)
3^d15	but we was at the pier, marked off	(a–s)
4^e14	and so we was doing the 50-yard dash	(a–s)
5^f13	there was about 8 or 9 of us, you know, going down, coming back	(a–s)
6^g0	and, going down the *third* time, I caught cramps	(a–g)
0^h0	and I started yelling 'Help'	(h)
0^i1	but the fellows didn't believe me, you know	(i–j)
1^j0	they thought I was just trying to catch up because I was going on or slowing down	(i–j)
0^k1	so all of them kept going	(k–l)
1^l0	they leave me	(k–l)
0^m3	and so started going down	(m–p)

13^n5	Scoutmaster was up there	$(a-s)$
6^o3	he was watching me	$(i-r)$
7^p2	but he didn't pay me no attention either	$(i-r)$

0^q0	and for no reason at all there was another guy, who had just walked up that minute . . .	(q)
0^r0	he just jumped over	(r)
0^s0	and grabbed me	(s)

In story 6, $a-f$ are freely permutable clauses, g and m narrative, i and j coordinated and n, o and p restricted clauses. The clause types can be well isolated and ordered on the basis of the indices.

Chronological sequence. The following is given as the condition under which two clauses are located in chronological sequence:

'Such a condition is met when the displacement range of a given clause does not extend past the actual location of some following clause, and conversely the displacement range of this following clause does not extend past the actual location of the given preceding clause. More concisely, their displacement sets do not include each other.' (Labov and Waletzky 1967, 25)

Two clauses defined on these lines are ordered chronologically in relation to one another. In story 6 there is thus a temporal link between g and h, h and i, j and k, l and m, m and q, q and r, r and s.

Definition of the narrative unit. The narrative unit can now be defined in terms of temporal link and displacement sets. It is a characteristic of the narrative clause that it cannot be displaced beyond a temporal link without altering the semantic interpretation of the chronological sequence. A narrative clause has therefore an *unordered displacement set*. A story A can be represented by a set of clauses $c^1, c^2, \ldots, c^n$, where $0 \leqslant 1 \leqslant n$. Then, according to the definition of Labov and Waletzky (1967, 27f.), it is true that:

1     $c^i \in \mathrm{DS}(c^j)$, if c^j and $c^j, \ldots, c^i$ yield the same chronological sequence in semantic interpretation (or when $c^i = c^j$).

2   If $c^i \in \mathrm{DS}(c^k)$ and $c^j \in \mathrm{DS}(c^k)$
and $c^i \in \mathrm{DS}(c^j)$ and $c^j \in \mathrm{DS}(c^i)$
(a) and $\mathrm{DS}(c^k) = A$, then c^k is a *freely permutable clause*.
(b) and $\mathrm{DS}(c^k) < A$, then c^k is a *restricted clause*.

3   When condition 2 does not apply, c^k is a *narrative clause*.

Definition of the story. Any succession of clauses that contains a temporal link is a story. Accordingly,

I know a boy name Harry	0^a2
Another boy threw a bottle at him right in the head	1^b0
and he had to get seven stitches	0^c0

is a story since there is a temporal link between b and c.

Before considering operations, which allow us to isolate narrative units from other clauses, brief mention must be made of the following. An important linguistic element of the narrative unit is the finite verb. It contains the tense marker and can therefore be termed the 'narrative head' of the clause; as such, it is an essential component of the definition of the story. Labov and Waletzky justify in a relatively detailed discussion why the '*a then b*' relation is a fundamental factor in stories. We shall, however, leave out a detailed account of this discussion, and simply take their conclusions for granted.

Isolation of primary sequences. Given the postulate of the '*a then b*' relation, one can attempt to isolate formally the underlying primary narrative sequence and to derive other equivalent narrative units from it (Labov and Waletzky 1967, 31).

This is done in four steps, as shown in story 6:

1   For each clause, the DS is specified by indices:
     0^a18 1^b17 2^c16 3^d15 4^e14 5^f13 6^g0 0^h0 0^i1 1^j0 0^k1 1^l0 0^m3 13^n5 6^o3 7^p2
     0^q0 0^r0 0^s0

2   Freely permutable clauses are placed at the beginning of the story:
     0^a18 1^b17 2^c16 3^d15 4^e14 5^f13 6^g12 7^g0 0^h0 0^i1 1^j0 0^k1 1^l0 0^m2 5^n3 6^p2
     0^q0 0^r0 0^s0

3   Restricted clauses are pushed as far forward as possible within the story:
     0^a18 1^b17 2^c16 3^d15 4^e14 5^f13 6^g12 7^g0 0^h0 0^n8 1^p7 2^i1 3^j0 0^k1 1^l0 0^m0
     0^q0 0^r0 0^s0

4   Coordinated clauses are combined into individual units:
     0^a $^n9$ 1^g0 0^h0 $0^{n-p}5$ $1^{i-j}0$ $0^{k-l}0$ 0^m0 0^q0 0^s0

The chain of 10 symbols in story 6 then represents the primary sequence of the account in which the '*a then b*' relation is explicitly worked out (Labov and Waletzky 1967, 31).

The operations carried out above can be summarized formally in one operation:

An account is composed formally of $c^1, c^2, \ldots, c^i, \ldots, c^n$ with left displacement ranges $a^1, a^2, \ldots, a^i, \ldots, a^n$, where $0 \leqslant 1 \leqslant n$. A left displacement function $y(E_i)$ is then defined for each permutation $E_1, E_2, \ldots, E_m$ of the clauses $c^1, c^2, \ldots, c^n$ (retaining the chronological sequence of the original semantic interpretation) as

$$y(E_i) = \sum_{i=1}^{n} a^i$$

If $y(E_j)$ is minimal, each sequence c^i, c^j (where DS $(c^i) = DS(c^j)$) is replaced by c^k; the displacement ranges are simultaneously reordered. The string resulting from this is the primary sequence of the range $E_1, E_2, \ldots, E_m$ (31f.).

If a comparison is made of the structure of several stories told by peer group members on the basis of the description arrived at by these operations, it becomes apparent that in the stories the clause types are distributed in a more or less specific way over five sections. These are fundamental for almost all BEV stories and may count as their overall structure: orientation, complication, evaluation, solution and coda. The following diagram illustrates the typical sequence for stories and shows 'evaluation' to be the central part of the structure:

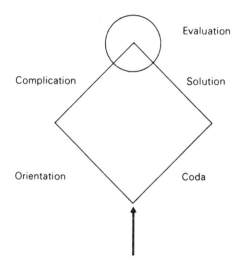

Fig. 6.11 Typical structure of BEV stories.

With *orientation* the speaker conveys the situation (persons, time, place etc.) in which the action took place: it consists to a large extent of freely permutable clauses, as figure 6.12 shows for story 6 (clauses *a–j*).

Complication embraces the immediate events of the action and is borne predominantly by narrative units (in story 6 the series *g–m*).

The *evaluation* or assessment of the story must be regarded as its most important part. A speaker who recounts a story in answer to the question, 'Were you ever in serious danger of being killed?' automatically feels obliged to prove that he actually was in a dangerous situation. With the evaluation of the event he justifies to the listener that what happened to him actually was highly dangerous and also assesses, in retrospect, what this event meant to him. The most complex sentences of the stories appeared in the evaluation section. Some of them contained four or five different embeddings, each of which was emphasized in different ways unknown to SE. Various comparative constructions, intensifiers and qualifiers were used to add weight to the evaluation vis-à-vis the listener and to contrast it with the rest of the story.

The *solution* follows the evaluation and is the ending of the sequence of action that has just been evaluated in the speaker's retrospective account (*q, r* and *s* in story 6).

Finally, the *coda* is a functional feature (absent in story 6) used by the narrator to mark the transition from the story to the present. It causes the verbal perspective to revert to the actual situation of the narrator and listener.

Labov *et al.* (1968, 314–38) conclude from an analysis of BEV accounts

Clause	a	p
a	0	18
b	1	17
c	2	16
d	3	15
e	4	14
f	5	13
g	6	0
h	0	0
i	0	1
j	1	0
k	0	1
l	1	0
m	0	3
n	13	5
o	6	3
p	7	2
q	0	0
r	0	0
s	0	0

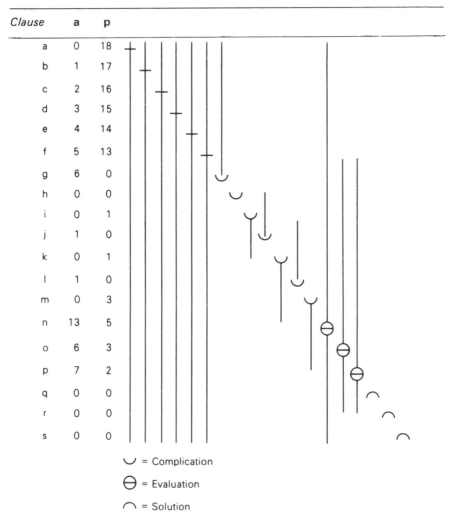

⌣ = Complication

⊖ = Evaluation

⌢ = Solution

Fig. 6.12 Displacement ranges of clauses and structure of story 6.
(Source: Labov and Waletzky 1967, 26)

(especially those of Black youths), conducted on the lines of the methods set out above, that:

1   BEV speakers have a command of various techniques of oral narration: captivating the listener by 'expressive phonology'; drawing out the action by inserting subordinate clauses and thus heightening the tension; making multilayered evaluations of events or actions; explaining events concisely. In stories, language is used with versatility to make an impression on the listener, to bring out the self-awareness of the individual's action, to display knowledge, to explain incidents and to shock. This is achieved partly by complex sentence constructions (chiefly in the sphere of evaluation), of

which only BEV is capable. The contents of stories are closely linked with the values of the peer groups.

2   A comparison of stories obtained from different age groups shows that the complexity of evaluation types or categories is greatest amongst adults and lowest among 10-year-olds (329). The 13- to 16-year-olds are, of course, not far behind the adults, but differ considerably from the 10- to 12-year-olds. Conclusions can be drawn from this regarding language acquisition.

6.4 Language and social structure

The correlation of language and social structure can be considered from four points of view:

1   Speech behaviour reflects the social structure
2   Speech behaviour can condition social behaviour
3   Social structure can determine speech behaviour
4   Speech behaviour and social behaviour are dialectically related to one another (cf. Grimshaw 1971a, 114).

With these possibilities in mind, we shall attempt to draw some conclusions from the empirical investigations into speech behaviour in its social context.

6.4.1 Reflection of social structure in speech behaviour

Most correlative studies (indeed these constitute the majority of investigations into speech behaviour) take social structure to be an independent variable and speech behaviour to be a dependent one. The terms of reference are thus established: speech behaviour reflects the basic categories of social structure. Most of the American investigations mentioned in 6.2 are of this type, especially the work of Labov. We shall give a synopsis of the most common categories that relates to the variables, age, social classification, ethnic differentiation and sex.

Age
On the strength of his investigations into New York speech, Labov (1964b, 91f.) distinguishes six stages in the acquisition of spoken English, based on results of the correlation of phonological variables with variables of age in connection with social class:

1   *Basic grammar.* In their early years, children learn basic words and grammatical rules so that they can communicate their most essential needs in their environment (cf. Bloom 1970). This stage is normally heavily affected by parental influence.

2   *Regional dialect.* The second stage is the decisive one from the point of view of language development. When aged between 5 and 12, children learn the regional dialect within their circle of friends and this undermines and partly diminishes the linguistic influence exerted by parents. The child also learns to read at school during this period.

3   *Emergence of social awareness.* In his early youth (12–15) the child becomes
more and more aware of the social significance of his speech as a result of
increasing contact with the outside world (adults, strangers, authorities etc.).
Systematic observations prove that the 15-year-old is just as aware of the social
significance of his speech norms as an adult is.

4   *Stylistic variation.* In this stage the child begins to modify his speech
behaviour towards the prestige norm (Standard). This applies particularly to
formal situations. Reorientation is accelerated as the child enters more advanced
schools or comes into contact with different social contexts. He develops the
ability to alter his speech behaviour according to situation. This stage also
determines the extent of the child's command of the rules of the Standard.

5   *Consistent use of Standard.* By no means all speakers are able to use the
Standard consistently over long periods of time. As a rule, consistent speech use
with only insignificant deviations from the Standard is not to be found outside the
middle class.

6   *Full range of stylistic repertoire.* Middle-class speakers sometimes exhibit a
stylistic repertoire for different situations and occasions that is particularly
marked in those who have a special interest in developing their speech behaviour
(e.g. students). The full range of Standard and prestige forms is restricted to
comparatively few speakers. Regional dialect is typical for lower-class speakers.

   Three factors inhibit the acquisition of the prevailing Standard: isolation, i.e.
the working class is more isolated from prestige forms than the middle class;
structural interference, i.e. linguistic attributes of the regional dialect make it
more difficult in the primary school years to learn the Standard because of
interference with forms of the Standard; value conflicts, i.e. peer groups inhibit
any deviation from regional dialect towards the Standard.

Social classification
Social class is the most reliable distinguishing feature in investigations of speech
behaviour in large cities (e.g. Labov, Wolfram, Fishman, Shuy and Reichstein).
Linguistic features reveal consistent stratification in correlation with education,
occupation and income. The phenomenon of hypercorrection is particularly well-
documented in the American investigations; this occurs when speakers of the
lower middle class use prestige forms of the dominant class over-correctly in order
to climb the social ladder more quickly. Hypercorrection is identified with
upward social mobility and is explained in terms of the norm and its social value.
Terms such as 'prestige norm' or 'social value' are not explained in any of the
works. Interest in social stratification is frequently aimed at 'discovering the
extent to which people . . . deviate from norms' (Labov, quoted in Grimshaw
1971a, 116).

Ethnic differentiation
Immigrant generations in the USA have various foreign accents which identify
them as non-Americans. There are nearly as many works devoted to ethnic

differentiation as to social classification (see in particular Fishman), and there is a functional correlation between the two. The Blacks, the group subjected to the worst living conditions and the most repressed in the USA, display the most consistent and greatest deviation from Standard English. This can be explained by their isolation in ghettos and their different social values (cf. 6.2 and 6.3). European immigrants in the USA have been integrated into society without difficulty, and their children have adapted their speech almost completely to Standard English (cf. Labov 1971a, 203–7).

Sex

The results of virtually all investigations show that women adapt to prevailing prestige forms more than men. Middle-class women are also far less tolerant of Non-Standard forms and taboo words (Labov 1971a, 207). The stylistic variation of women sometimes reaches extreme proportions. Labov's assessment (1971a, 207f.) of female speech behaviour among the middle and lower classes is typical of the American situation: 'Many middle-class women are critical of their husbands' speech and find it difficult to recognize the functional need for less cultivated speech patterns in daily business. The differences in the sexes do not seem to exist in rural or lower-class urban groups.'

Correlative studies, which see differences in speech behaviour as a reflex of social structure, generally explain these as a result of different living conditions or styles that are not further investigated, and as objective differences in social values and norms (measured according to deviations from the prevailing norms).

As Labov emphasizes, the social significance of language as a whole should not be over-estimated: 'Linguistic and social structure are by no means coextensive. The great majority of linguistic rules are quite remote from any social value; they are part of the elaborate machinery which the speaker needs to translate his complex set of meanings or intentions into linear form' (1970a, 77).

6.4.2 Determination of social behaviour by speech behaviour

This line is taken in some anthropological studies following the tradition of Whorf. It is argued that the social learning of language conditions social behaviour and therefore social perception. We have already dealt extensively with this in connection with Bernstein (cf. chapters 1, 2 and 3).

6.4.3 Determination of speech behaviour by social structure

Authors such as Gumperz and Fishman make the choice of verbal repertoire dependent on the social values of the speech community and on any given socially-defined speech situation. This principle was illustrated in 5.4 for domain-specific speech use (cf. also the ethnomethodological approach in 6.1.1). The general assumption is that the choice of a style depends on the speakers' characteristics and environment, in other words, on various intervening social factors; these represent varying restrictions for speech behaviour. Thus Grimshaw (1966), for example, demonstrated that the presence of listeners can have a considerable effect on the selection of style and topic. If, say, a professor (higher status) and a caretaker (lower status) interact with one another, the former's choice of style depends on the characteristics of the listener and his 'role-taking ability'. If the professor is not capable of adopting a flexible role his status awareness becomes the determining factor of his speech behaviour. He has three possibilities: he can use the style he presumes the caretaker will use; he can optimize the communication by simplifying his syntactic constructions; or he can resort to depersonalized speech behaviour (manifested in forms of address, indirect speech).

Another view also held by ethnomethodologists, namely that speech behaviour is a product of social and situational norms, has the following essential characteristics: social structure is equated with social roles, social status and social situations, which are again governed by social norms. These appear in turn as a result of the description of individual social situations etc. In short, explanations of different speech behaviour lose and exhaust themselves in the circular interaction of social situations and social (mostly cultural) norms.

6.4.4 Interaction of speech behaviour and social behaviour

It is only reasonable to assume that speech behaviour is dialectically linked with social environment. But so far no investigation has been able to demonstrate systematically how this mutual relation operates. All we can say is that speech behaviour and social behaviour are in a state of constant interaction. It can be taken for granted that syntax is least directly affected by social behaviour; at the same time the evaluation of language is the decisive link with social behaviour, which is again bound either directly or indirectly to material living conditions.

6.5 Summary

Correlative and functional studies are the two most important types of inquiry in American sociolinguistics.

Correlative studies link socially significant linguistic variables with social parameters (mostly, the former are considered dependent upon the latter). Functional studies deny the parallel between social and physical measurements by arguing that physical measurements can be carried out on the basis of simple registration, but sociological measurements necessarily involve a human intermediary interpreting the data in terms of categories common to both himself and the subject of investigation.

In correlative investigations, phonological and grammatical features are shown to display constant patterns of stylistic and social stratification. They reflect socially-determined differences in the speech behaviour of speakers, particularly with regard to age, sex, social class and ethnic membership. The notation of these differences in variable rules makes it possible to describe formally speech variation and linguistic change.

The analysis of speech events as related to situational contexts in functional studies includes only informally the social characteristics of speakers. The topic and content of utterances are the main points of interest. The communicative competence of speakers manifest in speech acts is described functionally in connection with their social values. Here the main priority should be to discover the invariant rules of verbal interaction.

The common aim of all investigations is to explain social values and norms by their manifestations in speech behaviour. Differences established are interpreted in terms of cultural diversity.

7 Applied sociolinguistics in the USA: the Variability Concept and its ghetto specialist[1]

Under the heading 'applied sociology of language' Fishman (1971b, 353) refers to Kurt Lewin's maxim that 'nothing is as practical as a good theory'. Well-founded sociolinguistic theory is therefore of great interest for the interrelation of 'planned social change' and 'planned language change', whenever

1   'Language varieties must be "developed" in order to function in the vastly new settings, role-relationships or purposes in which certain important networks of their speakers come to be involved', or
2   'important networks [particular groups of the population] of a speech community must be taught varieties . . . that they do not know well (or at all) so that these networks may function in the vastly new settings. role-relationships or purposes that might then become open (or more open) to them.' (*ibid.*)

   Instead of exploring the question of why certain specific language varieties should function in certain specific new environments and role-relations, Fishman, relying on 'commonsense', prefers to deal with existing practical problems: uneducated people must be educated, writing systems must be created and orthographic reforms implemented. Fishman does not specify what developments led to the situations where such measures must be implemented and where new branches of science are tackling these problems, although he is one of the founders of sociolinguistics. His extensive investigation of bilingual speech in New York (Fishman *et al.* 1968) might have raised the sociopolitical question of how such a vast and costly investigation could ever have been approved. Kjolseth appears to give a more realistic assessment of the roots of applied sociolinguistics: 'If . . . socioeconomic factors appear to require new branches of knowledge to satisfy newly-emerging needs but the necessary intellectual development is not forthcoming. then the development of a new field of inquiry is hardly conceivable' (1971. 10). In the USA the 'needs' were great and sociolinguistics rapidly developed from the mid-1960s to become one of the most important branches of the social sciences. Kjolseth gives his interpretation of the background to the boom in sociolinguistics in the USA in a sociological analysis. Problems of poverty are suddenly 'rediscovered':

1   'in complex, historical societies . . . many social differences are linked with language, i.e. language plays an important part in the unequal social

---

[1] I have formulated the following arguments in collaboration with Gisela Feurle.

distribution of positive and negative social values of a material and symbolic nature';

2 'in addition to the "rediscovery" of poverty, problems of education as well as of "development" have recently been regarded as social questions and have therefore become the aims of government programmes';

3 'disadvantaged groups who have recently organized themselves—such as the Blacks and Chicanos (Americans of Mexican origin)—look upon schools as an important lever for the realization of their social aspirations since these place a great deal of emphasis on the acquisition of certain linguistic capabilities. One hears, for example, that schools with a considerable concentration of cultural, ethnic and linguistic minorities are characterized by a "massive reading failure" (Labov). . . . This process of drawing attention to a social problem would not be ... conceivable without the recent social movements that have been set in motion by linguistic minorities in the USA.'

4 'In the last few years, the question of so-called development has been brought into the foreground as a result of the formation of a new supranational economic structure, and there seems to be a marked awareness that many of the existing problems are linked with language. This means that an important part of the programme for economic expansion is based on the erection of a "linguistic infrastructure". . . .' (Kjolseth 1971, 11–2).

Bearing these points in mind, Kjolseth finally indicates what may be understood by a language policy: 'It is clearly the task of the government to prove that they are capable of reacting to what are defined as social questions and problems by influential groups of the electorate whom they must "take into consideration" ' (12).

Thus if language policy is 'clearly the task of the government', on whose interests and financial backing the development of a branch of science such as sociolinguistics depends, we simply cannot accept the statement 'that poverty ... is "rediscovered" ... at certain points in time': instead we should inquire as to the sociopolitical factors determining such a 'rediscovery'.

In this respect the Variability Concept is more efficient than the Deficit Hypothesis, in content as well as technique.

7.1 Sociopolitical background to educational programmes in Black ghettos

In order to understand the full extent of sociolinguistic studies of the Variability Concept, it is not enough merely to pursue the internal academic discussion (Deficit Hypothesis v. Variability Concept). Sociolinguistic inquiry must be judged in the end by its success or failure in practical application (cf. chapter 3), as is already evident from the fact that criticism of the Deficit Theory was sparked off by the failure of speech compensation programmes derived from it (and carried out at great financial expense).

It is once again necessary to bear in mind what sociopolitical requirements lie behind the compensatory education programmes for deprived children in the USA (especially Blacks in the ghettos). This is because they also apply (and indeed become more critical after the failure of the programmes) to investigations in the framework of the Variability Concept, i.e. to investigations into language in its social context, the results of which are manifested in practical proposals for education.

In the USA, the richest industrial nation in the world, there is a stark contrast between wealth and poverty: at the beginning of the 1960s two fifths of the American population—77 million people—lived in a state of chronic poverty (du Bois-Reymond 1971, 25).

The hardest hit are the Blacks living in ghettos, and other ethnic minorities such as Puerto Ricans (Fishman *et al.* 1968), Chicanos (Stolz and Bills 1968) and Indians. There is a lack of jobs and the number of unemployed is increasing. The Blacks are the group most discriminated against on the labour market, in particular Black youths:

> 'In 1970 the number of unemployed youths (16–19 years) was 15·3 per cent (overall percentage of unemployed: 4·9 per cent). . . . Twice as many Blacks as Whites are out of work. In the same year about 30 per cent of Black youths were unemployed (as opposed to 13·5 per cent of White youths). . . . Between 1968 and 1980 the Black working force will have risen from 9 to 12 millions.' (du Bois-Reymond 1971, 39: 27).

On the other hand, between 30 and 40 per cent of all youths leave secondary schools before finishing and 5 per cent do not even complete the eighth grade. The number of jobs, especially technical ones, rose in recent years by 54 per cent (cf. 38ff.).

These few figures should show the dangers facing the economic and social stability of the country. This state of affairs is the cause of increased racial conflict. As a result, American crisis management was called into action in a coalition of government and private industry. Short-term measures were brought in to 'pacify the ghettos' by means of the police and the military, and conflict centres were set up (supposedly to ease tension and to develop methods for quelling ghetto riots); long-term measures for social integration were also planned: industrial investment in ghetto areas, creation of new jobs, compensatory education programmes for the deprived.

Yet all these measures do not attack the cause of the underprivileged conditions of this group: the contradiction that exists in the private appropriation of wealth by the society at large, i.e. the capitalist balance of power. They are rather corrective measures that do not get to grips with the basic economic and political reasons for inequality, and are symptomatic of the reaction (and absence of planning) of the capitalist state. Their avowed aim is to get the 'social dynamite' (du Bois-Reymond 1971, 40) under control and to adapt the Blacks (and other minorities) to the requirements of a highly-industrialized capitalist society engaged in international competition, i.e. to eliminate illiteracy and to satisfy the need for qualified workers (technicians etc.). The measures taken are embellished with the principle of equality of opportunity, which should be guaranteed by a suitable educational system. The contradiction that exists between the demand for equality of opportunity and that for competitiveness is glossed over. Yet competition, 'upward social mobility', is precisely the principle on which capitalist society is based. Little account is taken of economic and social inequalities which form each individual's starting handicap in the competitive society, and failure in competition is mostly attributed to *individual* shortcomings. It is typical that the motto should so often be 'equality of opportunity', rather than 'equality of results', although under any rational assumption equality of results (achievements) averaged over various social groups would be the most reliable test for the success of the current social development programmes. One task of the educational system, particularly that of compensatory education, is to conceal the fact that there exists a bias in favour of competition and against equality of opportunity.

In the mid-1960s, the research budget in the education sector increased roughly in proportion to the decrease in the military sector. In particular the Office of Equal Opportunity, the Department of Health, Education and Welfare and the Office of Manpower Policy benefited from this. At the same time educational research started to merge with private industry (du Bois-Reymond 1971, 50).

In his justification of increased state subsidies for the education sector, President Kennedy referred to the economic aspect of a competitive industrial nation that must fully exploit its intellectual resources, as well as to the Americans' belief in the basic right of every individual to develop his abilities to the full. Economic and technological pressures on individuals are intensified by this appeal to equality of opportunity: 'For the individual, education leads to the richest treasures of our free society: the power of knowledge; the training necessary for a productive job; the wisdom, ideals and cultural goods that enrich life, and a creative and *self-disciplined understanding of society*, which characterizes a good citizen in a world that is constantly changing . . .' (du Bois-Reymond 1971, 42; my italics). The 'war on poverty', initiated by Kennedy and continued under Johnson, must be seen against this background of economic and technological pressures and the necessity for a self-disciplined understanding of society. A series of laws were passed to alleviate the critical state of education, and to help the underprivileged: Civil Rights Act (1964); Economic Opportunity Act (1964); Elementary and Secondary Education Act (1965); Juvenile Delinquency and Youth Offenses Control Act (1961, supplemented 1965); Manpower Development and Training Act (1963); and Education Professions Development Act (1967) (cf. on individual points du Bois-Reymond 1971, 50ff.).

The failure of compensation programmes can be accounted for by pointing out the falsity of the premises and methods of research, as has already been done (cf. chapters 2 and 3; and especially Labov 1970b). It also illuminates the difficulties or even impossibility of getting children from the propertyless and repressed classes to perform in and adapt to the White business society, the so-called *mainstream culture*, when the basic contradiction (on which ideological contradictions are founded) in capitalist society continues to exist: the private appropriation of socially-produced wealth. It should be noted in passing that one of the most important and efficient instruments of adaptation is the language, Standard American (SE).

When the basic social conditions are not changed, but, instead, the symptoms of poverty and repression are merely corrected or compensated for to some extent, then, if some succeed in rising into the middle class out of the ghetto and obtain a 'mainstream job' (Baratz 1970b), the price to be paid for this will have to be a betrayal of home background and values, as a result of individual social mobility (cf. hypercorrection). The success achieved will then be used to justify in the eyes of the majority still living in poverty the well known phrases 'equality of opportunity', 'fair competition', 'land of opportunities', 'if you're prepared to work, you'll make it', etc.

7.2 New strategies for training pacification specialists

Now that we have outlined the sociopolitical background to sociolinguistic inquiries in the USA, we must examine the alterations and improvements (as a result of the failure of compensatory programmes) of the proposals for solving the educational problems of ghetto children.

The continued efforts to pacify the ghettos in the long term through the schools are to a large extent channelled into exact and very extensive inquiries (Labov *et al.* 1968; Fishman *et al.* 1968; Williams and Naremore 1969a and b; Wolfram 1969 and others) into the social conditions (family structure, peer groups, group solidarity etc.) and the values of the rival society in the ghettos, especially into BEV as a symbol of group solidarity (cf. 6.2.6 'Group norms v. individual norms'). The 'intellectual revolution' of the sociology of language (Kjolseth 1971, 14) started with Kennedy's campaign against poverty and proceeded roughly as follows (cf. 5.1):

Phase 1   1964: constitution of the new discipline, sociolinguistics, as a result of state interests; first publications.

Phase 2   1964– c. 1967: programmatic discussion of the academic status of sociolinguistics.

Phase 3   from about 1966: conclusion of the programmatic discussion with comprehensive, large-scale empirical studies (Blacks in ghettos, ethnic minorities).

Phase 4   1968 to 1972: theorizing in and about sociolinguistics (this process is still continuing), dealing with more specific linguistic problems and broader sociological ones (Labov 1970a; Grimshaw and Fishman in Fishman 1971b).

Phase 5   Evolution of methods for the application of sociolinguistic research, which are closely linked with the development of theoretical concepts and have been the main point of interest since 1969 (cf. Baratz and Shuy 1969; Fasold and Shuy 1970a).

It is no longer surprising that Hymes's well known concept of 'communicative competence' represents an attempt 'to contribute to the study of the language problems of disadvantaged children' and that it is motivated by the lack of a linguistic theory 'that practical research can turn to and has only to apply' (Hymes 1968a, 1). It is also understandable that the inadequate Deficit Hypothesis had to be replaced by more efficient methods and adaptational strategies as a result of the experience in fieldwork built up by social scientists (in particular anthropologists) over many years. On the basis of psychodevelopmental and sociolinguistic studies (Shuy, Wolfram and Riley 1967; Baratz 1969; Labov *et al.* 1968) specialists are now being trained to instruct 'disadvantaged children' in language and reading (cf. Baratz 1970b, 28).

7.2.1 Structural conflict

BEV speech and the reading difficulties resulting from it are regarded as decisive factors in educational problems, reading being the chief criterion for success at school,[2] and therefore in the general integration of Black children into society. Thus Labov writes: 'The principal educational focus of this research is the reading problems of the urban ghetto areas' (Labov *et al.* 1968, I, 13), and from this point of view 'reading failure' (*ibid.*, 1) should be understood and described as *structural* and *functional conflict* between SE and BEV. In the light of the structural conflict, the question is whether and how SE ought to be taught. There are three approaches:

1   'Eradication' consists of replacing BEV with SE by means of strict measures (correction, drill). This was the traditional method.
2   The second approach sees the aim of integration as a functional *bidialectalism*. The teaching of SE at school should not displace the use of BEV at home, on the contrary, the child should learn to switch between the two language varieties in different situations.
3   The third approach does not intend to change the speech behaviour of BEV speakers, but rather to reduce the prejudices of SE speakers towards BEV speakers. The efficiency (time, effort, success) of SE programmes for the disadvantaged is considered somewhat dubious (cf. on these points Fasold and Shuy 1970b).

The majority of authors (cf. Shuy 1964; Baratz and Shuy 1969; Fasold and Shuy 1970a) adopt the second method, and in recent years Baratz in particular has laid political emphasis on this (cf. Baratz and Baratz 1970). Baratz puts forward the argument that from the linguistic standpoint dialects and language varieties are of equal value, but from the social perspective some are regarded as more useful for particular contexts than others (in Fasold and Shuy 1970a, 24). She describes the progression towards standardization, towards the predominance of *one* language (i.e. its use in the essential social spheres) as a natural process: 'The existence of Standard English is not the result of a political conspiracy "to keep the black man down". But rather standardization is a *fact of life*. Societies are socially stratified. . . . One variety of the language becomes the standard' (*ibid.*, 25; my italics). With equal unconcern Fishman (1971b) depicts the *H* and *L* varieties (cf. 4.3.3 and 5.4.2 above), which are regarded as structurally equivalent but functionally complementary, as 'high' and 'low' language varieties that have been in existence from time immemorial: '. . . an *H*(igh) language . . .

[2] Deutsch estimates that up to 60 per cent of children from the lower classes are backward in reading when they leave primary school. A child in the seventh or eighth grade who lives in a slum is two to three years behind in reading compared with a middle-class child of the same age (see du Bois-Reymond 1971, 38).

[was] utilized in conjunction with religion, education and other aspects of high culture, and an *L*(ow) language . . . in conjunction with everyday pursuits of hearth, home, and lower work sphere' (Fishman 1971b, 287).

This is a clearcut instance of the idealistic concept (in the philosophical sense) of society as something naturally given, which negates the historical-materialistic processes of evolution in society and which, therefore, is not able to *explain* sociolinguistic facts and class conflicts as reflected in language conflicts. The ignoring or tacit acceptance of basic social conditions and of the élitist structure founded on them significantly determines the nature of the analyses and proposals for solving sociolinguistic problems: the Black child must simply accept the 'fact of life', i.e. he must learn SE or else he will be deprived of the opportunity of entering the 'mainstream' of American life. As Standard English is the language of the 'mainstream', it is clear that knowledge of the 'mainstream' system increases the chances of success in the 'mainstream' culture (cf. Baratz 1970b, 26 and n. 6). Thus it is evident that the aim of the educational system is to integrate the Blacks into capitalist society, or more precisely: 'to turn out literate citizens who can compete in and contribute to the mainstream culture' (*ibid.*, 26).

The 'contribution to culture' can here be interpreted as 'contribution to the production of private wealth'. We have already discussed the contradiction between the right to equality of opportunity and competition in the ideology of capitalist society. Williams gets entangled in this contradiction: 'Contributing monumentally to the problem in the United States is the *strong correlation between economic opportunity and being able to function in the mainstream society.* Here, we can equate at least part of being-able-to-function with being able to exercise the language of the society. . . . *As we ask a person to learn and use a way of speech, we are at the same time asking him to function* (if sometimes only to a small degree) *in that society*' (Williams 1970b, 396).

First of all, Williams points out the correlation between economic privileges and functioning in capitalist society. Then the ability to function is linked with command of the Standard, so that the underprivileged are taught to function in the society by speech education, whereby no account is taken of the economic reasons. As Sledd has rightly said: 'The fact is, of course, that Northern employers and labor leaders dislike black faces, but use Black English as an excuse' (Sledd 1971, 296). The majority of sociolinguistic studies on the comparison of BEV and SE, as well as the technical proposals that aim at a gradual transition from one to the other must be seen against this background.

7.2.2 Functional conflict

Most authors take into consideration the fact that the problems connected with Black children are only partly linguistic in nature (such as the interference of BEV and SE); rather, they stress the connection with the different cultural and social values and norms of the White middle class. 'Some of our findings clearly show that the overall problem is one of cultural conflict, for which the linguistic data provide us with only one indication' (Labov *et al.* 1968, I, 2). These values and norms, however, are not investigated, and therefore not *explained*, as an expression of actual material and political inequality, but described as necessary sociotechnical information required for developing school textbooks and educational material. At the end of a long passage in which every detail of the group values of BEV peer groups is described (cf. 6.2.6 for the 'bad' Black boy and 'good' middle-class boy), Labov *et al.* emphasize:

'We wish to make clear that we are not offering any "explanations" of deviant behavior or arguing that this frame of reference is the cause of delinquent acts. Nor are we making any statements about whether being "bad" is conceived of as being *morally* bad from the standpoint of members. . . . It is generally true of adolescent peer groups that they revolt against adult authority, and endorse values which are opposed to the dominant values of adult society.

Working-class adolescents admire train robbers, neighborhood gangsters, and big boys who stand up to the teacher; and this opposition of values affects many middle-class boys as well. We are not contending here that the values of being "bad" are confined to NNE culture. However, it can be said that whenever such oppositions are strongly entrenched in the peer group, there will be resistance to the school system; and to the extent that teachers and texts strongly endorse the notion of being "good", to that extent the NNE adolescents are apt to reject both, the form and the content of instruction.' (Labov *et al.* 1968, II, 44f.)

In his recommendations for changes in schools, Labov (Labov *et al.* 1968, II, 348) clearly states that schools must retain their own value system in order to give ghetto children a realistic view of the norms and practices of our society and to put across the value of a society based on law and order. As a tactical move he suggests that the teaching of SE in the first grades should be linked directly with the values that are already *there* if it is to have any success at all. This means that both the content of textbooks and the behaviour of teachers must, for reasons of efficacy, be tailored to BEV values.

From this point of view it is interesting to note the differences that Labov finds in the modes of behaviour of the peer groups and the 'lames' (isolated individuals). The peer groups constitute the core of resistance since their members display highly developed forms of solidarity. Under the heading 'Brothers should not fight with one another' (II, 32) Labov presents an example to show that organized adolescents have a principle whereby they never attack any group member from behind; he stresses this since in other literature there is evidence that Blacks are particularly criminal towards each other.

The 'lames', on the other hand, are adapted to the Standard; they are successful at school and in every respect perform better from the point of view of the 'mainstream culture'. If one is to adapt the peer groups to SE and the middle-class values associated with it, the group solidarity of ghetto children must necessarily be broken down; they will then lose their strength and the basis for resisting their oppressors.

Another example for the theory that 'value conflicts' are the only root of social conflicts is provided by an inquiry conducted by Gumperz (1970, 129–47), who investigates the speech of Blacks and Chicanos with its specific cultural and social significance in relation to school. The children's resistance and inability to learn is crystallized in the following statement: ghetto children associate what White

I

children consider to be normal teacher behaviour with the style of questioning used by welfare officials and automatically refuse to cooperate in any way. Gumperz concludes from this that the teacher must acquaint himself with the linguistic and ethnographic aspects of speech and communication behaviour of his pupils as well as their cultural values so that their inability to learn and inadaptability can be overcome by 'adapted methods' (Gumperz 1970, 142). Constant emphasis is placed on the necessity for the urban language specialist to study and learn the ghetto culture (e.g. in Baratz 1970b, 28ff.).

Along these lines, du Bois-Reymond (1971) gives a report of a training programme carried out in 1966 in conjunction with a project for school integration in the Riverside area of New York. The aim of this training was to prepare the teachers for the 'cultural diversity' of the population. They were to be sensitized to various problem areas: 'culture concept; evolution of Man and culture; the deep and all-pervasive influence of culture on the human personality and on human behaviour; understanding of social positions and subcultures in present day society, particularly in the USA; the role of the school in conveying the "general culture" of our nation . . .' (132).[3]

Du Bois-Reymond continues:

'Sensitivity training is perhaps one of the most sophisticated methods of harmonizing the materially based value distance between the middle-class teacher and the lower-class child, thus initiating social change as it were in a controlled manner and according to need.' (133)

Labov's discussion of the four basic tasks of the assistant teacher, a specially trained (male!) ghetto specialist (cf. 'Recommendations', at the end of 6.2.6) confirms this view and specifies it as a move towards an efficient harmonization (i.e. adaptation of the lower-class child).

7.3 Ideology and symptom correction

We can now summarize what we have repeatedly stressed. The sociolinguistic inquiries that have been made into the linguistic problems of Black and other ghetto children have the same fundamental aim as compensatory programmes: to adapt the Blacks and other ethnic minorities to the social conditions that repress them with the bait of 'upward social mobility', and to integrate them into capitalist society. They amount to a correction of symptoms which does not affect the basic fabric of social inequality and élitist conditions. This symptom-correction works with rather refined methods that have proved linguistically valid and efficient from the point of view of social engineering (cf. 6.2 and 6.3).

It is necessary to realize and to conclude from the practical proposals mentioned that a certain concept of society (or more precisely, the acceptance of existing society with its ideology) immediately impinges on the related field of sociology (cf. also chapter 3). This is very clear in the socioanthropological tradition (with its categories such as status, role, institution, cultural values and norms etc.) which presents its structural and functional analysis as absolute and

[3] 'Preliminary report and evaluation of the Riverside', 26 August 1966 quoted in du Bois-Reymond 1971, 132.

given for society as a whole. Society is considered a social system which is stable and permanent, and which functions by means of the interaction of its parts—an example of this interaction is the adaptation of the individual to social norms (his socialization).

Class oppositions are ignored in favour of categorization by occupation, formal/informal roles and individual interactions such as teacher/pupil, employer/employee, priest/parishioner, etc. No account is taken of the objective contradictions in society as a whole, nor of class oppositions and processes of development in society. The essential aspect is the equilibrium of the system, the 'deviation from the norms' which must be rectified ('this systematic deviation from the complex system which we wish to explain' (Labov *et al.* 1968, II, 217)).

The observations made above are only meant to provide some suggestions regarding the aims of a fundamental analysis of the role of language in society. They give expression to the feeling that most forms of current research are system-dependent to a considerable degree, even though they claim to be value-free in their theory, categorization and methodology. In short, insufficient notice is taken of the basic social and economic factors determining academic inquiry, the ensuing theories and their application. The connection between the two lies in the principles and the dominance of bourgeois ideology, and the result is an élitist knowledge that seeks to stabilize the system.

It is not difficult to see the tradition of this type of academic inquiry in the production of knowledge designed to pacify the ghettos: as early as the end of the nineteenth century, anthropologists and linguists were called in to pacify the Indians.[4]

[4] See Regna Darnell, *The development of American anthropology. 1879–1920* (quoted in Kjolseth 1971) and Neubert 1962. ch. 5, 117–37.

Annotated bibliography

The bibliography presents a selection of over 400 titles (from approximately 1000 works relevant to sociolinguistics), which have either been simply mentioned in the work or dealt with in detail. In that it comments on a series of works that are only touched upon in the text, it is to be regarded as complementary to the description of the literature. Some of the comments have been taken from Dittmar 1971.[1]

The reason why some titles have not been commented on is that they either do not contribute any essentially new points vis-à-vis the works that have been treated, or else they are of only marginal importance for the central core of questions with which this work is concerned. Theoretical, methodological and empirical works of general interest usually take precedence over more specialized investigations; likewise more attention is paid to sociologically-oriented linguistics than to the sociology of language.

Theme-specific grouping of bibliography numbers

1   Collections
1, 2, 7, 9, 13, 19, 37, 41, 55, 92, 93, 104, 117, 122, 135, 138, 139, 155, 161, 180, 182, 211, 217, 228, 230, 233, 239, 268, 276, 282, 284, 300, 310, 323, 329, 335, 349, 372, 374, 378, 392, 402, 403, 408, 415, 423, 424, 426, 431.

2   Research reports
50, 61, 62, 106, 118, 120, 129, 138, 145, 148, 160, 169, 196, 248, 254, 261, 262, 277, 278, 289, 308, 315, 316, 328, 331, 340, 361, 377, 412, 422.

3   Introductions
101, 120, 137, 143, 169, 188, 254, 275, 281, 328, 363, 391.

4   Programmatic essays
85, 128, 210, 212, 213, 214, 218, 393.

5   Theory of Sociology

5.1 General
73, 112, 114, 150, 151, 176, 184, 185, 186, 188, 189, 196, 260, 306, 318, 322, 405, 408, 409.

[1] The selection of and comments on the Soviet titles on sociolinguistics were made by Wolfgang Girke (Faculty of Linguistics, Federal Republic of Germany, Konstanz). I wish to take this opportunity to thank him for his cooperation.

5.2 Correlative method (see also 11.4)
184, 248, 262, 409, 412.

5.3 Ethnomethodology
73, 74, 150, 151, 176, 210, 304, 351, 352.

6   Sociology of language
132, 133, 134, 135, 136, 141, 169, 170, 230, 236, 237, 362.

7   Linguistic theory (see also 10.9; 10.10)
3, 11, 12, 42, 67, 70, 71, 108, 142, 144, 194, 232, 235, 253, 254, 258, 260, 269, 270, 275, 287, 288, 301, 306, 313, 315, 322, 346, 347, 354, 355, 356, 357, 358, 370, 371, 372, 373, 410, 411, 419, 420, 421, 435, 436.

8   Anthropoligical linguistics
145, 168, 175, 176, 180, 203, 210, 211, 212, 213, 214, 215, 299, 360.

9   Status, theory and method of sociolinguistics

9.1 Historical development of sociolinguistics
51, 218, 229, 254, 313, 399.

9.2 Deficit hypothesis
21, 22, 23, 24, 25, 26, 27, 28, 29, 30, 31, 32, 33, 34, 38, 39, 40, 41, 47, 54, 95, 96, 97, 118, 199, 202, 204, 205, 222, 277, 307, 316, 317, 318, 319, 323, 332, 337, 339, 340, 341, 359, 426, 427.

  9.2.1 Criticism of deficit hypothesis
  15, 16, 18, 51, 63, 83, 112, 115, 158, 255, 344, 364, 365, 435.

9.3 Variability concept
1, 11, 12, 15, 16, 17, 18, 19, 42, 48, 56, 89, 91, 116, 120, 121, 125, 141, 174, 208, 213, 245, 246, 247, 248, 249, 251, 253, 254, 257, 283, 287, 288, 302, 303, 377, 379, 380, 381, 396, 419, 420, 421, 433.

9.4 Marxist sociolinguistics
111, 112, 113, 115, 171, 188, 311, 312, 313, 322, 347, 385, 405.

10   Linguistic variation

10.1 Linguistic community
173, 175, 177, 236, 238, 245, 248, 257, 267, 290, 362, 419, 424.

10.2 Standard v. Non-Standard (see also 10.4; 10.8)
81, 94, 122, 123, 152, 153, 172, 239, 246, 248, 257, 267, 310, 334, 336, 397, 400, 412, 422.

10.3 Dialects
4, 10, 124, 125, 173, 174, 175, 208, 246, 248, 253, 258, 267, 273, 283, 286, 287, 288, 302, 303, 322, 328, 330, 374, 386, 396, 398, 420, 431.

10.4 SE v. *BEV* (see also 10.2; 10.8)
1, 10, 15, 16, 19, 95, 99, 208, 209, 240, 248, 252, 253, 256, 267, 286, 287, 288, 302, 303, 328, 374, 379, 380, 381, 382, 396, 398, 399, 407, 426, 427, 433, 434.

10.5 The Creole speech continuum
42, 90, 91, 92, 106, 170, 216, 217, 258.

10.6 Bilingualism
2, 75, 78, 79, 80, 98, 119, 124, 134, 136, 141, 169, 178, 181, 228, 271, 272, 290, 294, 295, 296, 297, 298, 348, 362, 419, 424.

10.7 Multilingualism
179, 230, 236, 237, 238, 308, 397, 424.

10.8 Norm (see also 10.2; 10.4)
73, 74, 81, 94, 125, 172, 220, 239, 246, 248, 249, 251, 253, 254, 257, 267, 310, 326, 331.

10.9 Variable rules and probabilistic grammars (see also 7)
42, 65, 66, 67, 92, 121, 144, 232, 242, 253, 261, 267, 350, 354, 355, 388, 394, 404.

10.10 Implicational scales (see also 7)
87, 89, 91, 92, 116, 121, 184, 355, 409.

11 Empirical principles and studies
11.1 For and against intelligence tests
109, 110, 146, 147, 154, 158, 255, 305, 333, 418.

11.2 Methods of field research
254, 353, 381, 387, 401.

11.3 Participant observation
45, 150, 151, 175, 267, 417.

11.4 Correlative studies (see also 5.2)
30, 31, 78, 79, 80, 130, 136, 141, 156, 199, 245, 246, 247, 248, 249, 251, 253, 256, 261, 262, 267, 271, 273, 283, 285, 286, 290, 318, 330, 336, 337, 339, 341, 376, 380, 412, 428, 433, 434.

11.5 Functional studies
45, 46, 119, 125, 127, 150, 174, 175, 191, 211, 213, 239, 259, 265, 266, 352, 429.

11.6 Attitude measurements
131, 137, 140, 156, 248, 254, 267, 271, 272, 273, 274, 320, 328, 343, 362, 367.

12 Language acquisition
46, 192, 215, 246, 249, 257, 286, 335, 338.

13 Linguistic change
11, 12, 93, 169, 170, 244, 246, 247, 249, 250, 251, 311, 322, 336, 398.

14   Style, verbal repertoire and communicative competence
86, 88, 125, 141, 173, 174, 175, 178, 191, 208, 210, 215, 239, 248, 254, 259, 265, 267, 286, 300, 309, 351, 352, 359, 364, 365, 395, 403, 427, 435.

15   Analyses of forms of address
5, 57, 58, 120.

16   Philosophy of language and speech-act theory
8, 102, 107, 111, 120, 164, 210, 243, 293, 299, 306, 346, 360, 366, 367, 368, 432, 435, 436.

17   Language and school
1, 2, 4, 14, 16, 17, 18, 19, 21, 22, 23, 43, 50, 51, 52, 53, 63, 64, 77, 97, 149, 156, 157, 158, 167, 179, 199, 200, 219, 221, 246, 255, 266, 277, 282, 286, 307, 318, 332, 337, 339, 340, 341, 369, 424, 426, 427.

17.1 Problems of reading and writing
96, 157, 158, 227, 239, 252, 256, 267, 282, 286.

17.2 Compensatory education
43, 47, 51, 97, 149, 167, 200, 219, 221, 227, 277, 307, 332, 337, 341, 390.

18   Language planning
197, 230, 238, 406.

19   Bibliographies
100, 129, 162, 231, 278, 289, 308, 315, 375, 384, 430.

20   Periodicals
Language in Society (Cambridge University Press)
Sociolinguistics Newsletter (Editor: E. Rose, Bureau of Sociological Research, University of Colorado, Boulder, Co. 80302)
Zeitschrift für Dialektologie und Linguistik

List of abbreviations

Journals

Amer. Anthropologist	American Anthropologist
Amer. J. Orthopsychiat.	American Journal of Orthopsychiatry
Amer. Sociol. Rev.	American Sociological Review
Anthropol. Ling.	Anthropological Linguistics
Brit. J. Sociol.	British Journal of Sociology
Canad. J. Ling.	Canadian Journal of Linguistics
Child Developm.	Child Development
Develop. Med. Child Neurol.	Developmental Medicine and Child Neurology

Educ. Rev.	Educational Review
Found. Lang.	Foundations of Language
Harvard Educ. Rev.	Harvard Educational Review
Int. J. Amer. Ling.	International Journal of American Linguistics
J. Child Psychol. Psychiat.	Journal of Child Psychology and Psychiatry
J. Soc. Issues	Journal of Social Issues
J. Speech Hearing Disord.	Journal of Speech and Hearing Disorders
LB	Linguistische Berichte
Lili	Zeitschrift für Literaturwissenschaft und Linguistik
Ling. Reporter	Linguistic Reporter
Merill-Palmer Quart.	Merrill-Palmer Quarterly of Behavior and Development
Mod. Lang. J.	Modern Language Journal
V. Ja.	Voprosy Jazykoznanija

Other abbreviations

BEV	Black English Vernacular (= NNE)
NNE	Non-Standard Negro English
NSE	Non-Standard English
SE	Standard English
SL	Sociolinguistics

1   ALATIS, J. E. (ed.) 1970a: *Report of the 20th annual round table meeting on linguistics and language studies.* Monograph Series on Languages and Linguistics **22.** Washington, DC.
Twenty contributions dealing with the problem of teaching SE to speakers of NSE; special consideration is given to sociolinguistic questions (theoretical or empirical in nature).

2   ALATIS, J. E. (ed.) 1970b: *Report of the 21st annual round table meeting on linguistics and language studies*–Bilingualism and language contact: anthropological, linguistic, psychological and sociological aspects. Monograph Series on Languages and Linguistics **23.** Washington, DC.
Twenty essays on the description of linguistic, sociological and psychological aspects of bilingualism. Almost half the essays are devoted to (political) questions of bilingual education. Authors include, Haugen, MacNamara, Fishman, Hymes, Mackey, Lambert, Tucker, Ervin-Tripp and Ferguson.

3   ALTHAUS, H. P. and HENNE, H. 1971: Sozialkompetenz und Sozialperformanz. Thesen zur Sozialkommunikation. Zeitschrift für Dialektologie und Linguistik **38,** 1–15.
Social communication can be observed in social interactions from the semiotic point of view, and can be analytically subdivided into speech communication and action communication. Linguistic subdisciplines describe the individuality of language (psycholinguistics), the duality of language (pragmatic linguistics) and the plurality of language (sociolinguistics) as speech competence, speech code and speech system in the *virtual* sphere, and as speech performance, speech discourse and speech norm in the *realized* sphere.

4   AMMON, U. 1972a: *Dialekt, soziale Ungleichheit und Schule.* Weinheim, Berlin, Basel, Wien.
Historical materialist analysis of the relation between dialect and Standard as affected by industrial and social development in the south of the Federal Republic of Germany.

5   AMMON, U. 1972b: Zur sozialen Funktion der pronominalen Anrede im Deutschen. *Lili* **7,** 73–87.
Explains in terms of the dialectico-materialist method how the social relations that are expressed in pronominal address are determined by the surrounding social structure. The three levels of social reality, its reflection in the consciousness of the society's members and linguistic expression are first kept strictly separate, and are then seen in their dialectical correlation. Demonstrates that German forms of address, for example, are on the linguistic surface only an apparent expression of social equality, whereas in the social reality, by contrast, their use corresponds to a fundamental inequality.

6   AMMON, U. 1974: *Probleme der Soziolinguistik.* Tübingen.
Sociolectal and dialectal class-specific linguistic differences are interpreted in terms of Bernstein's Deficit Theory. The data are taken from German as spoken in the Federal Republic of Germany. Properties of trade-specific variations are investigated, as well as the problem of how the notion of 'ideological linguistic variation' can be determined and made explicit.

7   ARBEITSGRUPPE BIELEFELDER SOZIOLOGEN (eds.) 1973: *Alltagswissen, Interaktion und gesellschaftliche Wirklichkeit*— I, Symbolischer Interaktionismus und Ethnomethodologie; II, ethnotheorie und Ethnographie des Sprechens, Hamburg.
Collection of essays central to anthropology and ethnomethodology, providing an adequate account of the theoretical and methodological state of this sociological development. Translated into German. The volumes include contributions by Blumer, Frake, Garfinkel, Hymes. The collection is preceded by a sizeable introduction and closes with a theoretical evaluation. The individual contributions are carefully annotated as for the notions and terms employed.

8   AUSTIN, J. L. 1962: *How to do things with words.* Cambridge, Mass.
A standard work on the philosophy of speech acts.

9   BADURA, B. and GLOY, K. (eds.) 1972: *Soziologie der Kommunikation.* Eine Textauswahl zur Einführung. Problemata 11, Stuttgart-Bad Cannstatt.
Eighteen essays, mostly reprinted, on the four themes of mass communication, communication and organization, dialogue communication, and language sociology. The language sociology part comprises the following contributions: A D. Grimshaw, Sociolinguistics and sociologists; S. R. Levin, 'Langue' and 'Parole' in American linguistics; W. Labov, The reflection of social processes in linguistic structures; K. Gloy, Die Normierung der Verständigung.

10 BAILEY, B. L. 1965: Toward a new perspective in Negro English dialectology. *American Speech* **40**, 171–7.
Recommendation for a transformational analysis of BEV.

11 BAILEY, C. J. 1969: Studies in three-dimensional linguistic theory II: Implicational scales in diachronic linguistics and dialectology. *Working Papers in Linguistics* **1–8**, 123–38.
See 5.2.4.

12 BAILEY, C. J. 1971: *Variation and language theory*, I – IV. Unpublished.
A drafted and as yet provisional version of two lectures on the time factor in synchronic description, which were given in 1971 at the Linguistic Institute in Suny (Buffalo). Bailey makes a plea for a new, dynamic paradigm in linguistics which will explain linguistic change. His theory of grammar describes the 'polylectal competence' of speakers, and is based on a wave model that orders linguistic features implicationally.

13 BAILEY, C. W. and SHUY, R. W. (eds.) 1973: *New ways of analyzing variation in English.* Washington, DC.
Collection of twenty-four essays on the analysis of variation, giving an up-to-date account of the discussions about the linguistic analysis of language variation. The essays are ordered according to six points of view: Variable rules, Squishes, Problems in variation, Other studies in variation, Creoles, and Variation in semantic reference. The contributions by Labov, Cedergren, Ross, Sankoff and Smith are particularly recommended.

14 BANDELOT, C. and ESTABLET, R. 1971: *L'Ecole capitaliste en France.* Paris.
A structural analysis of the French educational system based on an examination of educational economics.

15 BARATZ, J. C. 1969: A bi-dialectal task for determining language proficiency in economically disadvantaged Negro children. *Child Developm.* **40** (3). 889–901.
There are three ways of explaining why 'Negro children are disadvantaged': (1) The children do not have a functionally adequate and structurally systematic speech code. The reasons for deficient speech development are to be sought in environmental factors. (2) The children have a systematic, but underdeveloped speech behaviour which is determined by cognitive deficit. Hierarchial linguistic complexity (chiefly related to abstraction) corresponds to cognitive complexity (proponents: Bernstein, Bereiter and Engelmann, Deutsch). (3) The children have a *fully-developed, but different speech system* from that of SE, and for this reason their speech problem is not one of competence but of interference between their highly developed system and that of SE (Labov, Stewart, Wolfram and others). Criticism of tests of (1) and (2) is directed at typical 'middle-class test situations', the middle-class and SE criteria that are applied, lack of consideration for interviewer's race etc. A test is carried out with children of the 3rd and 5th grade from two schools: Blacks v. 'lower-middle-class' Whites had to repeat 30 sentences. 15 SE sentences and 15 BEV sentences. The Black children were significantly better for BEV stimuli, and the Whites for SE stimuli. The *results* show that (1) two dialects play a part in the education of Black children, (2) Black children are generally not bidialectal, (3) the interference of the individual's own dialect in learning SE is evident, (4) the speech behaviour of Black children must be tested for BEV *and* SE.

16 BARATZ, J. C. 1970a: Teaching reading in an urban Negro school system. In Frederick Williams (ed.), *Language and Poverty,* 11–24, Chicago.
Critical analysis of the reasons for the inadequacy of the Deficit Hypothesis from a theoretical and practical point of view and explanation why the adaptation of BEV speakers to the Standard cannot take place unless within the context of the Variability Concept.

17 BARATZ, J. C. 1970b: Educational considerations for teaching Standard English to Negro children. In Fasold and Shuy 1970a, 20–40.
See 7.2.1.

18 BARATZ, J. C. and BARATZ, S. S. 1970: Early childhood intervention: the social base of institutional racism. *Harvard Educ. Rev.* **40** (1), 29–50.
Critique of the Deficit Hypothesis which is interpreted as a 'pathology model' that promotes racialism.

19 BARATZ, J. C. and SHUY, R. W. (eds.) 1969: *Teaching Black children to read.* Urban Language Series 4. Washington, DC: Center for Applied Linguistics.
Essays on linguistic strategies for adapting BEV speakers to SE. Stewart, Baratz, Labov and Shuy propose a gradual transition from BEV to SE, controlled by linguistic description.

20 BARTSCH, R. 1973: Gibt es einen sinnvollen Begriff von linguistischer Komplexität?. *Zeitschrift für Germanistische Linguistik* **1** (1), 6–31.

21 BEREITER, C. and ENGELMANN, S. 1966: *Teaching disadvantaged children in the preschool*. New York.
See 3.1.

22 BERNSTEIN, B. 1958: Some sociological determinants of perception: an inquiry in subcultural differences. *Brit. J. Sociol.* **9**, 159–74. Reprinted in Fishman 1968b, 223–39.
Treats class-specific differences in the perception of children, which are determined by processes of family socialization, education and school practices. Types of cognitive expression, relations to the content and structure of objects are manifested in two class-determined speech forms, 'public language' (lower class) and 'formal language' (middle class). See chapter 1 for details.

23 BERNSTEIN, B. 1959a: A public language: some sociological implications of a linguistic form. *Brit. J. Sociol.* **10**, 311–26.
Linguistic, psychological and sociological characterizations of 'public' and 'formal language' (later 'restricted' v. 'elaborated code'). A systemization of the arguments put forward here can be found in Wunderlich 1970. Ten grammatical features are listed for the public form and eight features for the formal language. These characteristics are then explained in terms of their origin. The explanation given here of the linguistic features of the two speech forms can be regarded as Bernstein's most thorough work. At the same time the linguistic aspect is the most frequent theme. Three main aspects are distinguished:
1 *Psychologically* speaking, pronouns are seen as indices of (a) implicit meaning (public lang.) – explicit meaning (formal lang.) and (b) personal, individual qualification v. collective, cliché-type qualification. Short questions and commands identify the authoritarian style of public language without any chance of communicative feedback.
2 Continual use of idiomatic (socially-accepted) turns of phrase that have lost individual meaning acquires *sociological meaning*. Periodically recurring interpolations, such as 'I mean' or 'you know', are conceived as solidarity-seeking clichés and in abstract terms as 'sympathetic circularity'.
3 *Linguistic:* see 1.4.1. An important assertion is that sentence complexity correlates with the carrying through of logical operations. Speakers of the public language are therefore more illogical.
See chapter 1.

24 BERNSTEIN, B. 1959b: Soziokulturelle Determinanten des Lernens. In P. Heintz (ed.), *Soziologie der Schule*. Kölner Zeitschrift für Soziologie und Sozialpsychologie, Sonderheft **4**, 52–79.
The problem discussed is whether certain forms of speech use facilitate or impede learning, independent of measured intelligence. The first part is a comprehensive survey of the literature on these themes:
1 Innate intelligence and influence of the socializing environment;
2 Intelligence and socioeconomic status;
3 Educational practices in subcultural and lower-class milieus;
4 Effects of environment on language development (empirical tests);
5 Relationship between language and thinking.
Distinction of 'public' and 'formal' forms differs from that made in 1959a on the first two points. Bibliography with 163 titles.

25 BERNSTEIN, B. 1960: Language and Social Class. In *Brit. J. sociol.* **11**, 271–6.
See 2.1.

26 BERNSTEIN, B. 1961a: Social Structure, Language and Learning. *Educational Research* **3**, 163–76.
See 1.2 and 1.4.

27 BERNSTEIN, B. 1961b: Aspects of language and learning in the genesis of the social process. *J. Child Psychol. Psychiat.* **1**, 313–24. Reprinted in Hymes 1964a, 251–63.
There are essentially no new arguments that have not already appeared in previous essays. The distinction of 'elaborated code' and 'restricted code' is introduced for the first time in a postscript. The basic postulate of this postscript is as follows: 'The form of the social relationship acts selectively on the type of code which then becomes a symbolic expression of

the relationship *and* proceeds to regulate the nature of the interaction. Simply, the *consequences* of the form of the social relationship are transmitted and sustained by the code on a psychological level.'

28 BERNSTEIN, B. 1961c: Social class and linguistic development: a theory of social learning. In A. H. Halsey, J. E. Floud and C. A. Anderson (eds.), *Education, economy and society,* 288–314. New York.
Like some of the earlier essays, this is a combination of a research survey and an attempt to define middle-class and lower-class language.

29 BERNSTEIN, B. 1962a: Social class, linguistic code and grammatical elements. *Language and Speech* 5, 221–40.
See 2.3.4.

30 BERNSTEIN, B. 1962b: Linguistic codes, hesitation phenomena and intelligence. *Language and Speech* 5, 31–46.
See 2.3.4.

31 BERNSTEIN, B. 1964: Elaborated and restricted codes: their social origins and some consequences. In Gumperz and Hymes 1964, 55–69.
See 1.2.2 and 1.3.

32 BERNSTEIN, B. 1965: A sociolinguistic approach to social learning. In J. Gould (ed.), *Penguin survey of the social sciences,* 144–68. Harmondsworth, England.
See 1.2.2, 1.3 and 1.4.

33 BERNSTEIN, B. 1967: Elaborated and restricted codes: an outline. In Lieberson 1967, (4) 126–33.
The most condensed and clear explanation of the codes. Agrees basically with Bernstein 1965.

34 BERNSTEIN, B. 1970a: A critique of the concepts of 'compensatory education'. In Rubinstein and Stoneman 1970, 110–21.
Bernstein attempts to retract the Deficit Concept that he has represented in principle in his previous publications. At least, he no longer wants it to be understood as such. The reason for this is that in the USA application of the Deficit Theory, based on Bernstein's work, failed in its compensatory speech programmes. See also 3.2 and 3.5.3.

35 BERNSTEIN, B. 1970b: Education cannot compensate for society. *New Society,* 26th February, 344–7.

36 BERNSTEIN, B. 1971a: Social class, language and socialization. In A. S. Abramson *et al.* (eds.), *Current Trends in Linguistics* 12. The Hague.
See 1.2.2, 1.3 and 1.4.

37 BERNSTEIN, B. 1971b: *Class, codes and control–*1, Theoretical studies towards a sociology of language. Primary Socialization, Language and Education 4. London.
1972a: *Studien zur sprachlichen Sozialisation. Sprache und Lernen.* Band 7, ed. Werner Loch und Gerhard Priesemann. Düsseldorf.
Collection of Bernstein's 12 most important essays.

38 BERNSTEIN, B. 1972b: A sociolinguistic approach to socialization; with some reference to educability. In Gumperz and Hymes 1972, 465–97.
See 1.2, 1.3, 1.4 and 1.5.

39 BERNSTEIN, B. and HENDERSON, D. 1969: Social class differences in the relevance of language to socialization. *Sociology* 3, 1–20.
See 2.4.1.

40 BERNSTEIN, B. and BRANDIS, W. 1970: Social class differences in communication and control. In Brandis and Henderson 1970, 93–124.
Sociological analysis of the behaviour of lower and middle-class mothers.

41 BERNSTEIN, B., OEVERMANN, U., REICHWEIN, R. and ROTH, H. 1970: *Lernen und soziale Struktur. Aufsätze 1965–1970.* Schwarze Reihe.9. Amsterdam.
Collection of seven reprinted essays: two essays of Bernstein ('Lernen und soziale Struktur' and 'Der Unfug mit der kompensatorischen Erzriehung'), three by Oevermann ('Einige Thesen

über den Zusammenhang von Identifikationsprozessen und Sprachentwicklung', 'Soziale Schichtung und Begabung', 'Schichtenspezifische Formen des Sprachverhaltens und ihr Einfluß auf die kognitiven Prozesse'), one by R. Reichwein ('Sprachstruktur und Denkfähigkeit': see 2.3.5), and one essay by R. Roth (Die wichtigsten Ergebnisse der Gutachten aus dem Buch "Begabung und Lernen" ').

42 BICKERTON, D. 1971: Inherent variability and variable rules. *Found. Lang.* 7, 457–92. See 5.2.4.

43 BLANK, M. 1970: Some philosophical influences underlying preschool intervention for disadvantaged children. In Williams 1970a, 62–80.
Critical discussion of intervention programmes. The reasons for early intervention are found in the Deficit Hypothesis. Nevertheless it is not clear according to what norms deficit is defined. Many authors agree that the intellectual and verbal capacity of lower-class children must be increased. A summary is given of proposals for intervention which (i) presuppose perceptual dysfunctionality or (ii) regard the role of language as central (Bereiter and Engelmann). Blank makes some suggestions for programmes that are not based on group learning but on individual learning. Extensive bibliography.

44 BLOCH, H. B. 1948: A set of postulates for phonemic analysis. *Language* **24**, 3–46.

45 BLOM, J. P. and GUMPERZ, J. J. 1972: Social meaning in linguistic structure: code-switching in Norway. In Gumperz and Hymes 1972, 407–34.
Extended analysis of Gumperz 1966.

46 BLOOM, L. 1970: *Language development: form and function in emerging grammars.* M.I.T. Cambridge, Mass.
A study carried out under Labov which follows the syntactic development of three children aged between 19 and 27 months and attempts to give a generative description, taking into account the situation and context-specific function of utterances (linguistic analysis model: Chomsky 1965). The taperecorded utterances are compiled in a corpus which makes it possible to classify /describe *linguistic utterances* (individual words, noun + noun, noun + verb, noun + adj. etc.) according to the types and frequency of occurrence, by means of functional description of the speech event (Hymes's categorical frame). The different stages in the development of the grammar are compared for each child individually and for all three children in relation to one another. The appendix explains the methods of collecting/collating the material (sample, transcription) and gives a summary of the *linguistic data* (form of data evaluation, children's lexica, frequency/occurrence of individual word utterances and lexical units in syntactic contexts). Some of the results are: speech is essentially grammatical (which corroborates Labov's investigations). The most frequently used word classes are (i) 'syntactic markers' ('no', 'more', etc.), (ii) substantive noun forms. The two 'relational aspects of language' ('inherent meaning' of the substantives/'grammatical meaning' of the substantives varying with the syntactic constituent structure) are related to the description of the children's language as (1) 'telegraphic speech' (the child's attempts to manipulate substantive noun forms with variable grammatical meaning) and (2) 'pivotal speech' (the child's attempts to use an individual form with invariant function in different formal contexts). The children's learning strategies vary chiefly in (1) and (2). The linguistic competence results from different interaction and reciprocal influence of the three (ideal) components: (i) linguistic experience, (ii) nonlinguistic experience, (iii) cognitive-perceptual development.

47 BLOOM, B. S., ALLISON, D. and HESS, R. 1965: *Compensatory education for cultural deprivation.* New York, Chicago, San Francisco, Toronto, London.

48 BLOOMFIELD, L. 1927: Literate and illiterate speech. *American Speech* **2**, 432–9.
A discussion of 'good' and 'bad', 'correct' and 'incorrect' use of English. The linguist should avoid such labels and give neutral descriptions.
See 4.1 and 4.3.1.

49 BLOOMFIELD, L. 1933: *Language.* New York.

50 BOCK, I. 1972: *Das Phänomen der schichtenspezifischen Sprache als pädagogisches Problem. Erträge der Forschung.* Band 8, Wiss. Buchgesellschaft. Darmstadt.
A survey of works dealing with the Deficit Hypothesis, chiefly those of Bernstein. A resolute call for compensatory education and adaption of lower-class children to the elaborated code.

51 BOIS–REYMOND, M. du, 1971: *Strategien kompensatorische Erziehung. Das Beispiel der USA.* Frankfurt.
Materialist analysis of compensatory programmes and their social background in USA. See chapters 3 and 7.

52 BOTTROPER PROTOKOLLE 1968: Aufgezeichnet von Erika Runge. Frankfurt.
These protocols are the literal texts (based on tape recordings) of mainly biographical accounts given by speakers of various social classes from the town Bottrop in the Ruhrgebiet. They reflect particularly clearly the dialecto-sociolectal features of the highly-industrialized Ruhrgebiet. They led to extensive sociolinguistic discussions in the Federal Republic of Germany, in particular with respect to Bernstein's code theory. It was in this context that the first concerted attempts at refuting Bernstein's theory were made.

53 BOURDIEU, P. and PASSERON, J. C. 1970: *La Reproduction, Eléments pour une théorie du système d'enseignement.* Paris.
Chapter 2 discusses educational tradition and social conservatism from the point of view of academic speech use. Detailed analysis of the function of language as a selectional device in capitalism.

54 BRANDIS, W. and HENDERSON, D. 1970: *Social class, language and communication.* In B. Bernstein, ed. Primary Socialization, Language and Education 1, ed. B. Bernstein. London.
Introduction by Bernstein and summary of London investigations into class-specific speech behaviour. In chapters 1 and 2 Henderson investigates 'Type-token-ratios' (noun, verb, adjectives, adverbs) for 150 children from the middle class and 300 children from the lower class (aged 5 years) according to Halliday's principles of 'categorial grammar'. (Its basis is in every respect Bernstein's theory, even though certain empirical techniques have been improved.)

55 BRIGHT, W. (ed.) 1966a: *Sociolinguistics.* Proceedings of the UCLA Sociolinguistic Conference, 1964. The Hague, Paris.
Fourteen contributions, based on different methodological concepts; the questions treated originate mainly from ethnolinguistics, anthropological linguistics and social dialectology.

56 BRIGHT, W. 1966b: The Dimensions of Sociolinguistics. Introduction Bright 1966a, 11–15.
The task of SL is the systematic description of the covariance of linguistic and social structure. Linguistic diversity is a central theme. The seven analytical dimensions of SL are given in 5.1.

57 BROWN, R. and FORD, M. 1961: Address in American English. *Journal of Abnormal and Social Psychology* 62, 375–85. Reprinted in Hymes 1964a, 234–44.
Similar analytical methods and problematic questions to those in Brown and Gilman 1960.

58 BROWN, R. and GILMAN, A. 1960: The pronouns of power and solidarity. In T. Sebeok (ed.), *Style in language,* 235–76. Cambridge, Mass. Reprinted in Fishman 1968b, 252–75.
Discusses the social implications of pronoun use in France, Italy, Federal Republic of Germany and Spain: familiar pronoun (T) v. polite pronoun (V). Two types of use are revealed: (1) 'power semantics': no reciprocal relation (T:T; V:V), but asymmetry: one controls the behaviour of the other (the superior speaker uses T and receives V. (2) 'solidarity semantics': a symmetrical relation that expresses some kind of solidarity (T:T; V:V). Differences for the individual countries were established by questioning informants (male students of the upper middle class).

59 BUHLER, H. 1972: *Sprachbarrieren und Schulanfang. Eine pragmalinguistische Untersuchung des Sprechens von Sechs- bis Achtjährigen,* Weinheim, Basel, Wein.

60 BUTTERS, R. 1972: Competence, performance and variable rules. *Language Sciences* 20, 29–32. See 5.2.2.

61 CAZDEN, C. B. 1966: Subcultural differences in child language: an interdisciplinary review. *Merill-Palmer Quart.* 12 (3), 185–219.
An interdisciplinary review of numerous works which either deal with the problem of subcultural differences in child language or which are of relevance to it: (1) *linguistics:*

description of BEV, particularly contrastive studies; (2) *developmental psychology*: differences in language acquisition in children with different status characteristics; (3) *experimental psychology*: intra-individual (cognitive) role of speech behaviour; (4) *sociology and anthropology*: structural features of speech, inter-individual speech function within the subcultural context. One of the problems broached is that of the measurability of language development in children from the submilieu: the language development of children who have an NSE dialect should be measured in relation to the norms of this dialect and not to those of SE.

62 CAZDEN, C. B. 1968: Three sociolinguistic views of the language and speech of lower class children – with special attention to the work of Basil Bernstein. *Develop. Med. Child Neurol.* **10**, 600–12.
Reviews works of Bernstein, Lawton, Robinson. Amongst other things discussed is the influence of the test situation on speech strategies.

63 CAZDEN, C. B. 1970: The situation: a neglected source of social class differences in language use. *J. Soc. Issues* 26 (2) 35–60.
Cazden criticizes the Deficit model (Bernstein and others) and the Variability model (Labov and others) and calls for investigation into communicative competence.

64 CAZDEN, C. B., JOHN, V. and HYMES, D. (eds.) 1972: *The functions of language*. New York.

65 CEDERGREN, H. C. 1973a: On the nature of variable constraints. In Bailey and Shuy 1973, 13–22.

66 CEDERGREN, H. C. 1973b: *The interplay of social and linguistic factors in Panama*. Unpublished dissertation of Cornell University, Montreal, Canada.
Analysis of the variation of the consonants *s, ch, n* and *r* in Panama Spanish in various environments, differentiated according to extralinguistic parameters such as social class, style, age, sex. The method used is that of the variable rule in the multiplicative model (see Cedergren and Sankoff 1974), based on Chomsky's theory of grammar. Extensive collections of data are investigated statistically. The appendix contains a computer programme for the calculation of the values for the variable rules.

67 CEDERGREN, H. C. and SANKOFF, D. 1974: Variable rules: performance as a statistical reflection of competence. *Language* **50** (2), 333–55.
Formalization of the variable rule by means of the multiplicative model, and criticism of the original formulation of this type of rule as given by Labov (additive model). On the basis of the mathematical foundation of the variable rule, probability theory makes it possible to distinguish between competence and performance. The usefulness of the analytical tools is demonstrated for various collections of empirically gained data.

68 CHOMSKY, N. 1957: *Syntactic structures*. The Hague.

69 CHOMSKY, N. 1961: Some methodological remarks on generative grammar. *Word* **17**, 219–39. See 6.1.1.

70 CHOMSKY, N. 1965: *Aspects of the theory of syntax*. Cambridge, Mass.
Theory of transformational grammar.

71 CHOMSKY, N. 1966: *Topics in the theory of generative grammar*. The Hague.
See 6.1.1.

72 CHOMSKY, N. and HALLE, M. 1968: *The sound pattern of English*. New York.
Theory of phonology in the context of generative grammar and its application to English.

73 CICOUREL, A. 1970: Basic and normative rules. In Hans-Peter Dreitzel (ed.), *Recent sociology 2. Pattern of communicative behavior*, 4–45.
Ethnomethodological approach. The normative social patterns and rules existing in the deep structure of communication should be derived from language use.

74 CICOUREL, A. 1973: *Cognitive sociology. Language and meaning in social interaction*. Harmondsworth, England.
Collection of previously published essays on ethnomethodology and on the sociological analysis of the social meaning of language. Extensive discussion of the notion 'social norm'.

75 CLYNE, M. 1972: *Perspectives on language contact, based on a study of German in Australia.* Melbourne.
Study of the effects of linguistic contacts of German and English in Australia. Interference phenomena are analysed on different linguistic levels.

76 COHEN, R., FRAENKEL, G. and BREWER, J. 1968: Implications for culture conflict from a semantic feature analysis of the lexicon of the hard core poor. *Linguistics* **44**, 11–21.
Demonstrates the *language creativity* of the lowest and most isolated American subculture ('hard core poor') by means of semantic features of the lexicon, for which 11 (verbally formulated) rules ('distinctive features') are formed (these are illustrated by examples). The comparison with SE clearly shows the linguistic differences. The possibility of neologism (by morpheme and word combinations) is so great that subordinate clauses are hardly used. Meanings are linked chiefly to actions, direct observations, social situations and the social group concerned: in this respect the meanings are subject to more rapid change than those of SE. The *results* can serve to promote (1) a theory of cultural conflict and (2) a completely new educational strategy for the 'hard core poor'.

77 COLEMAN, J. S. *et al.* 1966: *Equality of educational opportunity.* Washington, DC: US Government Printing Office.
Report and proposals for equality of opportunity in education.

78 COOPER, R. L. 1969: Two contextualized measures of degree of bilingualism. In J. A. Fishman, ed. *Bilingualism in the Barrio. Mod. Lang. J.* 53 (3): 172–8.
Up till now measures of the degree of bilinguality have failed to relate to different social contexts. This investigation relates two (psychological) tests (word naming and word association) to five social spheres: family, neighbourhood, religion, education, work. *Word naming test:* the subjects had to name as many different words as possible in a minute. The test was conducted for both languages in the five social spheres. *Word association test:* the subjects had to give as many word associations as possible in one minute periods for specified English/Spanish stimulus words. These two tests were carried out for 4 ' Puerto Ricans (Span./Eng.) and related to six 'criterion variables': (1) number of years on the continent; (2) occupation; (3) accent; (4) command of English speech styles; (5) understanding of English passages read out loud; (6) understanding of read Spanish passages. *Results:* Spanish is dominant for the spheres of family and religion, English for the three remaining spheres. According to Fishman: 1965, 1966, it is therefore a case of 'language maintenance'.

79 COOPER, R. L. and GREENFIELD, L. 1969: Language use in a Bilingual Community. In J. A. Fishman 1969, 166–72.
Spanish/English language use of bilingual Puerto Ricans is investigated in five spheres of social interaction (cf. Cooper 1969). The hypothesis is that if Spanish is preferred to English in some spheres, it is established as 'language maintenance': if English is preferred in *all* spheres of life, then one must assume it to be 'language shift'.
Method: The language proportion per sphere is measured for each individual on a scale of 11 marks. Linguistic capabilities are ascertained (1) by means of a 7-mark scale for English and Spanish accent and (2) with a 6-mark scale to measure the English style repertoire. Demographic variables are sex, age, birthplace, occupation.

80 COOPER, R. L., FOWLER, B. R. and GIVNER, A. 1969: Listening comprehension in a bilingual community. In Fishman 1969, 235–41.
Demonstration of more precise methods of measuring bilingual language skill with regard to the comprehension of verbal interactions (role relationships, situations, communication intentions), and the linguistic capabilities of *speech* (interference, range of repertoire in both languages, speech fluency and skill), *reading* and *writing;* this is done with the help of empirical data obtained from bilingual Puerto Ricans. The technique of analysing comprehension is particularly revealing for the investigation of the communicative competence of bilingual speakers.

81 COSERIU, E. 1967: Sistema, Norma y Habla. In *Teoría del Lenguaje y Lingüística General,* 11–113. Madrid.
Criteria for the distinction of linguistic norm and system.

82 COULTHARD, M. 1969: A discussion of restricted and elaborated codes. *Educ. Rev.* **22** (1), 38–50.
See 3.4.1.

83 COULTHARD, R. M. and ROBINSON, W. P. 1968: The structure of the nominal group and elaboratedness of code. *Language and Speech* **11** (4), 234–50.
Empirical analysis which develops a complexity measure for Halliday's nominal group.

84 GRANDALL, V. J. and PRESTON, A. 1955: Patterns and levels of maternal behavior. *Child Developm.* **31**, 243–51.
An assessment of mothers' behaviour made by psychologists was compared with the mothers' self-assessment. Little correlation was found between the two assessments. The results are interpreted as an argument against the validity of the interview. See also 2.4.2.

85 CURRIE, H. C. 1952: A projection of sociolinguistics: the relationship of speech to social status. *Southern Speech Journal* **18** (1), 28–37. Reprinted in Williamson and Burke 1971, 39–47.
A programmatic essay, which uses the term sociolinguistics for the first time. See also 5.1.

86 DAVIES, A. 1969: The notion of register. *Educ. Rev.* **22** (1), 64–77.
A discussion of the relationship of linguistic utterances to the situation. By means of examples the dilemma of linguistics is shown in the fact that *grammatically deviant* sentences are not distinguished from sentences which are *appropriate in a specific situation*. SL investigates the ('double abstraction' of the) interaction of linguistic and sociological categories. A possible approach is the analysis of *verbal repertoire*. Two short scientific texts are analysed from the point of view of textual coherence. One of the conclusions drawn from the analysis is that a general approach towards a typology of text categories crucially implies an explicitation of the specific types of logical connections in texts.

87 DECAMP, D. 1969: *Toward a formal theory of sociolinguistics*. Unpublished, University of Texas.
See the definitions in 5.2.4.

88 DECAMP, D. 1970: Is a sociolinguistic theory possible? In Alatis 1970a, 157–73.
The chief topics of discussion are the three paradigms of theoretical linguistics – neogrammarians, structuralism and generative grammar in respect of the treatment of sociolinguistic questions. Generative grammar affords the best prospect of developing SL within a general linguistic theory. For the formal evolution of such a theory see 5.2.4.

89 DECAMP, D. 1971a: Implicational scales and sociolinguistic linearity. *Linguistics* **73**, 30–43.
See 5.2.4.

90 DECAMP, D. 1971b: Introduction: The study of Pidgin and Creole languages. In Hymes 1971, 18–23.
Exposé of the origins of Pidgin and Creole languages.

91 DECAMP, D. 1971c: Toward a generative analysis of a postcreole speech continuum. In Hymes 1971, 349–70.
Theoretical arguments similar to those in 87, 88, 89; cf. 5.2.4.

92 DECAMP, D. and HANCOCK, I. F. (eds.) 1974: *Pidgins and Creoles: current trends and prospects*. Washington, D.C.
Collection of eleven essays on the origin and delimitation of Creole and Pidgin languages, their acquisition and variation. The volume gives the latest results of empirical investigations. Of particular theoretical relevance is the contribution by Gillian Sankoff and Paul Kay. 'A language-universals approach of Pidgins and Creoles'.

93 DESNICKAJA, A. V., ŽIRMUNSKIJ, V. M. and KOVTUN, L. S. 1969: *Voprosy social'noj lingvistiki* (Questions of sociolinguistics). Moscow.
This volume contains nineteen essays on general problems of SL – the reciprocal influencing of languages, development of Standard languages and territorial and social language variants. All the works are concerned with the sociohistorical development of language as a means of communication, and together give a cross-section of the areas of inquiry pursued by Soviet SL. A particularly interesting work is that of V. M. Žirmunskij. 'Marksizm i social'naja lingvistika', which explains the ideological foundation of Soviet SL. As a social phenomenon, language reflects the processes of class differentiation and the class conflict in its development in the class society. The following are given as immediate problems in SL: (1) the social differentiation of the language of the class society at a particular stage of historical development: (2) the process of the social development of language, its history as a social phenomenon. Also of great importance is the question of the social norm in language in connection with language practice and matters of language policy.

94 DEUTRICH, K. H. and SCHANK, G. 1972: Redekonstellation und Sprachverhalten I. *Funkkolleg Sprache, Studienbegleitbrief* **11**, 12–24.
See 4.2.

95 DEUTSCH, M. 1965: The role of social class in language development and cognition. *Amer. J. Orthopsychiat.* **35**, 78–88.
See‑2.2.3.

96 DEUTSCH, M. *et al.* 1967: *The disadvantaged child.* New York.

97 DEUTSCH, M. 1970: Entwicklungsförderung bei Vorschulkindern. Gesellschaftliche und psychologische Aspekte. *Betrifft:Erziehung* **9**, 20–24.

98 DIEBOLD, A. R. 1964: Incipient bilingualism. In Hymes 1964a, 495–508.
A study linking methodological considerations with empirical investigations. Part I discusses and defines terms such as 'convergent'/'divergent change', linguistic integration and interference (which should be measured separately according to 'langue' and 'parole'). Part II contains results of an investigation of linguistic and social factors for the American Indian language *Huave* (Mexico) in contact with Spanish. There are three types of bilingual speaker, 'coordinate', 'subordinate' and 'monolingual' (quantitative data are listed for this). Phonemic/morphological examples are adduced for the integration/interference of linguistic units of the two languages. One of the conclusions drawn from the results is that interference is not determined solely by the linguistic structure of two languages in contact.

99 DILLARD, J. L. 1968: Nonstandard Negro dialects: convergence or divergence? *The Florida FL Reporter* **6** (2), 9–12. Reprinted in N. E. Whitten and J. F. Szwed (eds.), *Afro-American anthropology: contemporary perspectives,* 119–27. New York.
Explanations of the speech behaviour of BEV speakers by linguistic deficit (see Baratz 1969) are just as unsatisfactory as the purely technical descriptions of linguistic variability between BEV and SE. The deviant forms of BEV should rather be attributed to African language tradition (Creole *Gullah*), as is demonstrated by the work of Stewart (historical explanation).

100 DITTMAR, N. 1971: Kommentierte Bibliographie zur Soziolinguistik. *Linguistische Berichte* **15**, 103–28; **16**, 98–126.

101 DITTMAR, N. 1974a: Soziolinguistik. In Harro Stammerjohann (ed.), *Handbuch der Linguistik.* Munich.
Survey of the various paradigms, types of theoretical and empirical research in sociolinguistics, with reference to their spheres of application.

102 DITTMAR, N. 1974b: Pour un fondement empirique de la théorie des actes de parole. Paper read for the 8th World Congress of Sociology, Toronto, Canada (to be published).

103 DITTMAR, N. 1975: Review of Girke and Jachnow 1974. *Language in Society* **4** (1).

104 DITTMAR, N. and JÄGER, S. (eds.) 1972: *Soziolinguistik. Lili* **7**.
Seven essays on the status and application of sociolinguistics.

105 DITTMAR, N. and KLEIN, W. 1972: Die Code-Theorie Basil Bernsteins. In Klein and Wunderlich 1971.
See in particular 1.4.1, Excursus.

106 DITTMAR, N. and KLEIN, W. 1974: *Untersuchungen zum Pidgin-Deutsch spanischer und italienischer Arbeiter in der BRD.* Arbeitsbericht I des Forschungsprojektes der DFG 'Pidgin-Deutsch ausländischer Arbeiter', Germanistisches Seminar der Universität Heidelberg.

107 DUCROT, O. 1972: *Dire et ne pas dire. Principes de sémantique linguistique.* Collection Savoir. Paris.
Elaboration of the notion of 'implied meaning', in connection with the concepts of presupposition and conversational inferences.

108 DURBIN, M. and MICKLIN, M. 1968: Sociolinguistics: some methodological contributions from linguistics. *Found. Lang* **4**, 319–31.
SL is conceived as an autonomous field of interdisciplinary research with its own methodology. Up till now there have been three models for linking linguistic and extralinguistic data: the *association model*: the correlation of linguistic and sociological data on the lines of Labov: the

casual model: social stratifications causes linguistic variation; the *quasifunctional model*: different speech functions in lower and middle class produce cognitive differences (Bernstein *et al.*). The most important area of inquiry in SL is the *speech style*, which should be investigated from the paralinguistic, phonological and lexicographical points of view. According to current linguistic theory, speech differences are best analysed within the context of Chomsky's rules of subcategorization (1965). Such differences are shown for two examples on the basis of tree diagrams.

109   EELS, K. 1953: Some implications for school practice of the Chicago studies of cultural bias in intelligence tests. *Harvard Educ. Rev* **23**, 284–97.
Critique of the middle-class values of the intelligence test; see 3.3.1.

110   EELS, K. *et al.* 1951: *Intelligence and cultural differences.* Chicago.
See 3.3.1.

111   EHLICH, K. and REHBEIN, J. 1972: *Zur Konstitution pragmatischer Einheiten in einer Institution: Das Speiserestaurant.* Unpublished (Berlin).
Materialist analysis of speech acts in restaurants.

112   EHLICH, K., HOHNHÄUSER, J., MÜLLER, F. and WIEHLE, D. 1971a: Spätkapitalismus – Sozio-linguistik – Kompensatorische Spracherziehung. *Kursbuch* **24**, 33–60.
See 3.5.

113   EHLICH, K., MÜLLER, F. and WIEHLE, D. 1971b: Soziolinguistik als bürgerliches Herrschaftswissen – Marxistische Sprachanalyse. In Klein and Wunderlich 1971, 98–109.
Abbreviated version of Ehlich *et al.* 1971a.

114   EICHHORN, W. *et al.* 1969: *Wörterbuch der marxistisch-leninistischen Soziologie.* Berlin.

115   EISENBERG, P. and HABERLAND, H. 1972: Das gegenwärtige Interesse an der Linguistik. *Argument* **72** (3/4), 326–49.
Social interest in linguistics is determined both by the form of society and by the historical situation of scientific activity. The usefulness of formal and sociologically-oriented linguistics is demonstrated by reference to examples of American research practice; the analysis deals with (i) the role of the Wycliffe Bible translators in structuralism, (ii) the role of structuralism as a supplier of methods for teaching of foreign languages to the military in the Second World War, (iii) the development of machine translation since 1954 and its effect on computer linguistics and (iv) the function of sociolinguistic research as potential élitist knowledge and as preventive research into the avoidance of conflict. Chomsky serves as an example to demonstrate the separation of science and politics.

116   ELLIOT, D., LEGUM, S. and THOMPSON, S. A. 1969: Syntactic variation as linguistic data. In Robert I. Binnick *et al.* (eds.), *Papers from the 5th regional meeting of the Chicago Linguistic Society,* 52–6. Chicago.
See 6.2.5.

117   ENGEL, U. and SCHWENKE, O. (eds.) 1972: *Gergenwartssprache und Gessellschaft, Beiträgge zu aktuellen Fragen der Kommunikation.* Düsseldorf.
Fourteen articles on social communication. Theory of sociolinguistics and compensatory speech education.

118   ENTWISTLE, D. 1968: Development sociolinguistics: inner-city children. *Amer. J. Sociol.* **74** (1), 37–49.

119   ERVIN-TRIPP, S. 1964: An analysis of the interaction of language, topic, and listener. In Gumperz and Hymes 1964, 86–102. Reprinted in Fishman 1968b, 192–211.
See 5.3.2 and 6.3.2.

120   ERVIN-TRIPP, S. 1969: Sociolinguistics. In L. Berkowitz (ed.), *Advances in experimental social psychology* **4**, 91–165. New York. Reprinted in Fishman 1971b, 15–91.
See 5.3.2.

121   FASOLD, R. 1970: Two models of socially significant linguistic variation. *Language* **46** (3), 551–63.
Discussion of the most up-to-date methods of analysing the social significance of linguistic variation: (1) the variable rules (see 5.2.1), and (2) the implicational scale (see 5.2.4). The

central aim is to examine (1) and (2) with regard to their actual success and their potential combination. If (2) has the advantage of providing good results without the necessity for large-scale sociological background analyses, (1) overcomes the disadvantage of (2) by means of quantitatively-ordered variable rules. The attempt to describe data of each approach with the other method shows that the variable rules cannot readily be rewritten in implicational scales. The rewrite tests and the comparison of the two methods invite the résumé 'that the study of variable frequencies leads to deeper insights into the use of language in society than does strict implicational analysis'. In the application of sociolinguistic research in the education sector, however, both techniques must be combined: quantitative analyses can investigate speech use with precision and implicational scales can monitor, by means of the stages of present v. non-present features, speakers' success at gaining a command of the Standard.

122   FASOLD, R. and SHUY, R. W. (eds.) 1970a: *Teaching Standard English in the inner city*. Urban Language Series 6. Washington, DC: Center for Applied Linguistics.
Sociolinguistic questions are included in the main problems discussed, namely those of how SE should be taught to Non-Standard speakers: Baratz, 'Educational considerations for teaching Standard English to Negro children', is concerned with the Deficit and Variability Models. Fasold and Wolfram give an analysis of 'Some linguistic features of Negro dialect'. Wolfram, 'Sociolinguistic implications for educational sequencing', lists five points which show the importance of sociolinguistic inquiry for the preparation of linguistic material for teaching SE. The volume contains three further essays.

123   FASOLD, R. and SHUY, R. W. 1970b: Introduction to Fasold and Shuy 1970a, ix–xvi. See 7.2.1.

124   FERGUSON, C. A. 1959: Diglossia. *Word* **15** (2), 325–40. Reprinted in Hymes 1964a, 429–39. See 4.3.3.

125   FERGUSON, C. A. and GUMPERZ, J. J. (eds.) 1960: *Linguistic diversity in South Asia: studies in regional, social and functional variation*. Publication of the Research Center in Anthropology, Folklore and Linguistics **13**. Bloomington, Indiana.
Often-quoted volume containing linguistic studies on sociological and functional intraspeech variation. The position of such studies in a linguistic theory is discussed in the introduction.

126   FILIN, F. I. (ed.) 1968: *Jazyk i obščestvo* (Language and society). Moscow.
This collection of works discusses theoretical and practical questions of the problem of language and society. Special attention is paid to the social influence on language, language policy (e.g. creation of national literary languages) and the relation of intra- and extralinguistic factors in the development of language. Particular emphasis should be given to the work by the psycholinguist A. A. Leont'ev, 'Obščestvennye funkcii jazyka i ego funkcional'nye ekvivalenty' (The social function of language and its functional equivalents). Leont'ev stresses the necessity for a theory of 'parole', which should combine linguistic, sociological and psychological aspects (psychological phenomena are regarded as socially determined). According to Leont'ev, the mechanism of the social functioning of language cannot be revealed solely by relating the structure and development of language to the structure and development of society, but by making detailed analyses of the *functions of language*. Such functions are, for example, the communicative function, which occurs in three variants: individual-regulating function, collective-regulating function, self-regulating function; language as a reflection of reality (individual and social aspect); language as a medium for thinking; language as the form in which sociohistorical experience exists; national-cultural function; language as a means of acquiring knowledge.

127   FIRTH, J. R. 1958: *Papers in linguistics 1934–1951*. London. See 4.3.1.

128   FIRTH, J. R. 1964: On sociological linguistics. In Hymes 1964a, 66–70.
Programmatic essay on functional and context-specific linguistic analysis; cf. also 4.3.1.

129   FISCHER, G. 1971: *Sprache und Klassenbindung. Die Bedeutung linguistischer Kodes im Sozialisationsprozeß*. Hamburg.
Attempts to give as favourable as possible a reception to Bernstein's works and to his school of thought. The bibliography lists about 350 titles.

130   FISCHER, J. L. 1958: Social influences on the choice of a linguistic variant. *Word* **14**, 47–56.
        Reprinted in Hymes 1964a, 483–8.
        This investigation is reviewed in 6.2.1.2.

131   FISHBEIN, M. 1965: A consideration of beliefs, attitudes and their relationships. In Steiner and M.
        Fishbein (eds.), *Current studies in social psychology*, 107–20. New York.
        Discusses methods of measuring attitudes; see 5.4.4.

132   FISHMAN, J. A. 1965: Who speaks what language to whom and when? *La Linguistique* **2**, 67–88.
        The concept of the 'domains of language choice' relates sociocultural organization/contexts to
        language selection in multilingual situations. If domains of language behaviour are correlated
        systematically with other sources of variant language behaviour and are based on analyses of
        the relevant role-relationships and speech contents, they can make a decisive contribution to
        the formation of a general *dominance configuration*. An example is given by a distribution table
        of Yiddish-English maintenance and shift in the USA.

133   FISHMAN, J. A. 1966: *Language loyalty in the United States: the maintenance and perpetuation of
        non-English mother tongues by American ethnic and religious groups.* Janua Linguarum, Series
        Maior XXI. The Hague.
        Fifteen works by Fishman or Fishman *et al.* on the *language behaviour* (language maintenance
        v. language shift) of ethnic and religious groups in the USA, which is measured by several
        variables (e.g., degree of command of mother tongue, attitude towards mother tongue and
        other languages or dialects, distribution of languages in the USA according to ethnic groups,
        ideological orientation etc.).

134   FISHMAN, J. A. (ed.) 1968a: Sociolinguistic perspective on the study of bilingualism. *Linguistics*
        39, 21–49.
        See 5.4.1.

135   FISHMAN, J. A. (ed.) 1968b: *Readings in the sociology of language.* The Hague.
        Forty-four essays which, with three exceptions, had already been published elsewhere. Seven
        sections: (1) perspective on the sociology of language; (2) language in small-group interaction;
        (3) language in social strata and sectors; (4) language reflections of sociocultural organization;
        (5) multilingualism; (6) language maintenance and language shift; (7) the social contexts and
        consequences of language planning.

136   FISHMAN, J. A. (ed.) 1969: *Bilingualism in the Barrio. Mod. Lang. J.* **53** (3), 151–85, **53** (4), 227–58.
        Fifteen different (psycholinguistically and sociologically-oriented) essays, which are taken
        from the comprehensive report by Fishman *et al., Bilingualism in the Barrio*. Most of the
        investigations are concerned with the *language distribution* (English/Spanish) of bilingual
        Puerto Ricans in the five social spheres, *family, religion, education* institutions), *work,
        neighbourhood;* the language skill/ability in the two languages is measured by (1) 'word
        association tests', (2) 'word naming tests' (on (1) and (2) see Cooper 1969) and (3)
        questionnaires. One of the means of testing the *attitudes* towards each of the two languages is
        on bipolar scales according to Osgood's semantic differential. See also 6.2.3.

137   FISHMAN, J. A. 1971a: *Sociolinguistics: a brief introduction.* Rowley, Mass.
        An introduction to sociologically-oriented SL (with special consideration of anthropological
        works), which also has a digest of Fishman's numerous works. Chapters deal with (1)
        theoretical aspects/branches of linguistics, (2) basic concepts of SL: linguistic variation,
        measurement of attitudes towards languages, multilingualism, verbal repertoire in language
        community (related to social spheres); (3) interactional SL: speech acts/events in the context of
        social situations and social roles (distribution of rights /duties); (4) linguistic discontinuity (e.g.
        stratification of certain linguistic features), forces of diversification v. forces of the mass media
        (homogeneity pursuits); (5) bilingualism and diglossia; (6) discussion of the concept of
        linguistic relativity; (7) applied SL: use of sociolinguistic inquiries for language planning,
        school teaching, language learning etc.

138   FISHMAN, J. A. (ed.) 1971b: *Advances in the sociology of language–I, Basic concepts, theories and
        problems: alternative approaches.* The Hague, Paris.
        Four reprinted essays: Ervin-Tripp 1969, Grimshaw 1971a, Labov 1970a, Fishman, 'The
        sociology of language: an interdisciplinary social science approach to language in society
        (expanded version of Fishman 1971a).

139 FISHMAN, J. A. (ed.) 1972: *Advances in the sociology of language–II, Selected studies and applications.* The Hague, Paris.

140 FISHMAN, J. A. and AGHEYISI, R. 1970: Language attitude studies. *Anthropol. Ling.* **12,** 137–157. See 5.4.4.

141 FISHMAN, J. A., COOPER, R. L., MA, R. *et al.* 1968: *Bilingualism in the Barrio: the measurement and description of language dominance in bilinguals.* Final Report on OECD-1-7-062817. Washington, DC: Office of Education.
See Fishman 1969; 5.4 and 6.2.3.

142 FODOR, J. A. and KATZ, J. J. (eds.) 1964: *The structure of language: readings in the philosophy of language.* Englewood Cliffs, New Jersey.
A philosophical approach to language based on selected articles dealing with the theories, methods and results of linguistics.

143 FOWLER, R. 1971: *An introduction to transformational syntax.* London.

144 FRASER, B. 1973: Optional rules in grammar. In Shuy 1973, 1–15.
Fraser regards the variable rule (see Labov 1972b; Cedergren and Sankoff 1974) as a first but yet far from sufficient step towards a theory of optional rules. Such a theory should not merely describe observable linguistic behaviour and accumulate data, but should also, and mainly, *explain* the observed phenomena in a strict sense of the term. It is necessary, in Fraser's view, to assume degrees of optionality of rules; the degree will then depend on the role the rule plays in the actual use of the language. 'The notion of rule optionality should be extended beyond the narrow criterion of whether or not it affects the acceptability, or well-formedness, or grammaticality, of a sentence to the broader scope of how it functions in the language as a vehicle of communication.'

145 FRIEDRICH, P. 1971: Anthropological linguistics: recent research and immediate prospects. In O'Brien 1971, 167–84.
Survey of research carried out in anthropological linguistics over the last ten years. Numerous examples are given to show that it is founded on a relativistic linguistic theory. Works on lexicography are dealt with in detail.

146 FURTH, H. G. 1966: *Thinking without language: psychological implications of deafness.* New York.

147 FURTH, H. G. 1972: *Intelligenz und erkennen: die Grundlagen der genetischen Erkenntnistheorie Piagets.* Frankfurt.

148 GADET, F. 1971: Recherches récentes sur les variations sociales de la langue. *Langue Française* **9,** 74–81.
Survey which examines the most recent works (chiefly American) from three angles: geographical, sociological and contextual variations. Critique of French and other works that do not pursue SL systematically.

149 GAHAGAN, D. and GAHAGAN, G. 1970: *Talk reform: explorations in language for infant school children.* In the series Primary Socialization, Language and Education, ed. B. Bernstein. London.
Proposals for compensatory education based on Basil Bernstein's theory.

150 GARFINKEL, H. 1967: *Studies in ethnomethodology.* Englewood Cliffs, New Jersey.
Refutation of different empirical methods of measurement in sociology and explanation of 'ethnomethodology'.

151 GARFINKEL, H. 1972: Remarks on ethnomethodology. In Gumperz and Hymes 1972, 301–24. See 6.1.2.

152 GARVIN, P. 1964: The Standard language problem – Concepts and methods. In Hymes 1964a, 521–6.
Proposals for the definition and description of Standard languages. See 4.2.1.

153 GARVIN, P. and MATHIOT, M. 1956: The urbanization of the Guarani language: a problem in language and culture. In A.F.C. Wallace (ed.), *Men and cultures.* Selected papers of the 5th International Congress of Anthropological and Ethnological Sciences. 783–90. Philadelphia. Reprinted in Fishman 1968b, 365–74.
Criteria for the definition of Standard Language. See 4.2.1.

154 GETZELS, J. W. and JACKSON, P. W. 1962: *Creativity and intelligence*. New York.
There is virtually no correlation between creativity and scores of measured intelligence. See 3.3.1.

155 GIGLIOLI, P. P. 1972: *Language and social context: selected readings*. Harmondsworth, England.
Fifteen essays, some abridged, on five topics: (1) approaches to sociolinguistics (Hymes, Fishman); (2) speech and situated action (Goffman, Frake, Schegloff, Searle); (3) language, socialization and subcultures (Bernstein, Labov); (4) language and social structures (Gumperz, Ferguson, Brown and Gilman, Labov); (5) language, social change and social conflict (two essays).

156 GILES, H. 1970: Evaluative reactions to accents. *Educ. Rev.* **22** (3), 211–27.
Lambert's (1967) 'matched guise technique' for measuring stereotype evaluations of regional or dialectal accents is expanded by three evaluative dimensions: the *aesthetic* (liked v. not liked), the *communicative* (with regard to the facility of understanding in interaction) and the *status-oriented* dimensions (prestige value of an accent); the reactions to these dimensions are measured on 7 point scales. 177 subjects had to evaluate 13 regional and foreign accents: (1) taperecorded speech samples, (2) 'conceptual stimuli' by means of questionnaires. *Results:* (i) a general rank ordering of the accents right across the three dimensions; (ii) age, sex, social class and regional membership are the determinants of the evaluation. *Educational consequences:* The social prejudices against Non-Standard should be reduced. The Standard must be taught in schools in such a way that it can be produced in socially suitable situations.

157 GINSBURG, H. 1972: *The myth of the deprived child*. Englewood Cliffs, New Jersey.
Comprehensive (and chiefly psychological) critique of the Deficit Hypothesis. See chapters 2 and 3.

158 GINSBURG, H., WHEELER, M. E. and TULIS, E. A. 1971: *The natural development of academic knowledge: the case of printing and related graphic activities*. Final Report to the Office of Education.
Investigation into the natural learning of reading and writing of children from different classes. See also 3.3.2.

159 GIPPER, H. 1972: *Gibt es ein sprachliches Relativitätsprinzip? Untersuchungen zur Sapir-Whorf-Hypothese*. Frankfurt.

160 GIRKE, W. and JACHNOW, H. 1974a: *Sowjetische Soziolinguistik. Probleme und Genese*. Kronberg.
Research report on theoretical and empirical work in Soviet sociolinguistics from 1920 till the present day (post-revolutionary phase, Marxist phase, Stalinist period, post-Stalinist period). This is, so far, the only book which summarizes the results of Soviet sociolinguistics. It contains an annotated bibliography of 97 titles.

161 GIRKE, W. and JACHNOW, H. (eds.) 1974b: *Sprache und Gesellschaft in der Sowjetunion. 31 Dokumente aus dem Russischen*. Munich.
Collection of the most important essays on sociolinguistics published in the Soviet Union since 1917 (including contributions by Polivanov, Marr, Stalin, Filin, Žirmunskij). Most of the essays deal with the development of materialist linguistic theory, which has made its main contributions to the theory of linguistic change. The more recent studies on ethnic languages and linguistic varieties do not, in spite of their empirical orientation, take into account the notions of modern linguistics.

162 GIRKE, W., JACHNOW, H. and SCHRENK, J. 1972: Soziolinguistik in der Sowjetunion – Eine referierte Bibliographie. In *Lili* **7**, 131–54.
Bibliography with 63 titles.

163 GOLDMANN-EISLER, F. 1961: Hesitation and Information in Speech. In Colin Cherry ed. *Information Theory*. Fourth London Symposium. London.

164 GORDON, D. and LAKOFF, G. 1971: *Conversational Postulates*. Unpublished manuscript.
Attempt to formalize speech act conditions.

165 GOTTSCHALCH, W., NEUMAN-SCHÖNWETTER, M. and SOUKUP, G. 1971: *Sozialisationsforschung. Materialien, Probleme, Kritik*. Frankfurt.
Inquiry into socialization from the materialist point of view.

166　GRAY, S. and KLAUS, R. A. 1968: The early training project for disadvantaged children: a report after five years. *Monographs of the Society for Research in Child Development* **33** (120).
See 2.2.1.

167　GREENFIELD, P. M. 1966: On culture and conservation. In J. S. Bruner, R. Olver, P. M. Greenfield *et al., Studies in cognitive growth,* 225–56. New York.

168　GRIMSHAW, A. D. 1966: Directions for research in sociolinguistics: suggestions of a nonlinguistic sociologist. In Lieberson 1967, 191–204.
See 6.4.3.

169　GRIMSHAW, A. D. 1971a: Sociolinguistics. In Fishman 1971b, 92–151.
Survey which discusses the following points: (1) theoretical approaches (Whorf; correlative and functional sociolinguistics); (2) languages in contact (bilingualism, language conflict, language loyalty, Creole and Pidgin languages); (3) covariation of language structure and social structure (language as a reflection of social structure, sociocultural determinants of verbal repertoire, isomorphism of language and social structure); (4) integrated theory of descriptive sociolinguistics (taken over from Hymes 1967a). Extensive bibliography.

170　GRIMSHAW, A. D. 1971b: Some social forces and some social functions of Pidgin and Creole languages. In Hymes 1971, 427–45.
See 5.4.3.

171　GROSSE, R. and NEUBERT, A. 1970: Thesen zur marxistischen Soziolinguistik. *Linguistische Arbeitsberichte* **1,** 3–15. Leipzig.
Ten programmatic theses on the fundamental principles of SL as a Marxist theory. Thesis 6 specifies the *sociolinguistic differential,* consisting of the categories of sender, receiver, linguistic code and communication situation. In a broader sense, this serves to define the idiolect, sociolect and sociolinguistic system. Thesis 10 sums up: 'Sociolinguistics and pragmatics are the areas in which linguistics has to carry out the most important social tasks.'

172　GUCHMAN, M. M., JARCEVA, V. N. and SEMENJUK, N. N. (eds.) 1969: *Norma i social'naja differenciacija jazyka* (Norms and social differentiation of language). Moscow.
The seven Russian articles (with résumés in German) and the six German articles (with résumés in Russian), which were given at a jointly organized Soviet-German symposium in Moscow, are devoted to social differentiation. Special attention is paid to the functional aspect of linguistic processes, chiefly to the determination of the standard language norm and its relation to the regional standards, as well as to the historical relationship between the territorial, functional and social structure of language.

173　GUMPERZ, J. J. 1962: Types of linguistic communities. *Anthropol. Ling.* **4** (1), 28–40.
Linguistic communities ('social groups which are bound together by a multiplicity of social interactional patterns') with different degrees of social complexity can be investigated with regard to (1) the *code matrix* of their speakers (specific codes for different communicative roles) (2) the *role differences* of speakers analogous to social functions, (3) *language distance* (social/geographical) and (4) *language loyalty.* Different linguistic communities are shown to exist according to the different factors in (1)–(4).

174　GUMPERZ, J. J. 1964: Linguistic and social interaction in two communities. In Gumperz and Hymes 1964, 137–53.
SL investigates *speech use of groups* which is related to linguistically distinct dialects/styles and to variables of social interaction. The programme is implemented in (1) by giving definitions and in (2) by providing empirical analyses. (1) (i) *Verbal repertoires* are (a) grammatically and (b) contextually structured; linguistic interaction is a decision and selection process, related to (a) and (b); (ii) *selectional constraints* are grammatical in nature (intelligibility of sentences) and social in nature (acceptability of sentences), that is, social rules are learned with grammatical rules and help to determine selection; (iii) *interaction* in social relations and social situations is regulated by status; linguistic variants can be of a semantic kind (e.g. intralinguistic synonymity) and of a social kind (quality of relations); (iv) *speech variants* (styles/dialects) have specific linguistic rules of cooccurrence on all levels of grammar; verbal repertoires are thus distinct sets of speech variants. (2) contains a comparative analysis of groups of speakers from one Indian and one Norwegian village (cf. Gumperz 1966).

175   GUMPERZ, J. J. 1966: On the ethnology of linguistic change. In Bright 1966a, 24–49.
      See 6.3.1.

176   GUMPERZ, J. J. 1967: The social setting of linguistic behaviour. In Slobin 1967, 129–34.
      See 6.1.2.

177   GUMPERZ, J. J. 1968: The speech community. In *International Encyclopedia of the Social
      Sciences,* 381–6. MacMillan. Reprinted in Giglioli 1972, 219–31.
      See 4.2.

178   GUMPERZ, J. J. 1969: How can we describe and measure the behavior of bilingual groups? In
      Kelly 1969, 241–58.
      Bilingualism as a group phenomenon must be investigated in the context of the rules of verbal
      interaction, i.e. rules of selection from a single linguistic repertoire. Labov's concept of
      variables is taken up, and the *social significance* of an utterance is looked upon as the result
      of a process of selection of variants from a sphere defined by variables of linguistic
      structure. Cooccurrence rules determine sets of variable values. Cf. the comments of Labov
      in 5.2.3.

179   GUMPERZ, J. J. 1970: Verbal strategies in multilingual communication. In Alatis 1970b,
      129–43.

180   GUMPERZ, J. J. and HYMES, D. (eds.) 1964: *The ethnography of communication. Amer.
      Anthropologist.* Special Publication, vol. **66** (6), part 2.
      Twelve essays from the anthropological, sociological, linguistic perspectives, which Hymes
      relates in a detailed introduction, also outlining their theoretical basis.

181   GUMPERZ, J. J. and HERNANDEZ, E. 1971: Cognitive aspects of bilingual communication. In
      Whiteley 1971, 111–25.

182   GUMPERZ, J. J. and HYMES, D. 1972: *Directions in sociolinguistics: the ethnography of
      communication.* New York.
      Nineteen essays, most of them reprinted on three topics: ethnographic description and
      explanation, structural analysis of speech, and origin, maintenance and change of linguistic
      codes. Most of the analyses take an anthropological point of view.

183   GUTT, A. and SALFFNER, R. 1971: *Sozialisation und Sprache, Didaktische Hinweise zu
      emanzipatorischer Sprachschulung.* Frankfurt.
      Proposals for language teaching based on a Marxist social analysis.

184   GUTTMAN, L. 1944: A basis for scaling qualitative data. *Amer. Sociol. Rev.* **9,** 139–50.
      The most frequently-quoted basis of quantitative sociolinguistic works (e.g. Labov, Wolfram,
      Fasold); it is used as a theoretical framework for connecting linguistic and extralinguistic data.
      This essay is an explanation of the 'scale' as an adequate basis for the quantification of
      qualitative data, but it does not go into technical and mathematical details. It explains concepts
      of variables, simple function, universe of attributes, population of objects etc. *Definition:* A
      'scale' is a multivariant frequency distribution of a universe of attributes for a population of
      objects if and only if it is possible to derive a *quantitative variable* from the distribution, with
      which the objects can be characterized in such a way that each attribute is a simple function of
      this quantitative variable. Some of the scale's special features are: a *well defined* ordering of the
      'scale scores' (ordering of the objects according to their scores) and of the attribute scores; from
      a selection of attributes it is possible to draw conclusions about the universe of attributes; 'scale
      scores provide an invariant quantification of the attributes for *predicting any outside variable
      whatsoever.'* (Diochotomous, trichotomous) 'scales' and different types of representation are
      discussed with reference to examples: (1) 'scalogram'; (2) 'bar chart'; (3) 'four-fold table';
      (representation of correlation)

185   HABERMAS, J. 1967: *Zur Logik der Sozialwissenschaften.* Tübingen.
      Critical discussion of the theory and methods of the social sciences.

186   HABERMAS, J. 1968: *Erkenntnis und Interesse.* Frankfurt.

187   HABERMAS, J. 1971: Vorbereitende Bemerkungen zur kommunikativen Kompetenz. In Jürgen
      Habermas and Niklas Luhmann, *Theorie der Gesellschaft oder Sozialtechnologie – Was
      leistet die Systemforschung?* 101–41. Frankfurt.

188 HAGER, F., HABERLAND, H. and PARIS, R. 1973: *Soziologie + Linguistik: die schlechte Aufhebung sozialer Ungleichheit durch Sprache.*
Critique of bourgeois sociolinguistics, partly based on an analysis of the relationship between educational and economic interests.

189 HAHN, E. 1968: *Historischer Materialismus und marxistische Soziologie. Studien zu methodologischen und erkenntnistheoretischen Grundlagen der soziologischen Forschung.* Berlin (Ost).
Introduction to the materialist theory of knowledge and the methodology of Marxist sociology.

190 HALLIDAY, M. A. K. 1961: Categories of the theory of grammar. *Word* 17, 241–92.

191 HALLIDAY, M. A. K. 1964: The users and uses of language. In M. A. K. Halliday, A. McIntosh and P. Strevens (eds.), *The linguistic sciences and language teaching,* ch. 4, 75–110. London. Reprinted in Fishman 1968b, 139–69.
'Institutional linguistics' (as opposed to descriptive linguistics) is concerned with the relation between language and its speakers. Its four analytical tasks are: (1) language communities and languages in contact (bilingualism, Pidgin, Creole, Lingua Franca); (2) dialects (a) regional dialect v. Standard, where the accent is on phonetic transfer, (b) socioregional dialect, determined by class membership; (3) register (linguistic variation differentiated according to social role and situation; classification of the registers according to three dimensions: (a) field of discourse, (b) mode of discourse, (c) style of discourse; speakers use different registers in different situations); (4) speakers' attitude towards their own language and the variations in their attitude (moral, aesthetic, pragmatic value judgements lead to social sanctions and intolerance). Most of the works of the Bernstein school cite Halliday to support their case.

192 HALLIDAY, M. A. K. 1969: Relevant models of language. *Educ. Rev.* 22 (1), 26–37.
Distinguishes seven functions of children's language behaviour, to which correspond a similar number of language models.

193 HARMS, L. S. 1963: Status cues in speech: extra-race and extra-region identification. *Lingua* 12, 300–306.

194 HARRIS, Z. S. 1951: *Methods in structural linguistics.* Chicago.

195 HARTIG, M. and KURZ, U. 1971: *Sprache als soziale Kontrolle. Neue Ansätze zur Soziolinguistik.* Frankfurt.
As a commentary on this book see Christian Guksch's review of Hartig and Kurz, in *Language in Society* 1 (2) 271–5.

196 HAUG, F. 1972: *Kritik der Rollentheorie.* Frankfurt.
Discussion of the most important modern role theories, which, as a central part of bourgeois sociology, are rejected by the Marxist line of thinking.

197 HAUGEN, E. 1966: Linguistics and language planning. In Bright 1966a, 50–71.
Language planning is only necessary when there is hardly any, or only partial understanding between speakers in a speech community and when language problems arise ('secondary'/'tertiary speech community', e.g. Norway, Ireland). Language variation must be evaluated and a Standard established which must satisfy criteria of efficiency, adequacy, acceptability. When deciding on a particular Standard one should also take into account factors regarding the spread, the quality and the social justification of the language in question.

198 HAUGEN, E. 1967: Semicommunication: the language gap in Scandinavia. *Int. J. Amer. Ling.* 33 (4), 152–69.

199 HAWKINS, P. R. 1969: Social class, the nominal group and reference. *Language and Speech* 12 (2), 125–35.
See 2.3.5.

200 HÄNSEL, D. and ORTMANN, H. 1971: Kompensatorische Vorschulerziehung und sozialer Aufstieg. *Zeitschrift für Pädagogik* 17 (4), 431–52.
Compensatory education is not a means of attenuating social élitist conditions and the resultant inequality. In so far as its aim is to elevate the individual's social position it should be looked upon as an invasion of his identity. Only the full, politically-motivated integration of

an individual in his class of origin can be regarded as an act of emancipation. From this it follows that the only possible type of compensatory education is that which sees identity as a social category in which individuals develop capabilities such as combined action, linguistic skills etc. from a knowledge of their social position in order to change this position.

201 HELBIG,, G. 1971: *Geschichte der neueren Sprachwissenschaft. Unter besonderem Aspekt der Grammatiktheorie.* München.

202 HENDERSON, D. 1970: Contextual specifity, discretion and cognitive socialization: with special reference to language. *Sociology* **4**, 311–38.
See 2.4.1.

203 HENLE, P. 1958: *Language, thought and culture.* Ann Arbor, Michigan.

204 HESS, R. D. and SHIPMAN, V. C. 1965: Early experience and the socialization of cognitive modes in children. *Child Developm.* **36** (4), 869–86.
See 2.4.2.

205 HESS, R. D. and SHIPMAN, V. C. 1967: Cognitive elements in maternal behavior. In J. P. Hill (ed.) *Minnesota Symposia on Child Psychology,* **1,** 57–81. Minneapolis.

206 HINZE, F. 1966: *Deutsche Schulgrammatik.* Stuttgart.

207 HIRSCH, J. and LEIBFRIED, S. (eds.) 1971: *Materialien zur Wirtschafts – und Bildungspolitik.* Frankfurt.
Important analyses of and documents on German educational policy.

208 HOUSTON, S. H. 1969: A sociolinguistic consideration of the Black English of children in north Florida. *Language* **45** (3), 599–607.
Results of a linguistic investigation of 22 Black children in Florida (20 phonological rules). *Definition: dialects* are regional speech variants, which differ from socially/situationally/racially determined linguistic types; 'White English' and 'Black English' are genera of 'American English' (the author thus neutralizes the current term 'deprived'). The two genera are *CBE* (Child Black English) and SE. Different speech behaviour is described by the term 'register' (a broader concept than style). Black children have a 'school register' (1) and a 'nonschool register' (2). Features of (1): short utterances, slower speed of speaking than in (2), strong emphasis/high pitch, disjointed, word-for-word reading. Features of (2): in the family and amongst friends language is used creatively, spontaneously, fluently etc. The main differences between CBE and SE can be described (phonologically) by 'low level rules' (cf. Labov 1969). The 20 generative *rules* for CBE describe a speech level between competence and 'actualized performance' (cf. Houston 1970) and are optional. The phonemic notation has been taken over with modifications from Trager-Smith. In addition to the phonological rules, four syntactic differences are demonstrated between CBE and SE: (1) *Wh*-question: CBE does not use any inversion, no 'do'-transformation; (2) negation: 'have/be' + NEG. becomes 'ain't', (3) 'be' is deleted in all forms of the present tense; (4) use of pleonastic pronouns (cf. Smith 1969).

209 HOUSTON, S. H. 1970: Competence and performance in Child Black English. *Language Sciences* **12,** 9–14.
See 5.2.2.

210 HYMES, D. 1962: The ethnography of speaking. In T. Gladwin and W. Sturtevant (eds.), *Anthropology and human behavior,* 13–53. Washington, DC. Reprinted in Fishman 1968b, 99–138.
Highly regarded (anthropological) work on the theoretical basis for the analysis of speech behaviour, which had previously been neglected by linguistics and anthropology and which should be achieved by means of an 'ethnography of speaking'. Its subject: situation-specific speech, use of linguistic patterns and their functions, role of speech in socialization. *Programmatic starting-points:* (1) the speech behaviour of a group constitutes a system; (2) functions of speech and language vary with different cultures; (3) primary attention is devoted to the *actual heterogeneous speech use* of a speech community. Three problematic questions are discussed: language in cognitive and expressive behaviour (pragmatic dimension of speech use); descriptive analysis of speech (constituent factors of speech events, functions of speech etc.); and role of language in socialization.

211 HYMES, D. (ed.) 1964a: *Language in culture and society: a reader in linguistics and anthropology.* New York.
Sixty-nine articles, divided into 10 sections: (1) the scope of linguistic anthropology, (2) equality, diversity, relativity, (3) world view and grammatical categories, (4) cultural focus and semantic field, (5) role, socialization, and expressive speech, (6) speech play and verbal art, (7) social structure and speech community, (8) processes and problems of change, (9) relationships in time and space, (10) towards historical perspective. Hymes gives a detailed introduction to each section. The appendix contains a 39-page bibliography.

212 HYMES, D. 1964b: Introduction: toward ethnographies of communication. In Gumperz and Hymes, 1964, 1–34.

213 HYMES, D. 1967a: Models of the interaction of language and social setting. In MacNamara 1967a, 8–28.
An attempt to find concepts for an integrated theory of descriptive sociolinguistics and to outline the nature of its rules. Speech community, speech situation, speech event and speech act are defined as social units of such a theory; components *of speech* (speech event) are: (1) situation, (2) interlocutors, (3) intention, (4) form/content, (5) tone (paralinguistic), (6) channel/code, (7) norms of interaction/interpretation. *Rules* of speech take the form of statements about the relation between the relevant components of the specific speech event, which should be specified in a 'lexicon'. The sequential form of the speech act should be expressed in a syntax with context-free 'rewriting rules'.

214 HYMES, D. 1967b: Why linguistics needs the sociologist. *Social Research* **34** (4), 632–47.
Language should be investigated according to its functions, which are visible in the reciprocal relationship between language structure and social structure.

215 HYMES, D. 1968a: *On communicative competence.* Revised version of a paper given at the Ferkauf Graduate School, Yeshiva University, 1966. Unpublished manuscript: excerpts published in Pride and Holmes 1972.
See 5.3.1.

216 HYMES, D. 1968b: Pidginization and Creolization of language: their social contexts. In *Items: Social Science Research Council* **22** (2), 13–8.
Report of the international conference on Pidgins and Creoles at the University of Mona (Jamaica) 1968. *Pidgin* is defined as a stable (not primary) auxiliary language with reduced functions that are related to particular social situations; *Creole* is defined as a regular everyday language which is derived from 'Pidgin' and which has become the first language of a speech community owing to various circumstances. Geographic distribution of Pidgin and Creole languages as well as their specific linguistic and social features are pointed out and discussed.

217 HYMES, D. (ed.) 1971: *Pidginization and Creolization of languages.* Proceedings of a Conference held at the University of the West Indies, Mona, Jamaica, April 1968. Cambridge.
Forty essays on the description, origin and social situation of Creole and Pidgin languages.

218 HYMES, D. 1973: The scope of sociolinguistics. In Richard J. O'Brien (ed.), *Report of the 23rd annual round table meeting on languages and linguistics.* Monograph Series on Languages and Linguistics **25**. Washington, DC.
Survey report and genesis of sociolinguistics. Programmatic theses on its further development.

219 IBEN, G. *et al.* 1971: *Kompensatorische Erziehung. Analysen amerikanischer Programme.* Munich.

220 JÄGER, S. 1971: Sprachnormen und Schülersprache. Allgemeine und regional bedingte Abweichungen von der kodifizierten hochsprachlichen Norm in der geschriebenen Sprache bei Grund- und Hauptschülern. In Moser *et al.* 1971, 166–233.

221 JÄGER, S. 1972: Sprachbarrieren und kompensatorische Erziehung: Ein bürgerliches Trauerspiel. *LB* **19**, 80–99.

222 JENSEN, A. 1969: How much can we boost IQ and scholastic achievement. *Harvard Educ. Rev.* **39**, 1–123.
Genetic hypothesis of the inferiority of the Blacks.

223 JOAS, H. and LEIST, A. 1971: Performative Tiefenstruktur und interaktionistischer Rollenbegriff – Ein Ansatz zu einer soziolinguistischen Pragmatik. *Münchner Papiere zur Linguistik* **1**, 31–53.
The authors enlarge upon the arguments of Habermas on communicative competence. The connection between speech forms and roles is seen in performative terms.

224 KANNGIESSER, S. 1972a: *Aspekte der synchronen und diachronen Linguistik.* Tübingen.
Excursus on the preconditions for a sociolinguistic theory on pp. 146–70. See also 5.2.3.

225 KANNGIESSER, S. 1972b: Bemerkungen zur Soziolinguistik. In Engel and Schwencke 1972, 82–112.
See 5.2.3.

226 KANNGIESSER, S. 1972c: Untersuchungen zur Kompetenztheorie und zum sprachlichen Handeln. *Lili* **7**, 11–43.
In so far as speech is communicative practice and implies social behaviour, linguistics is *ipso facto* sociolinguistics. The socially-determined heterogeneities of and between speakers as well as their capacity for linguistic innovation should be analysed in an enlarged model of competence, which relates the traditional components of phonology, syntax and semantics to the description of *speech acts* in situational contexts. A conflict model with four states is outlined for the analysis of linguistic acts under conformity pressure.

227 KEACH, E. T., FULTON, F. and GARDENER, W. E. 1967: *Education and social crisis: perspectives on teaching disadvantaged youth.* New York, London, Sydney.
Proposals for compensatory education.

228 KELLY, L. G. (ed.) 1969: *Description and measurement of bilingualism: an international seminar.* University of Moncton, 6–14 June 1967.
Various articles discussing six topics: measurement of bilingual skill; measurement of the different role of the languages of a bilingual; measurement of the effect of one language on the other; behavioural description and measurement of bilingual groups; 'How and when do people become bilingual?' and measurement and description of range and distribution of bilingualism.

229 KJOLSETH, R. 1971: Die Entwicklung der Sprachsoziologie und ihre sozialen Implikationen. In Kjolseth and Sack 1971a, 9–32.
Sociological analysis of the development of sociolinguistics. See beginning of ch. 7.

230 KJOLSETH, R. and SACK, F. (eds.) 1971a: *Zur Soziologie der Sprache. Ausgewählte Beiträge vom 7. Weltkongreß der Soziologie,* Varna. *Kölner Zeitschrift für Soziologie und Sozialpsychologie,* ed. René König, Sonderheft 15. Opladen.
A number of sociologically-oriented articles on status, theory and methods in sociolinguistics, and on problems of linguistic interaction, multilingualism and speech planning.

231 KJOLSETH, R. and SACK, F. 1971b: Ausgewälte und gegliederte Literatur zu Soziologie der Sprache. In Kjolseth and Sack 1971a, 349–90.
Thematically-arranged bibliography of 870 titles.

232 KLEIN, W. 1974: *Variation in der Sprache. Vorschläge zu ihrer Beschreibung.* Kronberg, Taunus.
The assumptions of the 'ideal speaker-hearer' and the 'homogeneous linguistic community' must be given up. Each language contains numerous varieties according to social, regional, stylistic and historical factors. For the description of these varieties, a simple and readily applicable procedure is developed, based on suggestions by Labov, Suppes and Salomaas. The procedure is applicable to context-free rewrite rules as well as to transformations. The last chapter contains, among other things, a discussion of the notion 'variable rule', which is rejected on various grounds, partly theoretical, partly empirical.

233 KLEIN, W. and WUNDERLICH, D. (eds.) 1971: *Aspekte der Soziolinguistik.* Frankfurt.
The following titles listed in this bibliography are translated in this reader: Bernstein 1967, Coulthard 1969, Decamp 1970, Fasold 1970, Houston 1970, Labov 1970a, and an extract of 1970b, Loflin 1969. Original articles: Konrad Ehlich, Frank Müller and Dietmar Wiehle, 'Soziolinguistik als bürgerliches Herrschaftswissen – Marxistische Sprachanalyse' (condensed version of Ehlich *et al.* 1971a) and Dieter Wunderlich, 'Zum Status der Soziolinguistik'. The second edition (1972) replaces Bernstein's article by Dittmar and Klein 1972.

234 KLIMA, E.¹ S. 1964a: Relatedness between grammatical systems. *Language* **40**, 1–20.

235 KLIMA, E. S. 1964b: Negation in English. In Fodor and Katz 1964, 246–323.
One of the first extensive analyses of negation in English in terms of the theory of transformational grammar.

236 KLOSS, H. 1967a: Types of multilingual communities: a discussion of ten variables. *Int. J. Amer Ling.* **33** (4), 7–17.

237 KLOSS, H. 1967b: 'Abstand Languages' and 'Ausbau Languages'. *Anthropol. Ling.* **9** (7), 29–41.

238 KLOSS, H. 1969: *Grundfragen der Ethnopolitik im 20. Jahrhundert. Die Sprachgemeinschaften zwischen Recht und Gewalt.* Wien, Bad Godesberg.

239 KOCHAN, D. C. (ed.) 1971: *Stilistik und Soziolinguistik. Beiträge der Prager Schule zur strukturellen Sprachbetrachtung und Spracherziehung.* Berichte und Untersuchungen aus der Arbeitsgemeinschaft für Linguistik und Didaktik der dt. Sprache und Literatur. Series A, No. 1. Berlin.
Eight articles from the Prague school of functional linguistics dealing with stylistics and speech norm (written v. spoken language). *Introduction* by Eduard Beneš and Josef Vachek, 'The Prague School: its past and present'. *Essays:* Vilém Mathesius, 'Functional linguistics' (1929); Bohuslav Havránek, 'Theory of written language' (1969); Karel Hausenblas, 'Styles of linguistic utterances and speech stratification' (1962); Milan Jelínek, 'The stylistic range of the present-day Czech written language' (1969); František Daneš, 'Culture of spoken utterances' (1969); Miloš Dokulil, 'On the question of the norm of written language and its codification' (1952); Josef Vachek, 'On general questions of orthography and the written norm of language' (1964); Pavel Trost, 'On the causes of linguistic change' (1958).

240 KOCHMANN, T. (ed.) 1972: *Rappin' and stylin' out.* Urbana, Chicago, London.

241 KOSTOMAROV, V. G. 1968: Problemy kul'tury reči. In F. P. Filin (ed.) *Teoretičeskie problemy sovetskogo jazykoznanija,* 126–42. Moscow.
In Soviet linguistics a great deal of attention is paid to the problems raised by language culture. Kostomarov's essay provides a survey of the works that have been carried out in this field since the 1920s. He advocates a language policy which aims at correctness, greater precision and power of expression of collective and individual language. The work contains an extensive bibliography.

242 KREYSZIG, E. 1973: *Statistische Methoden und ihre Anwendungen,* 4th edn. Göttingen.
Detailed introduction to statistical methods; complex mathematical problems are not avoided.

243 KUTSCHERA, F. von, 1971: *Sprachphilosophie.* Munich.
Introduction to the syntactic and semantic descriptive problems of natural language. Ch. 4 deals with the complex 'Sprache und Wirklichkeit' ('language and reality') and discusses the linguistic relativity thesis of Whorf and others.

244 LABOV, W. 1963: The social motivation of a sound change. *Word* **19**, 273–309.
The social distribution of the diphthongs (ai) and (au) on the island of Martha's Vineyard is analysed with techniques which are applied in a more complex and precise manner in Labov 1966a. The aim of the investigation is to explain linguistic change. What is interesting, even in the light of later works, is the way he obtained four variants for (ai) depending on the 'degree of centralization'. The results of this investigation are condensed in Labov 1965.

245 LABOV, W. 1964a: Phonological correlates of social stratification. *Amer. Anthropologist* **66**, 164–176.
Suitable as a short introduction to Labov's quantitative methods. Same procedure in Chs. 2, 4, 6, 7, 8, and 10 of Labov 1966a: selection of the New York population, selection of linguistic variables, isolation of five contextual styles, stratification of variables (r) and (th) according to social class and distribution of other linguistic variables in social classes as well as in ethnic groups.

246 LABOV, W. 1964b: Stages in the acquisition of Standard English. In Shuy 1964, 77–104.
See 6.4.1 under 'age'.

247 LABOV, W. 1965: On the mechanism of linguistic change. In Charles W. Kreidler (ed.),
      Monograph Series on Languages and Linguistics **18,** 91–114. Washington, DC.
      Three problems of linguistic change – (1) the *transition problem* (development of one linguistic
      stage from another), (2) the *embedding problem* (tracing of continuous social and linguistic
      behavioural matrix in which the process of change takes place) and (3) the *problem of evaluation*
      (subjective or latent correlates of objective or manifest change) – are solved by means of two
      empirical investigations (Martha's Vineyard: linguistic variable (aw) and New York City:
      variable (oh)); this is done individually for each area of investigation and then for the two in
      comparison with one another. See Labov 1963, 1966a for the empirical methods of analysis.
      The most important relations of the (oh) variables to linguistic and extralinguistic variables are
      written in *variable notation.*
      The mechanism of linguistic change is summarized systematically in thirteen points (e.g.
      definition of 'changes from above', 'changes from below').

248 LABOV, W. 1966a: *The social stratification of English in New York City.* Washington, DC. Center
      for Applied Linguistics.
      See 6.1.3 and 6.2.2. This work is of central importance for all of Labov's published work up to
      and including 1966.

249 LABOV, W. 1966b: Hypercorrection by the lower middle class as a factor in linguistic change. In
      Bright 1966a, 84–113.
      The phenomenon of hypercorrection is described on the basis of the meth-
      odology/data/results of Labov 1966a for the four socioeconomic groups involved, as related to
      four contextual styles for the four phonological *variables* (th), (r), (eh) and (oh). The LMC
      shows overcorrect use of the variables (r), (eh) and (oh), i.e. the 'formal style' values for this
      group exceed those of the highest status group. Moreover, it reacts hypersensitively to 'prestige
      patterns' (reaction tests): those who themselves use stigmatized expressions unconsciously in
      'casual speech' give these the lowest evaluation. The LMC does not perceive its actual
      pronunciation, but that associated with the desired prestige. From this it follows that this
      group has a *high degree of linguistic instability* (a factor in linguistic change). Similar statements
      can be made for age groups: in contrast to other classes, the older members of the LMC (40–
      plus) exceed the younger members (20–39) in the use of prestige forms. This produces a
      feedback on the language acquisition of the children (acceleration of linguistic change).
      See 6.2.2.

250 LABOV, W. 1966c: The linguistic variable as a structural unit. *Washington Linguistic Review* **3,**
      4–22.

251 LABOV, W. 1966d: The effect of social mobility on linguistic behavior. *Sociological Inquiry* **36,**
      186–203. Reprinted in S. Lieberson (ed.), *Explorations in sociolinguistics. Int. J. Amer. Ling.*
      33 (4), 58–75.
      The analysis is based on the methodology and data of Labov 1966a, which are set out by way of
      introduction. The variables (r), (th), (dh) are investigated in connection with the four
      contextual styles for their function as indicators of the social mobility of the four
      socioeconomic groups. Each class is divided according to four categories: *upwards mobile,
      constant, downwards mobile* and *downwards and upwards mobile.* Comparisons are drawn
      within and between the class groups. Hypercorrection is shown to be a striking indicator of
      upward mobility. *Results:* (1) Upwards mobile people assume the norms of the next higher
      group with which they are in contact (rule). (2) A group which has a background of social
      stability (e.g. UMC), appears to be governed by its own (balanced) norms ('Consistent
      performance without a wide range of style shifting'). (3) A 'downwards mobile category' (set of
      individuals who are socialized in a subgroup) is deviant in that it does not accept the valid
      normative patterns. There is sufficient empirical evidence to show that linguistic stratification is
      a direct reflection of underlying social values.
      See also 6.2.2 and 6.4.1.

252 LABOV, W. 1966e: Some sources in reading problems for negro speakers of Non-Standard
      English. In A. Frazier (ed.), *New directions in elementary English,* 140–67. Champaign,
      Illinois: National Council of Teachers of English. Reprinted in Baratz and Shuy 1969,
      29–67.
      Summary of preliminary results of the contrastive analysis of SE and BEV from Labov *et al.*
      1968; see also 6.2.6.

253 LABOV, W. 1969: Contraction, deletion, and inherent variability of the English copula. *Language* **45** (4), 715–62.
Analysis of the English copula *be* and development of the theoretical concept of the Variable Rule. See 5.2.1 and 6.2.6 under 'Contraction and deletion of the copula'.

254 LABOV, W. 1970a: The study of language in its social context. *Studium Generale* **23** (1), 30–87. Reprinted in Fishman 1971b, 152–216.
At present the most suitable introductory reading on status, theory and methodology of SL. It gives a résumé of the state of discussion in recent years and examines the relation of SL to linguistic theory. See 5.1, 5.2.1, 5.3.3 and particularly 6.1.

255 LABOV, W. 1970b: The logic of Nonstandard English. In Alatis 1970a, 1–43.
Critique of the Deficit Theory supported by examples from Labov *et al.* 1968. See 3.1 and 3.4.3.

256 LABOV, W. 1970c: The reading of the *-ed* suffix. In Levin and Williams 1970, 222–45.
The analysis evaluates a variable from the investigation of Labov *et al.* 1968 from various points of view.

257 LABOV, W. 1971a: Variation in language. In Reed 1971, 187–221.
Explanation of processes of linguistic variation on the basis of Labov 1966a and Labov *et al.* 1968. See 4.2, 6.2.2 and 6.2.6.

258 LABOV, W. 1971b: The notion of 'System' in Creole languages. In Hymes 1968b, 447–72.
Variation is of central importance for the language system. It is the task of abstract linguistic analysis to explain it. For the problematic nature of this see 5.2.3.

259 LABOV, W. 1972a: Rules for ritual insults. In Sudnow 1972.
Revised version of the same analysis in Labov *et al.* 1968. See 6.3.3.

260 LABOV, W. 1972b: Some principles of linguistic methodology. *Language in Society* **1** (1). 97–120.
Methods of empirical linguistic description. Supplement to Labov 1970a.

261 LABOV, W. 1972c: *Language in the inner city: studies in the Black English Vernacular.* Conduct and Communication **3.** Philadelphia.
This volume contains the most important results of Labov *et al.* 1968, partly in revised form (such as the formalism of the variable rules, developed in Labov 1969). Part I deals with problems arising when linguistic variation is studied systematically. In Part II the social consequences of different linguistic varieties are analysed, and new insights are presented into the nature and function of linguistic norms. Part III gives an analysis of ritual insults as well as of stories of personal experience.

262 LABOV, W. 1972d: *Sociolinguistic patterns.* Conduct and Communication **4.** Philadelphia.
Collection of nine essays, summarizing mainly the results of Labov 1966a, but including also the general survey article 'The study of language in its social context' and the fundamental contribution to the study of linguistic change, 'The social setting of linguistic change'.

263 LABOV, W. 1972e: Negative attraction and negative concord in English grammar. *Language* **48** (4), 773–818.
See 6.2.6 (3).

264 LABOV, W. 1973: The boundaries of words and their meaning. In Bailey and Shuy 1973, 340–73.
Analysis of the semantic variation of the words *cup, bowl, dish, mug, glass, pitcher.* A procedure is proposed for the measurement of semantic vagueness, demonstrated with actual examples. The results are relevant for the organization of the English lexicon.

265 LABOV, W. and WALETZKY, J. 1967: Narrative analysis: oral versions of personal experience. In June Helm MacNeish (ed.), *Essays on the verbal and visual arts.* Proceedings of the 1966 Annual Spring Meeting, Seattle, 12–44.
See 6.3.4.

266 LABOV, W., COHEN, P. and ROBINS, C. 1965: *A preliminary study of the structure of English used by Negro and Puerto Rican speakers in New York City.* Final Report, Cooperative Research **3091.** US Office of Education and Welfare.

267 LABOV, W., COHEN, P., ROBINS, C. and LEWIS, J. 1968: *A study of the Non-Standard English of Negro and Puerto Rican speakers in New York City,* I and II. Final Report, Cooperative Research Project **3288.** Washington, DC: US Office of Health, Education and Welfare. See 6.2.6, 6.3.3 and 6.3.4.

268 LAIRD, C. and GORELL, R. M. 1971: *Reading about language.* New York, Chicago, San Francisco, Atlanta.
Collection of a number of essays on different language problems.

269 LAKOFF, G. 1970: Global rules. *Language* **46** (3), 627–38. Reprinted in Seuren 1974, 143–56.

270 LAKOFF, R. 1972: Language in context. *Language* **48** (4), 907–27.
Discussion of cases of pragmatic functions of utterances, whose description is said to require the incorporation of pragmatic aspects into grammar.

271 LAMBERT, W. E. 1967: A social psychology of bilingualism. In MacNamara 1967a, 91–109.
The 'matched guise technique' measures the *attitude* of speakers of a certain language towards the speech behaviour of speakers of another language. The subjects – who differ in sex, age, language/dialect, social class – evaluate taperecorded language samples which have different accents/phonemic qualities by assessing the supposed character of their speakers. (The very different language samples are spoken by *one* bilingual speaker.) Investigations into the speech behaviour of Anglo and French Canadians and speakers of BEV and SE show that groups who come from different ethnic/social backgrounds have a *stereotype* reaction to one another in that their social evaluation is either positive or negative. The second part deals with the sociopsychological aspects of *learning a second language* especially the role of motivation, which is decisively influenced by the cultural/social evaluation of the language to be learned. See 5.4.4.

272 LAMBERT, W. E. 1972: *Language, psychology and culture: essays.* Stanford, California.
Collection of twenty-one essays, previously published in periodicals, some going back to the mid-1950s. Most essays deal with problems concerning bilingualism.

273 LAMBERT, W. E. and TUCKER, R. G. 1969: White and Negro listeners' reactions to various American-English dialects. *Social Forces* **47** (4), 463–8.
Empirical application of the 'matched guise technique'. Six taperecorded speech samples (linguistic variations analogous to ethnic/social differentiation) are played back to groups of college students for evaluation so that their attitudes towards the speakers can be measured on an 8-point scale. The subjects made clear distinctions between the speech samples. The English of newscasters (most formal standard) is given the highest evaluation; Blacks and Whites gave the lowest assessment to each other's language.

274 LAMBERT, W. E., HODSON, R. C., GARDNER, R. C. and FILLENBAUM, S. 1960: Evaluational reactions to spoken languages. *Journal of Abnormal and Social Psychology* **66** (1), 44–51.
Theory of the 'matched guise technique'. See 5.4.4.

275 LANGACKER, R. 1968: *Language and its structure: some fundamental linguistic concepts.* New York.
Useful elementary introduction to the principles of language and grammar in a strictly transformational framework.

276 LAVER, J. and HUTCHESON, S. (eds.) 1972: *Communication in face to face interaction.* Harmondsworth, England.

277 LAWTON, D. 1968: *Social class, language and education.* London.
The sociopsychological background, which has led to the distinction of restricted and elaborated codes (Bernstein), is related in a complex argumentation to socialization and is discussed in the first four chapters with reference to numerous psychological/sociological/linguistic investigations for the *problem areas* of social class and educational opportunities, motivation, subculture and educability, relation of language to social origin, as well as language and thinking. Ch. 5 surveys Bernstein's works and criticizes them on various points (but does not question the basic concept of the codes). Results of empirical investigations of schoolchildren in formal school situations help Lawton to maintain that Bernstein's code theory is right. The appendix covers current compensatory speech programmes in the USA and Great Britain.

278   LENCEK, R. L. 1971: Problems in sociolinguistics in the Soviet Union. In O'Brien 1971, 269–301.
      Survey of Soviet SL 1920–30 and 1960–70. The background of the academic and sociopolitical
      interest in SL is explained. For results see 5.2.6. Bibliography of approx. 300 titles.

279   LENNEBERG, E. H. 1967: *Biological foundations of language*. New York.

280   LENNEBERG, E. H. and ROBERTS, J. M. 1956: The language of experience. *Int. J. Amer. Ling.,*
      Memoir 13. Bloomington, Indiana.
      Critical examination of the linguistic relativity thesis.

281   LEVELT, W. J. M. 1974: *Formal grammars in linguistics and psycholinguistics* 1, An introduction to
      the theory of formal languages and automata; 2, Applications in linguistic theory; 3,
      Applications in psycholinguistics. The Hague.

282   LEVIN, H. and WILLIAMS, J. P. (eds.) 1970: *Basic studies on reading*. New York, London.
      Fifteen essays on reading skills and capabilities, by Chomsky, Labov and others.

283   LEVINE, L. and CROCKETT, H. J. 1967: Speech variation in a Piedmont community: postvocalic r.
      In Lieberson 1967, 76–98.
      Results of an analysis of speech variation in correlation with social structure in a Piedmont
      community (North Carolina). Sole linguistic variable is *postvocalic (r),* which subjects
      pronounce bimodally (according to status, age, period of time spent in the community). The r
      values obtained reflect two r *norms:* r is preferred by higher status, immigrant and younger
      inhabitants; older inhabitants and those of longer standing tend towards r-less pronunciation.
      R pronunciation seems to develop into a prestige form.

284   LIEBERSON, S. (ed.) 1967: *Explorations in sociolinguistics. Int. J. Amer. Ling.* II, 33 (2) (also
      available as a separate volume).
      Thirteen essays, mostly by sociologists, dealing with social distribution of languages, socially-
      determined different forms of address and class-specific speech variation.

285   LINDENFELD, J. 1969: The social conditioning of syntactic variation in French. *Amer.*
      Anthropologist 71 (5), 890–98.
      Twelve persons (between 22 and 38 years old), six from the middle and six from the lower class,
      are tested for the *correlation* of class membership and formal/informal context by means of
      syntactic *complexity*. Complexity is measured by transformational history in respect of
      subordination, relativization and *nominalization*. Length of sentences is only a secondary
      measure. The results show a clear correlation between social variation (Class I v. Class II) and
      contextual variation (formal v. informal situation) with syntactic variation (especially with
      regard to nominalization).

286   LOBAN, W. D. 1963: *The language of elementary school children*. Champaign, Illinois: National
      Council of Teachers of English.
      See 2.3.3.

287   LOFLIN, M. D. 1969: Negro Nonstandard and Standard English: same or different deep
      structure? *Orbis* 18 (1), 74–91.
      See 5.2.3.

288   LOFLIN, M. D. 1970: On the structure of the verb in a dialect of American Negro English.
      Linguistics 59, 14–28.
      See the discussion in 5.2.3.

289   LUCKMANN, T. 1969: Soziologie der Sprache. In R. König (ed.), *Handbuch der Empirischen*
      Sozialforschung II, 1050–1101. Stuttgart.
      Survey of literature *on* and discussion of problems *of* sociologically 'relevant' questions of
      language, taking into consideration sociological, psychological and linguistic aspects. The
      bibliography lists 537 titles.

290   MA, R. and HERASIMCHUK, E. 1968: The linguistic dimensions of bilingual neighborhood. In
      Fishman *et al.* 1968, 636–835. Reprinted in Fishman 1972, 268–95.
      See 6.2.3.

291   MAAS, U. 1972a: Sprechen und Handeln – Zum Stand der gegenwärtigen Sprachtheorie.
      Sprache im technischen Zeitalter 41, 1–20.
      Historical-materialist analysis of modern linguistics.

292 MAAS, U. 1972b: Die neue Wissenschaft und ihr Funkkolleg. In Maas and Wunderlich 1972, 6–45. Analysis of the background of the radio lectures *Sprache* (language) in the Federal Republic of Germany, with regard to expenditure in the education sector.

293 MAAS, U. and WUNDERLICH, D. 1972: *Pragmatik und sprachliches Handeln. Mit einer Kritik am Funkkolleg 'Sprache'.* Frankfurt.
See in particular Maas's concept of speech as social work.

294 MACKEY, W. F. 1962: The description of bilingualism. *Canad. J. Ling.* **7**, 51–85. Reprinted in Fishman 1968b, 554–84.
Attempt to demonstrate the descriptive possibilities of bilingualism by means of definitions, diagrams and (measurable) variables. The main point of the arguments, which concentrate on *degree* and *function* of bilingualism, on alternative *language use* and *interference phenomena*, is on a theoretical and occasionally programmatic level. Bilingualism is mainly conceived as an individual phenomenon for which an interdisciplinary description can only be achieved by means of an integrated linguistic, psychological and sociological perspective.

295 MACKEY, W. F. 1970: Interference, integration and the synchronic fallacy. In Alatis 1970b, 195–223.

296 MACNAMARA, J. (ed.) 1967a: *Problems of bilingualism. J. Soc. Issues* **23** (2).
Ten articles on theory and empirical measurement of bilingualism; by Ervin-Tripp, Fishman, Hymes, Lambert and others.

297 MACNAMARA, J. 1967b: How can one measure the extent of a person's bilingual proficiency? In Kelly 1969, 80–97.

298 MACNAMARA, J. 1970: Bilingualism and thought. In Alatis 1970b, 25–40.
See 5.4.1.

299 MALINOWSKI, B. 1923: The problem of meaning in primitive languages. In C. K. Ogden and I. A. Richards, *The meaning of meaning,* Supplement I, 296–336. London.
See 1.2.4.

300 MARCELLESI, J. B. (ed.) 1971: *Linguistique et Société. Langue Française* **9.**
Sociolinguistic volume oriented towards the discourse in class-divided societies. Political speeches are analysed, particularly from the point of view of the relationship between linguistics and ideology. The analyses are of a morphophonological, syntactic, semantic and lexical nature (semiological school in France). Particular attention should be paid to the essay by Françoise Gadet (131) as it is the only contribution that deals with the social differentiation of the spoken language.

301 MCCAWLEY, J. D. 1974: Remarks on the lexicography of performative verbs. Unpublished paper, University of Chicago.

302 MCDAVID, R. J. 1966: Dialect differences and social differences in an urban society. In Bright 1966a, 72–83.
Three aspects of dialects in the USA are treated: (1) *historical aspect* (origin and establishment of dialects by the immigration of various ethnic groups, e.g. Blacks); (2) *linguistic deviations* of BEV vis-à-vis SE, and the sanctions associated with its use; (3) the problem of *speech programmes* for deprived NSE and BEV speakers; these should only concentrate on those linguistic features (e.g. postvocalic *-r*, invariant *be*, negation, stress) which are socially stigmatized.

303 MCDAVID, R. J. 1970: A theory of dialect. In Alatis 1970a, 45–62.

304 MCHUGH, P. 1968: *Defining the situation: the organization of meaning in social interaction.*
In a borrowing from ethnomethodological theory (e.g. Garfinkel, Cicourel), the definition parameter of situation is the 'knowledge' of interaction participants in time and space. The possibility of 'knowledge' is produced and limited by its 'emergence', the temporal dimension by activity and its relativity and the spatial dimension as an event in relation to other events. The acquired concepts ('emergence' and 'relativity' are characterized by a series of subconcepts) are validated in an empirical study.

305 MCNEMAR, Q. 1942: *The revision of the Stanford-Binet scale.* Boston.

306 MEAD, G. H. 1934: *Mind, self and society.* Chicago, London.

307 MILLER, H. L. 1967: *Education for the disadvantaged: current issues and research in education.* New York.
Discussion of compensatory education.

308 MOLNOS, A. 1969: *Language problems in Africa: a bibliography (1946–67) and summary of the present situation with special reference to Kenya, Tanzania and Uganda.* East African Research Information Center Information Circular **2.**
Research report and extensive bibliography.

309 MOSCOVIČI, B. 1967: Communication processes and the properties of language. In L. Berkowitz (ed.), *Advances in experimental social psychology* **3**, 225–70.

310 MOSER, H. (ed., with H. Eggers, J. Erben, H. Neumann, H. Steger) 1971: *Sprache und Gesellschaft. Beiträge zur soziolinguistischen Beschreibung der deutschen Gegenwartssprache. Sprache der Gegenwart 13.* Schriften des Instituts für deutsche Sprache in Mannheim, Jahrbuch 1970. Düsseldorf.
A total of fourteen thematically different articles by Hugo Steger, Hermann Bausinger, Roland Harweg, Hans Glinz, Hugo Moser, Eduard Beneš, Janos Juhász, Siegfried Grosse, Siegfried Jäger, Bernhard Engelen, Heinz Kloss, Els Oksaar and Ulrich Engel.

311 MUČNIK, I. P., PANOV, M. V., ŠMELEV, O. N., ZEMSKAJA, E. A., KRYSIN, L. P. *et al.* 1968: Principy sociologičeskogo izučenija russkogo jazyka sovetskoj èpoxi. In *Russkij Jazyk i Sovetskoe Obščestvo* (Leksika), 16–49, Moscow.
See 5.2.6.

312 NEGT, O. 1971: Sprachbarrieren und Lernmotivation. In *Soziologische Phantasie und Exemplarisches Lernen. Zur Theorie und Praxis der Arbeiter-bildung,* Ch. 3, 59–82. Frankfurt.
See 3.5.

313 NEUBERT, A. 1962: *Semantischer Positivismus in den USA. Ein kritischer Beitrag zum Studium der Zusamenhänge zwischen Sprache und Gessellschaft.* Halle.
Historical-materialist critique of the methodology of American linguistics. Ch. 3 (5) traces the genesis of anthropological linguistics (117–37); it is exposed as an ideological instrument of the dominant forces in the USA.

314 NIEPOLD, W. 1970: *Sprache und soziale Schicht. Darstellung und Kritik der Forschungsliteratur seit Bernstein.* Berlin.
The works of Bernstein – and those investigations of Lawton, Robinson, Reichwein, Oevermann and others, which work with his hypotheses – are discussed from a number of systematic points of view and a critique is given of their theoretical assumptions and empirical orientations.

315 O'BRIEN, R. J. (ed.) 1971: *Report of the 22nd annual round table meeting on linguistics and language studies* – Linguistics: developments of the sixties – viewpoints for the seventies. Monograph Series on Languages and Linguistics **24**. Washington, DC.
Articles on virtually all branches of modern linguistics (syntax, lexicology, structuralism, text linguistics, psycholinguistics, sociolinguistics, anthropological linguistics). Authors include Bach, McCawley, Fillmore, Pike, Lamb, Winter, Friedrich, Shuy, Fasold, Lenneberg, Oomen. A quarter of the book is devoted to the development of Soviet linguistics (surveys, extensive bibliographies).

316 OEVERMANN, U. 1969a: Schichtenspezifische Formen des Sprachverhaltens und ihr Einfluß auf kognitive Prozesse. In H. Roth (ed.) *Begabung und Lernen,* 297–355. Stuttgart. Reprinted in Bernstein *et al.* 1970, 138–97.
Extensive survey, selective analysis and assimilation of literature on/of problem complexes connected with language and social class, some of which are discussed in Oevermann 1970. Bibliography of 317 titles.

317 OEVERMANN, U. 1969b: Role structure of the family and its implication for the cognitive development of children. In M. A. Matthijssen and C. E. Vervoort (eds.), *Education in Europe.* The Hague.

318 OEVERMANN, U. 1970: *Sprache und soziale Herkunft. Ein Beitrag zur Analyse schichtenspezifischer Sozialisationsprozesse und ihrer Bedeutung für den Schulerfolg. Studien und Berichte 18.* Berlin: Institut für Bildungsforschung in der Max-Planck-Gesellschaft.
See the discussion in 2.3.6.

319   OLIM, E. G. 1970: Maternal language styles and cognitive development of children. In Williams
        1970a, 212–28.
        See 3.2.

320   OSGOOD, C. E., SUCI, G. J. and TANNENBAUM, P. H. 1957: *The measurement of meaning*. Urbana,
        Illinois.
        See 5.4.4.

321   PALMER, F. H. 1970: Socioeconomic status and intellective performance among Negro
        preschool boys. *Developmental Psychology* **3**, 1–9

322   PANOV, M. B. (ed.) 1968: *Russkij Jazyk i Sovetskoe Obščestvo: Sociologo-lingvističeskoe Issled-
        ovanie* (Russian language and Soviet society: sociolinguistic inquiries). Moscow. 1, Leksika
        sovremennogo russkogo literaturnogo jazyka. 2, Slovoobrazovanie sovremennogo russkogo
        literaturnogo jazyka. 3, Morfologija i sintaksis sovremennogo russkogo literaturnogo
        jazyka. 4, Fonetika sovremennogo russkogo literaturnogo jazyka.
        This collective monograph was initiated in 1958 by S. I. Ozegov and V. V. Vinogradov, and in
        1962 plans were already *sur le tapis* for a later monograph. Work began on it in 1963 with a large
        body of assistants. The *aim* was to elucidate the regularities of the development of the Russian
        language under new social conditions. *Methods*: the collection of material had to embrace all
        possible types of texts and records of spoken language. For this it was necessary to have an
        extremely extensive corpus of sociologically-qualified material if the results were to be
        statistically significant. A total of 13,000 questionnaires was evaluated, each with between 180
        and 768 questions on phonetics, morphology, word formation and syntax (approx. 5000 people
        were questioned). The subjective evaluation of individuals' speech habits was monitored by
        direct observation of spoken and written language. The monograph is not devoted to linguistic
        sociology, but to sociological linguistics. The language system is always treated in its socially-
        conditioned changes. Starting with the linguistic data, the social conditions are investigated
        which bring about these factors. *Results*: the investigation shows the close relationship between
        internal and external language development. No rigid norms and conditions can be derived
        from the results, but rather developmental tendencies, such as the trend towards increasing
        agglutination in the word formation system of Russian, or the tendency to simplify the vowel
        system etc. *Perspectives*: this monograph is the first in a series of investigations of theoretical
        and practical interest, such as the analysis of various speech genres ('Russkaja rec' i sovetskoe
        obščestvo') or the investigation of the development of the Soviet Belletrist language.

323   PASSOW, A. H., GOLDBERG, M. and TANNENBAUM, A. J. (eds.) 1967: *Education of the disadvantaged:
        a book of readings*. New York.
        Essays on compensatory education and the adaptation of BEV speakers to SE.

324   PAULSTON, C. B. 1971: On the moral dilemma of the sociolinguist. In *Language Learning* **21**,
        175–81.
        The moral dilemma of the sociolinguist is that, although he can diagnose and describe speech
        differences, change with a view to emancipation hardly seems possible without changing the
        whole structure of society. Paulston demonstrates the dependency of speech emancipation on
        political élitism with reference to Peru as an example. As economic change is at present
        unlikely, Paulston opts for a compromise: to highlight the dire economic and linguistic position
        of minority groups.

325   PIAGET, J. 1946: *La Formation du symbole chez l'enfant: imitation, jeu et rêve. image et
        représentation*. Neuchâtel.

326   POLENZ, P. von, 1972: Sprachnorm, Sprachnormung, Sprachnormenkritik. *LB* **17**, 76–84.
        Survey and proposals for a possible establishment of speech norm.

327   POLIVANOV, E. D. 1929: Der Kreis anstehender Probleme der gegenwärtigen Linguistik. *Russkij
        Jazyk v Sovetskoj Škole* **1**, 57–62. Reprinted in Girke and Jachnow 1974b.
        For the first time, tasks for sociolinguistic work are defined in a way which is still largely
        relevant: (1) language is to be defined as a sociohistorical fact; (2) languages and dialects are to
        be studied from a sociological point of view; (3) a given language should be investigated and
        evaluated as a means of communication; (4) causal relations between socioeconomic and
        linguistic phenomena must be investigated; (5) an explicit account must be given of the relation
        between stages in linguistic evolution and cultural history; (6) sociolinguistic results should be
        applied to political problems of language planning.

328 PRIDE, J. B. 1970: Sociolinguistics. In J. Lyons (ed.), *New horizons in linguistics*, 287–301. Harmondsworth, England.
Critical survey of the literature which points out the methodological difficulties of SL. Pride's work is based chiefly on anthropological investigations and it criticizes correlative SL.

329 PRIDE, J. B. and HOLMES, J. (eds.) 1972: *Sociolinguistics*. Harmondsworth, England.
Collection of well-known sociolinguistic essays, mentioned elsewhere in this bibliography.

330 PUTNAM, G. N. and O'HERN, E. M. 1955: The status significance of an isolated urban dialect. *Language* Supplement, Language Dissertation **53**.
See 6.2.1.

331 QUIRK, R. and SVARTVIK, J. 1966: *Investigating linguistic acceptability*. The Hague.

332 RAPH, J. B. 1967: Language and speech deficits in culturally disadvantaged children: implications for the speech clinician. In *J. Speech Hearing Disord.* **3** (32), 203–14.

333 RAVENETTE, R. T. 1963: *Intelligence and social class: an investigation into the patterns of intelligence and personality of working class secondary school children*. Unpublished dissertation, London.

334 RAY, P. S. 1963: *Language standardization*. The Hague.

335 REED, C. E. (ed.) 1971: *The learning of language*. New York: National Council of Teachers of English.
Eleven essays on eleven different topics: language acquisition in early childhood; development of natural language capabilities after the early years; learning psychology and analysis of the English language; speech variation; acquisition of a second language; foundations of speech; language pathology; ontogenetic problem of reference; lexicography; language at school; and teaching of foreign languages.

336 REICHSTEIN, R. 1960: Étude des Variations sociales et géographiques des faits linguistiques. *Word* **16**, 55–99.
See 6.2.1.

337 REICHWEIN, R. 1967: *Sprachstruktur und Sozialschicht. Soziale Welt* **18**, 309–30.
See 2.3.5.

338 RICCIUTI, H. N. 1965: Object grouping and selective ordering behavior in infants 12 to 24 months old. *Merrill-Palmer Quart.* **11**, 129–48.

339 ROBINSON, W. P. 1965: The elaborated code in working class language. *Language and Speech* **8**, 243–52.
See 2.3.7.

340 ROBINSON, W. P. 1969: Social factors and language development in primary school children. In M. A. Matthijssen and C. E. Vervoort (eds.), *Education in Europe*, 51–66. The Hague.
Survey of more recent inquiries on 'elaborated' and 'restricted code' under the direction of Bernstein: (1) class-specific behaviour of mothers towards their children; (2) class-specific speech behaviour of primary school children; (3) compensatory speech programmes.

341 ROBINSON, W. P. and CREED, C. D. 1968: Perceptual and verbal discriminations of 'Elaborated' and 'Restricted' code users. *Language and Speech* **11** (4), 182–93.
See 2.2.2.

342 ROEDER, P. M. 1968: Sprache, Sozialstatus und Schulerfolg. *Betrifft: erziehung* **6** (August), 14–20.

343 ROKEACH, M. 1968: The nature of attitudes. *International Encyclopedia of Social Sciences* **1**, 449–58.

344 ROSEN, H. 1972: *Language and class: a critical look at the theories of Basil Bernstein*. Bristol.

345 ROSENTHAL, R. and JACOBSON, L. 1968: Self-fulfilling prophecies in the classroom: teacher's expectations as unintended determinants of pupils' intellectual competence. In M. Deutsch, I. Katz and A. Jensen (eds.), *Social class, race and psychological development*. New York.

346   ROSS, J. R. 1970: On declarative sentences. In R. A. Jacobs and P. S. Rosenbaum (eds.), *Readings in English transformational grammar*, 222–72. Waltham, Mass.

347   ROSSI-LANDI, P. 1972: Kapital und Privateigentum in der Sprache. In *Ästhetik und Kommunikation: Beiträge zur politischen Erziehung* 7 (3), 36–48.
Attempt to establish a Marxist linguistic theory by transferring concepts of 'capital' to speech use.

348   RUBIN, J. 1968: *National bilingualism in Paraguay*. The Hague.
The coexistence of Spanish and Guarani is investigated for (1) their history and origin, (2) sociocultural data, (3) the attitudes of speakers towards each of the two languages, (4) the language skill in and acquisition of the two languages, (5) their stability, (6) their linguistic use. Ch. 6 on use (published with minor modifications in Fishman 1968b; 512–30) demonstrates by means of empirical data obtained from questionnaires (linguistic data are, for example, forms of address) the social roles and social situations in which the two languages are distributed.

349   RUBINSTEIN, D. and STONEMAN, C. (eds.) 1970: *Education for democracy*. Harmondsworth, England

350   RUNYON, R. and HABER, A. 1973: *Fundamentals of behavioral statistics*. Reading, Mass.
Introduction to theory and practice of statistical analysis, with problems.

351   SACKS, H. 1972a: An initial investigation of the usability of conversational data for doing sociology. In Sudnow 1972, 31–74.

352   SACKS, H. 1972b: On the analyzability of stories by children. In Gumperz and Hymes 1972, 325–45.

353   SAMARIN, W. J. 1967: *Field linguistics: a guide to linguistic field work*. New York.
Methodology of linguistic field research.

354   SANKOFF, G. 1973: Above and beyond phonology in variable rules. In Bailey and Shuy 1973, 44–61.
Three examples are given to discuss the many possibilities of application of variable rules in phonology, syntax and semantics. The examples are: (1) the variability of the future marker in Tok Pisin of New Guinea (syntactic analysis); (2) the variability of the conjunction *que* in *comme que, quand que, comment que* of Canadian French in Montreal (phonological conditions); (3) the semantic variation of the pronouns *tu, vous* and *on* in Montreal Canadian French.

355   SANKOFF, D. and ROUSSEAU, P. 1974: A method for assessing variable rule and implicational scale analysis of linguistic variation. In L. Mitchell (ed.), *Computer in the humanities*. Edinburgh.
Formal comparison and test of the degrees of success of the variable rule and the implicational scale in the light of examples, whose variability is analysed by means of statistical methods carried out by computer.

356   SAPIR, E. 1921: *Language: an introduction to the study of speech*. New York.

357   SAPIR, E. 1929: The status of linguistics as a science. *Language* 5, 207–14.

358   SAUSSURE, F. de, 1949: *Cours de linguistique générale*. Paris.

359   SCHATZMANN, L. and STRAUSS, A. 1955: Social class and modes of communication. *American Journal of Sociology* 60 (4), 329–38.
See 1.1 and 2.3.1.

360   SCHEGLOFF, E. 1968: Sequencing in conversational openings. *Amer. Anthropologist* 70, 1075–95.
Analyses of forms of conversational openings; see 5.3.3.

361   SCHERER, K. R. 1970: *Nonverbale Kommunikation*. IPK-Forschungsberichte Bd. 35. Hamburg.

362   SCHLIEBEN-LANGE, B. 1971: *Okzitanisch und Katalanisch: ein Beitrag zur Soziolinguistik zweier romanischer Sprachen*. Tübingen.
Analysis of the political situation of the two languages and of the awareness of their speakers.

363   SCHLIEBEN-LANGE, B. 1973: *Soziolinguistik: eine Einführung*. Stuttgart.
Short introduction to the history and problems of sociolinguistics.

364 SCHULZ, G. 1971: Satzkomplexität – Ein zweifelhaftes linguistisches Kriterium. *Diskussion Deutsch* **3**, 27–36.
See 3.4.2.

365 SCHULZ, G. 1972: Über die dürftige Syntax im restringierten Kode. *Lili* **7**, 97–116.
Inherent contradictions of Bernstein's sociolinguistic theory are described from a linguistic point of view. The theory of inadequate syntax in the restricted code is examined in the light of paratactic sentence construction plans and is rejected for the sentence type in question. This result shows that some points in the theory of linguistic codes are unproven and also indicates the problems raised in determining the sociological level in this theoretical concept.

366 SCOTT, M. B. and LYMAN, S. M. 1968: Accounts. *Amer. Sociol. Rev.* **33** (1), 46–62.
Attempt to distinguish social roles on the basis of performative utterances.

367 SEARLE, J. R. 1969: *Speech acts.* Cambridge.

368 SEARLE, J. R. 1971: What is a speech act? In J. R. Searle (ed.), *The philosophy of language.* London.

369 SELIGMAN, C. R., TUCKER, G. R. and LAMBERT, W. E. 1972: The effects of speech style and other attributes on teachers' attitudes toward pupils. *Language in Society* **1** (1), 131–42.
Correlative attitude measurement of teachers' behaviour. The social judgement of pupils by teachers is made on the strength of essays, drawings, photographs and voices.

370 SEUREN, P. A. M. 1972: Autonomous versus semantic syntax. In *Found. Lang.* **8** (2), 237–65. Reprinted in Seuren 1974, 96–122.

371 SEUREN, P. A. M. 1973: The comparative. In F. Kiefer and N. Ruwet (eds.), *Generative grammar in Europe,* 528–64. Dordrecht, Holland.

372 SEUREN, P. A. M. (ed.) 1974: *Semantic syntax.* Oxford.

373 SGALL, P., HAJIČOVÁ, E. and BENEŠOVÁ, E. 1973: *Topic, focus and generative semantics.* Kronberg.

374 SHUY, R. W. (ed.) 1964: *Social dialects and language learning.* Proceedings of the Bloomington, Indiana, Conference 1964. Champaign, Ill: National Council of Teachers of English.
Twenty articles, some very brief, on the topics: (1) social dialectology, (2) fieldwork projects, (3) speech programmes, (4) role of social factors in learning SE, (5) reaction of related behavioural sciences to aims and methodology of investigations of social dialectology, (6) consequences for further research, (7) summary of the results of the colloquium (see in particular the articles by Stewart, Labov, Pederson).

375 SHUY, R. W. 1968: A selective bibliography on social dialects. *Ling. Reporter* **10** (3), 1–5.
Annotated bibliography of 46 titles on works on social dialects, subdivided into three sections: (1) theory and programmatic aspects, (2) works of research, (3) educational application.

376 SHUY, R. W. 1970a: Subjective judgements in sociolinguistic analysis. In Alatis 1970a; 175–88.
The linguistic data that have been 'objectively' obtained by empirical investigations and differentiated according to social features (e.g. classes) can be verified by *language attitude tests,* which measure the reaction of speakers to linguistic forms. In addition, such tests provide information on the evaluation of BEV and SE.

377 SHUY, R. W. 1970b: The sociolinguists and urban language problems. In Williams 1970a, 335–50.
Comprehensive description of sociolinguistic techniques with a survey of current projects of the Center for Applied Linguistics in Washington. The following are put forward as strategies for sociolinguistic research: (1) correlative studies, (2) investigations of language attitudes, (3) studies of languages in contact and (4) switching between various linguistic varieties (regional, social varieties). Conclusions are drawn from the analysis for school practice.

378 SHUY, R. W. (ed.) 1973: *Sociolinguistics: current trends and prospects. Report of the 23rd Annual Round Table Meeting on Linguistics and Language Studies.* Monograph Series on Languages and Linguistics **25.** Washington, DC.
Collection of essays on sociolinguistics as a scientific discipline, on the analysis of variation in

K*

terms of grammar (optional rules), on the ethnomethodological analysis of face-to-face interactions, on the historical dimension of sociolinguistics, and on the application of sociolinguistics in the areas of language planning and of education.

379 SHUY, R. W. and FASOLD, R. W. 1971: Contemporary emphases in sociolinguistics. In O'Brien 1971, 185–97.
Survey article, which conforms essentially to Labov's views on theory and application.

380 SHUY, R. W., WOLFRAM, W. A. and RILEY, W. K. 1967: *Linguistic correlates of social stratification in Detroit*. Final Report. Cooperative Research Project **6-1347**, US Office of Education.

381 SHUY, R. W., WOLFRAM, W. A. and RILEY, W. K. 1968: *Field techniques in an urban language study*. Washington, DC: Center for Applied Linguistics.
Description of fieldwork methods which were employed in an empirical urban dialect study in Detroit (Shuy, Wolfram and Riley 1967). The book describes and discusses: (1) *Selectional procedure*: acquisition of the 'base sample' (random samples from schools) and of the 'ethnic sample' (random samples from linguistically-exposed districts); distribution in social classes according to three factors: (i) education, (ii) occupation, (iii) living conditions. (2) *Planning of fieldwork*: organization (administration, rapport with the families, time and place of interviews, technical instructions, e.g. for using taperecorders etc.). (3) *Training of fieldworkers*: precise details of the training programme (interview techniques, practice in phonetic transcription etc.). (4) *Questionnaires*: all the questionnaires are given in full; discussion of special cases in interviews: e.g. absence of several members of a family, etc. (5) *Practical information* on code books, computer programmes etc. and texts of two complete interviews. (6) *Assessment* of the fieldwork or of the fieldworker: *inter alia*, adequacy of transcription, problems of adaptability during the interview, e.g. if the speaker digresses, differences between interviewers, etc.

382 SHUY, R. W., BARATZ, J. C. and WOLFRAM, W. A. 1969: *Sociolinguistic factors in speech identification*. Final report, Research Project **MH 15 048–01**. Institute of Mental Health.
In the Detroit study, the reciprocal reactions of class-specified (white) SE speakers and BEV speakers to speech samples, which were spoken onto tape by speakers of both races and different classes, were measured on a seven-point scale of semantic differential. Race and status of the recorded speakers were clearly identified by the subjects. *Some results*: the lower the socioeconomic status, the easier it was to identify lower socioeconomic status and Blacks; the higher the socioeconomic status, the easier it was to recognize Whites.

383 SILVERMAN, S. H. 1969: A method for recording and analysing the prosodic features of language. In Fishman 1969, (4), 250–54.
A method of transcribing and analysing paralinguistic features (accent, 'juncture', intonation) is applied with a somewhat modified musical system of notation to the language of bilingual Puerto Ricans. Differences of prosodic structure were found for two different styles, i.e. paralinguistic shift accompanies style shift.

384 SIMON, G. (ed.) 1974: *Bibliographie zur Soziolinguistik*. Tübingen.

385 SLAMA-CAZACU, T. 1971: Die dynamisch-kontextuelle Methode in der Sprachsoziologie. In Kjolseth and Sack 1971a, 73–86.

386 SLEDD, J. 1971: Bi-dialectism: the linguistics of White supremacy. In Laird and Gorell 1971.

387 SLOBIN, D. I. (ed.) 1967: *A field manual for cross-cultural study of the acquisition of communicative competence*. Berkeley: US Office of Education, **4–7–008757**.
Survey of psycholinguistic and sociolinguistic inquiries into individual and social speech use, with contributions from S. M. Ervin-Tripp, J. J. Gumperz, D. I. Slobin, J. Brukman, K. Keenan, C. Mitchell and B. Stross. In addition to the concise summary of results of theoretical and empirical works, a number of suggestions are given for fieldwork and the layout of empirical investigations.

388 SMITH, R. N. 1973: *Probabilistic performance models of language*. Janua Linguarum, Series Minor **150**. The Hague.
Introduction to problems of probabilistic language analysis, with criticial discussion of various models and theories.

389 SMITH, R. B. 1969: Interrelatedness of certain deviant structures in Negro Nonstandard dialects. *Journal of English Linguistics* **3** (March), 82–8.
Two grammatical deviations of BEV from SE are discussed by means of examples (from a corpus of utterances obtained from 170 Black informants) in respect of their descriptive possibilities: (1) the 'pleonastic subject pronoun' (e.g. 'My mother *she* used . . .') and (2) the deletion of the 'subject relative pronoun' ('This here is one family *eat anything*'). A close relationship is assumed between structures of (1) and (2): the high frequency of deletion of the relative pronoun stabilizes the pleonastic subject pronoun, which thereby becomes a *disambiguating formative*. The sentence 'My sister plays piano' in SE does not have to be *a sentence* in BEV, it can be a nominal phrase with an embedded relative clause (disambiguated: 'My sister she play piano'). *Consequences for the teaching of SE*: teaching a speaker of BEV to omit the pleonastic subject pronoun leads to two serious consequences: (1) 'intra-code ambiguation' in BEV and (2) 'cross-code ambiguation' between BEV and SE. If rules of SE are to be prevented from producing ambiguous sentences in BEV, distinct rules must be written for the above examples; it is not clear how this is to be achieved in a transformational grammar.

390 SOZIALISATION UND KOMPENSATORISCHE ERZIEHUNG 1969: *Ein soziologisches Seminar an der Freien Universität Berlin als hochschuldidaktisches Experiment*. Unofficial publication, Berlin.

391 SOZIOLINGUISTIK. 1972: Block V des Funkkollegs *'Sprache'* (authors Bühler, Deutrich, Schröder, Schank, Schütz, Steger). Sendungen 47–55, Studienbegleitbriefe 10 and 11, Weinheim, Basel

392 SPRACHBARRIEREN. 1970: Beiträge zum Thema Sprache und Schichten. Verfaßt und herausgegeben von Mitgliedern des Seminars 'Soziolinguistik' (Bochum). Hamburg.
Critical articles and practical proposals on the topics: (1) language and classes (sociologists), (2) creativity v. intelligence (psychologists), (3) preschool programmes (educationalists) and (4) linguistic aspects of the seminar on sociolinguistics.

393 STEGER, H. 1971: Soziolinguistik: Grundlagen, Aufgaben und Ergebnisse für das Deutsche. In *Sprache und Gesellschaft. Beiträge zur soziolinguistischen Beschreibung der deutschen Gegenwartssprache* (Sprache der Gegenwart 13), 9–44. Düsseldorf.

394 STEGMÜLLER, W. 1973: *Probleme und Resultate der Wissenschaftstheorie und analytischen Philosophie; IV, Personelle und statistische Wahrscheinlichkeit*. Berlin, Heidelberg, New York.
Didactic presentation of probability theory, with critical discussion of the methodological premises of this theory, and of its applications in statistics.

395 STERNBERG, Y. 1970: A typology of verbal communicative situations as a basis for analysing cultural deprivation. *Educ. Rev.* **22** (2), 172–80.
Bernstein's investigations have diverted attention from the fact that 'cultural deprivation' is chiefly a result of *communicative interaction*. Four elementary communication situations – conversation, dialogue, discussion, argument – are discussed with regard to some dimensions with which they vary, and are related to some sociocultural and psychological factors with which they correlate.

396 STEWART, W. A. 1964: Urban Negro speech: sociolinguistic factors affecting English training. In Shuy 1964, 10–19.
The learning situation of SE for speakers of NSE is a 'quasi-foreign language' situation, in which the linguistic system of those being taught is regarded as socially inferior to the language being taught. An effective method of teaching SE depends on sociolinguistic research into NSE. The dialects of BEV, e.g. in Washington, result from regional dialect (long-established residents) and dialects of immigrants; they should be localized between the extremes of 'acrolect' (the most highly evaluated dialect in the sociolinguistic hierarchy) and 'basilect' (dialect of the lowest classes, spoken mainly by children). A list is given of linguistic features of both dialects. For the instructional situation, the linguistic interference of expressions of 'basilect' with those of 'acrolect' should be described by contrastive analyses.

397 STEWART, W. A. 1968: A sociolinguistic typology for describing national multilingualism. In Fishman 1968b, 531–45.
See 5.4.5.

398 STEWART, W. A. 1970a: Historical and structural bases for the recognition of Negro dialect. In
        Alatis 1970a; 239–47.
        The deviations of BEV from SE can only be explained *historically* (source: Creole 'Gullah' from
        African linguistic tradition): 'any distinctive characteristics of Negro speech have their origins
        in linguistic history rather than in oppression, and represent normal language differences rather
        than the direct effects of poverty, ignorance, or genetic inferiority.' From this point of view
        linguistic descriptions, particularly of the status of the copula *be* in BEV (Labov 1969; Loflin
        1969 and 1970), are regarded as inadequate. For those interested in this subject this essay gives
        many bibliographical suggestions.

399 STEWART, W. A. 1970b: Sociopolitical issues in the linguistic treatment of Negro dialect. In
        Alatis 1970a, 215–23.

400 STOLZ, W. and BILLS, G. 1968: *An investigation of the Standard-Nonstandard dimension of central
        Texas English*. Final Report to the US Office of Economic Opportunity, Austin. Child
        Development Evaluation and Research Center, University of Texas.
        See 6.2.5.

401 STROSS, B. 1967: Recording apparatus and techniques. In Slobin 1967, 71–83.
        See 6.1.3.

402 SUDNOW, D. (ed.) 1972: *Studies in social interaction*. New York.

403 SUMPF, J. (ed.) 1968: *La Sociolinguistique, Langages* **11**.
        In the various articles sociolinguistics is essentially regarded as an analysis of discourse.

404 SUPPES, P. 1970: Probabilistic grammars for natural languages. *Synthese* **22**, 95–116.
        By means of context-free grammars, whose rules are assigned probabilistic values, data of child
        language can be accounted for systematically, as a first step towards a fuller treatment of adult
        language. Grammars are fed information specifying theoretical and actual frequencies of
        applications of rules. Suppes gives the formal definition of a probabilistic grammar, which can
        be used for the analysis of performance without loss of the theoretical results of generative
        grammatical theory.

405 ŠVEJCER, A. D. 1971: *Voprosy sociologii jazyka v sovremennoj amerikanskoj linguistike*
        (Questions of linguistic sociology in modern American linguistics). Leningrad.

406 TAULI, V. 1968: *Introduction to a theory of language planning*. Uppsala.

407 TEMPLIN, M. C. 1957: *Certain language skills in children: their development and inter-
        relationships*. Minneapolis.
        See 2.3.2.

408 TOPITSCH, E. (ed.) 1968: *Logik der Sozialwissenschaften*. Cologne, Berlin.
        Thirty-one essays on the logic of science, problems raised by value judgements, dialectic and the
        relation of theory to practice in the social sciences.

409 TORGERSON, W. S. 1958: *Theory and methods of scaling*. New York, London, Sydney.
        The theory of the scaling procedure invented by Guttman is described in detail on pp. 307–36.

410 TRAGER, G. L. 1964: Paralanguage: a first approximation. In Hymes 1964a, 274–88.
        Human communicative behaviour should be investigated from the angles of language,
        paralanguage and kinesics. *Prelinguistics* defines the physical and biological processes which
        determine the 'voice set' of a speaker according to age, sex, social group etc. The features of
        'language' (microlinguistics) and 'paralanguage' (metalinguistics) are constructed on the voice
        set.

411 TROIKE, R. C. 1970: Receptive competence, productive competence, and performance. In Alatis
        1970a, 63–73.
        The model of 'analysis by synthesis' and therefore generally the competence of an ideal
        ('monodialectal' and 'monostylistic') speaker-hearer must be expanded towards a
        multidialectal, multistylistic and sociolinguistic competence. Tests with speakers of BEV lead
        to the hypothesis of *asymmetrical* competence (different receptive and productive competence):
        sentences of SE were clearly decoded by BEV speakers but reproduced exclusively in BEV.

412 TRUDGILL, P. 1974: *The social differentiation of English in Norwich*. Cambridge.
        First substantial instance of correlative work carried out in Great Britain. It is largely inspired
        by Labov's work on the social stratification of New York English.

413 TURNER, G. and MOHAN, B. A. 1970: *A linguistic description and computerprogram for children's speech.* Vol. 2 in the series Primary Socialization, Language and Education, ed. B. Bernstein.
Part I presents a detailed description of the (functional) linguistic theory of M. A. K. Halliday (up to 1965) which in most cases was used by pupils of Bernstein as a foundation for linguistic analysis of class-specific speech behaviour. (A critique of this theory, which relates to Halliday 1961, is to be found in Paul Postal, Appendix: Halliday's 'Categories of the theory of grammar' in Postal, *Constituent structure: a study of contemporary models of syntactic description,* Bloomington, Indiana 1964, 97–114). Part II contains a computer programme (operations, flow diagrams) for analysing speech behaviour.

414 UNGEHEUER, G. 1972: Aspekte sprachlicher Kommunikation. In Engel and Schwencke 1972, 16–30.

415 VACHEK, J. 1964: *Prague School reader in linguistics.* Bloomington, Indiana.

416 VACHEK, J. 1966: *The linguistic school of Prague.* Bloomington, Indiana.

417 VALENTINE, C. A. 1971: Deficit, difference, and bicultural models of Afro-American behavior. *Educ. Rev.* **41** (2), 137–57.
He argues against the Deficit Model and the Variability Model, the predominant descriptive models of Afro-American subculture. The Variability Model is attacked for its assumption of a homogeneous Black subculture and of the incompatibility of two different cultures in one individual. Instead, he advances the concept of 'biculturation', i.e. Afro-Americans are socialized simultaneously in two systems, (1) the (ethnic) Afro-American and (2) the Euro-American culture. The culture learned in (2) remains, however, to a large extent passive on account of structural conditions of poverty, discrimination and segregation. Not only the Deficit Model but also the Variability Model can have dangerous consequences in that they are used as an excuse for the failure of public educational institutions. With references to a paradigmatic individual case, an impressive demonstration is given of the consequences that occur when educational and social policy act on the assumption of a pathogenic Afro-American culture (=combination of the Deficit and Variability Models).

418 VERNON, P. E. 1965: Environmental handicaps and intellectual development. *British Journal of Educational Psychology* **35** (1), 9–20; (2), 117–26.

419 WEINREICH, U. 1953: *Languages in contact.* New York.
See 4.3.3.

420 WEINRICH, U. 1954: Is a structural dialectology possible? *Word* **14**, 388–400. Reprinted in Fishman 1968b, 305–19.
See 4.3.3.

421 WEINREICH, U., LABOV, W. and HERZOG, W. Empirical foundations for a theory of language change. In W. P. Lehmann and Y. Malkiel (eds.), *Directions for historical linguistics,* 95–195. Austin, Texas and London.
Comprehensive theoretical treatment of linguistic change and variation, which critically reviews theories developed by various authors (Paul, Saussure, Bloomfield, Chomsky, Halle and others) and corresponding theoretical paradigms (neogrammarians, structuralism, generative transformational grammar). Essentially, a discussion of the theoretical and empirical problems 1 to 3 in Labov 1965, taking into consideration a further point (4)– 'constraints' (influence of structural factors on linguistic change). Empirical foundations relates to: (1) empirical findings, which are of significance for theory and which indicate trends of research, (2) conclusions which can be drawn from (1) about the minimal complexity of linguistic structure and of the areas of definition of this structure, (3) relating methods, theoretical concepts to empirical evidence. Stages of the discussion are: (1) *isolation of the idiolect,* (2) *problems of structural change* (mainly phonology), (3) *language as a differentiated system* (linguistic geography, languages and dialects in contact, variability within a system etc.). The Variable Rule (cf. Labov 1965, 1969, 1970a) is proposed as a solution to problems 1–4 (see above).

422 WELLS, J. C. 1973: *Jamaican pronunciation in London.* Oxford.

423 WERKSTATTGESPRÄCHE 1971: *Forschung zur gesprochenen Sprache und Möglichkeiten ihrer Didaktisierung, Protokoll eines Werkstattgespräches des Goethe-Instituts am 10 und 11 Dez. 1970.* Munich: Goethe-Institut.

424 WHITELEY, W. H. (ed.) 1971: *Language use and social change: problems of multilingualism with special reference to eastern Africa.* London: International African Institute.
     Twenty-two essays on bi- and multilingualism in Africa, divided into two parts: (1) general and theoretical studies (Fishman, Robinson, Lambert, Gumperz) and (2) empirical studies within Africa (on language policy, language education, linguistic modernization, urban language problems).

425 WHORF, B. L. 1956: *Language, thought and reality.* Cambridge, Mass., New York, London.

426 WILLIAMS, F. (ed.) 1970a: *Language and poverty: perspectives on a theme.* Chicago.
     Nineteen essays on various aspects of the correlation between language and poverty.

427 WILLIAMS, F. 1970b: Language, attitude and social change. In Williams 1970a, 380–99.
     See 7.2.1.

428 WILLIAMS, F. and NAREMORE, R. C. 1969a: Social class differences in children's syntactic performance: a quantitative analysis to field study data. *Journal of Speech and Hearing Research* **12** (4). 778–93.
     The linguistic material of the urban language study of Shuy, Wolfram and Riley 1967 was tested against Bernstein's hypothesis (restricted v. elaborated code). In contrast to all the works from the Bernstein school, the analysis has three distinct advantages: (1) oral speech is investigated in a relatively favourable communication situation; (2) the measurement of syntactic complexity is based on 'Immediate Constituent' analysis (Gleason); (3) the quantification methods are theoretically evaluated in respect of their linguistic suitability. In (2), a finite set of 12 constituent levels (CL) is assumed (hypothetically) for English sentences; these levels are fully contained in a model. The hierarchical CLs are assigned a numerical code and alphabetical index for quantification. The following are counted as sentence units: (î) 'coordination ratio', 'subordination ratio', 'predicate clause ratio', 'relative clause ratio'. The quotients for 'complements' and 'compounds' are ascertained for *clauses*. In addition, an 'elaboration index' is measured. *Results*: it was possible to corroborate Bernstein's hypothesis for a series of indices. A variance analysis between the dimensions of race, sex and status revealed that status differences were not influenced by the variable 'sex', but that they did vary with the variable 'race'. In conclusion, a discussion is given of the strategy for analysing performance.

429 WILLIAMS, F. and NAREMORE, R. C. 1969b: On the functional analysis of social class differences in modes of speech. *Speech Monographs* **36** (2), 77–102.
     See 2.5.

430 WILLIAMS, F. and NAREMORE, R. C. 1970: An annotated bibliography of journal articles. In Williams 1970a, 416–56.   .
     160 titles, mainly on the Deficit Hypothesis.

431 WILLIAMSON, J. V. and BURKE, V. M. (eds.) 1971: *A various language: perspectives on American dialects.* New York.
     Fifty articles on linguistic variation and American dialects from approx. 1925. Because of the short articles, the volume is suitable as a reader for an informative synopsis. There are six main themes: (1) a various language, (2) inherited features (adoption of linguistic characteristics from other languages), (3) literary representation of American dialects, (4) aspects of regional and social dialects, (5) selected sounds and forms, and (6) studies of urban dialects.

432 WITTGENSTEIN, L. 1969: *The blue and brown books: preliminary studies for the 'philosophical investigations'.* Oxford.

433 WOLFRAM, W. A. 1969: *A sociolinguistic description of Detroit Negro speech.* Washington, DC: Center for Applied Linguistics.
     See 6.2.4.

434 WOLFRAM, W. A. 1970: Linguistic correlates of social differences in the Negro community. In Alatis 1970a, 249–57.
     Condensed survey of techniques, problems and results of analysis from Wolfram 1969; see 6.2.4.

435 WUNDERLICH, D. 1970: Die Rolle der Pragmatik in der Linguistik. *Der Deutschunterricht* **22** (4), 5–41.
     See 3.4.2 and 5.3.2.

436 WUNDERLICH, D. Pragmatik, Sprechsituation, Deixis. *Lili* **1,** 153–90.

437 WUNDERLICH, D. 1971b: Zum Status der Soziolinguistik. In Klein and Wunderlich 1971, 297–321.
See 5.3.1.

438 ZUNICH, M. 1962: Relationships between maternal behavior and attitudes towards children. *Journal of Genetic Psychology* **100,** 155–65.
A discussion of maternal influence on children's behaviour.

Index